The Sound of
Musicals

Edited by Steven Cohan

A BFI book published by Palgrave Macmillan

First published in 2010 by
PALGRAVE MACMILLAN

on behalf of the

BRITISH FILM INSTITUTE
21 Stephen Street, London W1T 1LN
www.bfi.org.uk

There's more to discover about film and television through the BFI. Our world-renowned archive, cinemas, festivals, films, publications and learning resources are here to inspire you.

Palgrave Macmillan in the UK is an imprint of Macmillan Publishers Limited, registered in England, company number 785998, of Houndmills, Basingstoke, Hampshire RG21 6XS. Palgrave Macmillan in the US is a division of St Martin's Press LLC, 175 Fifth Avenue, New York, NY 10010. Palgrave Macmillan is the global academic imprint of the above companies and has companies and representatives throughout the world. Palgrave® and Macmillan® are registered trademarks in the United States, the United Kingdom, Europe and other countries.

Cover image: *Hairspray* (Adam Shankman, 2007, © New Line Productions, Inc./© Ingenious Film Partners 2 LLP)
Set by Cambrian Typesetters, Camberley, Surrey
Printed in China

This book is printed on paper suitable for recycling and made from fully managed and sustained forest sources. Logging, pulping and manufacturing processes are expected to conform to the environmental regulations of the country of origin.

British Library Cataloguing-in-Publication Data
A catalogue record for this book is available from the British Library
A catalog record for this book is available from the Library of Congress
10 9 8 7 6 5 4 3 2 1
19 18 17 16 15 14 13 12 11 10

ISBN 978–1–84457–346–2 (pbk)
ISBN 978–1–84457–347–9 (hbk)

Contents

Acknowledgments

I wish to thank Rebecca Barden for inviting me to edit this collection and for the help provided by her staff, not least the tireless Sophia Contento. Thanks also to Roger Hallas, Ina Rae Hark and Linda Shires for their advice and suggestions; to my department chair, Erin Mackie, for her support; to my university for assisting me with a leave semester and funding for this project; and most of all to the contributors to this volume.

I dedicate this book to my students at Syracuse University who have taken my course on 'The Hollywood Musical' during the past decade: your unflagging enthusiasm for the film musical has made teaching this course a truly rewarding experience. I hope you never stop singing and dancing.

Notes on Contributors

RICK ALTMAN is Professor of Cinema and Comparative Literature at the University of Iowa. His research and teaching have concentrated on film sound (*Cinema/Sound*, 1980, *Sound Theory/Sound Practice*, 1992, *Silent Film Sound*, 2004), film genres (*Genre: The Musical*, 1981, *The American Film Musical*, 1987, *Film/Genre*, 1998) and narrative theory (*A Theory of Narrative*, 2008). His books and articles have won several prizes, and have been translated into eighteen languages.

KEVIN JOHN BOZELKA received his PhD from the Radio Television Film department at the University of Texas – Austin where he currently teaches. He has written popular music and film criticism for the *Village Voice*, *Chicago Reader*, *MTV* and *PopMatters*. His research interests include popular music in national cinemas, paracinema and queer theory.

STEVEN COHAN is Professor of English at Syracuse University. His books include *Telling Stories: A Theoretical Analysis of Narrative* (1988, co-authored with Linda M. Shires), *Masked Men: Masculinity and the Movies in the Fifties* (1997), *Incongruous Entertainment: Camp, Cultural Value, and the MGM Musical* (2005) and *CSI: Crime Scene Investigation* (2008). He co-edited with Ina Rae Hark *Screening the Male: Exploring Masculinities in Hollywood Cinema* (1993) and *The Road Movie Book* (1997), and edited *Hollywood Musicals, The Film Reader* (2001).

BRETT FARMER teaches Cultural Studies at Chulalongkorn University, Thailand. He is the author of *Spectacular Passions: Cinema, Fantasy and Gay Male Spectatorships* (2000) and numerous essays in cultural, film and media studies.

MATTHEW J. FEE is a lecturer in the Department of Cinema, Photography and Media Arts and the director of the Park Scholar Program in the Roy H. Park School of Communications at Ithaca College. He completed his doctoral dissertation at New York University on fantastic cinema and Irish national identity. He has presented and published in the areas of Irish cinema and contemporary Irish art, as well as on film genre, particularly horror films and post-9/11 cinema.

JANE FEUER is Professor of Film Studies and English at the University of Pittsburgh. She is author of *The Hollywood Musical* (1982; 1993) and *Seeing through the Eighties: Television and Reaganism* (1995).

DAVID A. GERSTNER is Professor of Cinema Studies at the City University of New York's Graduate Center and College of Staten Island. He is author of *Manly Arts: Masculinity and Nation in Early American Cinema* (2006) and the forthcoming *Queer Pollen: White Seduction, Black-Male Homosexuality, and the Cinematic*.

SEAN GRIFFIN is Associate Professor of Cinema-Television at Southern Methodist University. He is author of *Tinker Belles and Evil Queens: The Walt Disney Company from the Inside Out* (2000), and co-author of *Queer Images: A History of Gay and Lesbian Film in America* (2006) and *America on Film: Representing Race, Class, Gender and Sexuality at the Movies* (2004; 2009). He edited *Hetero: Queering Representations of Straightness* (2009) and co-edited *In Focus: Queer Theory, The Film Reader* (2004). He has also published a number of articles on the musicals of Twentieth Century-Fox.

ADRIENNE L. MCLEAN is Professor of Film Studies at the University of Texas at Dallas. She is the author of *Being Rita Hayworth: Labor, Identity, and Hollywood Stardom* (2004) and *Dying Swans and Madmen: Ballet, the Body, and Narrative Cinema* (2008). She is currently co-editing, with Murray Pomerance, a ten-volume series on stars for Rutgers University Press.

KAREN MCNALLY is a Senior Lecturer and Course Leader for Film Studies at London Metropolitan University. She has published several articles on postwar Hollywood film and is the author of *When Frankie Went to Hollywood: Frank Sinatra and American Male Identity* (2008) and editor of the forthcoming *Billy Wilder Collection*.

ANNA MORCOM is RCUK Academic Fellow at Royal Holloway College, University of London. Her research focuses on popular and 'traditional' performing arts in India and Tibet. Key recent publications include her monograph *Hindi Film Songs and the Cinema* (2007), the article 'Bollywood, Tibet, and the Spatial and Temporal Dimensions of Global Modernity' (2009) in *Studies in South Asian Film and Media*, and a book chapter 'Indian Popular Culture and Its "Others": Bollywood Dance and Anti-nautch in Twenty-first-century Global India' in K. Moti Gokulsing and Wimal Dissanayake (eds), *Popular Culture in a Globalised India* (2008).

LAWRENCE NAPPER teaches at Kings College, London. His book *British Cinema and Middlebrow Culture in the Interwar Years* was published in 2009.

PAMELA ROBERTSON WOJCIK is Associate Professor of Film and Director of Gender Studies at the University of Notre Dame. She is author of *Guilty Pleasures: Feminist Camp from Mae West to Madonna* (1996) and *The Apartment Plot: Urban Living in American Film and Popular Culture, 1945 to 1975* (forthcoming). She is editor of *New Constellations: Stars of the Sixties* (forthcoming), *Movie Acting: The Film Reader* (2004) and co-editor of *Soundtrack Available: Essays on Film and Popular Music* (2001).

BHASKAR SARKAR is Associate Professor of Film and Media Studies at UC Santa Barbara. He is the author of *Mourning the Nation: Indian Cinema in the Wake of Partition* (2009), and co-editor of *Documentary Testimonies* (2009) and a special issue of the journal *Postcolonial Studies* on 'The Subaltern and the Popular' (2005). His research interests include Indian and Chinese cinemas, globalisation and media, film sound and cultures of uncertainty. Currently, he is working on a monograph about 'plastic nationalisms'.

GAYLE SHERWOOD MAGEE is Assistant Professor of Musicology at the University of Illinois, Urbana-Champaign. She publishes on American music and film music. Her most recent book, *Charles Ives*

Reconsidered (2008), won a Choice Outstanding Academic Title Award. Recent publications include 'Song, Genre and Transatlantic Dialogue in *Gosford Park*' (2008) in the *Journal of the Society for American Music*. Other articles have appeared in the *Journal of the American Musicological Society*, *19th Century Music* and *Musical Quarterly*.

MATTHEW TINKCOM is Associate Professor in the Graduate Program in Communication, Culture and Technology at Georgetown University and the author of *Working Like a Homosexual: Camp, Capital, Cinema* (2002) and co-editor of *Keyframes: Popular Cinema and Cultural Studies* (2001).

Introduction: How Do You Solve a Problem Like the Film Musical?

The film musical was once closely identified with Hollywood's ability to deliver razzle-dazzle spectacle in the shape of those lavish, oversized production numbers of the sort Busby Berkeley was famous for directing. Although production of musicals was never confined just to Hollywood by any means, and the genre is still a thriving format in other national film industries like Bollywood in India, during the past several decades its obituary has been written again and again – at least within the context of the film industry in the United States.

But anticipation of a big revival for the genre has also persisted in the US during the past decade. As early as 2003, *Variety* noted that 'Hollywood has expressed excitement that the long-dormant musical is ready for a comeback'.[1] Two years later, the trade paper repeated how a 'comeback [has] been rumored since "Moulin Rouge" and "Chicago"'.[2] Baz Luhrmann's glitzy and self-consciously campy *Moulin Rouge!* (2001) was that exception to the rule for contemporary Hollywood: a moderately expensive (about $50 million) original musical produced by a major US studio, Twentieth Century Fox, albeit made at the Fox Studios in Australia. *Moulin Rouge!* grossed $57 million in the US and, to almost everyone's surprise, slightly more than twice that amount from international markets, including the UK, so its popularity was thought to signal renewed interest in the genre globally.[3] Yet what followed *Moulin Rouge!* were mostly filmic adaptations of big Broadway and West End stage musicals, with *Chicago* (2002) leading the way after being in development for over two decades.

Each time a new adaptation of a stage musical was released, the advance buzz prompted the kind of speculation about a comeback for the genre that *Variety* had noted in 2003 and again in 2005. Whether or not these adaptations have actually made an impact on the fortunes of the musical as far as the major studios and audiences are concerned is still uncertain. *Chicago*, which won many year-end awards, including the Academy Award for best picture, and *Hairspray* (2007), based on Broadway's musicalised adaptation of John Waters's 1988 movie, were critical and popular successes, with the former taking nearly $307 million worldwide and the latter, $202.5 million. Both *Dreamgirls* (2006) and *Sweeney Todd: The Demon Barber of Fleet Street* (2007), a rarity in being a transfer to the screen of a Stephen Sondheim work, repeated the degree of success that *Moulin Rouge!* had achieved at the decade's opening. While not wowing mainstream audiences, *Dreamgirls* and *Sweeney Todd* received their share of devoted cult appreciation, some year-end award recognition and decent grosses (each took in about the same amount as *Moulin Rouge!* and, significantly, in the same two-to-one proportion of international gross to that of the US).

At the other extreme, though, were several equally big flops which have not been forgotten. The highly anticipated film versions of *The Phantom of the Opera* (2004), *The Producers* (2005) and *Rent* (2005) were major critical and commercial disappointments, to put it gently. Their failures beclouded the genre's future yet again, causing the producer of *Hairspray*, Craig Zadan, to admit as his film began production in 2006: 'I'm optimistic about future musicals, but I think we're now in treacherous territory. … I think inevitably there will be a backlash.'[4] According to industry wisdom at that time, the magic bullet was to use movie stars instead of the original stage cast or unknowns with a stage background. This solution appeared to work well for *Hairspray* and *Dreamgirls* and then even more so for *Mamma Mia!* (2008). Earning nearly $610 million globally despite getting mostly negative reviews, *Mamma Mia!* was a hit in the US and even bigger elsewhere, breaking records in Britain. However, casting stars does not automatically guarantee box-office excitement. *Nine* (2009), the most recently released film musical, has a much-hyped all-star cast in another adaptation from Broadway; yet based on its very weak US opening and downbeat critical reception, it was pulled from cinemas prematurely and looks to be another of those big disappointments.

Whether succeeding or failing, none of these high-profile musicals has resulted in anything resembling a genuine comeback for the genre, certainly nothing compared to what happened in the US in 1933 when *42nd Street* and *Gold Diggers of 1933* did apparently bring a dormant genre back to life for audiences. Nor did *Variety* itself actually predict the movie musical's return seven decades later. When reporting on that rumoured comeback in 2003 following the successes of *Moulin Rouge!* and *Chicago*, *Variety* went on to observe: 'While some hope the two hit tuners will open the floodgates, so far it's a trickle. In fact, with rare exceptions, studio toppers don't even want to talk about musicals, as though not to tempt fate.'[5] Several small musicals released by independent or 'niche' distributors – such as *Hedwig and the Angry Inch* (2001), an adaptation of the Off-Broadway hit *The Singing Detective* (2003), inspired by Dennis Potter's 1986 television series in the UK, and *Camp* (2003), an original about a summer musical theatre camp – did nothing to change this viewpoint.

Variety's cover story on the musical's rumoured comeback in 2003 nonetheless makes for interesting reading. It offers insights worth summarising as an introduction to some of the issues organising this book: the genre's formal flexibility and varied histories, its currency for popular culture and global popularity beyond America, its contemporary reiterations and innovations. Writing from a perspective firmly located within the globalised Hollywood entertainment industries, the article's two authors, David Rooney and Jonathan Bing, carefully outline reasons why the time may be right for the genre's revival and, equally so, for why present conditions may be working against the genre's comeback.

On the plus side of the balance sheet are these factors: the youth audience has been raised on music videos and is therefore 'accustomed to seeing music and dance as part of a story-telling fashion'; the international success of *Moulin Rogue!* indicated that there is a global market for the genre (as *Mamma Mia!* went on to confirm in spades); new technologies like digital cameras and editing not only enable the 'machine-gun editing' associated with a 'cutting-edge, MTV-style aesthetic' but also have cut costs without fully sacrificing lavish production values; fans of musicals tend to be repeat viewers, making DVDs a 'robust after-market'; and 'tuners are a perfect fit for the soundtrack album, radio play and music vids'.[6] Apart from referring to the musical's commercial attractions in contemporary terms (e.g. the MTV-styled aesthetic of rapid editing), this list happens to describe much the same conditions that drove the genre during the 'classic' and 'new' Hollywood eras. After all, Busby Berkeley and Bob Fosse alike staged numbers using their own versions of rapid editing before anyone had thought of MTV; music videos have liberally borrowed from old musicals in order to incorporate song and dance into their storytelling; and the genre has a long history of exploiting new technologies and developing new filming and editing strategies. For that matter, the significance of 'soundtrack album, radio play and music vids' reaches back to a time when film musicals fed (and fed off) earlier versions of those ancillary markets such as the sales of sheet music and vinyl recordings, the promotion of the big bands and the crossover of the genre's big stars to and from network radio. The extra-filmic commercial value of musicals went hand in hand with its appeal to young moviegoers, moreover.

The studio-era musical preceded television as the major venue for developing new musical talent aimed at the youth demographic (teen performers like Mickey Rooney, Judy Garland, Deanna Durbin, Jane Powell). Today one may not think of Rooney and Garland, in their youth a very popular co-starring team in MGM musicals, as the entertainment idols for teens of the Depression and World War II eras, but they were in many respects the Justin Timberlake and Britney Spears of their generation.

'So what's the holdup?' Rooney and Bing ask *Variety*'s readers. They cite several negative factors beclouding a future for musicals. First, for an industry 'dominated by flashy tentpoles aimed at teenage boys', musicals are 'deemed negligible' by the studios, and this attitude perpetuates the 'conventional wisdom' that 'guys would watch volleyball on TV before they'd see musicals for free'.[7] Second, recalling their earlier point about the former centrality of musicals to popular music, Rooney and Bing wonder if there is even a need for 'tuners' given the vitality of what they call 'hybrids' as sources of profitable soundtrack CDs. They point to films like *What's Love Got to Do with It* (1993) and *8 Mile* (2002) which feature characters who are singers yet do not 'substitute spontaneous song and dance for dialogue'.[8] Related to these 'hybrids' are those films lacking any characters who sing and dance 'naturally' but which have a continuous musical soundtrack; 'music is crucial' to these films, Rooney and Bing comment, 'but few would define them as musicals' (yet they supply hit CDs too).[9]

Referring to the Broadway theatre's function as a bankable source of material for contemporary film musicals, the writers go on to observe that it has been many decades since stage musicals 'dominated pop culture' with their tune-filled scores. After the introduction of long-playing records, cast albums often reached the top of *Billboard* charts and, at the same time, their scores generated hits for singers performing cover versions of the most popular songs. Furthermore, the long-running stage mega-hits have slowed down the traditional pipeline moving properties from stage to screen, since the blockbusters have a much longer life in New York City and London than in previous decades.[10] Finally, Rooney and Bing remind readers of the earlier trail of 'clunkers', some made by high achievers like Robert Altman and Martin Scorsese, following the gigantic successes first of *The Sound of Music* (1965), then of *Grease* (1978). The chequered history of those past revivals does not augur well for the present, leading to the sad conclusion that 'perhaps most crucially, Hollywood is painfully aware that few people have the knack for making musical films'.[11] The one type of 'hybrid' that has repeatedly produced winners of late, the authors note, are the 'toon tuners', the Disney animated features such as *The Little Mermaid* (1989) and *Beauty and the Beast* (1991).[12]

I think the Disney animated features could successfully carry the banner of the traditional film musical during the 1990s, because their painterly two-dimensional animation and fairy-tale worlds worked in concert to make it easier for adult audiences to overcome their resistance, indirectly noted in the *Variety* cover story, to a cinematic genre that unabashedly allows characters spontaneously to burst into song or dance. The genre's detractors tend to blame the incredulity of someone breaking out into a musical number for their laughter and consequent sense of alienation as spectators, but I think that misstates their problem.

One of the film musical's distinctive – and to my mind most thrilling – formal conventions as a genre derives from the ease with which it creates a dual register, thereby breaking with the cinema's dominant codes of realism as a means of securing the unity of time and space for a film's fictive world or 'diegesis'. Consider the ease with which, through a frame narrative as in *The Wizard of Oz* (1939) or the fantasy ballet in *An American in Paris* (1951), the genre moves from waking reality to dream worlds and back again.[13] This convention creates multiple diegeses, and it is not limited to when characters have fantasies or dreams. From its beginnings, the genre has sustained a long tradition of building 'a shifting and volatile dialectic between integrative and nonintegrative elements': that is, of placing story and spectacle together in varying degrees of tension and harmony.[14] Governed by their own spatial-temporal logic, Busby Berkeley's numbers disrupt the diegetic unity of his musicals' backstage narratives, to be sure; but in their visualisation of 'configurations that are feasible only with a movie camera, or an editing table, or in a special effects lab and that would be either impossible or incomprehensible on a theatrical stage', his numbers imagine a truly cinematic space.[15]

A dual register further manifests itself every time a musical uses direct address in a number: that is, when performers 'cheat out', as it is also called, by facing the camera and hence the audience directly. This convention engages audiences with a double sense of being addressed: directly and extra-diegetically by the performer in the manner of a live performance and, simultaneously, by the performer's character expressing herself in musical terms within the diegesis. As Jane Feuer explains:

> Musicals are built upon a foundation of dual registers with the contrast between narrative and number defining musical comedy as a form. The dichotomous manner in which the story is told – now spoken, now sung – is a very different mode of presentation from the single thread of the usual Hollywood movie. The narrative with its third-person mode seems to present a primary level. But unlike other kinds of movies, a secondary level, presented in direct address and made up of singing and dancing, emerges from the primary level. The first-person interruption disturbs the equilibrium of the unitary flow of the narrative but, as we have seen, in an entirely conventional manner. Proof that the break into song does indeed exist at a different level of reality may be seen in the way present-day audiences (if out of tune with the conventions) may greet with nervous laughter any transition between modes in the classic musical films.[16]

While it may seem 'unrealistic' and hence laughable for characters to break the single register and 'unitary flow of the narrative' by breaking out in song or dance, especially when there is also a full orchestral accompaniment on the soundtrack, singing and dancing are central to the musical's ability to represent a heightened sensibility attuned to the lyricism, pathos or joy of music. In musicals, the cinematic can be contemplative or boisterous, romantic or 'torchy' in the feelings being performed, filmed and then edited without diminishing the medium's kinetic ability to 'move' the spectator. This is why the genre gives pride of place to performing; great stars like Fred Astaire, Judy Garland and Barbra Streisand *can* hold one's attention on screen while singing or dancing, even if their voices are pre-recorded and the sounds of their tapping feet achieved in post-production.

All of that probably goes without saying to anyone who knows and enjoys the genre. Or does it? Even famed Broadway composer Stephen Sondheim complains about musical numbers in a film, since he believes they find a comfortable home on a stage but work against the cinematic medium. As part of the publicity for the release of *Sweeney Todd*, Sondheim told *The New York Times* that he finds the film versions of his stage musicals unsatisfying, including the Academy Award-winning *West Side Story* (1961), considered by many to be one of the all-time great film musicals.

> In 'West Side Story' you see a gang dancing down a real New York Street in color-coordinated sneakers, and you just don't believe it. And then there are the songs themselves. The problem is, what do you shoot in something like 'Tonight'? You get a close-up of him, a close-up of her, a medium shot of the fire escape. It's the same problem with so many of those other movies. The director has to fill out three or four minutes of what is essentially a static song, which holds your attention on the stage because that's part of the theatrical convention. Whereas for me, as a movie buff, I want the action to move forward constantly, and

it doesn't. They have little camera diversions and a trick here or there, but they're just filming a stage musical, and that's not for me.[17]

I am not going to defend *West Side Story*, which I agree has its share of problems – starting with the casting of Richard Beymer as the male lead. Rather, what I find significant about Sondheim's complaint, at least in the careful way that he phrases it, is his notion that 'as a movie buff' he can only conceive of cinema as constant, forward-moving action. That is why, he reiterates elsewhere in this set of interviews, 'The only kind of movie I didn't like as a kid were musicals.'[18] And that is the principle, he goes on to explain, by which he cut down the score of *Sweeney Todd* for its filmic version. Numbers that worked well as quiet moments on stage were eliminated for being too 'static' if filmed; most of the others were shortened.

Sondheim's attitude toward film musicals – expressed, he says, from his viewpoint 'as a movie buff' – is symptomatic of a widespread and more commonly held prejudice against the genre that arises, it seems to me, out of a naive or at least unwarranted sense of fidelity to cinematic realism. Tommy Tune, who directed the original stage production of *Nine* in 1982, appears to share Sondheim's bias in his recent appreciation of Rob Marshall's 2009 film version: 'Today's screen characters, rooted in a certain reality, can't just burst into song when the temperature of a scene demands it. That could turn a heartfelt moment into a joke in these cynical times.'[19] This way of thinking maintains that musicals are, in effect, incompatible with the filmic medium as experienced today; so unless, as in the 'hybrids', singing and dancing are naturalised within the fictive world or, as in Marshall's *Chicago* and *Nine*, are represented as fantasies occurring only within a character's mind (thereby reunifying the dual register according to a psychologically 'realistic' explanation for the genre's doubting Thomases), today's audiences are expected just as a matter of course to find film musicals laughable for being out of sync with 'these cynical times'. Given, on the one hand, the film musical's history of having once been popular and appreciated precisely for exceeding the single register of classic realism and, on the other hand, the contemporary moviegoing audience's supposed postmodern sophistication in being able to see right through cinematic illusionism, this makes for a paradoxical state of affairs indeed. It helps to explain why speculation about the musical's comeback in the twenty-first century is typically phrased as an improbable possibility.

Back to School
So how do you solve a problem like the film musical within the context of today's tastes in popular entertainment? Rooney and Bing's comments about the conditions favouring a comeback of traditional (i.e. not 'hybrid') film musicals can help us see how it is now taking place: not in the form of all those splashy star-laden Broadway adaptations, but as more modest home-grown fare aimed at the youth market. I am talking about the Disney organisation's *High School Musical* (shown on cable in 2006) and its sequels, *High School Musical 2* (on cable in 2007) and *High School Musical 3: Senior Year* (released theatrically in 2008).

For starters, consider some statistics about the *HSM* juggernaut. *High School Musical* premiered in the United States on the Disney Channel on 20 January 2006 to an audience of 7.7 million viewers, at that point 'the biggest audience' in the cable channel's history'.[20] By September of that year, it had been seen by 37 million viewers in the US, sold 2.3 million DVDs and 8 million copies of the soundtrack album, and 'occupied pole position in the iTunes chart'.[21] Exploiting the musical's success, Disney spun it off as a sing-along version on the cable channel, a touring concert with almost the entire cast, an ice show, video games, and more than a hundred tie-in and souvenir products. In a stroke of merchandising genius, moreover, the screenplay was quickly adapted for licensing to high schools as an amateur stage version – there were nearly two thousand such productions in 2007.[22] Additionally, the musical was amazingly popular globally. Following a smash roll-out in Latin America and Australia, Disney gave the film a red-carpet Leicester Square European premiere in London, after which it was shown across Europe and Asia.[23] Local promotional events outside the US also indicated the musical's immediate currency with youth: in India, 'an online competition dubbed "My School Rocks"' was repeated across Asia; in South America, where a Spanish-language version of the musical produced for that market was later released in 2008, a live TV show aired for ten weeks and was planned for Spain. The musical created what *Variety* termed a 'global ripple effect' with 'more than 170 million viewers … worldwide' and equally strong DVD and CD sales. All told, it was estimated that *High School Musical*, shot in Utah on a budget of slightly more than $4 million, generated $100 million for Disney in 2006/7 alone.[24]

With a $7 million budget, the 2007 sequel, expected to be 'the Super Bowl of kidvid', rocked the Disney Channel with even stronger numbers than the first *High School Musical* had delivered, premiering to a 'cable record-busting 17.24 million viewers'. Since nearly a third of this number comprised adults (eighteen years or over) – a surprisingly high figure given the franchise's perceived 'tween' appeal – it was assumed that not all the viewers who comprised that 'over-age' demographic were parents watching with their kids.[25] Needless to say, the sequel did as well globally, breaking records in Australia, doing 'boffo' in the UK and setting 'a new high-water viewership mark' in Southeast Asia. A week after its US showing, *High School Musical 2* was 'seen by more than 44 million viewers worldwide'.[26]

In next to no time, a third entry in the franchise was in the works and, given the popularity of the first two, this one was released theatrically. Again, filmed entirely in Utah but this time on a somewhat larger budget of around $11 million, the more lavishly appointed *High School Musical 3: Senior Year* had an opening weekend in the US of $42 million, remained the number one film at the box office in its second weekend and repeated its success in a concurrent international release, 'whipping teens and tweens into a full-blooded frenzy', as *Variety* put it. In Britain, where the first and second instalments had been 'endlessly repeated to big viewership', cinemas took $2 million in advanced bookings three weeks before the official premiere of *High School Musical 3*, and merchandising for the third entry in the franchise was considered to be 'red hot' in that nation. In fact, the *High School Musical* calendar was already the biggest seller in the UK by then, 'beating out the ever popular Manchester United Football Club brand'.[27]

Because of its presence on the Disney Channel and sizeable fanbase of young females at the cusp of adolescence, the *High School Musical* trilogy has been written off as innocuous fare with 'no double-entendres, visionary artistry, or adult appeal', as *Rolling Stone* described the first entry. 'It is not even bubblegum enough to be enjoyable on an ironic level. It is plain vanilla, no sprinkles …'[28] No doubt that may be the level on which the large adolescent female audience watches these musicals repeatedly on cable and DVD. And to be sure, *High School Musical* and its progeny are neither stylistic game-changers as, say, Fosse's *Cabaret* (1972) and *All That Jazz* (1979) were for their generation or generic reboots as the cycle of post-1980s international art musicals analysed by Jane Feuer in this book proved to be for theirs. However, contempt for *High School Musical* as simply bland 'kidvid' fare misses its generic smartness, which is just as evident in the two sequels. As Kim Edwards observes, the charm and artistic merit of the original *HSM* movie lies in its ability to consider a sophisticated theatrical and musical heritage and consequently revise it for a modern audience … it simultaneously conforms to genre expectations and pays homage to its textual influences while taking a postmodern delight in exposing its own limitations and playing with some gentle pastiche of literary and cinematic predecessors.[29]

Underscoring its self-reflexive use of pastiche and allusion, the first *High School Musical* follows the genre's conventions almost to the letter, indicating director Kenny Ortega's and writer Peter Barsocchini's knowingness of the heritage of the traditional Hollywood musical which they are updating for the present-day youth audience. With its basketball-star hero Troy Belton (Zac Efron) and 'brainiac' heroine Gabriella Montez (Vanessa Hudgens), *High School Musical* faithfully unfolds according to the dual-focus structure analysed by Rick Altman in *The American Film Musical*.[30] Similarly, the trilogy of films follow the genre's convention of contrasting authenticity and spontaneity, which confirm the amateur's love of singing for singing's sake, with manipulated and engineered artistry, which depends upon the professional's well-rehearsed labour and derives from a profit motive (a 'profit' that here takes the form of scheming to procure the lead roles in the school musical as a means of acquiring more cultural capital within the high-school social system).[31] In all three of the films comprising the series, Troy and Gabriella are glossed as the extremely talented amateurs whose singing expresses their honesty and artlessness. In the first *High School Musical*, Gabriella compares singing with Troy to feeling like 'a cool other person inside you just came out'; her experience of such intense emotional transparency, she explains further, is because 'singing with you felt like you didn't have to be anything but yourself'. On the other hand, Sharpay Evans (Ashley Tisdale) and her twin brother Ryan (Lucas Grabeel), are just as talented but they want to overwhelm their audience with well-rehearsed, professionally arranged, razzle-dazzling performances that rely on engineered stagecraft and backup singers. When Troy asks Sharpay in *High School Musical 2* if she would 'ever try just singing without the lights and sets and backup people?', she fails to comprehend the value of artlessness. 'It'll be harder to get applause that way,' she replies. Accordingly, each *High School Musical* moves toward

Sharpay and Ryan inject Broadway razzle-dazzle into their audition number in *High School Musical* (2006), whereas Troy and Gabriella just sing, bringing the crowd to their feet

its conclusion in more or less the same way: a penultimate number, set in contrast with a preceding (and overly extravagant) one by Sharpay, who almost managed to steal the spotlight from Gabriella, reunites Troy and Gabriella on stage in a simple performance of 'just singing'; their duet engages the diegetic audience's participation – everyone claps and sways to the music's rhythm – as proof of these two performers' authenticity.

In the first *High School Musical*, musical theatre introduces Troy and Gabriella to a space of difference – the drama club – that challenges their otherwise conformist and rigidly hierarchical high-school world. It is here, I think, that this musical opens itself up to something more than a 'vanilla' reading. Performing does not, as in the dual-focus template of older musicals, reconcile the opposition of masculine priorities (jocks, sports) and feminine ones (brains, science) so much as reject that opposition in the interest of embracing one's difference through musical theatre to achieve a much fuller, more truthful expression of identity and desire. The number 'Stick to the Status Quo', moreover, recognises the possible queer signification of this theme. With Troy having in effect 'outed' himself by publicly signing up to audition with Gabriella for the school musical, other students confess their secret desires through this song. Their revelations challenge the apparent equivalence of stereotypical gender and social identities, musically reconfiguring the groups of jocks, cheerleaders, brainiacs, skater dudes and drama geeks who are all seated at separate tables in the school cafeteria, hanging out with their own pack, when the number begins. 'If Troy can tell his secret,' his teammate Zeke (Chris Warren, Jr) declares, 'I can tell mine: I bake.' As the number progresses, the social divisions fall apart vocally and

Zeke confesses he likes to bake in 'Stick to the Status Quo' from *High School Musical*, and by the end of this number the status quo has come undone

choreographically. The nonconformist implications of being drawn to musical theatre invest it (and, by implication, the film musical genre) with connotations of a progressive, utopian and – in the sense that it enables an alternative to rigid heterosexualised gender roles – queer politics. Such a resonance to Troy's refusal to stick to the status quo explains why, throughout the trilogy, he is characterised as loving musical theatre yet, as a jock, experiences conflict about his passion. In the third entry, he still finds himself in this position. Gabriella tells him to stop fighting it: 'You love it,' she reminds him. He agrees but asks, 'Why is it so hard to admit?'

The utopian politics I am attributing to the *High School Musical* trilogy also explains director Ortega's handling of the big finales. Contrary to generic expectations for a backstage musical, these do not occur on a stage but instead take place in the gymnasium following the big basketball win (in the first *HSM*), then a country club swimming pool (*HSM2*) and finally the athletic field after the graduation ceremonies (*HSM3*). On the one hand, these finales unambiguously celebrate the value of everyone 'getting along', articulating the 'vanilla' theme of the series as directed to its target audience: 'We're All in

The finale of *High School Musical*: 'We're All in This Together'

This Together', the entire cast sings at the close of the first *High School Musical*. On the other hand, the finales move musical theatre from its bounded space on stage in order to revel in its more carnivalesque energies. By the time the first *High School Musical* reaches its finale, Troy and Gabriella's friends, once antagonistic to musical theatre in the interest of winning sports and science competitions, have all been converted themselves and are now performing alongside the couple. When everyone exclaims in choral unison that they 'are all in this together', the indeterminate 'this' has a double reference: their social cohesion as a democratised community and their joy in communally singing and dancing on the gym floor. Indeed, there would be no unified high-school community to celebrate without musical theatre's transcendence of the jock/brainiac opposition, which the film heterosexualises as male/female. In picturing such unity, 'We're All in This Together' choreographs a successful takeover of the school gym – formerly the normalising yet restrictive space occupied by the jocks and their coach (who is also Troy's father) – by the utopian force of musical theatre.

The finale of *High School Musical* so successfully puts forward musical theatre as the fulfilling and more 'authentic' alternative to the gendered opposition of jocks and brainiacs that the two sequels really don't have much new work to do of their own in developing the series narratively or thematically. Consequently, the sequels simply replay the first film's conflicts by contriving to obstruct the couple's path with new obstacles that, as exploited by Sharpay, threaten to keep Troy and Gabriella from performing together in a show and temporarily break up the musicalised community.

What is more revealing about the series' commercial value for Disney and its import for our thinking about the genre's comeback in the twenty-first century is that, with their successively larger budgets, the sequels are more stacked with musical numbers, reminding us that plot is often of secondary consequence in a musical. Whereas the first *High School Musical* has eight numbers, counting reprises the second features thirteen and the third, seventeen. Each sequel, moreover, pays progressively greater attention to the over-the-top camp style of Sharpay's numbers (such as her rendition of 'Fabulous' in *HSM2* and her duet with Ryan, 'I Want It All', in *HSM3*). These are paradoxically (in another truism of the traditional musical) at once 'inauthentic' according to their over-theatricality within the diegesis and yet genuine camp crowd-pleasers for the extra-diegetic audience at home or in the cinema. Just as crucially, the sequels openly build up and play to the spectacular appeal of star Zac Efron, whose singing is mostly dubbed in the first *HSM* but not in the two sequels. By the time we reach *High School Musical 3*, I think it is not entirely amiss to surmise that the whole point of this film may be simply to enjoy the spectacle of Efron singing and dancing, not only with Vanessa Hudgens in their love songs and the full company in big production numbers, but also with co-star Corbin Bleu in

Zac Efron with Corbin Bleu in 'The Boys Are Back' and dancing his angst about his post-high-school future in 'Scream', both from *High School Musical 3: Senior Year* (2008)

a Michael Jackson-styled dance duet in 'The Boys Are Back' (which could stand alone as a music video) and in his own dance solo 'Scream' – in both numbers, the visual attention is directed squarely on Efron's body. In the two sequels, the many musical numbers do little to 'move' the formulaic narrative forward, yet their dominance indicates the filmmakers' realisation that they were the reason why so many millions of viewers were drawn to the first *High School Musical* more than once. I will also hazard a guess that the numbers are what enabled the trilogy to cross cultures so easily and as instantly.

High School Musical and its sequels make an illuminating point of departure for musing about the film musical's future in this century, particularly in contrast with the more high-profile adaptations of Broadway and West End blockbusters. Disney has been the one Hollywood studio persistently interested in reviving the original film musical on more than a one-off basis. Aside from its long-standing commitment to producing (and profiting enormously from) animated musicals, years before *High School Musical*, the studio had tried but failed with original youth-oriented musicals: *Newsies* (1992), directed by Ortega nearly fifteen years before he would go on to do the *HSM* trilogy, and *Swing Kids* (1993) did little business. For its ABC television network, Disney co-produced remakes of *Cinderella* (1997) and *Annie* (1999), but the return of the star-vehicle musical to TV, anticipated ever since the Bette Midler remake of *Gypsy* for CBS in 1993, never happened.

The significant factor in the film musical's 'comeback' with *High School Musical* in 2006, I believe, was the Disney Channel sponsorship. In addition to the first and second *High School Musical*, the cable channel presented three *Cheetah Girl* TV musicals (2003, 2006, 2008), and, at the same time that the *High School Musical* franchise moved to theatrical release with the 'senior year' entry in the series, the channel spun off to cinemas a concert (2008) and movie (2009) incarnation of its enormously popular *Hannah Montana* series (2006–present). Furthermore, the new cycle of teen dance 'hybrids' encouraged Disney to produce for theatres *Step Up* (2006), which then spun off two sequels of its own, *Step Up 2: The Streets* (2008) and *Step Up 3D* (2010). Supporting the production of musicals, the studio has synergistically developed a cohort of young performers (The Cheetah Girls, Miley Cyrus, the Jonas Brothers, some of the *High School Musical* cast members like Ashley Tisdale) for its Hollywood Records label as well as its cable channel, launching their careers 'in order to keep costs low and enable it to eke out more profits per project'. With the balance sheet in mind, Disney has retained few of its marquee names once their initial contracts expired and salaries increased, preferring instead to continue developing new, inexpensive talent.[32] Accordingly, a fourth entry in the *HSM* franchise currently in development will feature a new freshman class and new group of contract players. Comparable to the production of musicals by the MGM 'dream factory' during the studio era, the Mouse House of today may be the perfect Hollywood home for the production of original musicals like the three *High School Musical* films, which 'have low negative costs, good grosses and a healthy afterlife' on cable, DVD, CD, iTunes, touring shows and all the merchandising (video games, books, calendars, toys, etc.) that the target youth audience gobbles up, with everything produced by Disney itself or licensed in its name.[33]

Its ability to profit from a 'home-grown' musical on so many levels sets Disney apart from other contemporary studios, and may explain why the newest corporate incarnation of MGM, severely scaled down and nearly bankrupt, tried to replicate the Disney success in 2009 with a remake of its 1980 musical hit *Fame* but flopped big time. On the other hand, the success of *High School Musical* clearly paved the way for the TV series *Glee* (2009–present), which is co-produced by Twentieth Century Fox television for the Fox network in the US. Still midway through its first full season at the time of writing, *Glee* has already turned into a critical and ratings success, quickly generating a sizeable fanbase that includes well-known performers (some of whom have asked to do guest appearances on the show) and the musical theatre community.[34] *Glee* has more satiric edge (and more ironic perversity) than *High School Musical* and its sequels, but it follows the Disney franchise's template in its similar projection of a show setting – here, the high-school Glee Club called 'New Directions' – as the utopian alternative to and contestation of the more rigidly hierarchical and heterosexual structuring of 'normality' as otherwise upheld by high-school culture and as personified by jocks and cheerleaders.

Glee appears to confirm that several important lessons have been learned from the success of Disney's *High School Musical* trilogy. Let me elaborate upon three conclusions I draw from their popularity.

First, like *High School Musical*, *Glee* has successfully connected with popular music tastes in ways that other musicals have failed to do; after each weekly episode, cover versions of the three or four songs performed – which range from musical theatre anthems to pop standards, rock, even some rap – have continually been big sellers on iTunes, and the series has already generated two CDs from its soundtrack while still only in mid-season. The musical genre has usually been thought of as a family attraction, a gloss left over from the roadshow era and exemplified by the gigantic success of *The Sound of Music*, but historically it has thrived on forging its connection with youth audiences through popular music, as typified by the ominipresence of the big bands in the 1940s and the introduction during the following decade of rock 'n' roll music and teen idols from the record industry like Elvis Presley, Pat Boone and Fabian. The 'hybrid' teen dance musicals make this kind of connection with their soundtracks, too. Any viable comeback for the genre needs to revive this contact with popular music even if, as in the *High School Musical* trilogy, the songs are noticeably derivative or, as in *Glee*, are slick cover versions from the pop songbook.

Second, television may well turn out to be a key ingredient in any future revival of the more traditionally styled film musical on a large scale, especially when the significance of the youth market is factored in. In other words, Broadway-styled, star-studded entertainment aimed at the same demographic that attends theatre (i.e. upper-middle-class adults or tourists) may not be the secret either to the genre's longevity or to its bankable future. I suspect that in today's world of convergent electronic media home video – whether cablecast, streamed via the Internet or played back on DVD – will be crucial in grounding the exhibition of film musicals for a contemporary audience whose relation to the cinema multiplex is not their only means of accessing entertainment forms. From another perspective, too, while I doubt that the success of *Glee* will inspire the other networks to proliferate the genre as series television on a wide scale, through the course of a season comprising twenty-two or more episodes, a series like *Glee* can – much like the franchising of *High School Musical* via the Disney Channel – develop its inexpensive young cast into a repertory company. The institutional setting of a television network duplicates the role that the old Hollywood contract system once played in supplying and training creative talent (performers, music arrangers, choreographers, directors), and in building stars and a reliable fanbase for the genre.

Third, *High School Musical*'s projection of musical theatre as a progressive and liberating space of heterosocial nonconformity was fundamental, I think, to the trilogy's success in engaging its main 'femme' demographic of 'tween' to college-age women. While this segment of the moviegoing audience is not ordinarily well served by theatrical film, that group has consistently been diehard fans of new and old musicals, as I know from first-hand experience of teaching the genre for the past dozen years. The predominantly female audience of *High School Musical 3*, along with that of Disney's *Hannah Montana/Miley Cyrus: Best of Both Worlds Concert Tour* and the theatrical spin-off of *Sex and the City*, finally caused Hollywood to acknowledge the 'femme' demographic as more than a specialised market, making 2008 a sort of turning point in the studios' thinking: 'For the first time that anyone can remember', *Variety* reported, 'three femme-driven films … opened to No. 1 at the B.O., making it abundantly clear that fangirls are every bit as important as fanboys.'[35] It is probably no coincidence that all three 'femme' hits were derived from television antecedents. Of course, time will tell whether Hollywood remembers this lesson or has to relearn it again in two or three years, as has happened many times before. In any event, *Glee* is following the ground paved by *High School Musical* in addressing that same demographic of 'fangirls' – and some 'fanboys', too, it appears – while making much more visible the cohort of gay and lesbian fans that have always supported the genre.

The Sound of Musicals

Although central to any consideration of the musical's comeback in the US, the adaptations of big stage hits and traditional youth musicals obviously do not delineate the full range of the genre as it is currently produced globally; nor do the generic conventions which the adaptations and youth musicals draw upon capture the film musical's rich and varied formal history in its entirety. Reflecting further upon the genre's global variety and its varied history, this collection of original essays exemplifies the robust interest which the film musical continues to stimulate in scholars as well as fans.

Part One of this volume, 'Genre Matters', contains four essays which re-examine broadly based generic traditions that have previously been identified with the film musical's history in the United States, Britain and India. In the first chapter, 'From Homosocial to Heterosexual: The Musical's Two Projects', Rick Altman returns to his influential argument about the dual-focus template of the American film musical in order to explore the tension between homosocial and heterosexual currents within the form. In Chapter 2, 'British Gaiety: Musical Cinema and the Theatrical Tradition in British

Film', Lawrence Napper traces the Gaiety stage tradition in British musicals from the 1930s to the 60s, a period bookended for his essay by Jessie Matthews in *Evergreen* (1934) and Cliff Richard in *The Young Ones* (1961). In Chapter 3, 'The Mellifluous Illogics of the "Bollywood Musical"', Bhaskar Sarkar reconsiders, from the perspective of their formal uses and historical antecedents, the cultural significance of song-and-dance numbers in Indian popular cinema throughout that thriving industry's own history. And in Chapter 4, 'The International Art Musical: Defining and Periodising the Post-1980s Musical', Jane Feuer explores a cycle of films that flourished at the end of the last century and that 'almost' seem like musicals – such as the Japanese *Shall We Dance* (1995) and the British *Billy Elliot* (2000) – in order to propose how and why this group forms a subgenre that may be more respectful of the musical's long-standing traditions than the model perfected during the heyday of classic Hollywood.

The rest of this collection is arranged chronologically according to the chapter's topic. Part Two, 'Histories of the Hollywood Musical', returns to the classic-era musical but looks at it from fresh historical perspectives. In Chapter 5, 'Flirting with Terpischore: Dance, Class and Entertainment in 1930s Film Musicals', Adrienne L. McLean examines how the multiple styles of dance on view in early musicals were streamlined and made more uniform by the end of the decade, in large part due to the success of the Astaire–Rogers series. In Chapter 6, 'Star Spangled Shows: History and Utopia in the Wartime Canteen Musical', Steven Cohan looks at the seemingly ill-shapen all-star musical revues of World War II in order to examine their grounding of utopian spaces in stardom as a refraction of wartime labour issues. Karen McNally in Chapter 7, 'Sailors and Kissing Bandits: The Challenging Spectacle of Frank Sinatra at MGM', discusses the star's problematic image in 1940s musicals when, still the idol of bobby-soxers, he was a contract player at the Culver City studio and not yet the iconic 'swinging' Sinatra of the late 1950s and 60s. The eighth chapter, 'Bloody Mary Is the Girl I Love: US White Liberalism vs. Pacific Islander Subjectivity in *South Pacific*', is Sean Griffin's case study of the labour strife complicating and indirectly texturing the production of the Rodgers and Hammerstein musical when on location in Hawaii. This chapter also inaugurates a shift toward the big-budget musicals of the roadshow era. In Chapter 9, 'The Singing Sixties: Rethinking the Julie Andrews Roadshow Musical', Brett Farmer historicises the elements that made Andrews's musicals so popular with women and so industrially significant for their era; while in Chapter 10, 'The Streisand Musical', Pamela Robertson Wojcik turns our attention to the other female performer who achieved major stardom with her first musical film in the 1960s, analysing how the genre was significantly reshaped to fit the unconventional star image of Barbra Streisand.

Part Three, 'Beyond Classic Hollywood', concentrates on alternatives to the way the genre has usually been viewed through the output of classic Hollywood. In Chapter 11, 'The Music and Musicality of Bollywood', Anna Morcom analyses the 1975 Indian film *Sholay* in order to illustrate within the terms of a single narrative how songs and musicality work differently in Bollywood cinema – big-budget, star-laden Hindi films – compared to its western counterpart. In Chapter 12, 'Robert Altman and the New Hollywood Musical', Gayle Sherwood Magee looks at an auteur director one rarely thinks of in conjunction with the genre, examining Altman's three musicals in the aesthetic and industrial context of 1970s New Hollywood. Kevin John Bozelka in Chapter 13, 'The Musical as Mode: Community Formation and Alternative Rock in *Empire Records*', studies this 'hybrid' from 1995 with two objectives: to argue for the musical form's modality and to historicise the role of alternative rock in this film's reception, accounting for its theatrical failure and cult fandom on DVD a decade later. In Chapter 14, '"A Musical Dressed up in a Different Way": Urban Ireland and the Possible Spaces of John Carney's

Once', Matthew J. Fee looks closely at this critically acclaimed musical from 2006 in terms of its aesthetic adherence to the genre and its significance for the Irish film industry. Chapter 15, 'Christophe Honoré's *Les Chansons d'amour* and the Musical's Queer-abilities', finds David A. Gerstner analysing the queer affect of this 2007 French musical while also identifying its continuity with the earlier musicals of Jacques Demy. Finally, in Chapter 16, '"Dozing Off During History"': *Hairspray*'s Iterations and the Gift of Black Music', Matthew Tinkcom compares John Waters's 1988 original *Hairspray* and the Adam Shankman 2007 film adaptation of the fully musicalised stage version, tracing their different erasures of civil rights history in their representations of dance. Tinkcom's chapter emphatically reminds us, as do all of these essays, that while the film musical may be the most escapist of genres, it never escapes its placement in history.

My summary of the sixteen essays comprising this collection indicates how *The Sound of Musicals* tries to avoid rounding up all the usual suspects in its discussion of the film musical. Some essays in this volume return to the classic Hollywood era but do so in order to reconsider its generic historicity and cultural valences; others widen that lens to encompass national film industries beyond the US; and still others examine the US film musical in its many post-studio era incarnations, exploring how it intersects with social history, stardom, auteurist practices, the art film, alternative music, queer theory and camp. Yet while it aims to reflect contemporary scholarly interest in the musical from differing methodological, historical and global perspectives, this collection also makes no claim to be comprehensive in its coverage. The contents of an anthology like this one are always dynamically shaped by the current research of the contributing scholars as well as by the editor's own expertise and by the various time constraints that arise when publishing a book, so there will inevitably be some regrettable omissions. In this regard, I think of this volume as a report from the field, reflecting where scholars of the musical – many of whom are well known from their previous work on this enduring genre – are directing their energies at the present moment.

Notes

1. David Rooney and Jonathan Bing, 'Can Hollywood Carry a Tune? Despite Success of "Chicago", Studios Still Leery of Musicals', *Variety*, 10–16 March 2003, p. 1.
2. Gordon Cox, 'H'wood & Broadway's Love–Hate Relationship', *Variety*, 12–18 September 2005, p. 83.
3. Unless otherwise noted, my source for film grosses is the Internet site Box Office Mojo at <www.boxofficemojo.com>.
4. Nicole Laporte, 'Pics: Tune Deaf? Studios, Filmmakers on Shaky Ground with Movie Musical', *Variety*, 31 January–5 February 2006, p. 67.
5. Rooney and Bing, 'Can Hollywood Carry a Tune?', p. 1.
6. Ibid.
7. Ibid., p. 51. Rooney and Bing are quoting Harvey Weinstein, who at the time of this article was head of Miramax, the Disney subsidiary that produced *Chicago*.
8. The same can be said of the many teen films that feature dancers and dancing in a naturalised setting, an ongoing cycle which began with *Footloose* (1984) and *Dirty Dancing* (1987), and, according to *Variety*, was revived by the 'breakout' *Save the Last Dance* (2001), which 'ushered in a new wave of successful teen dance pics'. Tatiana Siegel, 'H'w'd's Musical Mania: Studios Find Juve Groove …', *Variety*, 6–12 October 2008, p. 63. Additionally, as Rooney and Bing's reference to *What's Love Got to Do with It* anticipates, biopics of singers – later ones in this renewed cycle include *Ray* (2004) and *Walk the Line* (2005) – are similarly 'hybrids' featuring song rather than dance, in which the protagonists perform in a naturalised setting.

9. Rooney and Bing, 'Can Hollywood Carry a Tune?', p. 51.
10. However, it also became clear with the release of *Chicago* and subsequent adaptations that, in an era of tourist-driven mega-hits, film versions stimulated the box office for the stage productions, which typically saw increased grosses during the film's run and then continued without further interruption after the film's theatrical life concluded. Gordon Cox, 'H'wood Tunes up Broadway's B.O.: Defying Old Axiom, Legit Gets Boost from Films', *Variety*, 30 January–5 February 2006, p. 67.
11. Rooney and Bing, 'Can Hollywood Carry a Tune?', p. 51.
12. Looking past the 2003 publication date of Rooney and Bing's *Variety* article, we might then appreciate how these features and their follow-ups like *The Lion King* (1994) were ultimately remade into Broadway mega-hits, their longevity fuelled in large part by tourists from around the world.
13. See Chapter 4 of Jane Feuer, *The Hollywood Musical*, 2nd edition (Bloomington: Indiana University Press, 1993).
14. Martin Rubin, *Showstoppers: Busby Berkeley and the Tradition of Spectacle* (New York: Columbia University Press, 1993), p. 12. For an elaboration of my point, see Steven Cohan, *Incongruous Entertainment: Camp, Cultural Value, and the MGM Musical* (Durham, NC: Duke University Press, 2005), pp. 43–5, 60–7. And for a comparable view of Indian cinema, see the chapter by Bhaskar Sarkar in this volume.
15. Rubin, *Showstoppers*, p. 39.
16. Feuer, *Hollywood Musical*, pp. 68–9.
17. Jesse Green, 'Back Story', *New York Times*, 16 December 2007, section 2, p. 12.
18. Jesse Green, 'Sondheim Dismembers "Sweeney"', *New York Times*, 16 December 2007, section 2, p. 12. Sondheim does admit to liking a few of the older film musicals – *Sous les toits de Paris/Under the Roofs of Paris* (1930), *The Smiling Lieutenant* (1931), *Love Me Tonight* (1932) 'and a couple of the MGMs'.
19. 'Tommy Tune on Rob Marshall of "Nine"', *Daily Variety*, 5 January 2010, p. A2.
20. Denise Martin, 'Smoke & Mirrors: TV Tuner Trills Teens', *Variety*, 30 January–5 February 2006, p. 9.
21. Steve Clarke, '"High School Musical" Is New Kid on Europe Block', *Variety*, 18–24 September 2006, p. 25.
22. Michael Schneider, 'Telepic Is Music to Mouse's Ears: "High School" Lifts Cabler, Creates Global Ripple Effect', *Variety*, 6–12 August 2007, p. 14.
23. Clarke, '"High School Musical" Is New Kid on Europe Block', p. 25.
24. Schneider, 'Telepic Is Music to Mouse's Ears', p. 14.
25. Cynthia Littleton, 'Back to "School" for Grown-Ups', *Variety*, 27 August–2 September 2007, p. 7. It is worth noting that in their attention to the 'tween' appeal of the *High School Musical* series, trade accounts of its audience tend to discount another important demographic, albeit one whose interest in the musicals (so I have been told) tended to peak rather quickly as new fads came their way: namely, very young girls in the five to nine age group.
26. Cynthia Littleton, '"Musical Scores Overseas"', *Variety*, 1–7 October 2007, p. 29.
27. Archie Thomas, '"High" & Blighty: Hot "HSM3" Advance Tix Set Record', *Variety*, 12–19 October 2008, p. 13.
28. Neil Strauss, 'The New American Heart Throb', *Rolling Stone*, 23 August 2007, p. 38.
29. Kim Edwards, 'The Cinematic Heritage of *High School Musical*: Restarting Something New', *Screen Education*, no. 52, Summer 2009, p. 19.
30. See Rick Altman, *The American Film Musical* (Bloomington: Indiana University Press, 1989), as well as his reappraisal of his dual-focus model in this volume.
31. See Feuer, *Hollywood Musical*, pp. 13–15.
32. Marc Graser, 'Runaway Teens: Disney Protégés Moving On', *Variety*, 23–9 March 2009, p. 4.

33. Siegel, 'H'w'd's Musical Mania', p. 1.

34. Patricia Cohen, 'A Market Segment "Glee" Can Call Its Own: Theater Folk', *New York Times*, 17 November 2009, p. C1.

35. Pamela McClintock, 'Femmes Show More Muscle: Brand-Name Pics Sashay to Top of Charts with Support from Girls, Women', *Variety*, 10–16 November 2008, p. 6.

PART ONE: Genre Matters

1 From Homosocial to Heterosexual: The Musical's Two Projects

Rick Altman

This article takes a fresh look at the beginnings of Hollywood musicals. I argue that existing treatments of the musical are so attendant to endings and to synchronic analysis that the beginnings of musicals have been lost in the shuffle. What we discover by transferring our attention away from repeated conclusions and stable structures is altogether surprising, and of more than passing importance for our understanding of the cultural projects at work in the musical.

Assumptions regarding the relative importance of endings, as compared to beginnings, are widespread. From Frank Kermode's classic *The Sense of an Ending* to the Conclusion ('Endgames and the Study of Plot') of Peter Brooks's *Reading for the Plot*, academic critics have made a cottage industry of writing about conclusions.[1] Not unlike the importance of deathbed conversions in certain religious traditions, endings somehow seem more meaningful, more important, more … final than other textual segments. There is a sense that endings have the power to transform all that came before. In terms of textual analysis, the danger lies not so much in the power of an ending to transform a beginning or a middle, but in the ever-present possibility that beginnings and middles will be forgotten or misremembered, hidden as they tend to be in the shadow of the ending. It's not that endings are unimportant, it's that the ending orientation of virtually all plot-based analysis enforces a sort of back-formation whereby beginnings and middles are read through endings, thereby robbing them of any potential independent importance they might have.

Musicals offer particularly strong incentives to attend to endings. Virtually every musical ends with a show-stopping number, designed to attract attention. Many musicals substantially expand this strategy, offering not one but a whole series of final numbers. The list includes such varied films as *Footlight Parade* (Bacon, 1933), *The Gang's All Here* (Berkeley, 1943), *Thousands Cheer* (Sidney, 1943), *The Band Wagon* (Minnelli, 1953), *The Glenn Miller Story* (Mann, 1954) and *Woodstock* (Wadleigh, 1970). It is hardly surprising that illustrations of these and other comparable films often privilege finales. Of the two full-page illustrations that Bruce Babington and Peter William Evans dedicate to their chapter-long exemplary treatment of *Easter Parade*, one is predictably of the film's final scene.[2] A similar effect is produced by the freeze-frame two-shots that end so many musicals; because they encapsulate the plot's conclusion, while providing a convenient image of both male and female stars, final freeze-frames often find their way into printed or video references to musicals. Academic analyses of musical films also regularly stress the film's plot and the couple's final clinch.[3] In fact, even the growing group of critics who actively champion alternative approaches to the musical typically begin by recognising the importance of endings for our traditional understanding of the genre.[4]

Critical attention to musical endings is not the only reason why the opening sections of musicals have been so regularly disregarded. An important contributing factor in the neglect of musical beginnings lies in the tendency of recent critics to apply the semiotics-inspired techniques of synchronic analysis to musicals. The more synchronic our analyses, the less access we have to the kind of diachronic concerns that might concentrate attention on the early portions of musicals.

A quick glance in the mirror reminds me that I am in all probability the culprit most responsible for skewing attention toward musical endings. A recent rereading of my book on *The American Film Musical*[5] convinced me that the analytical strategies presented there, while illuminating certain questions and portions of the text, left others all too much in the shadows. For example, in reading Chapter 3, on 'The Structure of the American Film Musical', I noticed a repeated tendency to consider the notion of structure as purely synchronic in nature. Through the use of section headings like 'Each separate part of the film recapitulates the film's overall duality', and 'The basic sexual duality overlays a secondary dichotomy', I was able to describe several essential structural features of the musical, but only to the extent that they fit comfortably into my overall dual-focus approach to the form. Recognising the musical's repeated pairing of opposite-sex stars, dual-focus analysis allowed me to show how the members of the primary heterosexual couple regularly serve as the repository of paired but opposed cultural values, ultimately united through the couple's eventual mating. For all practical purposes, this pattern sacrifices chronological considerations in favour of spatial pairings. With the exception of the final resolution, usually achieved through marriage of the principals, musicals are seen in this approach as stable and unchanging. While this analytical technique may offer substantial insight into each film's synchronic system, it virtually forecloses access to diachronic analysis, especially with regard to earlier portions of the film.

My suspicions regarding the potential danger of an approach that closes as many options as it opens were compounded by the memory of a passage from an earlier article in which I made some quite specific claims about the relative importance of beginnings and endings. In response to David Bordwell's claim that 'of one hundred randomly sampled Hollywood films, over sixty ended with a display of the united romantic couple ... and many more could be said to end happily', I blithely affirmed – as part of a general claim that Hollywood beginnings are retrofitted to a pre-existing ending, to which the beginnings must appear to lead – that 'it is safe to assume that, outside of formal similarities, the beginnings of Hollywood films have no such common content'.[6] On what basis I made this claim I have no idea. Instead of contesting the apparent tyranny of endings by careful analysis of beginnings, I simply assumed that there would be nothing to be gained by looking closely at beginnings, of musicals or of any other Hollywood genre.

The kind of synchronic analysis championed by *The American Film Musical* treats musicals as structured by a simple and thus mnemonically satisfying pattern. Individual films are thus seen through the regular alternation between the heterosexual partners whose union constitutes the text's conclusion. Because the text's closure mechanisms are all triggered by processes involving the primary heterosexual couple, other textual aspects tend to be excluded. Analyses of individual texts may well focus on details other than the central romance, but overall assessments of the genre regularly return to the fundamental dual-focus framework constituted by the romantic couple who carry both plot and thematic content. Whatever else may be going on in individual musicals, this approach affirms, the genre as a whole is about heterosexual partnerships.

Without abandoning this basic claim, would it be possible to discover additional things that the musical is 'about'? In order to do so, it seems evident, we would have to begin by turning our backs on the standard synchronic, ending-oriented approach presented in *The American Film Musical*. Were we to follow this path, what would we find? MGM's classic 1951 *An American in Paris* offers a useful test case. For traditional musical analysis, Vincente Minnelli's film is quite obviously about the romance between Gene Kelly and Leslie Caron, two dancers who discover each other thanks to the magic that is Paris. But if we were to break the film down into its successive scenes, we would find that only a small

In *An American in Paris* (1951), Gene Kelly dances with one 'wrong' partner after another, from men to children and old ladies. This dance with Leslie Caron is one of the few times when the romantic leads actually dance together

portion of the text is specifically dedicated to presentation of the Kelly/Caron romance. A substantial proportion of the film details Kelly's involvement with an older woman who offers to bankroll his painting. Apparently interested in much more than her younger charge's artistic skills, Nina Foch is however consistently presented as an inappropriate match for Kelly. Her age, financial situation and scheming personality are a poor match for Kelly's youth, poverty and all-American naïveté. Paralleling the many scenes devoted to Kelly's mismatch are a series of episodes in which French chansonnier Georges Guétary is presented as a possible – but equally inappropriate – partner for Leslie Caron. Older by far than Caron, Guétary consistently displays feelings for her that are more paternal than romantic. Much of the film is thus more about 'wrong' partners than Kelly and Caron as 'right' partners.

A closer look at the film's song-and-dance routines confirms the sense that the film is just as much about alternatives to a Kelly/Caron romance than it is about the apparently central couple. As Stephen Harvey has pointed out, *An American in Paris* is 'the only important musical of the era with an all-male vocal score'.[7] To be sure, Kelly and Caron do engage in a memorable dance sequence on the banks of the Seine. But they never sing together, and – as in many of his films – Kelly does far more dancing with others than with his eventual romantic match. An upbeat version of George and Ira Gershwin's 'By Strauss' offers Kelly an opportunity to waltz with a woman more than twice his age. Later, he involves a group of Paris street urchins less than half his age in a delightful rendition of the Gershwins'

'I Got Rhythm'. Soon Kelly will be involved in a still odder pairing. In what might easily seem an unlikely duet, he dances around and on Oscar Levant's piano, to the tune of 'Tra La La'. Before long, Kelly will be singing 'S'Wonderful' as a duet with Georges Guétary. When *An American in Paris* is configured as a traditional dual-focus musical, stressing the courtship of a young couple, these parts of the film receive relatively little attention. When we make a point of concentrating on scenes in which the successful couple are absent, however, something quite different appears. By far the majority of the film seems populated by mismatches, by potential couples that are unacceptable for one reason or another. Waltzing grandma: too old. Nina Foch: wrong age, wrong interests. Street urchins: too young. Oscar Levant and Georges Guétary: wrong sex. Even the culminating ballet, which gives Kelly and Caron the opportunity to dance together in what should be a final consecration of their romance, overwhelms couple-oriented considerations with Minnelli's over-the-top recreation of the Paris art scene in the first half of the twentieth century.

When understood as a traditional musical, using the tools provided by *The American Film Musical*, *An American in Paris* is clearly just as much about Kelly and Caron as *Gigi* is about Louis Jourdan and Caron or *Top Hat* is about Astaire and Rogers. However, a second look offers a different version of the film. Quantitatively, *An American in Paris* is apparently more about wrong matches than about the one right match that is usually stressed. Taken individually, each event involving a wrong match seems inconsequential. Taken together, the overall pattern of presenting one potential wrong match after another takes on greater importance. The obvious question that we must ask is this. If we were to apply the same kind of analysis to the genre as a whole, stressing beginnings and diachronic analysis rather than endings and synchronic analysis, what would we find? Would an attempt to consciously avoid synchronic analysis generated by a known and generically stable ending lead to a new understanding of the genre? Or would we simply find ourselves back where we started, with the 'wrong couple' syndrome simply serving as yet another way to draw attention to the central couple?

The Astaire/Rogers classic *Top Hat* (Sandrich, 1935) offers an appropriate starting point for an alternative analysis of the musical, just as attendant to beginnings and wrong matches as to the more obvious pairing of the principals. As a consummate Astaire/Rogers vehicle, *Top Hat* has understandably always been analysed through the primary couple's interaction. Typically, my own treatment of *Top Hat*[8] begins with Astaire awakening Rogers through his tapped rendition of 'No Strings'. Indeed, in terms of the Astaire/Rogers relationship, this is where the film starts. But the whole point of this article is to discover whether something is going on in Astaire/Rogers films that is not wholly dependent on the relationship between Astaire and Rogers. So where does *Top Hat* actually start? What images and sounds does the beginning provide us as a key to the rest of the film? True, the credits do offer images of Astaire and Rogers whirling to Irving Berlin's music. But that's not where the film's narrative begins. Instead, we are treated to a series of all-male scenes. First we watch (and listen) while Astaire is repeatedly shushed at the oh-so-stuffy Thackeray Club. As he waits for impresario Edward Everett Horton, Astaire is cast as a young noise-maker by repeatedly contrasting him with the silent and staid – even doddering – members of the Thackeray Club. As he leaves, Astaire taps out a loud wake-up call to his slumbering entourage, definitively distancing himself from the age and silence of his all-male neighbours and clubby surroundings.

The following episode continues the all-male motif, but in a different venue. Now located in Edward Everett Horton's hotel room, Astaire witnesses a delicious reconciliation scene between the effete Horton and his sassy butler Eric Blore. Like the film's audience, Astaire is more amused than interested by Horton and Blore's quibbles over how to tie a tie and other vestimentary essentials. These are

Fred meets Ginger in *Top Hat* (1935) – but not at the film's very beginning. By this point, he has already found time for an all-male scene at the Thackeray Club and for a hotel room haberdashery discussion with impresario Edward Everett Horton and his butler Eric Blore

clearly men who are more interested in haberdashery than in women. The scene that follows neatly demonstrates Astaire's quite different preoccupations. Though his encounter with Rogers is initiated by pure chance – sleeping in the room beneath, she is awakened by his tap dancing – the heterosexual nature of Astaire's interests is immediately demonstrated both by his dialogue with Rogers and by the bit of dance business that has him catching and cradling in his arms the statue of a woman. Later segments of the film will repeat this motif. Astaire is regularly paired with a man – including a whole male chorus in 'Top Hat, White Tie and Tails' – only to leave all male partners behind in favour of a romance with Rogers.

Rogers mirrors Astaire's repeated pairing with a soon-to-be-abandoned partner. When she arrives in Venice, she is at first presented in the company of Horton's wife (Helen Broderick). Later, Rogers will be followed around like a puppy by her prissy clothes designer Alberto Beddini (Erik Rhodes). Whenever Astaire or Rogers appears without the other, the film tends to be structured around the presentation of an inappropriate partner. As with Horton and Blore's fascination with apparel, Rhodes's effete attention to accoutrements and style makes him unacceptable as a partner for Rogers.

The obvious way to read *Top Hat* is the traditional approach through the central couple. After all, *Top Hat* isn't called 'an Astaire/Rogers film' for nothing. In one sense, the film is clearly built on alternation and parallelism between Astaire and Rogers. Seen this way, every part of the film prepares and/or cele-brates the union of the two principals. Yet if we look closely at the details of the film, we find something else going on. In addition to close attention to the 'right' couple – Astaire and Rogers – there would appear to be a studied attempt to define the nature of couples judged 'wrong' within the film's dynamic. The members of the Thackeray Club are not a good match for Astaire because of their age and preju-dice against noise (a situation partially remedied by a later change of attitude, marked by their atten-dance at Astaire's stage show). The odd couple of Edward Everett Horton and Eric Blore offers another unacceptable coupling choice – homosocial rather than heterosexual and overly attendant to vestimen-tary details. Eventually, we will witness the ultimate odd pairing: Horton and Astaire will (by this point, somewhat predictably) share the bridal suite. Rogers's potential partners confirm the pattern established with Astaire. Neither a same-sex partner nor a man more interested in clothing design than in women will do. Viewed in this manner, the Astaire/Rogers couple seems almost like an add-on to Top Hat's implicit discourse on proper partnerships. While Astaire and Rogers are clearly the 'right' match, they are only one of several matches considered (and, in all but this one case, clearly discarded) by the film.

In suggesting that critical attention to the central couple has kept us from perceiving other impor-tant aspects of the musical, I am of course criticising the central argument of my own study on The American Film Musical. However useful my dual-focus approach may have been a quarter-century ago, what is now needed is something different. As a complement to the dual-focus strategies presented in The American Film Musical, I thus propose two new hypotheses. The first is conservative and easily demonstrated. The second is both more radical and more speculative in nature. Hypothesis number one: far from safely assuming that the beginnings of musicals have little in common, I suggest that the diachronic aspect of musicals is regularly characterised by a progression from presentation of a series of 'wrong' couples – typically including same-sex matches – to establishment of one or more 'right' couples. While musicals may be oblivious to the kind of psychological causality usually associated with classical Hollywood narrative, a substantial amount of development clearly takes place in most of them. As is common with dual-focus texts in general – a topic treated at length in my recent A Theory of Narrative[9] – change in the musical takes place not through a traditional causal chain, but through a sequence of redefinitions or replacements, in this case eventually supplanting several wrong matches with the right one.

Textual structures based on sequential presentation of a series of wrong couples followed by even-tual exemplification of proper coupling are of course hardly unusual in the history of cinema – or of western literature, for that matter. From Greek 'new' comedy to British Restoration comedy and from classical French comedy to American screwball comedy, comic genres have often been built around the correction of romantic mismatches. Whether the mismatched partner is the wrong generation (as in Molière's The Miser), lacking a sense of humour (as in Frank Capra's It Happened One Night or Howard Hawks's His Girl Friday) or the wrong kind of dancer (as in Charles Walters's Easter Parade), the pat-tern varies little. In order to better define the 'right' type of couple, it is necessary to provide several contrasting examples of 'wrong' couples. In one sense, the successive presentation of unacceptable matches might be understood as an entirely normal aspect of the dual-focus process whereby con-centration on the central couple is maintained or at least implied even when both members of the couple are absent. Seen in this manner, 'wrong' couples are interpreted as nothing more than an episode in the musical's main project of championing the marriage of properly matched partners. The conservative nature of my first hypothesis is amply revealed by the ease with which attention to wrong couples can be interpreted as part of an entirely standard focus on the main couple.

A second hypothesis goes quite a bit farther. Instead of understanding musical beginnings as an integral part of the standard dual-focus structure, this second hypothesis suggests that there may be a quite specific second project operative in the musical genre. In addition to the musical's primary *heterosexual* project, which builds its structures and values around the romantic coupling of carefully paired opposite-sex partners, I propose that we recognise in the musical the operation of a carefully targeted *homosocial* project. When we look closely at the beginnings of musical films, we consistently find that at least one of the young lovers is initially presented in the company of one or more same-sex friends. In Lubitsch's *Love Parade* (1929), Maurice Chevalier is first presented in the company of his male servant and his male … dog. *Broadway Melody* (Beaumont, 1929) is built around the same-sex couple of Bessie Love and Anita Page. In *Gold Diggers of 1933* (LeRoy, 1933), Joan Blondell, Ruby Keeler and Aline MacMahon share an apartment. *Broadway Melody of 1940* (Taurog, 1940) provides Fred Astaire with George Murphy as a constant companion. Before considering heterosexual partners, Marilyn Monroe and Jane Russell are matched to each other in *Gentlemen Prefer Blondes* (Hawks, 1953). *Guys and Dolls* (Mankiewicz, 1955) gives Marlon Brando an entire gang of male cronies. *West Side Story* (Robbins and Wise, 1961) works similarly. *My Fair Lady* (Cukor, 1964) matches Rex Harrison's Henry Higgins with his friend Pickering (Wilfrid Hyde-White).

As noted by Steven Cohan, virtually every film featuring Gene Kelly begins with a same-sex pairing.[10] Throughout substantial portions of *Anchors Aweigh* (Sidney, 1945), *Take Me Out to the Ball Game* (Berkeley, 1949) and *On the Town* (Kelly and Donen, 1949), Kelly is practically inseparable from Frank Sinatra, with Jules Munshin rounding out the trio in the latter film. Phil Silvers joins Kelly in *Cover Girl* (Vidor, 1944) and *Summer Stock* (Walters, 1950). *Singin' in the Rain* (Kelly and Donen, 1952) provides Donald O'Connor as Kelly's primary male companion. *Brigadoon* (Minnelli, 1954) pairs Kelly with Van Johnson. In *It's Always Fair Weather* (Kelly and Donen, 1955), Kelly is partnered by Dan Dailey and Michael Kidd.

Military musicals regularly offer a full company of compadres, as in *Flirtation Walk* (Borzage, 1934) and *Shipmates Forever* (Borzage, 1935). Serving as an appropriate theme song for these films is Nelson Eddy's hearty rendition of 'Give Me Some Men Who Are Stouthearted Men' near the start of *New Moon* (Leonard, 1940). From *Roberta* (Seiter, 1935) to *The Glenn Miller Story*, musicals built around a band provide a ready-made male chorus for the central bandleader. Whether male or female, musical stars sometimes find homosocial society in the workplace, from *The Harvey Girls* (Sidney, 1946) to *Pajama Game* (Donen and Abbott, 1957). Often, it is a family that provides the same-sex matches, as in *Meet Me in St Louis* (Minnelli, 1944) and *Seven Brides for Seven Brothers* (Donen, 1954).

It would certainly appear that I was wrong – at least in the case of the musical – to claim that the beginnings of Hollywood films do not share the same level of commonality as endings. An extraordinary proportion of musicals commence not with the heterosexual couple that occupies the text's later portions, but with one or more homosocial pairs. Just what is going on in these films? Why, when we concentrate on musical beginnings, do we see something so different from what we find when we attend to musical endings? *Grease*, Randall Kleiser's 1978 portrait of high-school life, offers a particularly clear explanation of the stakes involved in the musical's investment in homosocial relationships.

From the outset, *Grease* presents its characters in unisex groups. The opening number ('Summer Nights') splits Rydell High into two separate worlds, with the Pink Ladies serving as a chorus for Sandy (Olivia Newton-John) and the Thunderbirds backing up Danny (John Travolta). By attributing the same lyrics alternately to the two groups ('Tell Me More … Those Summer Nights'), the film forces us to compare men and women as separate entities. When Danny discovers that Sandy – the object of his

From the very start of *Grease* (1978), the guys hang out with the guys and the gals hang with other gals. Here, the guys sing their part of the opening song, 'Summer Nights'

summer affections – has unexpectedly not left town, he at first reveals romantic emotions, apparently ready to bridge the gender gap, but the presence of his buddies soon forces him to adopt an entirely different approach. As Sonny (Michael Tucci) tellingly puts it a few minutes later, at the point where Kenickie (Jeff Conaway) deserts his buddies in favour of Rizzo (Stockard Channing), 'When a guy picks a chick over his buddies, somethin' gotta be wrong.' The entire first part of *Grease* follows this logic of enforced sexual separation. As Frenchy (Didi Conn) insists, explaining why all-female activities are a necessary part of high-school life, 'Men are rats. Listen to me. Fleas on rats. Worse than that. Amoebas on fleas on rats. The only man a girl can depend on is her daddy.' For women as well as men, the early portions of *Grease* argue strongly in favour of homosocial relationships.

But the film soon begins to push aside this logic of sexual separation. When National Bandstand comes to Rydell High, students are summarily informed that 'all couples must be boy/girl'. Soon afterward, the strength of single-sex relationships is compromised by the limits imposed on Danny and Kenickie's male bonding. In recognition of their longtime friendship, Danny agrees to serve as Kenickie's second at Thunder Road, but the physical expression of this arrangement – a friendly hug between Danny and Kenickie – is rapidly disavowed as inappropriate. Guys, the film insists, mustn't show emotional attachment to other guys.

Danny takes great pride in fulfilling a leadership role within his all-male group. One aspect of that leadership involves knowing just what kind of relationships are appropriate among group members. Whenever Danny is tempted to reveal even the slightest level of affection for another male, he instantly draws back, simultaneously demonstrating both the temptation of same-sex bonding and its inappropriateness. Sentimentality is simply not suitable among men, *Grease* tells us loud and clear.

While Danny is demonstrating both the importance and the dangers of male bonding, Sandy is being initiated into the parallel female group, where she learns both the pleasures of female togetherness and the potential dangers of heterosexual contact. On both sides of the sexual barrier, the characters spend substantial time and energy talking about the other group, but these conversations are consistently restricted to same-sex scenes. When the T-Birds turn their mechanical shop class into an ode to automobiles and the young men who drive and work on them, they are quite exceptionally accompanied by a woman – Mrs Murdock, the female shop teacher (Alice Ghostley) – but her entirely sexless demeanour only serves to prove the rule.

Grease's finale totally reverses the film's earlier dedication to single-sex logic. After Sandy clearly demonstrates to Danny that he's 'The One That I Want', we are subjected to an entire song explaining the diverse ways in which Sandy and Danny 'Go Together'. After over an hour of a fundamentally homosocial approach to life, Grease now switches strategies, insisting instead that heterosexual pairing is the better long-term course. Not just Sandy and Danny, but also Rizzo and Kenickie and even Coach Calhoun (Sid Caesar) and Principal McGee (Eve Arden) are matched in the film's final tableaux. A film that began by stressing homosocial relationships ends by vaunting heterosexual pairings. In addition, Danny's conversion from the homosocial world of the Thunderbirds to a heterosexual couple with Sandy is paralleled by his switch from T-Bird leather to an athletic letter sweater. Danny has graduated, the film implies, not only from high school, but from the homosocial ties of his past to the heterosexual relationship that will define his future.

When we concentrate on musical beginnings, we discover something quite different from familiar findings based on musical endings. Like Grease, many musicals appear under this new light to be about a

After one homosocial scene after another, Grease finally resolves its ambiguities by permanently pairing John Travolta and Olivia Newton-John

very specific rite of passage. Homosocial relationships, dominant in musical beginnings, must be put away in favour of the heterosexual relationships that dominate musical endings. It is important to note the mismatch between these two terms. Musical beginnings are typically homo*social*, while musical endings are almost always hetero*sexual* in nature. Why this slippage from the social to the sexual? In an important sense, I would suggest, this apparently insignificant shift is what the musical is all about. Many other texts – from popular psychology primers to buddy films and novels of development – champion a maturation process involving graduation from a narrow homosocial group to the broader heterosocial community. In contrast, the musical's insistence on a rite of passage that is specifically marked as progressing from the homo*social* to the hetero*sexual* has the effect of implicitly fore-grounding the absent homo*sexual* category. Whereas a movement from homosocial to heterosocial describes nothing more than the shift from childhood single-sex groups to mature mixed-sex society, the passage from homosocial to heterosexual specifically negates the alternative possibility of move-ment from relationships that are only homosocial to fully homosexual bonds.

It would thus appear that the musical as a genre forwards two separate but coordinated projects. The musical labours to eradicate homosocial bonds – or at least to keep them from turning into homo-sexual ties – just as hard as it works to establish durable heterosexual relationships. In order to be a productive citizen, the musical argues, we must not only put away 'childish' same-sex relationships in favour of 'mature' mixed-sex society, but we must also avoid allowing homosocial connections to turn into homosexual ties, adopting instead the solution of heterosexual courtship that the musical works so hard to represent as 'natural'. In this way, the musical imposes a restrictive ideology, offering implicit training in the conservative attitude that dominated American society during the decades when the musical thrived. Certainly, the restrictive nature of the musical's twin projects helps to explain why so many critics have felt the need to develop alternative approaches to the musical, stressing spectator-ship, style or a star persona as an appropriate alternative to the plot-oriented readings that long dom-inated the field.[11]

Stressing musical conclusions, we cannot help but attend to the genre's familiar support of coupling between the sexes. But a closer look at the musical's full agenda reveals a studied attempt to both present and reject the alternative of same-sex relationships. In order to understand the musical's cultural strategies, we must broaden our approach, attending to both of the musical's projects – the homosocial along with the heterosexual.[12]

Notes

1. Frank Kermode, *The Sense of an Ending* (New York: Oxford University Press, 1967); Peter Brooks, *Reading for the Plot: Design and Intention in Narrative* (Cambridge, MA: Harvard University Press, 1992), p. 313ff.
2. Bruce Babington and Peter William Evans, *Blue Skies and Silver Linings: Aspects of the Hollywood Musical* (Manchester: Manchester University Press, 1985), p. 41.
3. See, for example, Thomas Schatz, *Hollywood Genres: Formulas, Filmmaking, and the Studio System* (New York: Random House, 1981), p. 200ff; Alain Masson, *Comédie musicale* (Paris: Stock, 1981), p. 117ff; Patricia Mellencamp, 'Spectacle and Spectator: Looking through the American Musical Comedy', in Ron Burnett (ed.), *Explorations in Film Theory: Selected Essays from Cine Tracts* (Bloomington: Indiana University Press, 1991), pp. 3–14; Jane Feuer, *The Hollywood Musical*, 2nd edition (Bloomington: Indiana University Press, 1993), p. 77ff.
4. This is especially true of the growing number of critics who see the musical as a potential repository of gay values and/or as an object of gay appreciation. For example, while recommending a viewing strategy that

refuses and undermines it, Brett Farmer nevertheless recognises 'the musical's push toward closure' along with 'the clotural scenario of idealized heterosexual union promoted by the musical' (*Spectacular Passions: Cinema, Fantasy, Gay Male Spectatorships* [Durham, NC: Duke University Press, 2000], pp. 79, 81). In order to stress his point that 'there is more to the making of musicals beyond the plotline', and that gay readings appropriately subordinate plot orientation to spectacle sensitivity, Matthew Tinkcom must first recognise the heterosexual and end-loaded nature of that plotline (*Working Like a Homosexual: Camp, Capital, Cinema* [Durham, NC: Duke University Press, 2002], p. 53).

5. Rick Altman, *The American Film Musical* (Bloomington: Indiana University Press, 1987).

6. David Bordwell, *Narration in the Fiction Film* (Madison: University of Wisconsin Press, 1985), p. 159; quoted in Rick Altman, 'Dickens, Griffith, and Film Theory Today', *South Atlantic Quarterly*, vol. 88 no. 2, Spring 1989, p. 344.

7. Stephen Harvey, *Directed by Vincente Minnelli* (New York: Museum of Modern Art/Harper & Row, 1989), p. 98.

8. Rick Altman, *American Film Musical*, pp. 171–7.

9. Rick Altman, *A Theory of Narrative* (New York: Columbia University Press, 2008). See especially Chapters 2 and 3.

10. Steven Cohan, *Incongruous Entertainment: Camp, Cultural Value, and the MGM Musical* (Durham, NC: Duke University Press, 2005), pp. 152, 165.

11. See, for example, Farmer, *Spectacular Passions*, Tinkcom, *Working Like a Homosexual* and Cohan, *Incongruous Entertainment*, as well as the Conclusion of the second edition of Feuer, *The Hollywood Musical*.

12. It is interesting to note that the homosocial-to-heterosexual pattern treated here is by no means restricted to the musical alone. Many Hollywood films – including popular favourites like *Cocktail* (Donaldson, 1988) and *Wedding Crashers* (Dobkin, 2005) – slide nearly imperceptibly from homosocial situations to eventual heterosexual solutions, and thus from buddy film to romance. This basic pattern, along with the generic and cultural hierarchies that it implies, deserves further study.

2 British Gaiety:
Musical Cinema and the Theatrical Tradition in British Film

Lawrence Napper

As its title implies, *The Young Ones* (1961) is predicated on the notion of generational conflict. The film opens with a vision of modernity and regeneration – a panoramic view of London in the grip of the post-war building boom. The chimes of Big Ben drift across the rooftops as the camera swings around 180 degrees to reveal its location on top of a multi-storey office block in the process of construction. The film makes an immediate connection between this resurgent economy and the 'young ones' who are apparently its principal beneficiaries. 'It's Friday night! Time to go home now!' sings one of the young construction workers, initiating a credit sequence which follows him as he threads his way down through the scaffolding, picks up his wages from the pay office and finally disappears into the traffic on his moped. His song is taken up by the various principal characters as they too celebrate the arrival of Friday night. The camera picks up shop assistants, office workers, hairdressers, waitresses and students as they emerge from their various workplaces, greeting each other in the street and marking the division between work and leisure time in a song which emphasises their intention to 'see you at the dance tonight'.

As Kevin Donnelly has pointed out, *The Young Ones* initiates a successful cycle of British musicals which dramatise a transformation in the perception of youth from the delinquents of 1950s films such as *The Blue Lamp* (1950), *Cosh Boy* (1953) and *Serious Charge* (1959) into 'good kids' – a change which 'duplicates the subsuming of rock 'n' roll into established modes of popular music'.[1] It also represents probably the most ambitious attempt to replicate the Hollywood musical in Britain since Rank's disastrous experiment with *London Town* in 1945. On his DVD commentary for the film, the director, Sidney J. Furie, remembers the project as an explicit attempt to combine Hollywood musical conventions with the modern rock 'n' roll appeal and youth sensibilities of the film's star, Cliff Richard. Nowhere is *The Young Ones*' debt to Hollywood more evident than in this opening number, which absolutely demonstrates the popular cliché of characters bursting into song while walking down the street. This trope has the double effect of producing the street as a space available for appropriation by performers, and also of making that appropriation work towards benign ends. Whereas the previous films about youthful delinquency had represented the street as dangerous and frightening as a result of the presence of young people, the opening number of *The Young Ones* offers an alternative understanding, where the youthful presence is a force of utopianism.

This opening sequence, then, sets up two thematic concerns which one might suggest are intrinsic to the musical form more generally: first, a celebration of youth culture through its connection with popular music – but also the establishment of a continuity between that music and older forms of popular culture – and second, an interest in the city and city streets as the space for a utopian expression of that culture. Furie is right to offer the Hollywood musical as a key model for his film, particularly since by 1961 the musical genre had not held a prominent position in British production schedules for some time. Nevertheless, in this article I'd like to trace the recurrent appearance of these themes of youth and the city across a number of British musical films, and to suggest that these films, while drawing heavily on American models, are nevertheless also at pains to identify themselves as part of an explicitly British theatrical tradition, celebrating this heritage as a distinctive 'native' popular culture, separate from American jazz or European operetta forms. Drawing on popular memory of the 'Gaiety' theatrical shows associated with George Edwardes, films such as *Gaiety George* (1946) and *Trottie True* (1949) present the Edwardian musical comedy as both a break from previous Victorian forms, and as the initiation of a tradition which extends well into the mid-twentieth century. These two examples place the Edwardian Gaiety Theatre at the centre of their narrative, offering audiences nostalgic recreations of an Edwardian theatrical culture, which would still have been within living memory at the time of their release. However I'm also intrigued by the way in which even films which emphasise modernity and contemporary settings as their key pleasures still cite the Gaiety as a central reference point, obsessively referring backwards, it seems, to the Edwardian stage as a moment of inception for the pleasures of musical narrative. These British musicals, then, place a faith in the continuity of British popular entertainment, even as they introduce new musical styles, and draw on cinematic traditions from abroad.

Nowhere is this process more evident than in *The Young Ones*. The opening number, with all its show-tune chutzpah, is contrasted against the scene which follows, set at the dance which the young people have been anticipating. Here, rather than colonising the public street through music and dance, the young people are shown in a space already marked off as their own – the youth club to which they all belong. The music is also marked off as their own, both in style and presentation. Instead of an off-screen orchestra, it emanates from the on-screen guitar and percussion ensemble of the Shadows, fronted by Cliff Richard himself, playing Nicky Black, the unofficial leader of the gang, and singing the much more rock-inflected pop song, 'I've Got a Funny Feeling'. Whereas previously, the dancing and camerawork had both been highly choreographed, here the treatment is entirely naturalistic. This is a space, apparently, where the young people do not have to perform – they can be 'themselves'.

This space, though, is under threat, and from the very forces of modernity which the young ones themselves initially appeared to represent. Unbeknown to the rest of the gang, Nicky's father is the millionaire property developer Hamilton Black (Robert Morley). When we first discover Black, he is contemplating the symbol of his own modernity – an architectural model of a multi-storey office block reminiscent of the one which opened the film, and which I've already suggested is initially used to associate the young ones with the economic boom of the early 1960s. This scene, though, serves to modify that association, for it presents Hamilton Black as the true driver and beneficiary of that boom, and his values, though modern, as far from benevolent. The model is for a new development he is planning to build on the very site of his son's youth club, and in the dialogue with Nicky which follows, he uses an extended military metaphor to describe his plans to acquire the site and destroy the club. Unaware of his son's involvement in the club, his description of his opponents as 'a crowd of untidy adolescents, milling around in their leather jackets, brandishing bicycle chains' realises precisely the preconceptions about youth that the film itself is so keen to deny.

The narrative develops as a struggle over both the conception of youthful leisure and over the space in which that leisure may take place. This struggle involves an inversion of the oppositions between modernity and tradition that one might expect, as Black becomes identified with a destructive philistine modernity, while the gang at the youth club become increasingly identified with the maintenance of tradition. In time-honoured fashion, the gang resolve to raise enough money to save their club by putting on a show. They hire the Countess Theatre, only to find that they are unable to use it because Black has bought the theatre for himself, with the intention of converting it into a bingo

Cliff Richard and his pals attempt to save their youth club by recreating its pleasures on an Edwardian stage in *The Young Ones* (1961)

hall. Further setbacks follow, each of which threatens or restricts the relationship between the young people's performance and the 'natural' expression of their emotion. The relationship between Nicky and his girlfriend, Toni (Carole Gray), is placed under strain by the arrival of Dorinda Morrell (Sonya Cordeau), the busty and commercial – but undeniably vulgar – star who is set to replace Toni as the leading lady in the show. Nicky is unable to muster the requisite emotion when singing the love duet with Dorinda which he had originally written for Toni. Their relationship is further strained by the necessity of keeping Nicky's family connection to Hamilton Black from the rest of the gang. Significantly, the only space in which they can talk honestly is away from the club, outside London altogether, at Ruislip Lido – the setting for the rendition of the title song. Finally, in order to generate publicity for their show, the gang must devise a stunt involving a pirate radio station – literally breaking the law in order to carve out a space for their performance across the streets of London.

Thrown back on their own resources, the gang identify a derelict Edwardian theatre (actually the Finsbury Park Empire – itself demolished shortly after the film was released), and break into it with the intention of restoring it to its former glory as a fitting venue for their performance. The bricolage number which follows is by far the most elaborate and extended musical sequence in the film. It marks the point at which all the struggles of the backstage plot – the search for a venue and a star, and the

difficulty of writing original material for the show – give way to spontaneous and 'natural' group performance. Not surprisingly, given my argument, it is also the point at which the group are inspired by
the setting to connect with an Edwardian theatrical heritage. In its review of the film, *Kinematograph
Weekly* identified 'What d'ya Know, We've Got a Show' as the number most likely to figure in the hit
parade, commenting that 'during the music hall sequences old-time acts are cleverly parodied and the
artful tinge of nostalgia widens the film's appeal and scope'.[2] Donnelly points out that the reviewer is
mistaken in his prediction about the chart possibilities of the number – it was Cliff's pop solos which
had a life outside the film – but the intention of widening the generational appeal of the films through
the inclusion of 'old-time acts' is not in dispute, and indeed the technique reappears in Cliff's subsequent musicals, *Summer Holiday* (1963) and *Wonderful Life* (1964). Nevertheless, it would be an elderly parent indeed who, accompanying the teenage Cliff fan, had a direct memory of the performances
evoked here.

As they contemplate breaking into the theatre, one of the gang admits to stage fright. His mate
points out that this might be a little premature, since they have yet to find a stage, props, lights, costumes, make-up or script. That initial despondence turns to joy when they get inside to discover that
there *are* costumes and scenery littering the stage, even if they 'must be about a hundred years old'.
The transformation of their high-spirited fooling around with theatrical clichés into a spontaneous performance where the 'magic is working' is signalled by the miracle of the working stage lights, accompanied by three chords and a harp glissando (from an extra-diegetic orchestra), which segues into the
fully realised pastiche of a medley of Edwardian stage hits. Of these, the most 'recent' is an impersonation of Jessie Matthews singing 'Tinkle Tinkle Tinkle' from *Evergreen* (1934), complete with the
high kicks and crystalline elocution forever associated with Matthews's performance style. This song
(and the original film within which it appears) is itself concerned with the evocation of Edwardian
theatre, as I shall discuss below, but here it operates merely as a cultural staging post in the backwards
journey towards the origins of musical theatre celebrated by the number. Variously, we are treated to
a demonstration of the Vernon and Irene Castle style of dancing; an early film show in the style of the
serial queen melodrama of the teens; 'Have a Smile for Everyone You Meet' from 1918; 'Captain
Ginjah' from 1911; 'Where Did You Get That Hat?' from 1888 and rewritten in 1901; and 'The Piccadilly
Johnny with the Little Glass Eye' (albeit performed without the cross-dressing which so shocked Queen
Mary when it was sung by Vesta Tilley at the inaugural Royal Variety performance in 1912). The eclec-
ticism of this mixture, and the fact that the numbers are interspersed with comic routines reviving old
chestnuts, suggests music hall as much as the musical comedy associated with the Gaiety Theatre,
although, as I shall discuss later, there was considerable cross-fertilisation between the forms, and to
a certain extent they shared an extra-curricular culture as epitomised by the figure of the 'Piccadilly
Johnny'. The sequence is striking not only in the abundance of its Edwardian references, but also in
their specificity. Other than the film section and the comedians, these renditions are not stylistic generalisations – several of them are quite precise imitations of actual performances (Jessie Matthews, for
example) or iconic figures from the period (the Stage Door Johnnie in the Vesta Tilley number, for
example).

By the time 'What d'ya Know' is reprised as the closing number of the successful performance at
the end of the film, the Edwardian references and scenery have been excised in favour of modern costumes and a backdrop which self-reflexively represents the youth club itself. Nevertheless, the
Edwardian auditorium which hosts this performance, the fact that the reprise occurs straight after a
Cliff Richard rock number (complete with screaming audience) and the participation of Hamilton Black

himself on stage (now reconciled with his son and the youth club by his recognition and approval of their youthful 'enterprise') mean that the number can still be read symbolically as the point at which the generational conflict at the heart of the film is resolved, significantly through an emphasis on the continuity of entertainment values and styles.

I've already mentioned the use of Jessie Matthews's *Evergreen* as a staging post in the backwards journey towards the Edwardian numbers at the heart of *The Young Ones*. I'd like now to use that film in the same way for my own reverse journey through the history of the British musical. Like *The Young Ones*, *Evergreen* has a generational theme at its heart. It strives, both through its narrative and the range of musical styles it presents, to make a case for the continuity of popular musical forms, even as it celebrates the modernity and youthful exuberance of its central performer. Sarah Street has made a convincing case for seeing Jessie Matthews as an icon of modernity, through her association – established in this and later films – with art deco design.[3] Art deco, she suggests, should be understood as a design style which connotes a democratic conception of the modern through its use not only in mass-market films, but also in the consumer goods and modern interiors which they showcased, and in the variety of new leisure spaces designed to accommodate the popular audience of the 1930s – cinemas, most importantly, but also theatres, department stores, cafés and restaurants. Matthews is placed within such stylish settings in almost all of her films (the central 'Dancing on the Ceiling' number from *Evergreen* is instrumental in this argument), and with her lithe, streamlined body, the

Jessie Matthews turns back time in *Evergreen* (1934)

range of diaphanous but figure-revealing outfits she wears and her dancing style which emphasises a range of elegant, long-limbed, stretching poses, she could be seen as a physical embodiment of art deco's conception of ideal femininity, as portrayed in the ubiquitous table lamps, proscenium friezes and stylised posters of the period.[4]

Evergreen initiated a cycle of musicals which showcased Matthews in this way. Usually, as here, she plays a struggling actress who is only able to achieve her ambition of theatrical stardom through a series of impersonations – as a society hostess (in *It's Love Again*, 1936), as a male impersonator (in *First a Girl*, 1935), as a maid (in *Gangway*, 1937) and here, as her own mother. In each of these examples, the act of impersonation allows Matthews's character to move out of the obscurity of the chorus and into the elite spaces occupied by the producers and impresarios who can make her a star, through a series of spectacular publicity stunts. Each film turns on the question of whether the public and the producers will recognise her star quality and accept her even after her deception has been revealed (a question which is always, of course, answered in the affirmative). The films, then, place an emphasis on the democratic possibilities of modern patterns of consumption, display and publicity. Through these codes, the self can be constructed in such a way that social and professional barriers might be transcended – by behaving *like* a star, Matthews becomes a star *in fact*. One might contrast such a star image against Matthews's closest box-office rival of the period, Gracie Fields, whose films always emphasised her star quality as rooted in a class and region-specific *authenticity*. Fields's attempts at impersonation always fail. Whenever (as quite often happens) she is plucked out of her natural milieu to perform for the 'toffs' in the West End, she is either made to feel uncomfortable, or is unable to resist sending up the venue and the audience. Only when reunited with her roots is she able to produce successful performances. The social fluidity evident in Matthews's films, then, is quite specific to her association with modernity, and as Street suggests, with art deco.

Like *The Young Ones* (and in contrast to Gracie Fields's resolutely inexportable vehicles), *Evergreen* is also heavily indebted to Hollywood models. Andrew Higson has written extensively about the ways in which the narrative structure and the editing practices of the film draw on the classical Hollywood style, and he places this within the context of a production strategy at Gaumont-British which explicitly aimed to export the film internationally (a policy which appears to have been relatively successful in this instance).[5] Furthermore, it is adapted from a stage musical by one of the foremost American songwriting teams of the period, Richard Rodgers and Lorenz Hart, and was choreographed, both on stage and on film, by the black American dance trainer Buddy Bradley. The show – *Ever Green* – had been commissioned especially for the London stage by Charles Cochran, and opened (again starring Jessie Matthews) at the Adelphi Theatre in 1930. According to *The Times* review, it was as much a spectacular revue as a musical comedy, featuring set pieces involving a revolving stage, and ranging from a funfair at night to a Spanish village scene.[6] Nevertheless, the primary narrative idea (and, as I've suggested, the model for all of the Matthews films which followed) is credited to Rodgers and Hart, fleshed out by Benn Levy for the stage and refined by Emlyn Williams and the director Victor Saville for the screen.[7] Only a few of the original Rodgers and Hart numbers were retained in the screen adaptations, which introduced new songs by another American, Harry Woods, as well as using some original Edwardian popular hits.

Given the association with modernity mobilised by Jessie Matthews's star persona, and the influence of American personnel and musical styles on the film, it may come as a surprise to find that the narrative of *Evergreen* nevertheless revolves around the continuity between Matthews's character and an Edwardian stage tradition. The film opens with a prologue, heralded by a title card proclaiming simply 'Yesterday'. This dissolves to a view of an illuminated sign outside the Tivoli Music Hall in the Strand, advertising the 'Farewell Appearance of Harriet Green'. Inside, we discover Matthews as Harriet Green performing the 1892 hit 'Daddy Wouldn't Buy Me a Bow Wow', the song which apparently 'first endeared' her to the adoring audience who crowd the theatre in their top hats and bustles. She is giving up the stage, we learn, to marry her aristocratic sweetheart, thereby becoming the Marchioness of Staines. The finality of this decision is doubted by a couple of barmaids, who agree prophetically that, like all performers, she will be back on the stage, 'if not in two years, then twenty'; but all are agreed that whether on the stage or off, with her radiant beauty, she will never grow old, an observation which leads them to coin her soubriquet – 'Evergreen'. The scene dissolves to her engagement party at the Café Royal, where Harriet's friend Maudie (Betty Balfour) is also subject to a proposal of marriage (from another aristocrat, Lord Shropshire), a proposal which has not come unexpectedly, as the cutting remarks of a male chorus member, Leslie (Sonnie Hale), make clear. The two female stars are induced to dance on the supper table with a rendition of 'I Wouldn't Leave My Little Wooden Hut for You' (from 1905), but in the midst of these celebrations Harriet is called away. We learn in the following scene that she is being blackmailed by the father of her illegitimate child. In order to avoid the consequences of this, she resolves to leave her aristocratic fiancé and, placing the child in the care of her trusted dresser, she flees to South Africa. In our last glimpse of her, she is in a hansom cab, the strains of 'Little Wooden Hut' ringing in her ears as she regretfully removes her engagement ring. Passing the Tivoli, she looks up to see the illuminated sign advertising her name as it is gradually extinguished.

This prologue takes up less than 20 minutes of screen time, but it is packed both with incident and with incidental detail. The nostalgic recreations of both the performances and the performance spaces of pre-World War I London are matched by the recapitulation of a number of popular and iconic ideas about theatrical culture of the period. The extravagant feasting at the Café Royal (with Lord Shropshire drinking champagne from Maudie's slipper, for example) and the emphasis on the stage as a passport to aristocratic marriage offer a memory spectacle for the enjoyment of the audience, as well as sketching out a cultural and moral contrast with the modern storyline to come.

That story is introduced by a very descriptive establishing shot, a rhyme to the 'Yesterday' title which introduced the prologue. Whereas the 'Yesterday' title (matching the main credits of the film) appeared against a design suggesting an embroidered lace handkerchief, here the word 'To-Day' (in a deco typeface) is superimposed on a filmed image of the contemporary Tivoli Theatre, shot from a position in the middle of the Strand, with traffic passing by in front of it. The original Tivoli Music Hall had been demolished and rebuilt as a cinema in 1923, and it is this rather nondescript building that appears in this establishing shot. The camera lingers for a moment on the cinema before swinging round to the opposite side of the street and closing in on the Adelphi Theatre, clearly implying that this will be the setting for the modern portion of the story which is to come. The move is significant. The Adelphi itself had recently been demolished and rebuilt in a resolutely art deco style, reopening in 1930 with the production of *Ever Green* on which the film is loosely based.

The camera movement, then, implies a shift from the old fashioned to the modern implied by the 'To-Day' title. But it also contains another meaning. In the previous thirty years, the Adelphi had been associated not with music hall, but with a musical-comedy tradition. From 1908, it had been one of several theatres under the management of George Edwardes, expanding his business beyond the nearby Gaiety, and the home of a series of successful musical comedies starring Seymour Hicks and Ellaline Terriss (whose father, as any tourist to London will know, had been murdered outside the theatre's stage door in 1897).[8] The camera movement, then, also implies a shift away from the kinds of music-hall entertainments associated with the Tivoli, and towards a musical-comedy model of which the film itself might be understood as a direct descendant. Indeed, despite the clear associations with music hall in the performance scenes of the prologue (the bill number of Harriet Green's act displayed on the side of the proscenium, for instance), there remains in the film a certain blurring of the two forms – the depiction of aristocratic marriage and the scene at the Café Royal, for instance, suggest associations much more strongly aligned to musical-comedy (rather than music-hall) mythology.

At the Adelphi, we find Leslie, now a big producer, desperately searching for a stunt to boost his new show. It arrives in the form of Harriet Green's illegitimate daughter, herself a struggling chorine, who is persuaded by Maudie to impersonate her own dead mother, apparently miraculously youthful as befits her 'Evergreen' reputation. The film, then, even as it emphasises the difference between older and newer forms of entertainment, nevertheless proposes a continuity of appeal across the genera- tions in much the same way that *The Young Ones* does. I've already mentioned the centrality of the 'Dancing on the Ceiling' number in Sarah Street's account of Matthews as an art deco icon, showcas- ing her modern dancing style to Rodgers and Hart's hit number within an extraordinary example of Alfred Junge's set design at its most contemporary. That number, like the contemporary numbers in *The Young Ones*, expresses personal desire and emotion – the sense of frustration at not being able to declare publicly her love for her leading man (who, in the fraud they are perpetrating, is understood to be her son). It is balanced by the big production number which introduces her 'comeback' to the public, and which in its eclectic mix of performance styles drawn from the past can be seen as a par- allel to the 'What d'ya Know' number in *The Young Ones*. 'When You've Got a Little Springtime in Your Heart' gently pastiches the Edwardian musical style, framing a complex sequence which takes the audience back through 1924, 1914 and 1904, offering at the turn of an hourglass a version of the music and dance style of each period. By the end of the film, personal expression and performance skill coincide as the fraud, now discovered, comes to court. It is Harriet's ability to connect both emo- tionally and artistically with her mother's performance style, harmonising with a phonograph record- ing of the older Harriet singing 'When You've Got a Little Springtime in Your Heart', which persuades the judge to set aside the case, allowing a finale which offers Harriet stardom in her own right.

Like *The Young Ones*, then, *Evergreen* presents its young protagonists as both restricted by, and indebted to, an older generation. I've chosen to focus on these two films because I think they offer a way of thinking about the relationship between cinematic musicals and the theatrical tradition which hopefully moves us away from a simplistic emphasis on adaptation, or a focus on the development of musical entertainments from a 'primitive' to a 'sophisticated' form, and towards an understanding of what the tradition of musical culture more generally represented to historical audiences. Noting the wealth of films of the 1930s which draw on theatrical sources, for instance, Stephen Guy has accused British producers of a 'lack of imagination in their reliance on a theatrical perspective'.[9] In contrast, I would suggest that these explicit references to a theatrical heritage offered producers a rich resource for presenting youthful pleasures as part of a continuing history of the relationship between contem- porary pleasures and popular memory.

In both *The Young Ones* and *Evergreen*, generational conflict is represented through the struggle of young people to carve out a space to 'be themselves', culturally through the assertion of new musi- cal styles, fashions and social interactions, commercially through consumption both of entertainment and of leisure goods, and finally literally through the requisitioning of actual space within the city. In both examples, the reference to older theatrical forms leads directly to an acknowledgment and understanding by older protagonists of this struggle as legitimate due to its long history. Hamilton Black acknowledges the 'enterprise' of the young people at the end of *The Young Ones*, just as the young Harriet Green's elderly 'fiancé' admits that he will collude with her fraud because he admires her 'pluck'.

Moving back once again, we can see that these central themes are integral to the very origins of the musical-comedy form, to which I suggest these key texts centrally allude – the Gaiety Theatre itself. Nobody, wandering around London's West End, could fail to acknowledge the extraordinary influence exerted by the theatrical model which emerged from the Gaiety Theatre in carving out new spaces of leisure within the city. The theatre building boom at the turn of the century was arguably a result largely of the financial success of this new type of show: numerous major venues were funded directly out of musical-comedy profits, contributing to the refocusing of the West End as a key site of leisure consumption during this period.[10] Developed famously by the impresario George Edwardes (who in his early career had been involved in producing the Gilbert and Sullivan operas at the Savoy Theatre), and fully inaugurated around 1893 with the productions of *In Town* and *A Gaiety Girl*, the Edwardes style musical comedy was a development from the more familiar operetta and the popular burlesque forms of the preceding period. Several key features differentiated it from these models.

First, an emphasis on the contemporary was a key aspect of the Gaiety's appeal, enabling the display of high fashion in the costuming and settings displayed on stage. Indeed, fashion and consumption were central themes, as evidenced by the number of shows set in shops and department stores (*The Shop Girl*, 1894, *The Girl from Kays*, 1902) and the wide circulation in popular papers and postcards of the image of the Gaiety chorus girl resplendent in the latest styles. This concern with the modern extended to the form of the shows themselves – loosely constructed around their narratives, they were designed in such a way that they could be 'refreshed' during long runs with the introduction of new numbers (often incorporating hits from successful American shows, for instance), as well as being entirely re-costumed.[11] This emphasis on fashion and contemporaneity went hand in hand with the other central appeal of these productions – the Gaiety Girl herself. It is this 'rhetoric of the girl' which Peter Bailey places as the central and lasting influence of the Gaiety in his discussion of the form, and there is little doubt that she was a phenomenon of the age. Beautiful, fashionable, independent and 'naughty', the Gaiety girl represented the culmination of the possibilities for modern female success and celebrity at the limits of respectability. That she was a professional working girl was emphasised both by the publicity surrounding the theatre and by the shows themselves, which showcased her persona as a shop-girl, a factory worker, a showgirl, an artist's model, and so forth. The Gaiety girl's work was not restricted to the stage, though, since, as with modern celebrities, it also encompassed the entire package of personality and lifestyle which she represented. Edwardes apparently exerted a strict control over the extramural activities of his actresses, dictating their choice of restaurants and other resorts, reputedly through a series of financial deals, which ensured that the endorsement of their custom did not go unrewarded.[12] Jon Burrows suggests that this managing of the whole package of personality by Edwardes can be seen as a model for the star-system which emerged in the film industry shortly afterwards.

Within the narratives of the shows themselves, of course, the virtuous working girl who managed her beauty, talent and fashion sense appropriately was always rewarded with an advantageous marriage, often one involving a startling leap of class status. A number of similarly propitious marriages for Gaiety actresses were well publicised during the period and became central to the popular conception of the theatre – the aristocratic unions in the prologue of *Evergreen* suggest the longevity of this association, and tensions within such alliances form the central theme in the representation of the Gaiety in films such as *Trottie True*, *Gaiety George*, *Fanny by Gaslight* (1944) and others. This interconnection between the fantasies of social betterment offered on the theatrical stage and the apparent off-stage reality of social advancement enjoyed by the actresses representing those fantasies points to another defining aspect of the Gaiety – its astonishing level of self-reflexivity. Almost every Gaiety show offered a paean to the lifestyles and pleasures which the Gaiety itself represented. Most particularly, this is embodied in the figure of the Gaiety girl herself, and her male equivalent, the man-about-town and stage-door Johnny who was her fan. George Grossmith's song 'Beautiful Bountiful Bertie' from *The Shop Girl* provides a typical example. Among his various pleasures – such as dressing in style, flirting with girls and promenading around the fashionable West End – the singer describes himself as a patron of the theatre. However, it is a particular type of theatre which catches his approval – not Shakespeare, not a theatre of tragedy or indeed one with a plot, but rather one which 'don't tax the intellect' and into which he can stroll at will 'to sit out half an hour or so … I must confess in Hamlet no interest I've found/I much prefer *The Gaiety Girl* or else *Morocco Bound*'.[13] After the show, it transpires, his delight is to bribe the stage doorman and mingle with the girls themselves. Such songs were not merely the prerogative of male singers, as the number 'I Like London' from *The Arcadians* (1909) demonstrates: here, the female singer confesses that contrary to what she's been led to expect, London men are 'good and kind', always smiling at her when she meets them in the street. She endeavours to teach them that 'love is king', and finds that not one of them is a dunce in his lessons, particularly when it comes to 'the kissing part'.[14]

This sense of a utopian world of leisure consumption and sexual opportunity which extends beyond the stage, transforming both the theatre itself and the West End streets in which it is located into a space for the entertainment of the younger generation is central to the appeal of the Gaiety, and, I would suggest, is the key reference point for later film-makers when they evoke the Edwardian stage as an inspiration for the carving out of youthful pleasures in the musicals discussed above.

Peter Bailey notes that theatrical historians have until recently given the Edwardian musical comedy scant attention, preferring instead to concentrate on the social-problem plays and the 'New Drama' of figures such as Ibsen and Shaw. Nevertheless, he suggests, 'familiar and apparently unproblematical forms can reveal much of social and ideological significance', citing the serious attention given by film studies to the Hollywood musical as a demonstration of this fact.[15] I must confess that part of my own motivation in this essay has been to draw attention to a form which, it seems to me exerted a profound influence on later film musicals, and yet which remains largely obscure. Compared even to shows from the 1920s, these entertainments are almost never revived, and appear to have largely dropped out of popular memory. Nevertheless, as I hope I have demonstrated, it is precisely the popular memory of such shows, even as late as the 1960s, which formed the model and the springboard for the entertainment of generations.

Notes

1. Kevin Donnelly, 'The Perpetual Busman's Holiday: Sir Cliff Richard and British Pop Musicals', *The Journal of Popular Film and Television*, vol. 25 no. 4, Winter 1998, p. 147.

2. *Kinematograph Weekly*, 7 December 1961, p. 10.

3. Sarah Street, ' "Got to Dance My Way to Heaven": Jessie Matthews, Art Deco and the British Musical of the 1930s', *Studies in European Cinema*, vol. 2 no. 1, 2005, pp. 19–30.

4. One might cite here the bas-relief friezes of dancing figures which decorate the auditorium of the Odeon, Leicester Square (built 1937), or the stylised design of Apollo above the proscenium of the Novello Theatre, Aldwych (formerly the Strand Theatre at the time of this interior addition in 1930).

5. Andrew Higson, *Waving the Flag: Constructing a National Cinema in Britain* (Oxford: Clarendon Press, 1995), pp. 98–175.

6. Susan Rusinko, *The Plays of Benn Levy: Between Shaw and Coward* (Cranbury, NJ: Fairleigh Dickinson University Press, 1995), p. 173.

7. Victor Saville and Roy Moseley, *Evergreen: Victor Saville in His Own Words* (Carbondale: Southern Illinois University Press, 2000), p. 74.

8. Alan Hyman, *The Gaiety Years* (London: Cassell, 1975), p. 164.

9. Stephen Guy, 'Calling All Stars: Musical Film in a Musical Decade', in Jeffrey Richards (ed.), *The Unknown 1930s: An Alternative History of British Cinema, 1929–1939* (London: I. B. Tauris, 2001), p. 119.

10. Peter Bailey, ' "Naughty but Nice": Musical Comedy and the Rhetoric of the Girl, 1892–1914', in Michael Brooke and Joel H. Kaplan (eds), *The Edwardian Theatre* (Cambridge: Cambridge University Press, 1996), p. 38.

11. Jon Burrows, 'Girls on Film: The Musical Matrices of Film Stardom in Early British Cinema', *Screen*, vol. 44 no. 3, Autumn 2005, p. 317.

12. Hyman, *The Gaiety Years*, p. 98.

13. Lyrics by George Grossmith Jr, quoted in the sleevenotes to the CD recording, *Lionel Monckton: Songs from the Shows* (Hyperion CDA67654).

14. Lyrics by Arthur Wimperis. Transcribed from the CD recording, *Monckton & Talbot: The Arcadians Highlights* (Classics for Pleasure 094633598225).

15. Bailey, ' "Naughty but Nice" ', p. 36.

3 The Mellifluous 'Illogics' of the 'Bollywood Musical'

Bhaskar Sarkar

The song-and-dance number is to the Indian film industry as the martial arts sequence is to its Hong Kong counterpart: for a global cinematic imagination, each form constitutes the dynamic 'essence', the defining characteristic, of its respective cinematic formation. Such essentialism effectively frames these behemoth culture industries as idiosyncratic exceptions to Hollywood, the presumed global benchmark, even as Hollywood itself keeps mutating through its encounters with its others. The caricatural impression of cheesy, upbeat, fantastic musical sequences reduces Indian popular cinema – now misconstrued as 'Bollywood' – to an odd curiosity, even as Indian film songs routinely infiltrate Hollywood soundtracks as songs or aural samples. The current transnational purchase of 'Bollywood musicals' begs the question: to what extent is the *musical*, as theorised in relation to a Hollywood genre, an apt or useful conceptualisation for Indian cinema? This is not an altogether new question, but now it becomes more pressing as the Indian film industry rapidly reinvents itself and as many of its reinventions appear to be organised around its core musicality.

Two recent attempts at producing Bollywood-style musicals in the West, *Moulin Rouge!* (2001) and *Bride and Prejudice* (2004), unwittingly stage the contradictions precipitated by the conflation of the Hollywood genre with Indian cinema's ubiquitous song-and-dance sequence, foregrounding certain questions with which any analysis of Indian 'musicals' must engage. The former, an Anglo-American co-production set in *fin-de-siècle* Paris, was, according to its Australian director Baz Luhrmann, inspired by Bollywood. However, this 'influence' transpires mainly in the exotic India-themed spectacle staged by the film's bohemian Parisian characters (indexical of late-nineteenth-century Europe's orientalist preoccupations), and is most evident in the set design (including the heroine's elephant-shaped living quarters) and in the final production number (based on a hit song from the 1998 Hindi film *China Gate*); otherwise, the plot remains quite Hollywood-ish in its focus, style and length, owing more to classic musicals such as Rouben Mamoulian's *Love Me Tonight* (1932) than to Hindi films as such. *Bride and Prejudice*, an Anglo-European co-production helmed by diasporic-Indian director Gurinder Chadha, adapts Jane Austen's novel into a 'Bollywood musical' set in the present. But in a significant departure from the Indian industry's practice of having actors lip-synch to songs recorded by 'playback singers', and more in keeping with Hollywood norms, Chadha has her actors sing their own songs, generally with disastrous results. One is left with the impression that *Bride and Prejudice*'s intention is to lampoon Bombay films.

In their marked distinction from their imputed inspiration, these two 'global' attempts at simulating 'Bollywood musicals' help us to approach the singularity of the song-and-dance sequences of Indian popular cinema. I will couch my analysis of Indian 'musicals' in terms of a larger claim: thinking through these musical sequences is tantamount to confronting head on the ontological and epistemological specificities of Indian cinema. Those of us who teach Indian cinema in contexts outside South Asia become acutely primed to this broader project. Students (and colleagues) often remark that the grandiose musical numbers in *Mughal e Azam* (1960) are 'just like' those associated with Busby

Berkeley, or that the long dream sequence in *Awara* (1951) 'reminds' them of the one in *Singin' in the Rain* (1952). There is much to be said of these commonalities, without necessarily slipping into the hoary questions of 'influence' and 'derivativeness'. The core challenge is: how to establish the cultural specificities of Indian cinema without dismissing the trans-cultural synergies? At stake is a shift of focus, enabling research methodologies that attend to the extraordinarily generative interactions between Indian philosophical and aesthetic traditions, evolving industrial conventions and global cinematic trends.

Lately, there has been a happy spate of scholarship on Indian film music that focuses on industrial practices and material circuits to produce thick descriptions of the 'hows' and 'whys' of the Bombay industry (including various stages of producing song numbers, integrating songs in the narrative, orchestral procedures, commercial life of film songs and cross-cultural circulations).[1] My aim in this essay is far more modest. I begin with some reflection on the expediency of the 'musical' as an analytical concept in the context of Indian cinema. Next, I briefly consider a range of functions of the song-and-dance number to complicate, if not counter, the prevalent impression that it is simply a *masala* diversion, a spectacle-oriented 'interruption' of the narrative. Finally, I situate these performative interludes in relation to local aesthetic genealogies to establish how they operate as synaesthetic elements within a singularly Indian film language. While the bulk of my analysis holds for Indian popular cinema taken as a whole (in its myriad regional and linguistic manifestations), most of my examples are drawn from Hindi films produced in the Bombay industry.

Beyond Genre

Characters breaking into song-and-dance routines, the defining element of the musical genre, also remains its chief enigma: how to make such behaviour plausible to audiences? For Jane Feuer, the 'self-referentiality' intrinsic to the preponderance of backstage musicals in 1930s Hollywood had to do with letting audiences feel 'more comfortable viewing musical numbers within the context of a show'.[2] A related challenge is to render the spectacle, the exuberance and the utopianism typical of the genre intelligible without transgressing the limits of audience credulity. Such considerations lead Martin Rubin to characterise the musical as an 'impossible genre'.[3] As Steven Cohan elaborates, the 'impossibility' of musical numbers derives from them being 'motivated, performed, and/or photographed in spatial, temporal or logical contradictions to the otherwise realistic fictive world of the movie's plot'.[4] When ordinary characters sound like seasoned performers (Asha Bhosle, Mohammed Rafi), or when a song number transports characters unaccountably to a distant picturesque setting (glaciers in Kashmir, tulip fields in the Netherlands) just for its duration, the rising implausibility/impossibility quotient challenges – or *ought to challenge* – realist tenets. Thus, the musical genre appears to stretch the customary 'suspension of disbelief' that is part of the contract between any film and its audience. The flipside of this is the observation that the musical genre constantly reminds audiences they are watching a film. Rick Altman has noted the irony that 'the most escapist of the entertainment arts' also happens to be 'the most reflexive, the most aware of its status', and therefore 'the most complex of all the Hollywood genres'.[5]

The song-and-dance sequence is only the most obvious of various forms of 'interruption' that characterise Indian popular cinema: films routinely feature multiple genres and narrative strands, subplots of wildly disjunctive tones and exegetical digressions. If the beginning and the resolution etch a linear arc, even achieve cyclical closure, the plot in between is peppered with coincidences and foretellings, detours and redundancies. Already, to speak of narrative interruptions is to presume a hermetic and complete narrative, whose communicative efficacy would increase in the absence of such disturbances. Such streamlined linearity is not innate to South Asian narrative traditions, which tend to be sprawling, meandering and polyvocal. In its multi-perspectival discursivity, the typical Indian commercial film is *epic*. It is this epic sensibility that calls for a matrixial hermeneutic, in which the repetitions, detours and excesses ('interruptions') signify as much as any imputed core – not as extraneous embellishments, but as key narrative elements.

Film-maker Mani Kaul makes a strong case for the distinctiveness of a vernacular narratology generalisable across commercial and alternative forms. He takes the ubiquitous perspectivalism of post-quattrocento western art as his point of departure, arguing that what began as a brilliant reorganisation of human relationship to space, and enabled 'secular appropriations' of space, eventually also led to modernist cartography and the production of a 'universal geography' that, in turn, made colonialism possible.[6] In the visual arts, perspective produced an illusion of contiguity between fore-, middle- and background, while at the same time isolating the object for our sight. Instead of the *presentation* of a figure, art now aimed for *representation* of an entire reality through the illusive unification of ground and figure. Soon this perspectivalism would be extended to other aesthetic realms – for instance, to orchestral music (where every instrument was at once isolated from and conjoined to the others), and to Italian chronicle (introducing convergence and climax). Thus, perspectivalism consisted of a 'notion of convergence wherein argument and counter-argument were poised in opposition of each other and fought a battle to reach a point of resolution'.[7] Kaul argues that the hegemonic understanding of screenplays influenced by Hollywood embraces 'this particular shape of narrative' as 'something eternal, handed down from the ancients, as something that forms a "biological" heart of story telling'. Countering this vitalist universalism of narratology, Kaul points to the persistence of narrative forms 'replete with distractions of song and dance' in many contemporary cultures that 'do not much care for that tense movement of events heading for a climactic close'.[8]

This is not to say that no attempts are made to streamline plots; the point is that commercial Indian film-makers have had a differential understanding of 'narrative economy'. In her recent book-length study of Hindi film music, Anna Morcom documents the efforts that go into integrating the musical numbers within the story: 'details of the situation, drama, emotion, character, location, action and cinematography' are made to interact with the songs.[9] Generally, the composing and recording of songs takes place after the preliminary drafting of the film script, but before the completion of the screenplay and the dialogues, and well before the shooting of the film and the 'picturisation' of the songs. How the audio recordings pan out often compels directors to rethink their scripts, add or delete scenes, even reconsider casting and location.[10] What emerges from such details is the notion that songs are fundamental to the narrative structure, rather than mere additives. While Morcom agrees in principle with earlier estimations of the Hindi film narrative 'as modular, "an assemblage of pre-fabricated parts"', she also insists that the song sequences are 'cinematically conceived'.[11] At the same time, she points to the ways in which film songs exceed the film narrative because of their commercial life beyond the film: they generate *audio value* (as records, cassettes and CDs, now as ringtones) and, in recent years, *video value* (to be shown as stand-alone music videos on television channels, and compiled as song clips on DVDs).[12]

Besides working with trans-perspectival narratives with web-like causality, Indian popular cinema happens to be epic in a rather direct sense: it draws on what may be called civilisational repositories of dramatic situations, moral quandaries and discursive structures. I am referring to the mythologies contained in the two epics, *Ramayana* and *Mahabharata*, and in the religious texts, the *Puranas*.

Then there are the Sanskrit classical literary works: plays such as *Mrichchhakatika* and *Abhijnanasakuntalam*, and narrative poems such as *Meghdoota*. These ancient texts remain a vital presence in everyday life: as India's 'living traditions', they continue to provide guidelines for aesthetic experiments and ethical dialogues. Not surprisingly, landmark films such as *Awara*, *Mother India* (1957), *Guide* (1965) and *Deewar* (1975) have incorporated epic allusions and mythic excursuses to establish their verisimilitude. More than a quest for narrative novelty, it is the familiarity of a recognisable cosmology, an already intelligible moral universe, which drives these cinematic references to aesthetic-epistemological mores. It is routine to 'solve' moral conundrums by asking what Seeta or Arjun, hallowed protagonists of the epics, would do in similar situations, or by making light of the dilemmas in a comic vein. The epic sensibility of Indian cinema is culturally specific; it is also historically situated, as the references partake in a discursivity that is thoroughly modern, deeply invested in questions of nationhood, contemporary cultural life and social transformation.

Intertextuality and self-parody, annotative digression, and melancholic or sarcastic commentary: such hallmarks of reflexivity abound in Indian commercial cinema. However, reflexivity here may not even imply making audiences aware that they are watching a film, let alone foster a critical optic. It is not that Indian popular cinema does not pretend to be a slice of real life; rather, 'real life' itself is understood to be highly dialogical and disjunctive. The 'spatial, temporal or logical contradictions' simply fold into a different logic of realism: thus, every character being able to sing and dance like professionals, the arrest and upstaging of the storyline by performances or the unaccountable flight to dazzling locales for the song sequences *ought* to violate notions of what is credible, but they *do not*. These 'contradictions' need not be value-neutral, but they need not constitute a radical political gesture either. If there are no ruptures in relation to a vernacular epistemology, then the epistemological status of reflexivity changes. Tropes of reflexivity are so much a part of local hermeneutical systems that they get subsumed under standard 'codes of cinematic realism'. One is tempted to ask, rephrasing Altman's provocation – 'Isn't Indian narrative by nature reflexive?' – with the proviso that reflexivity be decoupled from an obligatory radical disposition. Rather, reflexivity is best understood as a modality of realising negotiated, collective signification.

A pivotal scene in Raj Kapoor's *Awara*, in which Raghunath throws his pregnant wife out due to erroneous suspicions about the paternity of their yet-to-be-born child, brilliantly exemplifies the reflexive negotiation of meaning. As the disconsolate wife drags herself out, a song begins on the soundtrack, but its source remains unclear for over a minute and a half. The result is a dense, noir-ish *mise en scène*: long shots of Raghunath in his baroque mansion; the wife stumbling in the rain-drenched night; a shot of dark clouds with jagged edges tracing a crack in the sky. The song recounts a well-known story from the *Ramayana*, in which the mythical monarch Rama abandons his wife on the basis of false suspicions. Eventually, the singers come into view, without the preamble of an establishing shot, the sound-bridge of the song securing the contiguity of the narrative space. As the audience on screen joins in the singing (typical in such oral performances), we, the film's audience, are interpellated to participate. The song becomes a searing commentary on the patriarchal oppression of women, by situating the current injustice within a shared hermeneutic framework. That Raghunath happens to be another name for Rama underscores the cultural connection. This epic address directly implicates the film's viewers in an act of reflexive commentary. In a typical melodramatic move, the unfairness of the expulsion is intensified: emotional intensity bears the burden of an oblique critique, even as injustice is perpetrated once more. In many other instances of such epic allusions, reflexivity will simply invoke a shared milieu, a common frame of cognition, without a shred of criticality.

Just as the song in *Awara* swings effortlessly from the non-diegetic to the diegetic, so does the archetypal song sequence boast multiple costume changes, seamlessly traversing between locations, between dreams and waking hours, between objective and subjective registers. Thus, in so many films of the period between the 1960s and 90s, a crescendo of strings ushers in a song sequence on the slopes of Kashmir or the Swiss Alps, when the narrative warrants no such voyage, and when the adjoining sequences are played out in Bombay or Delhi. Mani Ratnam takes such routine incongruities and plays them up to dazzling effect in *Dil Se* (1997): in a narrative that sends the hero on a wild chase across North India after the heroine, the song sequences are so phantasmatic that viewers trying to piece together the duo's itinerary would be left somewhat baffled. There is a surreal quality to the musical sequences: for the title track, the realism of television news (armed patrols, bomb explosions, burning tyres, barbed wire) is intermingled with ludic shots of the would-be lovers and dancing children; in another song sequence ('Satrangi re'), the duo dances (sometimes lip-synching, sometimes not) in a Buddhist monastery, amid the ruins of a fortress, and against constantly changing landscapes (desert, rocks, lake, snow), the choreography invoking a mish mash of Sufi idioms, dervish dancers, Martha Graham, Pilobolus and, finally, the *pietà*. In both sequences, there is considerable intimacy between the two characters – in stark contrast to the 'reality' of their relationship. Here, too, the jump-cut transitions, the blurring of fantasy and reality, and the wild mixing of styles and iconographies become a matter of convention: from within the set of codes that contour Indian popular cinema, the shifts seem quite acceptable, if not quite realistic. It is only when movie critics and certain elite sections of the audience look at these films in terms of Hollywood or art-cinema norms that they appear implausible and unrealistic, perhaps even asinine.[13]

The point here is not to launch a romantic primordialism, but to understand how a peculiarly Indian aesthetic modernity is fashioned through the creative gerrymandering of vernacular precepts of perception-cognition *and* post-Enlightenment European tenets of rationality. Art historian Kajri Jain locates such a process occurring in the post-colonies 'across *epistemically disjunct yet performatively networked worlds*: the worlds of bourgeois-liberal and neoliberal modernism on the one hand and those of "vernacular" discourses and practices on the other'.[14] Thus, while Indian cinema adopts Hollywood-derived continuity editing and narrative principles, their implementation is always circumscribed – even waylaid – by vernacular aesthetic practices and forms: in addition to the ones discussed above, Ashish Rajadhyaksha draws attention to the persistence of premodern strategies such as frontality and tableau,[15] while Geeta Kapur points to the continuing centrality of a logic of revelation (in contradistinction from modernist scepticism).[16] The 'interruption' of film narrative by song-and-dance sequences is one such moment within a vernacular cinematic modernism.

If standard theoretical discussions of the musical genre have very limited applicability for Indian cinema's song-and-dance number, then the question arises: can we even demarcate a well-defined genre in the Indian context? One can locate occasional films that approximate the received definition of musicals: for instance, the *Sant* films of the first decade after the coming of sound are biopic-musicals. Oddly enough, it is the modernist master Satyajit Ray, rather than any of the more commercially oriented film-makers, who can be credited with having produced three films (*The Goopy-Bagha Trilogy*, 1968, 1973, 1991) that come closest to the formalised idea of populist musicals – films that boast an organic spontaneity, and a thoroughly Bengali folksiness. Be that as it may, the very ubiquity of the song-and-dance numbers across all commercial genres – romantic melodramas, caper films, thrillers alike – presents a further practical difficulty in isolating a musical genre. Perhaps the musical is best thought of as a *mode* that permeates various genres of Indian cinema.

Functions and Genealogies

What does such a pervasive musical mode do for Indian cinema? I will focus on the song sequence, widely taken to constitute Indian cinema's singularity: even a partial list of its syntactic and semantic functions begins to flesh out its polyvalent role beyond mere ornamental or entertainment value. The most obvious instance is that of a show, a performance: the site could be a stage, royal court, party, school or college function, club, bordello and, increasingly from the 1990s, weddings. The performance is often complicated in its address, indexing a covert, melodramatic function: directed at a diegetic collectivity, at another character (present or absent) and/or at the film's audience. For instance, Rosie's stage performance of 'Mose chhal kiye jaye' in *Guide* is pointedly directed at Raju's apparent betrayal; the dance ends with Raju surrounded by a group of women dancers, and ensnared in a giant mesh – is this actually a part of the performance, or a visualisation of the characters' fantasy/nightmare? Within the space of the song sequence, Rosie's public life as a dancer becomes entangled with her conjugal tensions. In a more direct vein, *Kismet* (1943) uses the ruse of a stage performance ('Aaj himalay ki chhoti se') to stir up patriotic fervour at the height of India's struggle for independence: the audience on screen is posed in a metonymic relation to the film's audience. 'Aage bhi jaane na tu' (*Waqt*, 1965) stages the drama of outsiders infiltrating high society against the backdrop of the plush lifestyle of the 1960s' nouveau riche; while 'Aare re aare yeh kya hua', from *Dil To Pagal Hai* (1997), is as much about putting on a show as it is about 'finding true love' in contemporary life, and about changing habitus and consumption patterns in an Indian 'global city'.

Like underscoring, song numbers generate and organise filmic affect; but since characters (appear to) sing, a more direct subjectivity is materialised. It is possible to differentiate between emotional registers associated with a spectrum of subjectivities. The simplest is the exuberance of romantic love, exteriorised in verdant rural settings, landscaped gardens, on mountain slopes and sea beaches, riverbanks and lakes, in forts, palaces and temples, in the bazaar, on bustling streets, on cars and trains, and – sometimes – indoors. For the picturisation of such love songs, the camera pans across the landscape, circles the lovers, swoops down on their intimate moments, often tracing the dynamic of the music in its very movement. The palimpsestic iconography of these sequences invokes multiple romantic legends – Radha–Krishna, Laila–Majnu, Romeo–Juliet – and palpable sensations associated with the moods of *ragamala* paintings (see below), retro screen memories and the populist, intensely haptic depictions of romance and conjugality in Indian 'calendar art'.[17] The audio inspirations range from light classical *ghazals* and *thumris*, folk musical forms like *kajri* and *bhatiyali*, to western classical music, pop songs, Arabic music, latin jazz and funk. Sometimes the scene focuses exclusively on the couple, the camera moving with the melody and the actors' shifting proxemic relations. 'Abhi na jao chod kar', from *Hum Dono* (1960), offers a subtle assemblage of an intimate sphere that the lovers inhabit as they wander languorously among trees in the woods; this affective space is replete with held glances, yearning sighs, tender gestures, the anxiety of separation, the heroine's gendered reticence, the possibility of misunderstanding and the sheer buzz of being in love.[18] At other times, the picturisation involves entire groups in the background, the energy of the chorus line and intricate choreography framing and amplifying the lovers' rapture. In such instances, the supporting performers may be the main protagonists' peers; but quite often, they are human props that fit in with the natural settings – 'children of the soil' exotica produced by/for an ethnographic gaze. Case in point: the exuberant and brightly costumed fisherfolk of the Goa coastline who dance with Rishi Kapoor and Dimple Kapadia in the 'Jhoot bole kauva kate' number from *Bobby* (1973).

Beyond romantic love, cinematic exuberance expresses emotions that are emphatically collective, in songs celebrating a sense of togetherness arising from being part of a close-knit community. These songs may be set in a village, in the lap of nature, a topos that, as modernity's idyllic other, invites a form of organic primitivism: in the 'Oori oori chhayi ghata' sequence from *Amar* (1954), the actress Nimmi is a doe-eyed nymph at one with her bucolic environment; her performance channels modern, calendar art depictions of Shakuntala and Damayanti, mythic characters from classical antiquity known for their connections to nature and for a trans-species ecological sensibility. The songs may take place in a *chawl* or urban tenement building, a boarding house, a slum, or in a minority *mohalla* or neighbourhood: the immigrant Pathan community extolling friendship in 'Yaari hein imaan mera' from *Zanjeer* (1973), or the young lodgers of *Naukri* (1954) hoping for employment ('Ek chhotisi naukri ki talabdaar hoon mein'). In both rural and urban versions, the vicissitudes of proletarian life bring the characters together, and they toast their fond aspirations and hard-earned achievements in the midst of their daily struggles. The ritualistic celebration of various festivals not only marks the passage of time in films, but also honours community life. It is telling that the spirited Holi (spring festival) sequence in *Sholay* (1975) is interrupted by marauding bandits under the vicious Gabbar Singh: this threat of savage lawlessness underscores the precarity of the charming hamlet of harmonious, hard-working people. The fundamental thrust of these sequences is a passionate utopianism: for the characters, as for the audience, the plenitude of nature helps compensate for all that is lacking in real life, and a highly romanticised ideal of unity seeks to ameliorate the feeling of alienation and drift.

A sense of community also comes from labouring in the field as a *kissan* or peasant, and in a factory; from serving in the army as a *jawan* or soldier; and more recently from the inebriated bonhomie of gangsters. Of course, with the *kissan* and the *jawan*, the two paradigmatic nationalist figures in the early decades following independence, exuberance is often tempered by memories of sacrifice and toil: a sad note enters the songs. For the haunting composition 'Kar chale hum fida jaan-o-tan saathiyon' from *Haqeeqat* (1964), images of suffering and sacrifice are intercut with documentary footage, marking an introspective moment in the nation's history when the euphoria of independence ended with the defeat in the Sino-Indian war of 1962, and with Nehru's death in 1964. Likewise, while the melodious 'Dharti kahe pukar ke' number from *Do Bigha Zameen* (1953) honours the farmers' hard work, contrapuntally it frames the protagonist Sambhu's migration to the big city in search of a better life. The song stages one of the central contradictions of India's modernisation: the compulsion to leave behind one's home and hearth even as one constantly exalts one's roots. Such contemplative attempts at negotiating post-colonial challenges and projecting utopian futures are discernible even in the commercial ventures of Filmistan, Mehboob Productions, Navketan or R. K. Studios.

If the songs work in relation to the embedding narrative, they also stand alone as apertures to the emotional life of the characters – particularly when they develop and cue us in to a sense of the characters' interiority. While interiority is best understood in relation to the bourgeois individualism advanced by literary forms such as the novel and the essay, and raises spectres of a disembodied consciousness, even a mystified soul, such inward inflection can never quite transcend the muck of social and material entanglements – certainly not in cinema. Individualist interiority remains, at best, a heuristic fiction, helping to foreground (in Kaul's sense of perspectivalist isolation) moments of affective intensity, allowing for the expression of invisible – even non-linguistic – feelings: at the same time, it is always splayed out, displayed, on screen and transmitted as sound all over the auditorium, in terms of cultural and formal-technological ingredients. In short, interiority is crucially a matter of a poetics of cinema, a poetics that is always culturally rooted.

Satyajit Ray, who was a vocal critic of the Bombay industry's melodramatic excesses, particularly the affected song embellishments, provides us with a remarkable instance of musical interiority in his most rigorously realist film, *Kanchanjungha* (1962). At a pivotal moment in the narrative, which seems to unfold in real time, the ageing matriarch, silently suffering her despotic husband's handling of family matters, sits alone on a bench as the afternoon fog rolls over the mountainside, and sings a song – an act that appears to assuage her apprehensions. The camerawork is remarkably restrained: only four shots, two of them involving a slow, nearly imperceptible dolly-in, make up the sequence. The contemplative song, figuratively about modern displacement and loneliness, happens to be a famous composition by Rabindranath Tagore, and is of considerable import to a modern bourgeois Bengali sensibility. Even in this realist work, Ray follows an established industrial practice: the actor lip-synched the song recorded by a well-known exponent of Tagore's music (a particularly profitable segment of the Bengali culture industry). Interiority is still mediated by local conventions of cinematic representation, and by a shared cultural patrimony. And the sequence begins and ends with another character, the woman's elder brother, who appreciatively listens in: one person's 'interiority' is framed by another's presence. That this silent listener is none other than Pahadi Sanyal, an iconic singer-actor known for some legendary playback singing in the 1930s and 40s, brings in a reflexive dimension: Ray seems to be commenting on the function of the song sequence in cinema, framing it not as a generic component, but as a mode of signification.

Affect in cinema, whether couched in terms of individualised interiority or social experience, must of necessity spring from the interaction of formal strategies and common codes of intelligibility. I have been gesturing toward some of these formal cinematic techniques and cultural resources. With respect to the musical numbers, it is worth stressing the *non-representational* aspects of representation: at the auditory level – tonal progression, rhythm, dynamics, pitch, fading in and out, echo and reverberation effects – and the visual – colour, texture, camera movement, angle and framing. Richard Dyer reminds us that these elements produce *structuration*: operating largely at a subconscious, even corporeal level, they orchestrate affect and meaning.[19] Crucial to the performativity of song sequences, these non-representational cues impinge on our senses, shaping intuitive, embodied understanding. Culturally rooted signs, as shared signifying shorthands, are efficient tools for structuring comprehension. Stories from the epics, iconography of mythic figures and their exploits, tableau arrangements, types of tonal patterns, folk performance forms: these components often work in semi-conscious ways, as familiarity induces automatic, connectionist processing, shifting interpretation away from the deliberative and towards the intuitive. Somewhat paradoxically, this type of intelligibility is at once embodied *and* intersubjective, fostering something like an incarnate social consciousness. This is one of the larger claims we can make for cinema in general; in the Indian context, specifically, popular cinema has facilitated a sense of collective belonging that, at least emotionally, is far more compelling than anything the nation-state has been able to provide.

The claim about an embodied intersubjectivity needs to be substantiated by further research, well beyond the scope of this piece. For now, I will briefly enumerate three sources/influences for Indian cinema's musical numbers – forces that contribute to the formation of such a public. First, as many accounts of Indian cinema have suggested, the use of song and dance has its roots in vernacular theatrical traditions. Two particular strands are often mentioned: folk theatrical and oral performance forms (including *ramlila, kuravanci, nautanki, yakshagana, jatra, bhavai*); and modern stage from the nineteenth century – especially Parsi theatre, which, in spite of its roots in one linguistic community, turned itself into a multilingual form with wide appeal.[20] Along with its Bengali, Gujrati, Marathi and

Tamil counterparts, the Parsi stage instigated new ways of seeing, introducing audiences to novel aesthetic-sensorial pleasures – including proscenium stage, painted backdrops and architectural sets, and original music.[21] While a received view of modern Indian stage and screen stresses the influence of *Natyashastra*, a nearly two millennia-old treatise on Sanskrit theatre, poetics, dance and music, any such influence has to have been critically inflected by modern aesthetic exigencies, tastes and social values. Modern Indian stage, and especially Parsi theatre, combined European and Indian conventions, imbibed cosmopolitan values and fostered an urban bourgeois sensibility.[22] Such articulations are evident in the song-laden Parsi-Urdu plays of Munshi Bedil and Agha Hashr Kashmiri, or in the Bengali dance-dramas of Tagore and satires of Kshirodprasad Bidyabinod. With the coming of sound to Indian cinema in the early 1930s, reels of stage performance recordings were put together for public screening in Bombay and Calcutta, before actual films were released. The two earliest Indian talkies released in 1931, *Alam Ara* and *Shirin Farhad*, featured seven and forty-two songs respectively. But as Ashok Ranade reminds us, many of these 'songs' were, in fact, 'verses, couplets, and partial recitations', following the vernacular stage's custom of melodeclamation.[23]

A second vernacular aesthetic tradition deserving our attention includes musical forms like *kirtan*, *qawwali*, *baul* and *bhajan*, known for their ability to induce a state of trance in singers and audiences alike, transporting them to an intersubjective space of rapture. These forms are often associated with the populist *bhakti* and *sufi* movements aimed at religious reform, seeking to achieve a direct spiritual awakening among the masses without the mediation of organised religion. A direct reaction against religious orthodoxies and corrupt hierarchies, these movements conflate devotion and love, producing a complex phenomenology of experience in which the distinction between body and soul is transcended. Popular films abound in scenes of ecstatic singing: often staged at temples, mosques and gurdwaras, leading to miracles; often performed by blind fakirs and wandering minstrels, yielding profound revelation. An early and notable example is *Sant Tukaram* (1936), a Marathi film produced at Prabhat Studios, in which sheer faith brings its own miracles. By the time we get to Bimal Roy's *Devdas* (1955) or Guru Dutt's *Pyaasa* (1957), a passionate social commitment recasts devotional fervour into reformist zeal, all along presenting the need for social transformation in populist terms – *as love* (for instance, in the famed 'Aaj sajan mohe ang lagalo' sequence from *Pyaasa*).

Miniature *ragamala* paintings constitute our third vernacular inspiration for musical

Raga Megh, c. 1800

sequences. A *raga* is a particular sequencing of tones set to a single scale; since variations using augmented or diminished tones change the *raga*, one scale may be the basis of multiple *ragas*; a single *raga* may be interpreted and improvised in performance in a wide variety of ways. Each *raga* is associated with a particular mood, often attributed to a specific time of the day or night, or to a season. Thus *Bageshri*, a romantic *raga*, is supposed to be sung around midnight, while the *Malhar* group of *ragas* is associated with the rainy season. From the fourteenth century, *ragas* come to be described by short Sanskrit verses: each *raga* is personified as a god, a hero or heroine of romantic legends, or a figure of particular disposition/emotion – such as an ascetic, a warrior prince, a jealous woman, a yearning lover. By the seventeenth century, these referents find iconic representation in paintings: these are the famed *ragamala* paintings. Thus, the *raga* system articulates music, poetry and painting, comprising synaesthetic assemblages of great expressive capacity. If the musical *ragas* have a visual dimension, then the *ragamala* paintings boast a musical component; both conjure up feelings involving multiple sensory registers. Standardised narratives of lovers' tiffs, infidelities and longings, of worshippers' devotion, of royal subjects' grandeur, are mapped onto hours, seasons, gardens, balconies, courts, temples. These representations circulate as condensed tableaux, as compelling chronotopes – precursors to cinematic *mise en scène*. Thus, a painting depicting the *raga Megh* will always include rain clouds, possibly peacocks, verdant trees and lovers – ideally Krishna, the love-god, surrounded by adoring women. For Indians, such an image is likely to invoke sensuousness: the tactility of moist air, smell of jasmine, furtive trysts, a listless melancholic longing. It resonates with a long tradition of literary allusions, most notably Kalidasa's famous poem *Meghdoota* about an exiled lover intimating his lovelorn thoughts to his beloved through the monsoon clouds. What we have here is an intermedial sensorium of emotions, which in the modern era is taken up and developed by mass media. So there is a popularisation, and thus revitalisation, of what was once a primarily elitist art form. Just as film music composers such as Naushad, Vasant Desai and Madan Mohan harness the capacity of *ragas* to elaborate and engage emotions, art directors and choreographers draw on their sensorial-aesthetic cognates to flesh out entire lifeworlds. The lavish 'Mohe panghat pe Nandalal chhed gayo re' sequence from *Mughal e Azam*, conceived within the global context of epic film-making in the 1950s, surely includes an emulative nod to Busby Berkeley, but it draws its expressive energy more directly from calendar-art refractions of *ragamala* idioms.

Mughal e Azam (K. Asif, 1960)

Such sensorial associations are not always obvious: the cinematic use of the *ragas* is usually far more abstruse. Take the example of *Kedar*: a solemn, contemplative *raga*, usually sung late evening to early night; often represented by the figure of an ascetic, possibly a devotee of Shiva, lost in music or meditation. So profound is his commitment that he himself becomes an object of others' reverence.

In the paintings, we see 'An ascetic, often with a vina, and a noble visitor, seated on a tower or terrace. Often the visitor's horse, or boat, and his attendants are included.'[24] From the Mughal era, c. 1610, we have a description, original in Sanskrit: 'in penance, adorned, grey [with ashes,], dark, a young man beauteous in every limb, [this is] Kedara Raga'.[25] An alternative imagination, c. 1650, original in Hindi: Kedara is the woman separated from her lover. She has 'taken the Yogi's form' and

> has besmeared [her] body with ash. [Her] body is reduced to a skeleton. The emaciated … holds a vina and plays on it: 'Piu Piu' (o lover, o lover). [She is] absorbed in the love passion and sings the praise of the lover … Kedara's [pangs of] separation do not abate, how could [she] reach the day's dawn?[26]

If we are to glean an elemental mood-picture from these descriptions, it will be one of deep absorption, sober contemplation.

It is this disposition that seems paramount in the song sequence from Mehboob Khan's landmark film *Andaz* (1949), starring Nargis in the role of Neeta, a woman who inherits her industrialist father's business and wealth; Dilip Kumar, as Dilip, her friend, who looks after her business and is secretly in love with her; and Raj Kapoor, as Rajan, her dashing, playboy husband whom she loves with all her heart, but who is jealous of the bond between her and Dilip. Caught in the oppressive tension of this triangle, Neeta expresses her suffering through a song – 'Uthaye ja unke sitam' – set to music by Naushad, sung by Lata Mangeshkar:

> Go on living, bearing his cruel ways
> Keep on smiling like you do, swallowing your tears.
> This is the way of love, my heart
> He causes you anguish, you keep wishing him well.

Neeta sings the song sitting alone on the edge of a chaise longue in the resplendent living room (indexical of the life of a new capitalist class). The romantic triangle is established spatially, with great economy, through a relay of looks. As a callous Rajan gets ready to go and play tennis at the club, he seems indifferent to Neeta's anguish – not unlike a god to the devotee's penance. This structure of adoration/indifference is repeated in Dilip's silent devotion to Neeta, which she seems to ignore. Nevertheless, more than any precise link to the descriptions of the Raga Kedar, I will stress the general pensive mood, a troubled interiority that we, as spectators, are privy to.

Pinning down cinema's use of classical music in reductive terms would go against the very principle of creative improvisation that animates the Indian classical tradition (what Mani Kaul describes as 'moving intensely into something' without congealing 'into a junction', akin to 'a narrative elaboration without the perspectival development').[27] The fundamental point here is that the invocation of *ragas* lend paradigmatic depth to cinematic narration, simultaneously allowing for the enjoyment of the song numbers beyond their original narrative context. This enjoyment stems not only from the songs' 'audio value' or 'video value'; by now, they constitute a contemporary cultural heritage, the object of endless nostalgic invocation and recycling in India, and an anchoring peg for life in the diaspora.

Coda

The reflexivity about Indian cinema's song sequences – already evident in the elevator sequence from *Ek Duje Ke Liye* (1981), in which the Tamil-speaking hero woos the Hindi-speaking heroine by cobbling together a 'love song' from titles of well-known Hindi films, thereby acknowledging Hindi cinema as multilingual India's effective lingua franca – has taken centre stage from the 1990s. With India's entry into a neoliberal world order, as Bollywood idioms infiltrate and recalibrate global circuits of culture and entertainment, lifestyle and leisure activities, Indian cinema becomes more and more self-conscious about its own modalities. In its new role as a global arbiter of tastes, the industry finds itself at once empowered *and* embarrassed by its 'illogics' and 'idiosyncrasies' – particularly its musical and melo-dramatic proclivities. But what exactly happens when a cultural formation begins to internalise stereo-typical views of itself, to reflect obsessively on its conventions and practices, to make that knowledge a part of its repertoire? On the evidence of recent hits, from *Dil Chahta Hai* (2000) to *Om Shanti Om* (2007), it appears that Indian commercial films will continue to feature song-and-dance sequences as a vernacular idiom, but will increasingly feel compelled to somehow bracket these sequences as a mark of their globality, as if it does not behove well for a mature industry to serve up such excessive con-coctions without a self-confident formalist accentuation or a dollop of self-disparaging irony.

Notes

Thanks to Moinak Biswas, Charles Wolfe and Bishnupriya Ghosh, and to Steven Cohan for his editorial feedback.

1. Gregory Booth, *Behind the Curtain: Making Music in Mumbai's Film Studios* (New York: Oxford University Press, 2008); Sangita Gopal and Sujata Moorti (eds), *Global Bollywood* (Minneapolis: University of Minnesota Press, 2008); Anna Morcom, *Hindi Film Songs and the Cinema* (Aldershot, Hants.: Ashgate, 2007); Ashok Da. Ranade, *Hindi Film Song: Music beyond Boundaries* (New Delhi: Promilla, 2006).
2. Jane Feuer, 'The Self-reflective Musical and the Myth of Entertainment', in Rick Altman (ed.), *Genre: The Musical* (London: Routledge and Kegan Paul, 1981), p. 160.
3. Martin Rubin, *Showstoppers: Busby Berkeley and the Tradition of Spectacle* (New York: Columbia University Press, 1993), p. 37.
4. Steven Cohan, 'Introduction: Musicals of the Studio Era', in Cohan (ed.), *Hollywood Musicals: The Film Reader* (London and New York: Routledge, 2002), p. 2.
5. Rick Altman, 'Introduction', in Altman, *Genre: The Musical*, p. 7.
6. Mani Kaul, 'The Rambling Figure', in Larry Sider, Diane Freeman and Jerry Sider (eds), *Soundscape: The School of Sound Lectures 1998–2001* (London: Wallflower, 2003), p. 211.
7. Ibid., pp. 216–18.
8. Ibid., p. 211.
9. Morcom, *Hindi Film Songs and the Cinema*, p. 60.
10. Ibid., Chapter 2, 'The Production Process of Hindi Film Songs', pp. 25–60.
11. Ibid., pp. 59–60.
12. See Corey Creekmur, 'Picturizing American Cinema: Hindi Film Songs and the Last Days of Genre', in Pamela Wojcik and Arthur Knight (eds), *Soundtrack Available* (Durham, NC: Duke University Press, 2001), pp. 375–406.
13. See the discussion of the critique of Hindi commercial films – including a summary dismissal of their penchant for convoluted plots and musical numbers by Satyajit Ray and others – in Ravi Vasudevan, 'Shifting Codes, Dissolving Identities: The Hindi Social Film of the 1950s as Popular Culture', *Journal of Arts and Ideas*, vol. 23 no. 24, January 1993, pp. 51–79. A related controversy around cinema's alleged bastardisation of music led to the state-run All India Radio placing restrictions on the broadcast of film songs between 1952 and 1954. See Bhaskar Sarkar, *Mourning the Nation* (Durham, NC: Duke University Press, 2009), pp. 57–8.

14. Kajri Jain, *Gods in the Bazaar* (Durham, NC: Duke University Press, 2007), p. 14 (emphasis in original).

15. Ashish Rajadhyaksha, 'The Phalke Era: Conflict of Traditional Form and Modern Technology', *Journal of Arts and Ideas*, vol. 14/15, 1987, pp. 47–78.

16. Geeta Kapur, 'Revelation and Doubt: *Sant Tukaram* and *Devi*', in Tejaswini Niranjana, P. Sudhir and Vivek Dhareshwar (eds), *Interrogating Modernity* (Calcutta: Seagull Books, 1993), pp. 19–46.

17. 'Calendar art' refers to *bazaar* appropriations of classical sculptures and paintings, influenced by Raja Ravi Varma's nineteenth-century chromolithographs; it includes a wide range of artifacts, from posters and painted billboards to commercial calendars.

18. More boisterous depictions of love, in which the lovers run around trees and roll on the ground, have instigated a dismissive stereotype of Bombay-style romance. The title track from *Junglee* (1964), complete with the hero's loud yelp 'yahoo!', may well be the paradigmatic number of this ilk.

19. Richard Dyer, 'Entertainment and Utopia', in Altman (ed.), *Genre: The Musical*, p. 178.

20. Kathryn Hansen, 'Language, Community and the Theatrical Public: Linguistic Pluralism and Change in the Nineteenth-century Parsi Theatre', in Stuart Blackburn and Vasudha Dalmia (eds), *India's Literary History: Essays on the Nineteenth Century* (Delhi: Permanent Black, 2004), pp. 60–86.

21. Anuradha Kapur, 'Impersonation, Narration, Desire, and the Parsi Theatre', in Blackburn and Dalmia, *India's Literary History*, pp. 87–118.

22. See Ananda Lal (ed.), *The Oxford Companion to Indian Theatre* (Oxford: Oxford University Press, 2004).

23. Ranade, *Hindi Film Song*, p. 110.

24. Klaus Ebeling, *Ragamala Painting* (New York: Ravi Kumar, 1973), p. 62.

25. Ibid., p. 126.

26. Ibid., p. 134.

27. Kaul, 'The Rambling Figure', p. 217.

4 The International Art Musical:
Defining and Periodising Post-1980s Musicals

Jane Feuer

Very early in my career, I encountered a student who insisted that I name the precise number of musical performances that a film must have in order to be considered a musical. When I asked him what number he had in mind, he said emphatically, 'Six.' While this degree of empirical certitude is admirable in its way, it does not begin to tackle those borderline cases wherein a film 'feels like' a musical but has only one or two 'numbers' (e.g. *Lili*, 1953), or those in which a film has multiple performances but does not 'feel like' a musical (e.g. *Applause*, 1929). Nor does it account for my labelling John Waters's *Hairspray* a teen musical before it had even been made into a Broadway and then a film musical, with the odd result of my analysing what came to be known as the 'non-musical' version of *Hairspray* in a book on the musical. Rick Altman's distinction between the semantic and syntactic musical[1] goes a long way towards solving this problem, but his distinction does not work as well for films after 1981, because the basic building blocks themselves have altered so much with changes in the nature of popular musical performance. How do we recognise and periodise post-1980s films as musicals? This is the question I want to address in this paper by, in a sense, 'genre-fying'[2] a group of films not originally considered to be musicals.

In my previous attempts at periodising the musical, I sought to update Rick Altman's original schema by adding to it a 'reconstructive' period in the 1980s. For Altman, the musical's 'experimental' period, during which the semantic elements accumulated in all three subgenres, lasted from 1929 to 1933.[3] The genre's classical period lasted from 1933 to the mid-50s and can be defined by a semantic field coalescing into a stable syntax. With the deconstructive period (from the mid-1950s to 1981 and after), there was a return to the semantic genre with a consequent unravelling and critique of that stable syntax. What I added to this was the development after *Dirty Dancing* (1987) of a 'reconstructive' period which established a new set of positive conventions for the musical and often restored the classic syntax. Many of these films were 'teen' musicals, which also meant that they targeted a different, younger audience. Since then, the deconstructive and reconstructive tendencies have worked in tandem so that sometimes one needs to argue whether a given moment in a given film is one or the other.

For example, is the ending of *Pennies from Heaven* (1981) deconstructive or reconstructive? Previously, I argued that this film represents the furthest reach of deconstruction within a commercial Hollywood film.[4] But my reading depends upon how one reads the tacked-on 'reconstructive' turnaround at the very end of the film. I think that most of us would see 'The Glory of Love' add-on as a feeble attempt at reconstruction of the obligatory happy ending of a traditional musical. It is the kind of 'fake happy ending' often noted in melodramas of the 1950s. On the other hand, Dennis Potter felt the need to offer us a reconstructive moment, however brief. Such an acknowledgment of the dialectical nature of deconstruction/reconstruction occurs in even the most pessimistic films, such as at the ending of *Dancer in the Dark*. Given this qualification, I still find the idea of a 'reconstructive' cycle of (mostly teen) musicals in the 1980s useful, because in creating new conventions for the musical genre under the influence of music videos, the process of genre-fication was able to continue. In this way, the teen musical of the 1980s becomes the 'dance film' of the 2000s, a cycle of musicals now defined to the point that a parody of them was made.[5]

Many scholars distinguish between a 'genre' and a 'cycle' or a 'genre' and a 'subgenre'. A cycle would be a temporally brief but numerically and aesthetically significant outpouring of related films, such as the Warner Bros. gangster films of the early 1930s. A subgenre is usually, but not always, historically broad-based and characterised by shifts in its semantic field over time. Subgeneric division shows us these shifts within a synchronic field within a historically long-lived genre, such as the 'folk musical' described by Rick Altman. Cycle and subgenre are easily confused, because, as Altman points out, either can develop into a fully-fledged genre through a process of genre-fication, and also because, in a given case, it is sometimes hard to differentiate between a cycle and a subgenre. For example, the 'folk musical' developed during the 1940s and 50s from a particular historic concern with Americana. Since one can find precedents for it much earlier in the all-black musicals made around 1929, and since its influence persists to the present day in films like *Hairspray*, it is not exactly a cycle, yet the films made between 1944 and 1952 could be described as a cycle. In addition, the term cycle has an industrial and commercial ring to it, whereas subgenre seems more of an academic distinction. Here one is reminded of Todorov's distinction between a historical genre and a theoretical one, a cycle being more historical and a subgenre more theoretical.[6] Recent work on film genre theory has suggested that a cycle may or may not become a genre. Yet no one has suggested that the musical is not a genre; Altman even says that the musical is not typical of the coming and going of cycles in Hollywood because of its longevity.[7]

In the 1990s, a different kind of small-scale musical emerged as part of an international cycle of films. They were not called 'musicals', but I will argue that they can be construed as a new 'period' or 'cycle' in the historical development of the musical as I have sketched it above. This cycle includes:

- *Strictly Ballroom* (Australia, 1992)
- *Everyone Says I Love You* (US, 1996)
- *Shall We Dance* (Japan, 1996; remake US, 2004)
- *Little Voice* (UK, 1998)
- *Dancer in the Dark* (Denmark co-production, 2000)[8]
- *Billy Elliot* (UK, 2000)

These films – released during a single decade – could be considered a cycle of independent art films, but I am going to argue for them as a subgenre of the long-lived Hollywood musical genre. The main characters are not professional entertainers, neither are they fairy-tale kings and princesses nor Midwestern farmers and cowboys. Rather, they are amateurs in the truest sense of the term – lovers of song or dance. Instead of representing the lead performers in old Hollywood musicals, they take up the position of spectators of old Hollywood musicals in a world where it is no longer possible to be Fred Astaire. For me, these films are a more significant and aesthetically successful continuation of the musical's constant enquiry into the nature of musical entertainment and its effect on audiences than any of the so-called 'new musicals' of recent years such as *Chicago*, *Dreamgirls*, *Phantom of the Opera*, *Hairspray* and *Nine*. In their insistence on the deconstruction and reconstruction of the ideals of musical entertainment, they fit better with my own genre model for musicals than do other, bigger films which have six or more 'numbers' in them.

Unlike the reconstructive teen musical cycle inaugurated by *Dirty Dancing* in 1987, they do not necessarily reconfigure the musical for a new generation. They do not all – although some do – conceptualise the musical number as a little music video. Yet a closer look at their structure reveals a surprising unity. Most were distributed by Miramax, at that time an 'art-house' distributor which catered to the international art-house audience. They continued an important thematic thread in the musical that I would call the 'glorification of entertainment'. But now this tradition is linked to an older, more European idea of 'art for art's sake' or aestheticism. In this sense, if not in scale, the cycle culminated in the big-budget studio musical *Moulin Rouge!* (2001).

All are what I would call 'reconstructive' musicals – they reconfigure the old conventions in a positive direction – but unlike the teen musicals that do this, they are not geared to the youth audience, but rather the art-house audience. Many return to the classic syntax whereby success in an artistic endeavour and success in love go together. Despite the many deconstructive elements within them, these films close on a 'feel-good' note whether or not the couple comes together in a wedding ritual at the end. Thus, they affirm the spirit if not the letter of classic Hollywood musicals. But they do so with an acknowledgment that our love for old musicals cannot be anything but a form of nostalgia. This combination of nostalgia for past forms of musical entertainment with a declaration of the greater realism of present-day models has always characterised musical films.

In *Strictly Ballroom*, the couple/show syntax is classical, as in *Dirty Dancing*: he creates art, she is art; dancing together leads to falling in love; the message is that being true to one's ideals and dreams can result in a happy ending. Indeed, *Strictly Ballroom* is the perfect example of the way in which musicals reproduce themselves not through surface similarities but through structural homology. Very different on the surface and in terms of authorship and style, *Dirty Dancing* and *Strictly Ballroom* nevertheless share an underlying 'deep structure' to the extent that, at this level only, one could consider the latter to be a 'remake' of the 1987 film. The endings – in which a diegetic audience spanning three generations joins the happy couple on the dance floor in a communal celebration – are remarkably similar. They attest to the significance of the reconstructive moment across national boundaries and directorial signatures.

If Baz Luhrmann has a distinct authorial voice that nevertheless can be analysed away at the level of generic structure, surely Woody Allen's voice had become hyper-authorial by the 1990s. And yet his – dare I say sweet and nostalgic? – musical film displays a profound knowledge of the classic genre and the music that enabled it. *Everyone Says I Love You* peaks at the bittersweet moment of reconstruction of a typical dance number reminiscent of a Fred and Ginger romantic couple dance. 'I'm Through with Love' finds the ex-spouses, played by Goldie Hawn and Woody Allen, on the banks of the Seine in a quotation from *An American in Paris* (1951) and ends with the stern gaze of a policeman directed at the couple in a quotation from the title number from *Singin' in the Rain* (1952). In between, she sings the downbeat lyric and he partners her in a dance. But presumably because they are not Fred and Ginger, he does not sing, and her dancing is enhanced by special effects that cause her to fly through the air and slide endlessly. Any description of this number could not but suggest that it is a deconstructive parody of a real romantic dance number.

Woody Allen and Goldie Hawn in *Everyone Says I Love You* (1996)

But this is not the whole story. Because Goldie Hawn is capable of singing and dancing (although not especially known for it), her song and dance have an eerie beauty to them which the effects enhance but do not destroy. She is able to hold the dance poses so that the effects appear to extend her own body posture rather than mocking an inability to dance at all. It is a far more paradoxical use of CGI than is found in those films that employ a dance double. And Woody Allen just manages to disappear into the role of partner so that we do not quite laugh at him. The number harks back to the most nostalgic moment in the history of the musical, the number in *Gigi* wherein Maurice Chevalier and Hermione Gingold reminisce but do not quite remember their youthful romance. As such, it is a reconstructive moment, because nostalgia for youthful passion and the kind of dancing that used to represent it is always a metaphor for an audience's nostalgia for old Hollywood musicals.

The desire to imitate Fred and Ginger runs deep in more recent musicals. Quite literal quotations from their romantic dances are inserted into the most dramatic number in *Pennies from Heaven*,[9] and an excerpt from the 'Top Hat' title number is inserted into *Billy Elliot* in a moment early in the film in which the quotation represents his grandmother's desires as well as what would come to be his. At the same time, the quotation serves as a non-diegetic insert for the audience, reminding us that Billy's desire to be a *male* dancer has deep precedents in musical films.

Perhaps the most bizarre example of an Astaire quotation occurs in the US remake of *Shall We Dance* when the coterie of ballroom dancers are transfixed by a display of television monitors in a store window, all showing the jazziest section of the 'The Girl Hunt' ballet from *The Band Wagon* (1953). Clearly not a reference addressed to purchasers of TV sets, the quotation begs to be deciphered by the film's audience. But the scene can only be addressed to those audience members familiar with the history of the musical film. Only for this audience can the glorification of the dance signify. There could also be a deconstructive move at work in the quotation. Perhaps the film-makers are acknowledging the fact that their film will never be *The Band Wagon*, because they will never be Vincente Minnelli, and no matter how much money they spend, their films can never be MGM musicals. Ultimately, however, the quotation, despite its apparent desire to connect historically to a golden age, actually 'misreads' *The Band Wagon*. The jazz ballet stands as a monument to classic musicals, but in fact it was an innovative type of number in 1953. Now we know that every generation of artists intentionally misreads the previous one. So what does this particular misreading tell us?

It interprets *The Band Wagon* as a cheerful, upbeat classic musical. The film's reconstructive impulse had centred on redeeming the persona of Fred Astaire from historical obscurity. Perhaps 'The Girl Hunt' does this by giving Astaire 'modern' choreography. And yet, the film's ending was quite a lame attempt at asserting Astaire's contemporaneity in 1953, much less in the 2000s. But for today's students, *The Band Wagon* is depressing, its ending more like Brecht than MGM. *Shall We Dance* (2004) needs to redefine the previous generation of musicals as innocent and simplistic in order to assert its own sophistication and modernity.

Supremely reconstructive moments need not always occur at the end in these films. In *Little Voice*, for example, reconstruction occurs at the moment when the title character manages to fulfil her dream of recreating on stage the numbers she has taught herself to imitate from her deceased father's record album collection – numbers by such singers as Judy Garland, Marilyn Monroe, Marlene Dietrich and Shirley Bassey. In an uncanny performance, Jane Horrocks even recites the patter from Judy's Carnegie Hall album creating a kind of nostalgia recognisable only by those devoted Garland fans who have listened endlessly to the original. This film is no *A Star Is Born* – the character is unable to sustain a career – but she does find love and, to some extent, finds herself in

Jane Horrocks in *Little Voice* (1998)

the effort at imitation. The notion of class mobility through musical talent is shared with the other British film in the group, *Billy Elliot*.

Thus far, I have demonstrated that an international group of independent films made during the 1990s bear a close relationship to the Hollywood musical and seem to be commenting nostalgically on the original genre. One could argue, however, that I have not yet established that these films are actually *musicals*. Perhaps they are more like 'theory films', commenting on earlier kinds of cinema without actually being them, in the way that a deconstructive impulse is more suited to criticism than it is to art. In this way, I might be noting an influence of the musical on later films rather than a generic development.

Nevertheless, I want to make the more extreme case that the films under analysis here are more than art films that reference musicals. Rather, I want to say that they are musicals, in keeping with the way in which musicals have always quoted from previous generations of entertainment texts, usually not in the same medium as the quoting text. If vaudeville served as an intertext for film musicals from the 1920s to the 50s, and older Hollywood musicals were 'recycled' into films of the 1980s, then the 'art musicals' I am attempting to periodise work by, in a sense, taking the musical number out of the diegesis of the film and placing it in a nostalgic past. Only Woody Allen's film has diegetic 'numbers' in the traditional sense, and yet these numbers are totally historical in terms of the songs borrowed and in terms of their insertion into the diegesis of the contemporary 'Woody Allen film' that surrounds the numbers. You can't exactly take the numbers away – they are diegetic – but you can trace out a narrative of a contemporary family that resembles the director's other films far more than it resembles a 'folk musical'. The folk musical impulse is carried by the numbers, beginning with the opening of the film, which is right out of *Meet Me in St Louis*. 'Just You, Just Me' references the (urban) folk musical in every way: it shows ordinary folks (not professional entertainers) singing because the 'sounds of the earth are like music'. New York City – a site of nature not urbanity – awakens in the spring, and this 'passed along song' is carried by a community that spans generations. Reminiscent of many opening numbers in folk musicals, 'Just You, Just Me' brings a kind of innocent joy to a narrative that in its non-musical moments carries the kind of angst more suited to a Woody Allen film.

In *Strictly Ballroom*, the numbers are not quite diegetic, in the sense that they are motivated by the dancers' profession rather than life itself, and yet there is clearly a level that elevates the dancing to a higher, less realistic realm in the way that numbers functioned in Busby Berkeley musicals. The DVD of the film actually lists the musical 'numbers' according to the music playing under them, and the song 'Time After Time' makes a Coca-Cola neon sign into a dream space. The camera pans up and down to the father dancing his own crazy steps, thus using dance to narrate the story and link the generations. So many of these films invoke the fairy-tale musical tradition of creating a contrast between a real world and a dream world and then in the end dissolving the harsh real world into the musical dream world.

Stephen Daldry's *Billy Elliot* (2000)

Little Voice, for example, is entirely about this contrast. When the eponymous heroine performs at the club, the entire film is lifted up into a spectacular sphere in which the world of working-class English realism dissolves into the cabaret space of a musical.

Although it does not exactly use musical 'numbers', *Billy Elliot* also employs non-diegetic music in a way that links the film to musicals. The fact that this film was eventually made into a theatrical musical shows us that the structural underpinnings for numbers were already present in the original film. We like to think that in adapting a non-musical text into a musical, the main task is inserting 'numbers' into an already existing 'straight' play. Since so many London/Broadway musicals today are adapted from films not plays, in a case such as *Billy Elliot* or *Hairspray*, one would look for moments in the original text which can inspire musical performance. The adaptation would involve adding diegetic numbers to a text for which the diegesis was not musical in nature. Yet there are moments in the film *Billy Elliot* that could already be described as 'numbers'. The film uses non-diegetic music throughout to create a binary opposition between the masculine, working-class world of the miners and the effete feminine world of *Swan Lake* to which Billy aspires. These binaries are mediated in the 'number' where Billy dances out his anger at his father by incorporating the more masculine Irish dance steps into his balletic vocabulary, thus proving, as Gene Kelly always tried to do, that ballet can be for men. Indeed, the film ends with Billy performing in Matthew Bournes's *Swan Lake*, surely the most masculine version ever of that classic ballet. (Curiously, the stage adaptation omits this flash-forward.) The establishing of simple binaries which eventually merge through a dance performance was typical of classic Hollywood musicals, and it remains the structuring device behind *Billy Elliot*.

The question for me becomes: which is more 'musical' – the film version which integrates music and performance into a more or less realist text, or the stage adaptation which creates more traditional 'diegetic' numbers? What is the status of the 'number' in post-1980s film musicals? Has not this questioning of its status been part of the deconstructive move since at least 1955 when *It's Always Fair Weather* chose to use a series of quasi-Brechtian 'non-numbers' in the place of conventional MGM diegetic numbers. I want to argue that this group of international art musicals is truer to the history of the genre than other more traditional musicals with diegetic numbers. I want to argue that a film without 'numbers' can be defined as a musical for our times. Furthermore, I want to state my opinion that John Waters's original *Hairspray* represents a more interesting development for the genre than does the film version of the Broadway show *Hairspray*.

One of these numberless films, *Shall We Dance*, resonates with a discourse about the value of dancing that harks back to the song lyrics of old musicals I described in *The Hollywood Musical*. For example, the sensei tells the hero that 'dance begins with a dancer's feelings', just as Ira Gershwin had told us long ago:

All you preachers
Who delight in panning the dancing teachers,
Let me tell you there are a lot of features
Of the dance that carry you through
The gates of Heaven.[10]

Shall We Dance also invokes such tried and true musical ideologies as 'dancing from the heart' and 'finding one's true partner'. As ever in musicals, dance becomes a metaphor for life, as when Mai tells the hero that practising with him for his first competition has changed her. When she herself was a champion, she was dancing 'only for [her]self'. But now she shares her gift with him. As in *Strictly Ballroom*, the final dance between Mai and the hero inspires others to dance, including the detective who has been following the hero at the request of his wife. The words 'shall we dance' are spoken in English, seeming to invoke not only *The King and I* but also the ballroom dream world of Fred and Ginger. *Shall We Dance* also invokes the fairy-tale tradition of contrasting a mundane world with a dream world. The dream world is first represented by the dance studio where the hero gazes at Mai as she looks out of the window. Later, Mai's dream world is represented by the seaside town of Blackpool, the English working-class resort where the international ballroom dancing competitions take place. Even though this film has nothing that would correspond to the typical musical 'number' in a classic musical (although it does have dances), it carries a nostalgic discourse about the world of musicals that links it to the Hollywood and Broadway show-business traditions, even though the film takes place in Japan.

I have said that this group of small-budget art musicals culminated in the spectacular *Moulin Rouge!* or perhaps prepared the way for the re-emergence of the 'big' musical. *Moulin Rouge!* follows *The Band Wagon* model of a show-within-a-show. The Pitch number 'Spectacular, Spectacular' follows 'That's Entertainment' in form and function and mode of address. *Moulin Rouge!* even includes lines from *The Band Wagon*, as when Jeffrey Cordova's declaration that no one's going to play (the devil) but him is quoted directly in the film.

But the show is now so deeply interwoven with the primary story of the lovers to the point where at the end, the story of the show and the story of the film become merged. Now there was a long tradition of a show-within-a-show in the classic Hollywood musical as well. Typically, as Altman says, the energy that drives the lovers goes into the show and vice versa.[11] But the emphasis in the classic musical, the *raison d'être* for the lovers and the focus for all the energy of the film, was always the show. Even though *Moulin Rouge!* echoes the cry of 'the show must go on', ultimately the film is not about the glorification of show business. There seems to be an imbalance between the importance of love and the importance of the show. But it is only the internal show, 'Spectacular, Spectacular', that is secondary. The real work of art is the account Christian is writing of his great love affair, and that show is the film *Moulin Rouge!* Thus, the theme of eternal love does in the end run parallel to the creation of a work of art, but the work of art is no longer the show-within-the-film but rather the film itself. Art rather than entertainment is what is ultimately affirmed, making the 'message' of *Moulin Rouge!* opposite to that of *The Band Wagon*. And yet, the postmodern pastiche of the film's score relies heavily upon popular songs.

The interweaving of the show with the plot of *Moulin Rouge!* is much closer than in any classic musical. The *mise-en-abyme* structure is more like Pirandello than a Hollywood musical. Again, the emphasis is on an art form rather than an entertainment form. And yet, *Moulin Rouge!* is itself a pastiche of numerous forms of cheap entertainment: the cancan of Paris at the turn of the century, Bollywood cinema and a collection of American pop songs of the most commercial type. The film's style and tone extend the mock seriousness of the fairy-tale musical as described by Rick Altman:

> We are too sophisticated to accept such a banal plot without dissociating ourselves from it; in order to permit belief, we must cover that belief with … a mask of unbelief in the form of irony, parody, and the numerous other winks … yet in spite of initial protests and insistent pride, each member of the couple eventually succumbs to the goddess of love, as do we to their charm. The fairy tale musical's distancing devices are heavily front-loaded, with fewer and fewer occurrences toward the end of the text.[12]

This description of the 1929 Ernst Lubitsch film *The Love Parade* could just as easily apply to *Moulin Rouge!* What Altman calls the 'mock seriousness' of the fairy-tale subgenre of musicals, Baz Luhrmann calls the 'heightened interpretation of end-of-century Paris seen through a very contemporary lens, a shockingly operatic, high pop, high camp kind of lens'. Nevertheless, we are meant to take the ending as 'tragicomedy'.[13]

The function of classic Hollywood musicals was to glorify entertainment of which they were also a part. The function of the international art musicals is to glorify art, as defined by art cinema, of which they are also a part. Yet in glorifying bohemian art, *Moulin Rouge!* makes use of the most popular forms of entertainment: in being a pastiche of old musicals and in selecting music that is far more removed from the opera house than anything Rodgers and Hammerstein ever wrote. In many ways, *Moulin Rouge!* makes *Oklahoma!* look like opera.

But what about the tragic ending? Doesn't this present at least a variation on the traditional happy ending of the musical? I believe the answer to this question brings us back to the periodisation of the musical I offered at the beginning. For it is only by taking the model of the classic period as the model for the genre as a whole that one can generalise that musicals have happy endings. In fact, during both the experimental period and the deconstructive period, the musical typically combined musical numbers with melodramatic or tragic plots, not comic ones. The more we learn about the 1929–33 early period of films about performers,[14] the more we realise that a film like *Applause*, with its tragic ending, was not atypical of a 1929 musical.

Of course, it's perfectly possible to interpret *Moulin Rouge!* as ending with the lovers together forever in eternal love. But even if we read the ending as experimental or deconstructive, it is in no way out of line with the history of the musical genre considered as a whole and not just as a form of classical Hollywood cinema.

While it is a truism that almost every film has music in it – whether diegetic or not – I think it is misleading to define the film musical as a film with diegetic numbers. This is to mistake a period of musicals for the genre as a whole. In fact, if we take 1929 as a starting date, the notion of diegetic singing only held sway for about thirty of the next eighty years. What's more, if we consider diegetic dancing to be definitional of a musical film, then 1929 is far too late a starting date for the genre, because some of the earliest films contain diegetic dancing accompanied by music. While I am not especially interested in having six numbers dancing on the head of a pin, I do think it is important at least to consider these shifts in definition of the genre in a historical context. What is it about diegetic singing that makes it so hard for audiences to accept? Why does this mode of singing appear to be more acceptable on the Broadway stage than on film? Why is the musical today once again defined as a *dance* film? These are all questions that a genre critic must take into account in deciding which films to include in her own theoretical genre.

For me, the self-reflexive nature of the musical genre has always been definitional. As a quasi-modernist form of popular entertainment, this genre can easily move from popular cinema to art cinema. At the same time, the re-emergence of ballroom dancing and hip-hop dance films (and TV dance competitions) can take the place of popular musicals of the past. To focus on blockbuster films in talking about the rebirth of the musical is to mistake one (not very successful economically or artistically) cycle for the entire genre. It is to forget that musicals are there to be discovered but rarely in the places you might expect to find them.

Notes

1. Rick Altman, *Film/Genre* (London: BFI, 1999), pp. 216–26.

2. Ibid., p. 62ff.

3. Jane Feuer, *The Hollywood Musical* (Bloomington: Indiana University Press, 1993, 2nd edition), pp. 130–3; Rick Altman, *The American Film Musical* (Bloomington: Indiana University Press, 1987), p. 116ff.

4. Feuer, *Hollywood Musical*, p. 128.

5. *Dance Flick* (Damien Wayans, 2009).

6. Tzvetan Todorov, *The Fantastic*, trans. Richard Howard (Ithaca, NY: Cornell University Press, 1975).

7. Altman, *Film/Genre*, p. 30ff.

8. Because of its more avant-garde background, I chose not to include this film in my discussion. Nevertheless, it bears resemblance to the films I will be analysing.
9. I analysed this number at greater length in the second edition of *The Hollywood Musical*, pp. 128–9.
10. George and Ira Gershwin, 'I'll Build a Stairway to Paradise', in *George White's Scandals* (1922). Recycled into *An American in Paris* (1951).
11. Altman, *American Film Musical*, p. 227.
12. Ibid., p. 146.
13. Baz Luhrmann, *Moulin Rouge!: The Splendid Illustrated Book That Charts the Journey of Baz Luhrmann's Motion Picture*, 1st edition (New York: Newmarket Press, June 2001), p. 10.
14. See, for example, Richard Barrios, *A Song in the Dark: The Birth of the Musical Film*, 2nd edition (New York: Oxford University Press, 2009).

PART TWO: Histories of the Hollywood Musical

5 Flirting with Terpsichore:
Dance, Class and Entertainment in 1930s Film Musicals

Adrienne L. McLean

The title of this essay, as perhaps any fan of the musicals of Fred Astaire and Ginger Rogers knows, is from their 1936 film *Swing Time*. Astaire, dressed in spats, pin-striped trousers, a tailcoat and top hat, has pursued Rogers to the dancing school where she teaches, after embarrassing her in front of a policeman on the street when she accuses him of stealing a quarter from her – a ridiculous charge, the policeman thinks, because of Astaire's upper-class attire. We already know that Astaire is a professional stage dancer, although we haven't seen him do much yet. But the only way he can force the angry and humiliated Rogers to communicate with him is to hire her as his dancing instructress, and when Eric Blore, playing the school's proprietor, begins to list the thrills of learning 'to dance, to move', Astaire cuts in with 'To flirt with Terpsichore', prompting one of Blore's famous double-takes ('Yes ... What??'). When Blore asks Astaire what kind of dance he's interested in, Astaire professes ignorance as to the varieties available; Blore tells him they have 'tap dancing, and ballroom dancing, and aesthetic dancing', to which Astaire responds, 'If it's all the same to you, I'll take a little of each.'

Astaire and Rogers flirting with Terpsichore in the 'Pick Yourself Up' number from *Swing Time* (1936) (Collection of the author)

But the films of Astaire and Rogers had already 'taken a little of each'; the numbers the team performs all employ tap, ballroom and aesthetic dancing. There were many other types of dancing available to and displayed by Hollywood musicals throughout the 1930s, however, and the point of this essay is to discuss how Terpsichore herself, as it were, turned from being the inspiration for a wildly eclectic and energetic range of performance styles at the beginning of the decade into the more cultivated, polished and professional muse of the relatively limited repertoire of familiar dance techniques – variously inflected forms of ballet, tap and ballroom – that populate most of the canonical integrated musicals from the mid-1930s through the 50s. Although a few film musicals appeared in 1929 – *The Broadway Melody*, for example, which became the first sound film to win an Academy Award for best picture, or *Glorifying the American Girl*, supervised by Florenz Ziegfeld himself – it was in the 1930s that the form also acquired its crucial generic structures and meanings: utopian energy; sexual chemistry leading to a semantic and syntactic emphasis on the heterosexual couple and the community it implies and represents; a drive toward increasing integration of narrative and number, with dance serving as the locus of emotion, communication, self-expression and desire.[1] Moreover, across the 1930s, dancing, partly but hardly exclusively through the popularity of stars like Astaire and Rogers, became the 'controlling factor', in Jerome Delamater's words, of the musical's status as an eventually auteur-defined art form.[2] Using a range of film texts, this essay explores how dance, and the bodies that performed it, participated in creating the Hollywood musical as a genre during the 1930s, and how that dance and those bodies in turn were literally and figuratively shaped by ongoing and often strenuous debates about class, national identity, modernity and art and/as professional entertainment, and by the processes of recording, representation and preservation – and the ability to reach previously unimaginably vast audiences – that sound film enabled.[3]

Small, Active and Pretty

The first US periodicals devoted to dance began publication in the 1920s, in concert with dance's increasing visibility in motion pictures, especially during the first 'musicals boom' ensured by the success of *The Broadway Melody*. Although Hollywood, as is well known, sought to profit from the fame or prestige of theatrical performers lured away, temporarily or permanently, from vaudeville and

Backstage in *The Broadway Melody* (1929). Bessie Love, Charles King and Anita Page (*Movie Star News*)

Broadway, and, occasionally, the concert stage, even before the transition to sound was complete, the US film industry seemed to offer potentially the greater opportunities to the ambitious professional dancer than other venues ever had, with Los Angeles being heralded as 'The New Mecca of the Dance World' by 1930. Albertina Rasch announced the 'opening of a Hollywood studio' in 1929, with 'direct contact with MOTION PICTURE ACTIVITIES [being] assured to qualified pupils'; the following year, ads proclaimed the 'Cyclonic Success' of the 'Albertina Rasch Dancers in Hollywood'. Larry Ceballos, a dance director from Broadway, advertised his participation in eleven musical films in 1929 and 1930, and in 1930 Earle Wallace, who had also opened a studio in Los Angeles, claimed to be 'now rehearsing a unit of sixteen girls' who would be 'the first of a series of units to be featured in forthcoming screen productions for Warner Brothers and First National Studios'. In addition, numerous articles sought the opinions of leaders in the dance world about 'screen dancing' and how best to arrange or present it, on 'Talkies – Past and Future' and on the 'New Hollywood Dancing Girl'.[4]

The clear sense of Hollywood movies as both potential employer of the dance professional and as a performance venue is interesting, as is the emphasis on the gender of the movie performer as female; these are issues that I will return to later. What also stands out from the ads is the astonishing variety of show-business dance training available. Although Rasch's choreography for films usually involved ballet or 'toe dancing', even her studio (both the New York and Los Angeles branches) taught 'modern forms of ballet, jazz rhythms, tap and acrobatic, physical culture, [and] interpretive dancing'. Michel Fokine, whose stature derived from his association with Diaghilev's Ballets Russes and the fact that he was Russian, also offered an extensive roster of classes: 'Ballet, character, esthetic, Greek dances, plastic and expressive movements'. Jack Clark, known as the 'Radio Tapper', offered 'musical comedy, acrobatic-dancing, dance routines arranged [in] military, soft shoe, waltz, clog, buck, tap, nerve roll and broken rhythms' in New York, while Jack Stone, 'Tap Dancing Specialist', trained pupils in 'eccentric, acrobatic, musical comedy, soft shoe, syncopation buck, military broken rhythm, stair dance, waltz clog, exhibition ballroom, etc.'. Ernest Belcher's Los Angeles studio (Belcher's daughter Marjorie later became famous as Marge Champion) taught 'Toe ballet, Grecian, Oriental, acrobatic and all branches of stage dancing, including tap, buck and wing, waltz, clog, etc.'. Claude Alviene, advertising 'Pupils Fred and Adele Astaire, Lee Tracy, Mary Pickford, etc.', taught 'exhibition

Full-page ad for the Earle Wallace studio in Hollywood from *The Dance*, April 1930. The 'ballet dancer' in the upper left is Betty Grable. Note that the artist's rendering of the dancer's body in the upper centre represents an idealised version whose muscularity and attenuation would soon become the actual standard for the 'normal' professional dancing body (Collection of the author)

team dances, tangos, adagios, Spanish, toe and tap dancing', and although his studio was located in New York, his ad, like many others had begun to do by 1930, also offered training for 'Talking Pictures'.

The bounty of the types of dance instruction offered in a studio setting in the late 1920s and early 30s is supplemented by the routines, numbers and training one could also acquire by mail (routines were published in the magazines too). Every other appurtenance of dancing – costumes, wigs, makeup and shoes, including toe shoes, tap shoes (with 'resonating heel and toe plates' or 'wood clog tap' options), 'dancing oxfords', 'soft toe ballets', 'nature sandals', 'flats and musical comedy ties', 'Grecian sandals', and on and on – was available through the mail, suggesting the spread of interest in dance to areas not yet served by resident teachers, but also indicating that the nature of dancing, and by implication of the dancer, was understood to be somewhat different from the way both are charac- terised now. That is, at this time dancing was a patchwork set of skills, acquired by whatever means and however quickly, not – except in the case of certain revered ballet dancers, like Russian ballerina Anna Pavlova, who died in 1931 after fulfilling her ambition to take ballet 'to the masses' – an avo- cation that involved lengthy training, or even unusual or virtuosic talent. To be sure, certain types did require specific physical abilities, especially acrobatic and eccentric dancing, in which strength and flex- ibility and a good degree of extension were necessary to perform the contortions, balances and other 'tricks' that each form depended upon. But even there, if you could keep time and do the splits or bal- ance in a pair of toe shoes, you could end up as one of the 'new Hollywood dancing girls' featured in the 'Wedding of the Painted Doll' in *The Broadway Melody*.

While it is impossible to make direct correspondences between the simultaneous burgeoning of mail order as well as studio dance training and the heyday of the 'All-Talking, All-Singing, All-Dancing' musical film, articles in fan as well as dance magazines that focused on the requirements for becom- ing a Hollywood dancing girl fed the notion that it wouldn't take much to become one of the many 'chorines' employed in Hollywood after the transition to sound. Once the Broadway dancer learned that 'the stories from Hollywood were fact and not fairy tales', then for 'the first time, New York could no longer boast of being the undisputed Mecca of the dancing girls', wrote *The Dance* in December 1929.[5] For the film dancer, a 'fresh' face and body, of slightly shorter stature than the Broadway chorus girl, were necessary; 'certain New York chorus girls are still in demand at thirty', reported *Photoplay* the same year, but you 'wouldn't find a girl past twenty-five among the entire two thousand in Hollywood'.[6] Instead, the chorus girls 'at First National, Warners, Paramount, and Radio Pictures are pretty much the same type – small, active and pretty' (Albertina Rasch's 'girls' were allowed to be 'larger and apparently stronger' because ballet was a little more 'exacting').[7] Although it is claimed that they all could dance, and musicals of this era, especially the revues (*Hollywood Revue of 1929*, 1929, *The March of Time*, 1929, and *King of Jazz*, 1930), do contain examples of many, if not all, of the dance styles named in the dance-studio ads of the period, the decision to become a film dancer, even a musical star, required no great soul-searching or dedication. Bebe Daniels, according to *Photoplay*, simply decided that she would 'change her whole style of acting' when she made her debut as a 'talkie star' in 1929, 'going in for singing and dancing' instead of the 'stunts' she had heretofore been performing in 'tomboy comedies'.[8] Despite some reverence directed at Europeans like Rasch, then, the forms that the early musical drew upon understood dance, even ballet, to be a bag of tricks, not an underlying technique; and the dancer, whether female or male, to be whoever could perform those tricks to the most applause.

In his book on US dance in the 1930s, Mark Franko describes a scene from *Glorifying the American Girl* in which the heroine, played by Mary Eaton, unsuccessfully auditions for the Ziegfeld Follies by performing a 'shuffle dance' with her vaudeville partner: 'Given another chance, she performs an impromptu ballet variation in pointe shoes which succeeds in landing her a starring role in the Follies.'[9] Franko interprets this segment as indicating that 'classical ballet was a way of moving the chorus girl never studied, but rather discovered as a native resource in herself'. I would argue instead that it would have been assumed that she *had* studied it – she has toe shoes, after all, although she doesn't dance *en pointe* in the audition – but only enough (perhaps by mail) to be able to perform satisfactorily when the situation demanded it, in this case because the Ziegfeld Follies was a classier venue than vaudeville. While Franko invokes the scene in order to argue that the boundary between ballet and 'show dance' had always been 'permeable', a claim with which I agree entirely, it also throws light on the place and meaning of *all* show dance in film musicals of the period.[10] Eaton's character passes muster when she demonstrates, through her performance of a more aestheticised type of dancing, that – combined with her blonde beauty – she has the necessary skills for the job. Extreme technical competence is not required, just the ability to perform the right steps for the context.

When dancing of obvious virtuosity does occur in the early 1930s musical, it is likely to be in forms that are no longer familiar to us – 'legomania' or 'rubber legs' eccentric dancing, for example – or located in the scale of a number, such as a huge precision tap-dancing chorus line working in complete synchronisation. Thus, when Al Norman takes the (sound) stage to do amazing things with his body in the 'Happy Feet' section of *King of Jazz*, he draws gasps (even now) both because he *is* exemplifying a virtuosity that is otherwise rare in the film's dancing and because that virtuosity, as such, is recognisable to us today (and if some of what he does looks remarkably like moonwalking and other forms assumed to be novel and contemporary now, this only underscores the spurious history that *King of Jazz* promulgates, that jazz is a white musical form derived from a 'melting-pot of music', as its final number is called, of strictly European forms). When the film musical went out of favour in 1931, the reasons that are usually given are the high number of similar films released at once and the fact that the public no longer found them entertaining. Too much too soon, the standard history goes, but at least one commentator found it 'curious' that just as the Depression was deepening, 'the public did not choose to find a welcome escape in as artificial a form as the musical, but it simply did not'.[11]

At this point, the argument becomes complicated: on the one hand, there were a variety of interesting dance styles from which the musical could draw and which could have been used to differentiate one vehicle, and dancing star, from another; but on the other hand, with few exceptions, much of the dancing and many of the dancers that the musical *did* use became identifiable by an increasingly sophisticated public as being not much better than amateur. When the musical returned in 1933 with the success of *42nd Street*, which 'inaugurated a New Deal in entertainment!' according to its ads, the argument becomes more complicated still. Conventional wisdom has it that the topical and gritty 'backstage' narrative, especially the snappy dialogue and racy innuendo, of *42nd Street* was at least as important an element of its success as its elaborate and gigantically populated production numbers, under the direction of Busby Berkeley; but those numbers also represent the successful *return* of what Martin Rubin calls the 'tradition of spectacle', which makes Berkeley's musicals part of 'an important and lively tradition demonstrating that musicals can have much to offer outside the achievement of [stylistic and narrative] consistency'.[12] So *42nd Street*, and Berkeley's numbers especially, seems to continue many of the traditions that had made the musical passé just a year before, while reinvigorating the genre for the rest of the decade and beyond. Moreover, while Berkeley had already done his part to increase the employment prospects of the 'chorine' (*42nd Street* was Berkeley's eighth Hollywood musical), his new 'girls' needed even less dance training than they had

A range of dancing skills and bodies in *42nd Street* (1933). Ginger Rogers, Ruby Keeler and Una Merkel in the middle, and note that Merkel has the wrong arm in front (*Movie Star News*)

previously, just a level of physical pulchritude and a few standard tap combinations, as well as the ability to sway from side to side in unison or, for *Footlight Parade* (1933), to swim underwater while smiling at the camera. When Berkeley's peripatetic camera stops to focus on someone who *is* dancing, like Ruby Keeler in the title number of *42nd Street*, it generally means that the virtuosity has switched registers, now being located not in the camerawork or editing, nor only in the dancer's alluring body, but in the dancer's abilities and competence – a competence in which Berkeley himself supposedly had little interest.

Unfortunately, because today we are taught so little about the history of even well-known concert dance forms like ballet much less that of antique modes of show dancing, Ruby Keeler has come in for a lot of unjustified criticism in regard to the dancing she does on top of that taxi in *42nd Street*. Keeler is not graceful, she does stare at her feet, she does stomp, and loudly. By comparison with Fred Astaire or Ginger Rogers, Keeler's movements seem heavy, her tapping a bit stolid. But that was precisely the goal of the 'buck' dancer, which Keeler was (among other things) – she was performing a virtuoso turn in a mode that valued the loudness and clarity of the tap, its perfection of rhythm, never ahead of or behind the beat set by the music (buck dancing contests were judged from under the stage, out of view of the body producing the sounds).[13] If one looks closely, one can see that she is wearing shoes with a split wooden sole, which help her to make the rhythm so dark-sounding; and if they look to us like shoes a comedy granny might wear – big thick lace-up oxfords – that is because of our own ignorance, not Keeler's deficiencies. Moreover, we can see elsewhere in the film, for example in the rehearsal scene where she is being drilled by the show's director before being sent out on stage to 'come back a star!', that she is also able to do standard hoofing.

While Keeler would not have been perceived as an amateur by educated audience members who had been trained in the different forms of tap or who had acquired familiarity with it through vaudeville or other live performance venues, generally it is not the dance content that is discussed in Berkeley's Depression-era films but rather the numbers as cinematic spectacle and his equation of women's bodies with riches and abundance. The narratives point to situations of lack and scarcity that are ameliorated with overwhelming displays of gender-inflected plenitude in the numbers. In *Gold Diggers of 1933*, 'We're in the Money' is first performed by beautiful girls dressed in costumes made figuratively of golden coins, before the show is closed down by the police because the bills have not been paid; as Morris Dickstein writes, 'Escapist illusions are what this number is *about* – pretending you're in the money when there isn't any.'[14] By the latter half of the decade, though, there is more dancing in both Berkeley and 'Berkeley-esque' films like MGM's *Broadway Melody of 1936* (1935) and *Broadway Melody of 1938* (1937), and Sam Goldwyn's *The Goldwyn Follies* (1938), among others, and it is less idiosyncratic and more virtuosic, with a stronger element of technical proficiency. A wide range of other tap styles – even tapping in toe shoes – does continue to appear sporadically in what Rubin has named the 'aggregate' (non-integrated) film musical as late as the 1940s;[15] but the competition between dance as a speciality, as 'pure' entertainment and as a more or less spectacular irruption into narrative continuity and cohesion, was arguably decided by the enormous popularity at the box office, in the midst of the terrible Depression that the plots of Berkeley's *42nd Street*, *Gold Diggers of 1933*, *Footlight Parade*, et al. invoke so overtly, of the musicals of Astaire and Rogers. (That Rogers was also a player, something more than a chorine – she had great lines – but was not required to dance much, in both *42nd Street* and *Gold Diggers of 1933*, is an interesting irony, as is the fact that the first film that teamed Astaire and Rogers, *Flying Down to Rio*, was released the same year as *42nd Street*.)

The success of the Astaire–Rogers films derives partly from their nature as escapist fantasies as well (Rick Altman places the films in his 'fairy-tale' subgenre, in which sexual tension is displaced onto battles of will, class and style, in an often exotic or foreign setting supposedly far away from the Depression realities of daily existence), and Dickstein writes that 'it's no accident that so many screwball comedies, stage musicals, and the Astaire–Rogers films are set in the world of the very rich, for that world had not only the money but the mobility that was denied to most Americans during the Depression'.[16] But, in contrast to the Berkeley-esque musical, 'Dancing is not simply what [Astaire and Rogers] do; it's what their films are about.'[17] Dickstein, like many others who have written about the continued transcendence of Astaire and Rogers in the musical pantheon, believes that it was the use of dance as a metaphor of *transformation* that made their musicals so significant, and, before turning to a final discussion of dance, class and entertainment in the Astaire–Rogers films, I want to explore how transformation also resonates in relation to dance and dancing in the US more broadly during the decade.

It Would Have to Come Painlessly

In 1930, Albertina Rasch was interviewed for an article called 'Dancies Preferred' in which she was asked to comment on 'screen ballet technique'.[18] At this time, ballet could refer to any non-tap form of aesthetic dancing, and among Rasch's most interesting points was that, while the 'talkie' was still hampered by technical difficulties, the 'dancie' had learned to function 'smoothly and effectively'.[19] She was also one of the first film-affiliated choreographers to equate cinema dancing with dancing as such, to take for granted that what audiences saw in the movies was true of dancing in other venues:

The developments in the direction of the cinema dance seem to indicate that our attitude in the art of dance is not the working out of a specific style or school as the Italians, the French and the Russians did, but the fusing and melting of all dances of all nations and ages.[20]

Just as *King of Jazz* had denied jazz its non-white origins (beyond a cartoon showing Paul Whiteman in Africa making musical instruments out of animal parts), there is no reference in Rasch's writing, nor in the dances she choreographed in Hollywood (although her studio did offer training in 'jazz rhythms'), to non-white contributions to American concert or show dance.[21] But she was correct in her assertion that virtually all of the screen dancers whose work we admire to this day did perform an amalgamation of many dance styles, and her statement can usefully be extended to the gradual synthesis of the distinct types and subtypes of tap, ballet and ballroom dancing into larger, more inclusive but also more difficult *techniques*. That is, Fred Astaire, Ginger Rogers and Eleanor Powell, to name three of the most famous dancing musical stars of the decade, did not, could not, become stars by learning military, soft shoe, waltz, clog *or* buck dancing; rather, they had to be able to do most of them, all under the rubric of tap or 'rhythm tap', in addition to being proficient in 'exhibition ballroom' and 'adagio' styles. And Astaire and Powell, at least, do their share of ballet dancing too in the 1930s, Astaire in *Shall We Dance* (1937) (Rogers represents the tap and swing which Astaire wants to merge with ballet) and Powell in *Broadway Melody of 1936* (in a Rasch number). Moreover, the technical requirements increased not only for dancers desiring to become stars but for

Eleanor Powell and Albertina Rasch dancers in the 'Lucky Star' ballet in *Broadway Melody of 1936* (1935) (BFI)

chorines as well – there's even a ballet plot underpinning Berkeley's dance direction in *Gold Diggers in Paris* (1938).

Indeed, in US dance history, the 1930s are largely understood as the period in which classical ballet assumed a final dominance over modern dance, and in which ballet became 'American' rather than Euro-Russian.[22] In a 1931 article called 'Creating a Dance Public' by Leon Leonidoff, then-director of the dancing unit at the Roxy (and on whom the James Cagney prologue director in *Footlight Parade* was reportedly modelled), he explains how he 'led' the 'great mass audiences' to an appreciation of ballet ('It would have to come painlessly').[23] He started by 'slipping' into his programmes 'clogs and jigs and taps, wooden shoe specialties, tarantellas, gavottes, and Russian and Spanish specialties'.[24] Then, in 'tiny doses, like solid food administered to a starved man, the ballet was introduced to the great American public. (The same public that everyone was sure could never respond to higher forms of dancing.)'[25] If ballet's increasing popularity in the 1930s was based less on live performance than its presence in motion pictures, the preponderance of dancing in musicals by mid-decade was swing-inflected tap and ballroom (see 'The Waltz in Swing Time' in *Swing Time*); ballet numbers were common only in operettas. But ballet was circulating powerfully as a presence in non-musical films too, as a mood, a set of outward appurtenances rather than dance technique (toe shoes, tights, tutus) and melancholy or tragic narratives based on the lives of 'dying swan' Pavlova or the insane Russian dancer Nijinsky (girls enrolled in ballet classes after seeing Garbo play a ballerina in *Grand Hotel* in 1932, in which no one dances a step).[26] These narratives represented ballet as something that required extensive dedication, devotion and training but that could now prove significant to achieving stardom. Even C. L. Ebsen, who ran a dancing school and was the father of eccentric/tap/ballroom dancers Buddy and Vilma Ebsen, told *The American Dancer* in 1936 that 'Ballet is now the foundation of the Ebsen school'.[27] There were no 'finer physical specimens, or better examples of the value of this physical and mental development which comes only from dancing' than ballet dancers who are 'trained from their early childhood'.[28] Ebsen ends with the proclamation that 'When all children have adequate dance instruction we will have a stronger and healthier race of Americans.'[29] The same year, *Life* magazine put ballet on its cover in the form of dancers from George Balanchine's new American Ballet, as part of a twelve-page portfolio on dancing that began with 'Lindy Hoppers' in Harlem (but who might 'soon be on Broadway') and included a section on Fred Astaire, a 'hard-working professional'.[30] Of ballet, *Life* writes it is '[n]o amateur hobby [but] a hard, steady, painstaking job, requiring five years of training in the prime of youth to attain a properly professional degree of skill'.[31] Signally, nowhere in this portfolio is modern dance so much as mentioned, and the only kind of 'amateur dancing' covered is the social type taught by Arthur Murray.

The Americanisation of ballet in the 1930s occurred, then, partly because it *was* hard, and because it was turning to 'American characters' and 'American themes' as subject matter, thereby borrowing and undercutting some of the identity of modern dance. Jane Feuer has written of the way that the backstage musical affirmed its own value for popular audiences by offering alternative forms of entertainment to the 'stiff, formal, classical art of ballet', and certainly there are a number of comic or parodic uses of ballet in 1930s musicals (for instance, the Balanchine-choreographed 'Romeo and Juliet' number in *The Goldwyn Follies*, in which ballet and tap engage in a dance battle that ends with both forms still standing, or the various crazy dancers or effete ballet-associated characters in films from *Gold Diggers in Paris* to *Shall We Dance*).[32] But it's not true that 'in the 1930s the musical either shunned ballet or made a travesty of it';[33] rather, ballet no longer looks to us the way it did in the 1930s, and this is in part because of its representation and visualisation in film – just as

Vera Zorina and George Balanchine's American Ballet in *The Goldwyn Follies* (1938) (BFI)

the disappearance or consolidation of other earlier forms of show dancing that were popular at the beginning of the decade derives in some sense from the way people looked while dancing that way in the movies. The type of dance employed in 1930s musicals is less significant than its increasing presence as something *more* than entertainment, as something that resonated in ways that arguably it never did in musicals again quite as profoundly. Dickstein uses dance as a metaphor for the Depression – dancing in the dark, aimless movement 'heading nowhere' (the dance marathon emblematic of this), but also dance as mobility, real or imagined, dance offering 'a lift to those who [felt] "down in the dumps", a sense of movement and relationship to those who [felt] hemmed in and isolated, a democratic kind of classiness, available in fantasy if not in fact, to replace stiffly hierarchical notions of class'.

   But there is also a 'tension in thirties culture', in Dickstein's words,

> between a naturalism or populism, with its emphasis on social reality, and a technically innovative modernism, stressing the complications of individual experience. These forms of seeing, which often overlapped, were part of a debate about the role of the arts in a period of social crisis.[34]

What Mark Franko calls an 'issue of amateurism versus professionalism' in dance came to a head in 1937 in a series of strikes in New York in which modern dancers, largely amateur, were accused of 'usurping the legitimate identity of performative workers', the professional ballet dancer and chorus girl. As these last two became more and more identified as one through the linkage of *corps* and chorus, 'the politics of skill' came to replace the 'political radicalism' of the modern dancer.[35] Yet the chorus girl, while the most professional of dance workers, was the lowliest as well. Dickstein claims that by the end of the 1930s, the chorus girl in film was a 'tired stereotype',[36] but in reality she was working even harder, and with many more bills to pay due to the tremendous number of classes she now had to take – including ballet – to maintain her skills at an elevated level of virtuosity and her body as a toned and proficient choreographic instrument (she still had to be pretty too). Like many other elements of American art and letters during the Depression, dance was transformed into a complex and often contradictory set of relationships that at once made it an avocation as well as a profession, increased the requirements for being recognised as proficient in that profession, and also insisted upon the necessity that the labour performed by the dancer should ideally be, no matter what its roots, modern and American.

As If Invented by Terpsichore, Herself

The effect of motion pictures on the popularity and meaning of dance in American culture during the 1930s is almost impossible to overestimate. 'As if invented by Terpsichore, herself, for that very purpose, the cinema has suddenly turned to the dance for its themes, its stars, and its scenes,' wrote *Dance* in late 1936.[37]

> Even the small towns now see Fred Astaire, Eleanor Powell, Marie [*sic*] Gambarelli and the De Marcos as well as the leading line-ups and dance groups of the world right in their small local theatres, and they see them not once but several times a year. It won't be long now before every one, whether he lives in Squedunk or New York, will have seen the finest dancing of the day … Already we are experiencing a general improvement in the dance standards of the general public.[38]

Astaire and Powell for tap, Maria Gambarelli for ballet and the De Marcos for ballroom – while the same article writes that the public was 'ready and waiting' for 'all kinds' of dance, including modern, in fact it sums up the issue succinctly: the movies were 'improving standards' at the same time that they were actually closing down the types of dancing to which audiences would have access (modern would never become a significant screen dance form).

Fred Astaire and Ginger Rogers were the only dancers (besides Shirley Temple) to be *Motion Picture Herald* top-ten box-office stars in the 1930s (from 1935 to 1937), and their popularity sent droves of people to dance classes. 'All teachers agree that … dance activity on stage and screen has a definite influence on school enrollments', wrote *The American Dancer* in 1938,[39] and increasingly even show dance was associated with training, with dedication, with the dancer's body as an instrument of choreographic art, not only of entertainment. Certainly, I can admire the transcendence and sublimity of the Astaire–Rogers vehicles, and I'm happy to agree that they create, in Dickstein's words, a 'song and dance world in which seemingly mismatched people can connect beautifully to form a little community of two, in which all awkwardness and inhibition are soon banished and all movement is unimaginably graceful, fluid, purposeful, and lovely'.[40] But the point of this essay has been to show that there were other types of dance in musicals – even in some Astaire–Rogers films – from which 'all awkwardness and inhibition' have *not* been 'banished' and in which 'all movement' is *not* 'unimaginably graceful, fluid, purposeful, and lovely' (and which are not interested in romance, authentic or otherwise). *Flying Down to Rio*, *The Gay Divorcee* (1934), *Top Hat* (1935) and *Shall We Dance* feature Berkeley-esque finales that include static displays as well as hoards of 'extra dancers',

Fred Astaire as a ballet dancer in *Shall We Dance* (1937)
(*Movie Star News*)

and there are a few peppy but unpolished specialities (see, for example, Betty Grable and Edward Everett Horton in 'Let's K-nock K-nees' in *The Gay Divorcee*) dotted throughout the series that represent the continuing presence of a mode emphatically uninterested in technical proficiency and grace. Astaire called himself a dancer with an 'outlaw style', so named as a 'new blend of his own' of ballet, tap and ballroom[41] – a blending represented most programmatically in the opposition of ballet and musical comedy in *Shall We Dance*, in which Astaire, really an American named Peter P. Peters, has been masquerading successfully as a Russian ballet dancer named Petrov. The finale showcases both, although the ballet is treated perfunctorily (Astaire never wears tights, but he's sporting a floppy satin shirt when he dances with American ballerina Harriet Hoctor), and the synthesis of ballet and swing that Astaire/Petrov/Peters desires resembles most of his other performances of the decade and after (can a style still be described as 'outlaw' when it goes on to dominate a genre for more than three decades?).

In addition, the films' self-reflexivity, the fact that Astaire plays a professional dancer of some kind in most of them (see *Roberta*, 1935, *Top Hat*, *Follow the Fleet*, 1936, *Swing Time*, *Shall We Dance* and *The Story of Vernon and Irene Castle*, 1939; Rogers does too in all but *Top Hat*), also implies the shift from dance as something in which anyone with energy, desire and a few skills could potentially find work towards an increasingly specialised and compartmentalised avocation, where idiosyncrasy and individuality are replaced by versatility just as tap, ballet and ballroom subsume all other varieties under a broader rubric. And more and more, in Astaire–Rogers films, it's the stars who dance. There are still 'extra dancers', but they, too, are required to demonstrate an increasing degree of proficiency and versatility.

In the end, I would argue that Astaire's style is considerably less 'outlaw' than that of Eleanor Powell, whom Dickstein does not so much as mention but who was Astaire's equal in skill and appeal across a number of successful star vehicles, beginning with *Broadway Melody of 1936* and concluding in the 1930s with *Broadway Melody of 1940* (1940), in which she danced opposite him. Powell was the subject of numerous features in dance magazines, a source of inspiration to many women dancers during the decade and regarded as the 'female equivalent' of Astaire.[42] That she seems so anomalous to us now (there's really no one to compare her to; Ginger Rogers performs exactly one tap solo in the entire Astaire–Rogers series) indicates the other 'transformations' in the musical that occurred during the decade: of dance from something idiosyncratic, energetic but at times a bit amateurish to a codified assortment of difficult techniques that were expensive and time-consuming to

Publicity photo of Eleanor Powell in 1936 (Collection of the author)

acquire and even more expensive and time-consuming to maintain; of jazz and swing from black dance (and music) forms to white; of dance as the province of powerful, competent and joyous women to dance as an expression of heterosexual romance, with male performers and choreographers leading in every sense of the term. Dickstein believes that Astaire and Rogers 'preserved in wit, rhythm, and fluidity of movement what the Depression almost took away, the high spirits of Americans, young and modern, who had once felt destined to be the heirs and heiresses of all the ages'.[43] But many other films preserved these things as well; as I have shown here, wit, rhythm and even fluidity of movement were never in danger in the 1930s dance musical. Although it's hard to feel much sense of loss while watching Astaire and Rogers flirt so wonderfully with Terpsichore in any of their 1930s musicals, from time to time we might go back to all those 'other' musicals too, in which dance is something you do rather than something you are, need not express emotional or psychological truths and is a little awkward or raw but also fresh, entertaining and full of the giddiness of promise yet to be fulfilled.

Notes

1. For more on these, see Rick Altman, *The American Film Musical* (Bloomington: Indiana University Press, 1989); Jerome Delamater, *Dance in the Hollywood Musical* (Ann Arbor, MI: UMI Research Press, 1981); Jane Feuer, *The Hollywood Musical* (Bloomington: Indiana University Press, 1982).

2. Delamater, *Dance in the Hollywood Musical*, p. 98.

3. Much has been written about the paucity of 'real' dance training in the US, especially 'real' ballet training, until the 1930s; see, for example, Adrienne L. McLean, *Dying Swans and Madmen: Ballet, the Body, and Narrative Cinema* (New Brunswick, NJ: Rutgers University Press, 2008), esp. Ch. 1. The general outline of American theatrical dance history characteristically begins with the Puritanist denial of the body and the lack of any indigenous dance traditions; moves through the rise of vaudeville, the opera house, Broadway and, eventually, motion pictures as venues in which the dedicated (white) dancing body could find work, bodies which had often been trained in schools founded by expatriates from Europe or Russia; and, finally, in the 1930s with the institutionalisation of ballet as well as 'modern' dance, whose competition for the status of the 'true' American form of dance became the subject of heated debate during the decade. The founding of the School of American Ballet in New York in 1933 by George Balanchine and Lincoln Kirstein, and the companies which spun off from the school, became the basis for America's rise to prominence in the concert dance world after World War II. Simultaneous with the increasing attention paid to the aristocratic

Euro-Russian and centuries-old techniques and vocabulary of classical ballet was a burgeoning interest in dance as abstract self-expression and as a form of spirituality, embodied first by Isadora Duncan at home and abroad and subsequently linked to modern dance, which, partly through a rejection of ballet as anachronistic and un-American and show-dancing as frivolous and exploitative, saw dance and the working body as a means of political expression and social solidarity as well, with the Depression forming a natural ground on which these cultural debates about the identity of American dance and the American dancer could be played out.

4. All material from ads in this and other paragraphs is taken from the author's collection of dance magazines; ads are bracketed off into a separate section, usually at the front of the magazine.

5. Sidney Marshall, 'The New Hollywood Dancing Girl', *The Dance*, December 1929, p. 11.

6. In Miles Kreuger (ed.), *The Movie Musical: From Vitaphone to 42nd Street* (New York: Dover, 1975), p. 104.

7. Ibid.

8. Ibid., p. 43.

9. Mark Franko, *The Work of Dance: Labor, Movement, and Identity in the 1930s* (Middletown, CN: Wesleyan University Press, 2002), p. 109.

10. Ibid.

11. Kreuger, *Movie Musical*, p. 257.

12. Martin Rubin, *Showstoppers: Busby Berkeley and the Tradition of Spectacle* (New York: Columbia University Press, 1993), p. 14.

13. For more on different types of tap, see Marshall and Jean Stearns, *Jazz Dance: The Story of American Vernacular Dance* (New York: Schirmer Books, 1968).

14. Morris Dickstein, *Dancing in the Dark: A Cultural History of the Great Depression* (New York: W. W. Norton, 2009), p. 234.

15. Rubin, *Showstoppers*, pp. 14–21.

16. Altman, *American Film Musical*, pp. 129–99; Dickstein, *Dancing in the Dark*, p. 358.

17. Dickstein, *Dancing in the Dark*, p. 360.

18. Ivan Narodny, 'Dancies Preferred' [Albertina Rasch on Film Ballet Technique], *The Dance*, April 1930, pp. 27, 64.

19. Ibid., p. 27.

20. Ibid., p. 64.

21. For further information, see Brenda Dixon Gottschild, *Waltzing in the Dark: African American Vaudeville and Race Politics in the Swing Era* (New York: St Martin's, 2000).

22. For more on the history of ballet in American culture, see Franko, *Work of Dance*, Ch. 5; McLean, *Dying Swans and Madmen*.

23. Leon Leonidoff, 'Creating a Dance Public', *The Dance*, March 1931, pp. 40, 62.

24. Ibid., p. 40.

25. Ibid.

26. McLean, *Dying Swans and Madmen*.

27. Betty Carue, 'A Famous Father Speaks', *The American Dancer*, September 1936, p. 8.

28. Ibid.

29. Ibid.

30. *Life*, 28 December 1936, pp. 30–41.

31. Ibid., p. 40.

32. Jane Feuer, 'The Self-Reflexive Musical and the Myth of Entertainment', in Barry Keith Grant (ed.), *Film Genre Reader II* (Austin: University of Texas Press, 1995), p. 442. See also McLean, *Dying Swans and Madmen*.

33. Feuer, *Hollywood Musical*, p. 8.
34. Dickstein, *Dancing in the Dark*, p. 507.
35. Franko, *Work of Dance*, pp. 151–4. Others who doubted modern dance's future did so specifically with reference to technique: as one critic wrote in 1935, 'just because a number is named *Conflict* is no reason that it is a good dance and should be lauded to the skies. Does not the finish of the performance mean something? Does not the manner of production have some value? Rebellion and conflict have existed since time immemorial, so why are they now hailed as something new and important? Other elements are equally important in life.' Moreover, it is 'our American modernists who are often the worst offenders'. Dorothy S. Lyndall, 'Subject Matter of the Modern Dance', *The American Dancer*, August 1935, p. 7.
36. Dickstein, *Dancing in the Dark*, p. 241.
37. W. Carranza, 'The Cinema Projects the Dance', *Dance*, September 1936, p. 5.
38. Ibid.
39. Ruth Eleanor Howard, 'Summing Up', *The American Dancer*, September 1938, p. 8.
40. Dickstein, *Dancing in the Dark*, p. 379.
41. Quoted in Stearns and Stearns, *Jazz Dance*, p. 226.
42. See Adrienne L. McLean, 'Putting 'Em Down Like a Man: Eleanor Powell and the Spectacle of Competence', in Sean Griffin (ed.), *Hetero: Queering Representations of Straightness* (Syracuse, NY: SUNY Press, 2009), pp. 89–110.
43. Dickstein, *Dancing in the Dark*, p. 393.

6 Star Spangled Shows:
Utopia and History in the Wartime Canteen Musical

Steven Cohan

During the three-year period between 1942 and 1944, the Hollywood studios produced a series of patriotic backstage musicals directly addressing wartime audiences at home and on the European and Pacific fronts: Paramount's *Star Spangled Rhythm* (1942), United Artists's *Stage Door Canteen* (1943), MGM's *Thousands Cheer* (1943) and *Two Girls and a Sailor* (1943), Twentieth Century-Fox's *Four Jills in a Jeep* (1944), Universal's *Follow the Boys* (1944), and Warners' *This Is the Army* (1943), *Thank Your Lucky Stars* (1943) and *Hollywood Canteen* (1944). The musicals in this cycle are noteworthy for their nationalism, topicality and all-star casts. They celebrate the diversity of US entertainment, typified by an eclectic array of numbers performed by an equally eclectic assortment of performers: stars from screen, stage, radio and the recording industry. These musicals are not plotless, but their thin narratives contrive mainly to find an excuse for staging an extended all-star show – whether a canteen revue, a benefit for the war effort or a USO tour – in order to project, through the trope of entertainment, a reassuring vision of a unified, confident nation at war.

With only a few exceptions, these films refrain from using 'the story characters', as *Stage Door Canteen*'s cast listing refers to them, in the star-powered musical portions, so they make little effort to integrate narrative and number. And while these musicals frame the revue mix with a romance plot, they most often conclude with the couple's union interrupted by the war, perhaps for good. In *Star Spangled Rhythm*, to give an example, sailor Eddie Bracken can leave his ship to marry Betty Hutton only if she arranges for Paramount's stars to do a show at the navy canteen in San Pedro. 'No show, no wedding,' the commanding officer informs him, making a negative out of the show/couple equation that backstage musicals usually reiterate. Even though Hutton manages to pull the show together, there is still no wedding, since Bracken's company receives its orders to depart before the couple can marry.

That this cycle of canteen musicals would have trouble imagining the stable formation of couples in wartime as a means of reaching narrative closure is not surprising. According to Dana Polan, the couple's fate was a historical problem for films of the 1940s generally. World War II not only intensified cultural awareness of sexuality and encouraged promiscuity but, in the uncertainty of its outcome, the war was always present extra-filmically: wartime profoundly challenged the ability of a Hollywood narrative to achieve the kind of determinate, future-oriented closure represented by a couple's union. Polan argues that a high degree of narrative incoherence characterises this era's films, with musicals epitomising the alternative to narrative closure in 'an endless repetition of spectacle', the power of which 'comes from its ability to turn back onto moments of the social totality and infuse them with the qualities of spectacle'.[1] No musicals do this more successfully than these canteen films.

Although often disparaged on formal or aesthetic grounds, the wartime canteen cycle is thus worth a closer look. For in heightening the asymmetry of story and spectacle that is always central to the genre, in their star spangled patriotism these musicals project a historically concrete, if also highly contradictory, representation of entertainment as a metaphor of social unity. As a result, the canteen cycle makes more explicit what other musicals of the 1940s may not represent as directly but nonetheless refer to: namely, the genre's tense, often incoherent immersion in the volatile social history in which these films were produced and consumed – and they *were* enormously popular. Rather than being an exceptional case, then, the cycle's indifference to narrative coherence and formal integration helps to reveal an inescapable historical dimension to what Richard Dyer calls 'the utopian sensibility' of entertainment.[2]

For a musical, this utopian sensibility is most vividly realised when, without breaking character, performers effortlessly burst into song or dance to express their feeling of liberation from the regulation, boredom, deficiencies or spatial confinement of everyday life. As Dyer explains,

> Entertainment offers the image of 'something better' to escape into, or something we want deeply that our day-to-day lives don't provide. … Entertainment does not, however, present models of utopian worlds … Rather, the utopianism is contained in the feelings it embodies. It presents, head-on as it were, what utopia would feel like rather than how it would be organized.[3]

In Dyer's view, with its transformative energies mostly bursting forth as musical numbers, the genre is able to imagine utopia only in metaphoric terms, the 'as if' of representing 'what utopia would feel like'. Still, he recognises, 'To be effective, the utopian sensibility has to take off from the real experiences of the audience', and this imperative consequently requires the management of contradictions arising from 'the gap between what is and what could be'.[4] There are, in short, unavoidable historical pressures – 'real experiences' – motivating but also complicating what utopia 'feels like' in a musical.[5]

The canteen cycle is a case in point. Given its historical motivation, a utopian sensibility would appear to be never more secure or unproblematic than in this cycle. Yet none of these musicals are notable for their numbers, which is where Dyer locates the genre's utopian sensibility. Rather, the pleasure they generate occurs from the sheer accumulation of numbers performed by well-known artists; these are backstage musicals in which a revue is not condensed into a single production number but presented more or less in its entirety. These musicals imagine what utopia 'would feel like' in the spatial terms of the all-star canteen show. In this setting, stardom functions for the cycle to personify the canteen's utopian ethos; but since the cycle also views what stars do there as labour (and unpaid labour at that), stardom simultaneously registers the historically immediate social tensions which the canteen itself attempts to reconcile as a privileged yet democratic space in order to achieve that utopian aura. Stardom is then made even more problematic by the way the cycle not only features numerous guest stars but as often incorporates versions of a star's 'real' personality into the diegesis. Although all the musicals comprising this cycle use stardom in this way, *Hollywood Canteen*, as I will show, pushes to its extreme limit this strategy of attempting to embed 'utopia' in 'history' through stardom.

'All them famous people being democratic'
Taken at face value, the cycle's patriotic sentiments seem perfectly consistent with the official view of the home front which the Office of War Information wanted to project on screen, 'a picture of a prosperous, wholesome, democratic America'.[6] The studios obliged with product such as the canteen musicals because the morale-boosting role of movies justified the government's special exemptions to the film industry.

In a book about Hollywood's contribution to the war effort published in 1945, the editors of *Look* magazine reported that surveys revealed servicemen's preference for 'movies whose components –

street scenes, normal people on the streets, women who look like mothers, wives, sweethearts – bring them near home'.[7] Heading the list of their favourite genres were musicals (followed by comedies, mysteries, romantic dramas, documentaries and newsreels). Sometimes shown to troops months before their theatrical release, these films did more than assuage soldiers' loneliness and raise their morale, for they also served as distractions, filling up the long stretches of time in between armed conflicts. In his memoir about heading one of the army's entertainment units, C. Tyler Carpenter recounts how he organised live shows for the troops at night and ran movies during the day. As what turned out to be the Battle of the Bulge approached in mid-December 1944, he notes that he could tell

> Something big was happening. Our orders were to show films around the clock. Thank God, headquarters kept us well supplied with new movies. For two days, I ran three escapist musicals which the fellows liked: *Here Come the Waves* with Betty Hutton and Bing Crosby warbling 'Accentuate the Positive'; the all-star *Hollywood Canteen* with Bette Davis and our dancing friend, Joan McCracken; and *Music for Millions* with Marsha Hunt and June Allyson.[8]

At around this same time, these three musicals with stage shows were the year-end holiday attractions in New York City at the Paramount, Strand and Capitol theatres, respectively.

The canteen musicals stand out for being such highly specialised wartime product, as much preparation for battle as the stuff of R & R. At the close of *Stage Door Canteen*, a voiceover reminds viewers that the canteen offers soldiers 'momentary escape from the war, from homesickness'. Slim Green (Robert Hutton), the young GI protagonist of *Hollywood Canteen*, makes the same point when, as the millionth man to enter, he addresses his fellow soldiers from the stage:

> We've seen people we've dreamed of up close, and we found them all as real as they are famous. They wait on us. They wash dishes. They come up here every night to make us laugh, or even choke up a little. Whatever they do, they make us forget where we've been or where we're going.

Earlier in this film, Slim's friend Nowland (Dane Clark) defines the canteen as a microcosm of American democracy: 'All them famous people being democratic. Democratic. Democracy – that's what it means, Slim. Every boy equal, like tonight. All them big shots, listening to little shots like me. Being friendly.' The logic of American 'democracy' applies to the canteen entertainment too, which brings together the most diverse talents of show business to '[assure] us', as Gerald Mast notes about *Follow the Boys*, 'that we *are* all alike, different but the same, one nation …'.[9] Midway through *Hollywood Canteen*, the number 'You Can Always Tell a Yank' (sung by Dennis Morgan, Joe E. Brown and the entire canteen audience) momentarily allows the film to visualise how the USA is indeed a 'united nation' within the canteen space: the groups of people shown to illustrate the song lyrics are multicoloured and ethnically diverse, their ancestry hailing from all over the globe.

Of course, the home front was not as homogeneous and democratic as the OWI wanted Hollywood to picture it. During World War II, not only did 6 million women get jobs in industry, but 16 million people entered the military and another 15 million relocated because of war work; such massive social dislocations challenged established patterns of family and community. Social life was further disrupted by race riots in big and small cities throughout the country, by local wildcat hate strikes as industry became integrated, and by widespread labour agitation, despite the official no-strike policy agreed upon by the government, big business and unions. 'Thousands of small strikes and work stoppages interrupted production throughout the war,' George Lipsitz points out, citing the large number of strike days halting industrial production.[10] In Lipsitz's view, these actions by labour were utopian, having less to do with wages and more to do with making work a collective enterprise in which all employees had a share. Organised by union locals, often in direct conflict with their national leaders, labour's goals were for the most part responding to 'unsettled grievances about working conditions, anxiety over the post-war world, and a desire by workers to assert some control over their lives'.[11] Nor was the entertainment industry itself exempt from such actions by labour, with the cartoonists strike, the investigation of the IATSE's corrupt leadership and their ties to organised crime, the musicians' strike and the CSU strike of the studios all occurring between 1941 and 1945.[12]

Because the canteen cycle evades overt reference to that social disruption, the films can represent the home front only by imagining it in the utopian terms of 'as if' – or what Slim calls 'paradise' – located somewhere other than home: that is to say, in either one of the two centres of show-business life, Hollywood or Broadway, or its military equivalent, the USO. These musicals offer domestic consumers the opportunity to watch the kind of star-studded entertainment which the USO put on for the armed forces, and these same musicals supply troops with the popular entertainment associated with 'home'. For either audience, the canteen cycle projects a utopian depiction of 'America' by imagining it as someplace else: as a specialised site of cultural unity defined by the spectator's own historical exclusion. Because a military uniform was the price of admission, the trailer for *Hollywood Canteen* begins by announcing, 'The only way you can see the canteen is … to see the picture!' The trailer casts the Warner Bros. musical as a privileged glimpse of what domestic audiences or soldiers not on home-leave would otherwise be unable to see: a version of the typical all-star revue performed nightly at the canteen by film and radio personalities after completing their regular work.

The canteen itself is imagined in these musicals as a liminal space, set off from the war yet owing its very existence to it. *Hollywood Canteen* and *Stage Door Canteen* use their specialised setting to imagine the impossible, a space which joins together, through entertainment, the separate spheres of militarisation and domesticity, soldiers and civilians, men and women, performers and audience, workers and patrons. The two *Canteen* movies, both written by Delmer Daves, foreground this hybridity: the canteen is located on the home front and comprises the daily life of tireless volunteers in New York City or Los Angeles but caters to servicemen from other states who are on leave; its audience is the average American male but it is staffed by extraordinary talents, the most famous of them working women; it celebrates the nation's determination to win but reflects the harmful psychological impact of war; it is racially integrated (it was in reality and, for a few moments, is openly so on film) but services a segregated institution; it is sexually innocent but redolent of frustrated heterosexual desire; it requires anonymity in the encounters between hostesses and guests but encourages their intimacy; it is labour-intensive and dependent on capital acquired from the entertainment industry for its maintenance but relies upon unpaid workers and lacks paying customers.

In the two *Canteen* films, as in others of this cycle, an odd juxtaposition of camp performance, romantic sentiment and jingoistic, patriotic fervour in the numbers brings out the utopian liminality of the canteen setting while also registering its historical inability to secure the unity of the home front. What Martin Rubin refers to as the 'aggregate' style of the revue format, which prizes 'heterogeneity' and 'as much diversity as possible',[13] prevents the variety show from sustaining either a singular stance toward a 'normative' American identity or a stable representation of the home front.

At one point in *Stage Door Canteen*, for instance, British performer Gracie Fields sings a jaunty ditty about an American soldier killing three Japanese fliers, set to the cadence and structure of 'Three

Blind Mice'; then she abruptly delivers 'The Lord's Prayer' in song. At another point, Ethel Waters sings 'Quicksand' with Count Basie's Orchestra and then Gypsy Rose Lee follows with a mock striptease. In *Hollywood Canteen*, Golden Gate Quartet, an African-American group, perform 'The General Jumped at Dawn', and then Eddie Cantor comes out to sing 'We're Having a Baby' with Nan Martin. Roy Rogers enters the canteen astride Trigger, singing 'Don't Fence Me In' (and the horse even dances to it), and moments later The Andrews Sisters perform a swingy reprise of this number (their duet with Bing Crosby of this tune was a hit single for them at the same time as the film's release). Later on, classical violinist Joseph Szigeti solos on Schubert's 'The Bee' and afterward performs a comic duet with Jack Benny.

A comparable instance of the canteen show's disunifying aggregate style occurs when non-musical stars play themselves doing numbers that are either incompatible with their screen image or exaggerations of it. *Thank Your Lucky Stars* parades one after another of Warners' biggest dramatic actors, and their numbers theatricalise the performer through the performance, casting the stars as amateur entertainers while italicising the authenticity they are supposed to personify by playing themselves. John Garfield sings 'Blues in the Night' as if it were a gangster song. Errol Flynn, bowler hat and all, cavorts in a working-class British pub to the tune of 'That's What You Jolly Well Get'. At what seems to be a slumber party, Ann Sheridan advises her sorority sisters to be sexually aggressive, because, as her song puts it, 'love is not born, it is made' ('and that's why every window has a window shade'). Bette Davis, out nightclubbing, complains that there are no sexually attractive men left on the home front because 'they're either too young or too old'. Ida Lupino and a gum-chewing Olivia de Havilland join George Tobias in a hokey jive version of 'The Dreamer', complete with pseudo-scat singing and zoot-suit costuming.

One last example of the canteen show's disunifying effect arises from the way its eclectic mix also marks what is left out. That jive number in *Thank Your Lucky Stars* implicitly points to the absence of African-American blues or jazz from this show. What *Thank Your Lucky Stars* offers instead is Hattie McDaniel's up-tempo 'Ice Cold Katie', in which she recounts how Katie keeps rejecting her lover's entreaties to wed until the draft board arrives to cart him away. This so-called 'Harlem number' is in keeping with racial stereotypes of the times, evoking blackface in both its broad performance style and depiction of the uptown ghetto. There are similar numbers featuring black talent in *Star Spangled Rhythm* and *This Is the Army*. As done in all three films, as well as recalling minstrelsy, the Harlem number shares its conventions for representing a black working culture with comparable proletariat numbers done by white performers in 1930s musicals, as in Alice Faye's 'Slumming on Park Avenue' in *On the Avenue* (1937). This type of number makes momentarily evident how, when the canteen films incorporate race into the patriotic show, it has the residual effect of effacing class and the unsteady political situation of labour as it troubled home-front stability.

Labouring for Utopia

This does not mean, though, that labour plays no part in the canteen films; on the contrary, it is fundamental to the cycle's representation of 'democracy' as the interaction of stars with ordinary people. The story characters in *Thank Your Lucky Stars* live collectively with other rank-and-file performers in Gower Gulch, a kind of squatters' village constructed out of used movie sets. Star Eddie Cantor plays a double role: himself as an arrogant, domineering celebrity who almost ruins the show, and his humbler, working-class double, Joe Simpson, who masquerades as Cantor in order to save it. Dinah Shore is under contract to Cantor's radio show, as she was at the time, and in the film cannot perform elsewhere without his permission. Somewhat similarly, *Hollywood Canteen* and *Stage Door Canteen* each portray hostesses as young, single women working as rank-and-file employees in the entertainment industry. The hostesses serve the war effort at the canteen but it is still another job for them, albeit an unpaid one; as they go about their tasks, the young women's behaviour is subjected to the same degree of supervision that characterises their paid employment. The women must have passes to enter the canteen, are unable to date GIs who interest them or to share in the free food they dole out. As GIs queue to enter, move single-file to be served food, and then pair up for dancing and talk with the next available hostess, the canteen's labour is as well managed as any factory's mass-production line.

Making an effort to characterise the common bonds of its audience, the canteen cycle associates the show's operation with a working culture but does so without taking much overt notice of labour's often tenuous relation to management, despite the booming wartime economy. However, the set-up for the all-star show in *Star Spangled Rhythm* does reverberate with awareness of the film industry's anxiety about its labour force: this musical's farcical 'no show, no wedding' plot gets rolling when the lead characters leave their service jobs at Paramount Studios to masquerade as management. Betty Hutton is a switchboard operator and Victor Moore, a guard at the front gate. Since he has been pretending to be head of the studio in his letters to son Eddie Bracken, once the latter arrives back home in Hollywood, Moore and Hutton disrupt the studio's orderly operations in order to keep this masquerade going, even tricking the actual studio head into thinking he has been fired. After being kicked off the lot for her insubordination, Hutton has to sneak back inside in order to convince the studio's stars to walk off their sets early so that they can do the show as planned at the San Pedro canteen. The suspicious sight of stars such as Veronica Lake, Paulette Godard, Alan Ladd, Ray Milland, Dorothy Lamour, not to say Bob Hope and Bing Crosby, all bringing the company to a screeching halt as they march out en mass at 4.30 p.m. so outrages (and, as a work stoppage of sorts, implicitly terrifies) the 'real' studio head that, in retaliation, he makes every possible effort to prevent their show from going on.

Hollywood Canteen (1944): 'And the movie unions in town said we're with you a hundred per cent.'

By comparison, *Hollywood Canteen* celebrates labour's utopian goals. Midway through, co-founder John Garfield steps up to the stage and recounts to the audience how the canteen originated as a collaboration of studio management and its labour, from actors to designers to carpenters and electricians. 'And the movie unions in town said we're with you a hundred per cent,' Garfield declares, as imagery of men and women toiling to design, build, fit out and manage the canteen flashes on screen. This montage provides a frame with which to view the continual sight of stars working in the canteen as proof that its democracy flattens social hierarchies. 'I thought movie stars got paid enough not to have to work,'

Slim comments as he watches the famous faces dishing up food and clearing tables (and the same joke is made in *Stage Door Canteen*).

Needless to say, Garfield's utopian view of labour ideals obscures the conditions in which industrial work occurs in a wartime economy, even with everyone patriotically doing their part. Production of *Hollywood Canteen*, in fact, was stopped midway through because of a dispute between Warners and the Screen Actors Guild about fair payment to stars not contractually affiliated with the studio. Within the industry, the patriotic all-star films, their profits divided between the producing studio and some charitable organisation like the Hollywood Canteen, were informally called 'pressure' pictures, because the studios pressured stars and other entertainment players to perform in guest spots or as speciality acts at reduced rates. The temporary abandonment of *Hollywood Canteen* due to guild objections, it was also reported, caused the industry-wide cancellation of nine other planned 'all-star' films, 'for which players were to be asked to perform at reduced salaries'.[14] Several months later, filming on *Hollywood Canteen* resumed but only after the studio and the guild had reached a compromise for such 'charitable or "pressure" pictures': Warners agreed to 'a week's usual salary as the minimum for free-lance players', while SAG 'waived jurisdiction over deals between a studio and its contract players'.[15] When production began again, Warners' 'girl-next-door' Joan Leslie replaced its 'oomph girl' Ann Sheridan (who thought the script was simply unbelievable) as the female lead.

That all-too-rosy view of studio labour described on screen by Garfield nevertheless identifies an important way the canteen cycle makes contact with the 'real experiences' informing its utopian sensibility. These musicals call attention to their historical referentiality, and just as inevitably raise questions about it, because their entertainment value depends upon featuring so many stars playing themselves. When Slim praises the canteen for proving that stars are 'as real as they are famous', his comment summarises how the all-star casts that distinguish the canteen musicals function to put utopia in conjunction with history. Playing a representation of themselves that is marked as both 'real' (the authentic person) and 'famous' (the screen persona), the stars portray an industrially manufactured fictional image *as if* it were a historical referent.

'Joan Leslie Night' at the Hollywood Canteen

Although all of the films in the cycle award stardom this significance, *Hollywood Canteen* gives this trope its most audacious twist by fabricating an on-screen romance between the fictional Slim and the real-life Joan Leslie. Stationed in New Guinea when the film opens, Slim dreams about her, indeed becomes obsessed with thoughts of her, because she is a movie star who convinces him, as he says, that 'she's just like the girls back home'. 'Joan Leslie's my kind of girl', he informs Nowland while, despite rain and a malfunctioning sound system, the GIs watch her in what appears to be *The Hard Way* (1943). 'She looks like a guy could go right up to her and say hello ... You can tell by her eyes she's nice.' When Slim and his buddy arrive on medical leave in Los Angeles, all he can think and talk about is 'Joan Leslie'. Of course, she is the one star he longs to meet at the Hollywood Canteen, which is what Slim informs Jack Carson, Jane Wyman, Barbara Stanwyck and every other performer he encounters there. John Garfield contrives to give Slim his wish by arranging for a phoney contest with a kiss from Joan Leslie as the prize. 'You know it's all too rarely in these hectic times that a man has his dreams fulfilled,' Garfield tells the surprised Slim.

After unexpectedly encountering Joan again the next day at Farmer's Market, Slim is lucky enough that same night to win a genuine contest, this time as the millionth man to enter the canteen, the one

Who 'just represents every fellow who's ever come here'. His prize? A date with any starlet present at the canteen, and there is no question about Slim's choice. Forgoing the Sunset Strip nightspots because of the photographers there, Slim sits with Joan in the back-yard of the house she shares with her parents. As they talk, it appears she has begun to return Slim's strong feelings. Following one more date, this time to meet the parents, the soldier's leave ends and he has to return to the front. 'It's all right to keep on dream-ing about you?' he asks Joan as his train begins to pull out of the station. She readily and warmly con-sents. 'Maybe if I get back—' he continues but stops before finishing his thought. 'You'll get back,' Joan insists, which enables Slim to say, 'Goodbye, sweet-heart.'

The transparency with which this contrived romance presumes that male viewers of *Hollywood Canteen* effortlessly identify with their on-screen 'representative' Slim, thereby validating the wish-fulfilment that Hollywood entertainment eagerly satisfies, is pretty obvious. Yet underlying the film's apparent naivety in imagining such an intimate rela-tion between stardom and moviegoers is the utopian logic by which the fabricated romance

Hollywood Canteen: Slim (Robert Hutton) meets Joan Leslie's actual sister (top). Slim bids 'goodbye sweetheart' to Joan Leslie (bottom)

claims to democratise Hollywood entertainment within the canteen space. This utopian view, more-over, became attached to Leslie's star image by way of *Hollywood Canteen*, as columnist Sidney Skolsky reminded his readers a short time after the film's release:

> She seldom misses putting in an appearance during the week at the Hollywood Canteen. It's supposed to be Warner night, but regulars call it 'Joan Leslie night.' The soldiers even phone and ask if she is going to be there. The soldiers are thrilled to see her and often comment that it is like the movie, Hollywood Canteen, come true.
>
> They want to go to her house afterwards. In fact, they want to enact the picture in every detail.[16]

Skolsky is registering here how successfully *Hollywood Canteen* locates its utopian sensibility in extra-filmic 'reality' through Joan Leslie. What authenticates Slim's belief that she is 'just like the girls back home at heart' is the same set of attributes Warner Bros. promoted through her other screen roles and publicity, which the GI repeats in his dialogue and which the diegesis of *Hollywood Canteen* recreates in the ordinary Southern California bungalow house in which she lived with her parents (played by actors) and her sister Betty (played by the actual sibling). But when she develops feelings for Slim, does not seem to mind that newspaper headlines wonder if the couple has eloped, invites him to a family dinner, swears their dates were not a publicity stunt and gives every appearance of promising to wait for him, *Hollywood Canteen* fictionalises Joan Leslie's agency, too. This film brings the 'real' Joan Leslie into the space of the canteen setting in order to imagine a utopian solution to a soldier's loneliness, but it also uses her stardom to displace the extra-filmic history of wartime female labour that 'Joan Leslie' represents in the diegesis as a Warners contract player. Joan Leslie is real in that she plays herself, a working movie star who, with no sense of paradox, is portrayed as being as genuine as the fan magazines have documented to fans like Slim.

Joan Leslie's star image, however, actually marks several crucial disjunctions between her naturalistic screen persona and the extra-filmic discourse surrounding it at the time.[17] Although exemplifying the ordinariness of the girl-next-door, she came from a show-business background, first in vaudeville with her family's act and then in the movies as a child performer under her real name, Joan Brodel. Although often representing an independent, career-minded woman in her twenties on screen, she was a teenager when Warners created that image for her in the early 1940s, attending high school and still wearing braces when not working. Although cast as spunky romantic leads, often opposite much older actors – Gary Cooper in *Sergeant York* (1941), James Cagney in *Yankee Doodle Dandy* (1942) and Fred Astaire in *The Sky's the Limit* (1943) – she was depicted off screen as an innocent teenage girl, dutiful daughter and devout Catholic who did not date or go out nightclubbing. Although portrayed by the press as a loyal company player, one never put on suspension by her studio, she was bound to Warners by a minority contract – and sued to terminate it as soon as she reached her legal majority in 1946.[18] As *Hollywood Canteen* brings these contradictions together – diegetically representing her stardom as studio labour over which she has control, while simultaneously fictionalising her agency for narrative purposes and so exploiting her as a studio commodity – the referentiality of Joan Leslie's star image exerts historical pressure upon the film's utopian vision of democratised labour in the canteen.

As a star already closely associated with this cycle of musicals – she plays a major story character in *This Is the Army* and *Thank Your Lucky Stars*, too – Joan Leslie plays 'herself' in *Hollywood Canteen* in order for the film to dramatise how stardom extends the utopian space of the canteen toward the historical world outside it. In both ideological and practical terms, this grand finale of the canteen cycle exploits stardom to mediate history and utopia. But that is also to say that this musical does what the other all-star canteen musicals do, although they do it less extravagantly. By incorporating Leslie's star image so thoroughly if improbably into its diegesis, *Hollywood Canteen* magnifies how the cycle as a whole works to use the utopian sensibility of the canteen show to manage the instabilities of both wartime and wartime labour. Indeed, although the imminent ending of the war was obviously responsible for bringing the cycle to its own conclusion with *Hollywood Canteen* in 1944, Warners' dispute with SAG may well have hastened the canteen musical's demise, insofar as the controversy made public 'that the studios now are not willing to loan talent to competing companies for such pictures'. This disclosure belied the claim that these all-star musicals were an 'industry undertaking', which had been Warners' justification for paying guest artists reduced salaries.[19] Henceforth, utopia could not be bought quite as cheaply – unless the performers were, like Joan Leslie, already under contract.

Notes

1. Dana Polan, *Power and Paranoia: History, Narrative, and the American Cinema, 1940–1950* (New York: Columbia University Press, 1986), pp. 115, 295.

2. Richard Dyer, 'Entertainment and Utopia', 1977, reprinted in Steven Cohan (ed.), *Hollywood Musicals, The Film Reader* (London: Routledge, 1992), p. 22.

3. Ibid., p. 20.

4. Ibid., p. 26.

5. One of these historical pressures, as I emphasise in this essay, was labour; but another was racial segregation. The liberatory energy of performers in these older musicals, as Dyer points out in a follow-up piece occasioned by the release of *That's Entertainment! III* (1994), is a privilege afforded only to white stars and 'the space they take over is already a white space, one that they are socially entitled to'. 'The Colour of Entertainment', in Bill Marshall and Robynn Stilwell (eds), *Musicals: Hollywood & Beyond* (Exeter, Devon: Intellect Books, 2000), p. 26.

6. Clayton R. Koppes and Gregory D. Black, *Hollywood Goes to War: How Politics, Profits and Propaganda Shaped World War II Movies* (Berkeley: University of California Press, 1990), p. 143.

7. The editors of *Look*, *Movie Lot to Beachhead: The Motion Picture Goes to War and Prepares for the Future* (Garden City, NY: Doubleday, 1945), p. 105.

8. C. Tyler Carpenter and Edward H. Yeatts, *Stars without Garters! The Memoirs of Two Gay GIs in WWII* (San Francisco: Alamo Press, 1996), p. 125.

9. Gerald Mast, *Can't Help Singin': The American Musical on Stage and Screen* (Woodstock, NY: Overlook Press, 1987), p. 227.

10. George Lipsitz, *Rainbow at Midnight: Labor and Culture in the 1940s* (Urbana: University of Illinois Press, 1994), p. 27.

11. Ibid., p. 87.

12. On Hollywood labour during this era, see Mike Nielsen and Gene Mailes, *Hollywood's Other Blacklist: Union Struggles in the Studio System* (London: BFI, 1995), and Gerald Horne, *Class Struggle in Hollywood 1930–1950: Moguls, Mobsters, Stars, Reds, & Trade Unionists* (Austin: University of Texas Press, 2001).

13. Martin Rubin, *Showstoppers: Busby Berkeley and the Tradition of Spectacle* (New York: Columbia University Press, 1993), p. 14.

14. Fred Stanley, 'Warners and Actors Guild Smoke Peace Pipe: Controversy over Salary to Players in Benefit Films Settled – Other Items', *New York Times*, 30 April 1944, p. X3. For an account of the dispute with the union when it began, see Fred Stanley, 'The Warners vs. the Screen Actors Guild: The Controversy That Halted Filming of "Hollywood Canteen" – Other Matters', *New York Times*, 2 January 1944, p. 3X; and 'Sues over Acting Curbs: Warners Asks Writ against Rules of the Screen Guild', *New York Times*, 12 January 1944, p. 27.

15. 'Film Wage Row Settled: Studio and Actors Compromise on "Hollywood Canteen"', *New York Times*, 20 April 1944, p. 12.

16. Sidney Skolsky, 'Close-up of Joan Leslie', *Motion Picture*, October 1945, n.p. The source of this article is the 'Joan Leslie Page', a defunct fan page devoted to this star which was at <http://www.picturegoer.com> until 2007.

17. The fan magazine and newspaper articles collected at the defunct Joan Leslie Page well represent the persona I am about to describe. As some of their titles exclaim, Warners promoted her as 'Glamour Girl in Socks' (by Jane Porter in *Hollywood*, May 1941), 'Sixteen and Unkissed!' (by Henry P. Malmgreen in *Modern Screen*, September 1941) and a 'Canteen Kid' (by Marcia Daughtrey in *Modern Screen*, April 1944).

18. While initially declared a free agent in 1946 by Los Angeles Superior Court, a decision that also challenged the binding force of minority contracts, Leslie's victory was reversed when the studio took it to the California District Court of Appeals. She then petitioned the US Supreme Court in 1948, which declined to review the case. At that point, with the legal validity of minority contracts confirmed, Warners released Leslie from her contract (which was just weeks away from its expiration anyway). But few roles of any note followed her departure from Warners, suggesting that she may have been blacklisted in Hollywood. The studio certainly took umbrage, since Leslie had to go to court yet again to prevent her billing from being lowered on her final

Warners film, *Two Guys from Milwaukee* (1946), after it was sneak previewed with her as the female star; just as spitefully, Warners refused to exhibit in its own theatres her first starring vehicle as an independent agent, *Repeat Performance* (1947), produced by Eagle-Lions films. Several decades later, Leslie claimed that the result of her lawsuit was a 'gentlemen's agreement' among the Hollywood studios because she was branded as 'difficult' to work with. Thomas F. Brady, 'Hollywood Contract Blues', *New York Times*, 2 June 1946, p. X1; 'Court Enjoins Film in Joan Leslie Suit', *New York Times*, 24 August 1946, p. 6; 'Film Star Fights Ruling: Joan Leslie Carries Contract Battle to Supreme Court', *New York Times*, 21 August 1948, p. 8; 'Joan Leslie Loses Pay Suit', *Oakland Tribune*, 19 October 1948, p. D27; Bill Ruehlmann, 'Joan Leslie: An Interview', *Classic Images*, January 2006, p. 13.

19. Stanley, 'Warners vs. the Screen Actors Guild', p. 3X.

7 Sailors and Kissing Bandits:
The Challenging Spectacle of Frank Sinatra at MGM

Karen McNally

In the 1945 musical *Anchors Aweigh*, Frank Sinatra, cast as a sailor on leave, attempts to enter the MGM studio lot, only to be physically removed by a security guard. This passing moment of interest in Sinatra's first film with the studio only hints at the star's uneasy fit within the MGM musical of the 1940s. The screen musical genre and its refined format at MGM articulated at its core a sense of flexible boundaries in relation to definitions of gender and sexuality. Nevertheless, the screen image developed around Sinatra in his musical films with the studio unsettles even these wide parameters. Predictably drawing on Sinatra's early persona as a singer, the films equally attempt to contain the more troubling aspects of the star's unconventional male image. In redefining the problematic elements of Sinatra's image for the screen, the resulting characterisations and narratives conversely construct a male identity which challenges still further the musical's accepted notions of masculinity and male sexuality, locating Sinatra in surprisingly uncomfortable ways in the MGM musical.

Gender, Sexuality and 'The Voice'

Sinatra's early musical persona was developed as the singer moved from stints with the Harry James and Tommy Dorsey orchestras to the solo status that provided the route to his unparalleled popularity and success as the idol of the bobby-soxers. Sinatra's rise to prominence during the years of American involvement in World War II meant that the singer was closely associated with the musical soundtrack to the war and, more specifically, the ballads popular with the largely female audience on the home front. While the appeal of popular music rather than patriotic war songs was consistent among the female population at home and the men overseas, there were clear gender distinctions in the particular musical styles and performers to which they were drawn. Serving men found relief in big-band swing, gratified by the racial diversity of its performers and audiences, which fulfilled the requirements of a democratic form of American music, and warmed by the escapism it provided as a reminder of home and civilian life. In contrast, on the home front, women responded to ballads which articulated their emotional experience of war, most often interpreted by female performers.[1] Songs such as 'I'll Never Smile Again', 'I'll Be Seeing You' and 'I'll Walk Alone', which Sinatra performed frequently throughout the early 1940s, evoked a sense of loss and separation to which female audiences easily related. Sinatra's expression of a female perspective on the wartime experience through these ballads, combined with his 4-F status due to a punctured eardrum and rise to prominence during the war years, invested his image with a core sense of emotional and physical vulnerability, positioning the star in relation to the feminine in opposition to a climate of masculine excess.

Sinatra's style of performance as a singer accentuated further the star's development of an unconventional male image. His performances at the Paramount Theater in New York in December 1942 and October 1944 launched Sinatra as what E. J. Kahn, Jr, in a series of articles for *The New Yorker*, termed an 'American phenomenon'.[2] The extreme response of young female fans, who screamed and fainted through Sinatra's performances, encouraged journalists, psychiatrists and social commentators to muse as to the provocation for such unprecedented behaviour. While significantly, some noted a sense of identification between Hoboken-born Sinatra and his working-class audience that would remain a central element of his appeal, a recurring theme of the commentators' analyses was the apparent air of safe sexuality evoked by the combination of romantic expressions of vulnerability and a 'choirboy' vocal quality.[3] As journalist Martha Weinman Lear reported on the eve of Sinatra's Madison Square Garden concert in October 1974, however, the conclusion that a comforting image of asexuality lay at the root of the response to Sinatra was fundamentally flawed. At the same time as Sinatra's female audiences were drawn to his empathetic expression of their emotional experience through his ballad singing, they responded in equal measure to his highly sexualised style of vocal performance:

> The voice had that trick, you know, that funny little sliding, skimming slur that it would do coming off the end of a note. It drove us bonkers … whatever it's called, it was an invitation to hysteria. He'd give us that little slur – 'All … or nothing at aallll …' – and we'd start swooning all over the place … It was like pressing a button. It was pressing a button … the thing we had going with Frankie was sexy.[4]

As Weinman Lear's recollections highlight, Sinatra's trademark use of glissando, the erotic skimming over notes he injected into his performances, was identified by both the singer and his audience as a highly sexual aspect to his vocal style intended to provoke a comparable response, and sexually objectifying Sinatra as a male performer. Equally significant is the location of Sinatra's appeal solely in his voice. His lack of conventional good looks in part roused the initial curiosity of commentators, and, as Weinman Lear confirms, the bobby-soxers' attraction was framed around the singer's vocal style rather than the 'frail frame' and 'cabbage ears' he presented in physical form.

Sinatra drew attention to his body in ways which again challenged gender norms, cultivating a style of dress incorporating bow ties which he then threw out to the audiences, and prefacing the distinctive visual image of suits and fedoras that would accompany him through the 1950s and continue to complicate his image of masculinity. However, Sinatra's sexuality was initially drawn almost exclusively around his voice, enhanced by the soubriquet 'The Voice'. Parker Tyler's analysis in 1947 of the overwhelming significance of Sinatra's voice to his image emphasises the shift from singer to actor on the screen, noting that he 'reverses many a personal chronicle of the screen by having practically originated as a voice and gradually added to it a body'.[5] For Tyler, Sinatra's 'detachable voice' acts as the ventriloquist to Frank's 'glamourized dummy', making the singer's voice the active physical form in his image as a performer. Tyler goes on to confirm the sexuality central to this distinct physicality:

> It makes little difference what songs he chooses or whether on the screen he is visible from the neck or the knees down. On his lips is the theme song of a boudoir Tarzan – not everything he might be in weight, it is true, but swinging, if the lady has a radio, from end to end of the Hit Parade and naked to the larynx.[6]

Tyler's analysis highlights the extent to which Sinatra's body becomes an irrelevance in relation to his sexual persona and to the voice by which it is subsumed. Sinatra's vocal performances instead reveal the 'naked' singer's intentional self-objectification and sexualisation, and form the active masculinity of this 'boudoir Tarzan'.

Visualising 'The Voice'

The sexual imaging that existed around Sinatra and the singer's core sense of vulnerability and uncon-ventional gender positioning are key to examining the characterisation of the star in his early musical screen roles. The visual medium makes problematic the definition of Sinatra's self-objectifying sexuality solely around his voice, and additionally emphasises a physical lack – slim frame and unconventional movie-star looks – which continuously provokes questions around both his sexual appeal and mascu-line persona. Moreover, the screen musical and its central dance performances highlight still further the sense of inadequacy that exists around Sinatra's body. One of the characteristics of the musical as a film genre is the narrative space it provides for non-traditional representations of gender and sexuality. As Richard Dyer's classic essay on the utopian mythology of entertainment articulates: 'Entertainment offers the image of "something better" to escape into ... the sense ... that something other than what is can be imagined and maybe realized.'[7] While Dyer ostensibly examines the form's core concern to satisfy utopian ideals through capitalist means (for example, abundance through consumerism and energy through individualism), the aspects of fantasy and difference that are integral to the themes and mythologies of the musical as a prime entertainment form, combined with the emphasis on perform-ance, almost require unconventional readings of images to counter conventional narratives of hetero-sexual romance. The interventions provided through disruptions which emphasise the qualities of female performance/stardom and which display the male body through dance create space for the alternative reception of both gender and sexual imaging by normally disempowered female and gay audiences.[8]

Even within this arena of movable boundaries for sexual and gender imaging, Sinatra's star image proves a challenging spectacle. The hysteria created around Sinatra as a solo singer led to a seven-year optional contract with RKO and two films which illustrate the extent to which characterisation would continuously draw on his existing image as a singer, and, equally, the ways in which disruptive ele-ments of that image were contained. In the 1943 musical comedy *Higher and Higher*, Sinatra appears as 'Frank Sinatra', an unmarried singer living across the street from the bankrupt Mr Drake (Leon Errol) and his household staff, including a fainting bobby-soxer. This curious mix of character and star com-mences the development of a screen image in which Sinatra's star persona consistently intervenes in the characterisation. Equally, the film reveals the ways in which key elements of his developing image as a singer begin their transference to his screen persona, while those which would prove problematic in the visual medium are reformatted to present a less unconventional male persona, an intervention which ultimately results in a far more challenging image of masculinity. Sinatra's performance of songs such as 'I Couldn't Sleep a Wink Last Night' and 'This Is a Lovely Way to Spend an Evening' therefore both emphasises the ballad singer's romantic and vulnerable appeal, and transforms his sexualised image into innocent asexuality as these songs are performed to his character's platonic female friend, scullery maid Millie (Michèle Morgan) posing as Mr Drake's debutante daughter, rather than to a love interest. The only sexual imagery circulating around Sinatra in the film comes via the unwelcome atten-tions of the bobby-soxer maid, a prospective coupling with a rival debutante merely suggested in the closing reel. As a budding playwright to George Murphy's wily producer in *Step Lively* (1944), RKO's musical remake of the Marx Brothers' *Room Service* (1938), Sinatra's musical performances draw a sexual response from female characters. The elimination of Sinatra's active intent and self-objectification, however, leaves his character, Glen Russell, in the feminised position of passive object of desire. The naivety which replaces this sexualising intent reinforces this positioning, demonstrated when Russell is chased around a hotel room by one sexually aggressive female, ultimately fleeing down a staircase and out of the building.

An MGM Misfit

Sinatra's roles in these RKO musical comedies point towards the much more problematic placement of his star image in the musicals of MGM. Sinatra's arrival at the studio coincided with MGM's developing status as the home of the musical, eclipsing studios such as Warner Bros. and RKO, who had enjoyed success with, respectively, the backstage musicals and Astaire/Rogers films of the 1930s. MGM's specialist units run by producers Arthur Freed, Joe Pasternak and Jack Cummings, which included the talents of songwriters, musicians and other craftsmen dedicated to the film musical, and which had access to performers such as Fred Astaire, Gene Kelly, Judy Garland and Eleanor Powell, associated the studio with the development of the genre in relation to both style and format through high production values and the assimilation of narrative and performance in the integrated musical. In the year prior to Sinatra's arrival, Vincente Minnelli's *Meet Me in St Louis* (1944) heralded this emerging era for the MGM musical, thrusting Sinatra into a studio and genre at its pinnacle. The initial arrangement was a single-picture loan-out for *Anchors Aweigh*, following which Sinatra was released from his seven-year contract with RKO and signed to a five-year deal with MGM. Aside from his film performances, Sinatra's developing star image placed him at odds with the wholesome image MGM attempted to promote around its stars. Press reports of a trip to Havana to meet with the exiled Charlie 'Lucky' Luciano, a physical dispute with journalist Lee Mortimer in the same year, for which Sinatra was arrested, and the public breakdown of his marriage to first wife Nancy and relationship with Ava Gardner shifted his image in ways which conflicted starkly with the MGM ethos. Thus, despite being named *Modern Screen*'s most popular screen star in 1945, Sinatra became such a problematic figure, his overall career in steep decline, that in 1950 MGM declined to extend their option on his contract.

As the epitome of its genre, the MGM musical illustrates the variety of representations of sexuality and gender that are central to its form. As Steven Cohan has argued, the MGM musical, in particular, provides space for specifically camp readings of its narratives and characterisations. Even more specifically, Cohan suggests, a concentration of gay personnel working within the Freed unit, high production values and extravagant musical numbers

> signified to some audiences money lavishly spent on a musical's spectacle while allowing for recognition by others of a camp sensibility at work in the style. Its double valence, the potential to be legible as camp commentary or noncamp entertainment, was thus a result of industrial and aesthetic intentions combining.[9]

For Cohan, then, the combination of the natural perspective of its core contributors and the heightened sense of spectacle which became a central element of MGM's musicals enables the films to be comprehended as both normative and camp representations of gender and sexuality. The openness to camp readings is only accentuated by the aggregate form which Cohan, converse to accepted readings, contends the musicals take, emphasising further the films' focus on display and signalling the possibilities for interpretations of camp.

Sinatra's representation in MGM musicals of the 1940s leaves him occupying an unidentified space between definitions of normative and camp masculinity. His roles define the star's masculinity in ways which challenge either standard or typically transgressive readings in the context of the musical, as visual objectification and transposed gender positioning combine with physical inadequacy, desexualisation and unsettling male relationships. Sinatra's incoherent screen image at the studio stems from the extent to which his characterisations draw on aspects of his image as a singer while attempting to neutralise its problematic core of intentional sexualisation and self-objectification. Positioned in MGM's definitive construction of the genre, Sinatra's misplacement is all the more acute as, even at a superficial level, his films fail to conform to the standard musical narrative of 'boy meets girl, boy loses girl, boy gets girl back' played out through the combination of dramatisation and song and dance. Instead, his films frequently follow a format of 'boy fails to get first girl, second girl gets boy, boy's friend gets first girl', immediately indicating Sinatra's passive feminised role in the films' gender relationships and the disruption caused by male bonding. This narrative trend in the star's films at MGM, while challenging, disguises the more significant complexities of Sinatra's imaging in the studio's musicals, as the films attempt to reconcile the various conflicting elements of his image as a singer in the visual and vocal form of the film musical.

The Sinatra/Kelly musicals, considered as a subgenre later in this essay, reveal additional shifting imagery around this particular buddy dynamic. However, the films most clearly intended as Sinatra vehicles equally demonstrate the tensions of the star's location in the MGM musical. In *It Happened in Brooklyn* (1947), Sinatra appears as World War II veteran Danny Miller attempting to recommence life in the New York district following his time overseas. Early scenes at a camp in England introduce Sinatra's shy and insecure soldier, repeating the format initiated by RKO and continued by MGM which transforms the vulnerability of his early persona as a singer into a characterisation of anxious timidity. Prompted by an American nurse from his neighbourhood (a small role for Gloria Grahame) who refuses to believe his Brooklyn origins, because 'a Brooklyn guy is a friendly guy', Miller assumes a confident identity, convincing Peter Lawford's even more inhibited Englishman (Jamie Shellgrove) and his uncle (the impossibly titled Duke of Dunstable) of his natural self-assurance, resulting in Shellgrove later joining Miller in Brooklyn. The assumption and performance of a normative masculine identity forms a further key theme for Sinatra at MGM. Here, the Brooklyn male references Hollywood's frequent use of the figure as an archetype of working-class American masculinity and Miller's distinction from it, just as it connects the character to the male image established through Brooklyn-born Clarence in *Anchors Aweigh*. Sinatra's problematic sexual persona is therefore in evidence as he directs his opening love song to the Brooklyn Bridge, a photo of which Miller has carried with him overseas. Following Sinatra's by now familiar trend, the narrative initially positions Miller in pursuit of Kathryn Grayson's schoolteacher and aspiring opera singer, Anne Fielding, who ultimately falls for Lawford's English gentleman. Miller's realisation in the final reel of his feelings for Grahame's Brooklyn nurse is complicated by the character's nameless status. While her Brooklyn identity points to narrative closure, with the consolidation of a normative masculinity finally achieved by Danny, the character's lack of a name conversely emphasises the fantasy aspect of a number of Sinatra's screen relationships at MGM.

Notions of a troublesome masculinity requiring correction, performed identities and imaginary relationships, combined with constantly challenging sexual and gender imagery, paint a disruptive and ultimately irreconcilable picture of American masculinity in Sinatra's MGM musicals. Central to this extraordinary imaging is the problematic visualisation of Sinatra. His sexualised vocal performances as a singer clearly articulated an active intent at self-objectification and the provocation of a corresponding audience response. As Parker Tyler's analysis suggests, the potency of Sinatra's sexual styling and the innate basis of his sexuality in vocal expression make his physicality almost an irrelevance. Notably, though Tyler refers to Sinatra's visibility on screen as evidence of this irrelevant body, the singer's invisible radio performances provide the perfect forum for this 'boudoir Tarzan … swinging … and naked to the larynx'. Sinatra's sexuality finds limited expression on screen, even in vocal performance. The physical and visual manifestation of 'The Voice', whereby Sinatra's body is unable to maintain its irrelevant status, combined with the physicality inherent in the genre's musical performances, necessarily problematises his sexual persona and its active self-objectification for the MGM musical. Sexually naive characters, while drawing on early misinterpretations of Sinatra's vocal style and appeal, work towards neutralising this most troublesome aspect of his sexual image. At the same time, Sinatra is constantly visually objectified in these films, a seemingly safe sexualisation of the star whose male physique is undermined through regular joking references to his characters' lack of weight and shape. Representing Sinatra passively as a sexual object stripped of male active sexuality, however, places him in a feminised position that moves him further across the gender trajectory away from traditional masculinity. While his persona as a singer disrupted traditional ideas of masculinity through its combination of sexual objectification, active intent and emotional expressiveness, Sinatra's imaging in the MGM musical retains little, if any, sense of masculine placement.

Consider, for example, his appearance in the 1946 Jerome Kern biopic *Till the Clouds Roll By*, Sinatra's first film under contract to the studio. As one of the film's succession of musical illustrations of the composer's work, Sinatra's performance of 'Ole Man River' from *Show Boat* stands out as an excessively stylised production number performed by a cast dressed collectively in white (providing separate incompatibility issues around the song's subject matter). Surrounded by an orchestra and a male and female chorus in a white setting of columns and drapes on a stage floating in the clouds, Sinatra provides the main feature as he sings atop a dais raised to separate him from the accompanying crowd, or is shot alone against a backdrop of lush, sweeping drapery. The heightened glamour of this setting, reminiscent of a Ziegfeld production number, and Sinatra's role as the ultimate object to be viewed, positions him as a musical performer in ways much more familiarly linked to female screen performance. The feminising effect of this type of objectifying imagery is only compounded by narratives in which Sinatra's gender-swapping roles reverse the genre's standard routes to musical seduction.

The challenges stimulated by these sexual and gender displacements are evident in the extreme imaging of *The Kissing Bandit* (1948), a low point in the Sinatra canon which the star frequently ridiculed in later years. Returning from Boston Business School to take over his late father's saloon in Spanish California, Ricardo (Sinatra) is confronted by his father's true identity as a bandit chief famed for kissing his female victims and causing them to faint. A clear reference to Sinatra's sexualised performance style is immediately neutralised as Ricardo faints into the arms of his uncle on seeing his father's 'Wanted' poster. Required to assume the identity of the 'kissing bandit' for the sake of the family finances, Ricardo is able to master only the visual appearance of this sexually aggressive outlaw, setting Sinatra up on screen in costumed excess that continuously draws attention away from his

The kissing bandit asks, 'What's wrong with me?'

female co-star, Kathryn Grayson, as the local Governor's daughter, Teresa. Frequently falling off his horse, and unable to kiss Grayson due to his inexperience, Ricardo cannot physically perform his father's role. His ideals of masculinity are gleaned from the mythology of the 'kissing bandit' and Robin Hood, and therefore either remain in the imaginary or result in failure, exemplified by Ricardo's attempt to emulate Romeo by serenading Teresa and climbing up to her balcony, only to be shot at by the Governor's guards. The relationship is able to be realised only when the characters reverse their prescribed roles, instigated by

Teresa, who serenades Ricardo beneath his balcony, enabling him to reveal his true identity, kiss her and finally cause her to faint. The degree to which the film pulls his image as a singer directly into the text, while at the same time deactivating the sexual and gender conflicts that result, is evident in its excessive feminisation of Sinatra. This extends to the representation of the film's vocal performances as a demasculinising problematic as Sinatra sings 'What's wrong with me? Why didn't I kiss her?', expressing his character's sexual confusion, and projects something close to sexual terror when confronted by a female dancer who cracks her whip while chanting suggestively, 'I like you, if you like me'.

The Sailor Suit and the Buddy

These films constructed around Sinatra articulate his problematic placement in the MGM musical. Attempts to neutralise his active sexual imaging and therefore make safe his screen persona inversely have a more troublesome effect in positioning the star in extreme ways which challenge conventional cinematic images of gender and sexuality. Those films in which Sinatra plays an increasingly supportive role to established film and MGM star Gene Kelly nevertheless reveal further testing complexities in the negotiation of his image. The roles which best represent Sinatra's MGM career in the popular imagination emphasise a screen image brought into sharper focus and complicated further through a formatted contrast with Kelly's persona as a musical screen star, which in itself provokes further questioning. The first and last of these films equally establish a generic strand as Sinatra and Kelly play sailors on shore leave, joined by Jules Munshin in *On the Town* (1949). Both this film and Sinatra's MGM premiere *Anchors Aweigh* nominally provide the ultimate utopian musical space via narratives which position the servicemen in the complementary arena of the city (Los Angeles and New York respectively) for a limited time, made more specific in *On the Town*'s twenty-four-hour story. While this liberating space is constructed to enable the alternative experiences of the films' characters and equally provides generic room for challenges to conventional imagery, the conflicts inherent in the transference of Sinatra's image to the screen remain to problematise these representations of masculinity.

The familiar tropes of sexual naivety and reversed gender positioning are evident in both films. The narrative of *Anchors Aweigh* has its basis in Clarence Doolittle's (Sinatra) insistence that shipmate Joe Brady (Kelly) teach him the art of attracting a girl so that he can spend his leave in the conventional manner rather than reading books at the local library. This leads to Clarence initially falling for aspiring singer Susan Abbott (Kathryn Grayson), who, in the unorthodox boy meets girl format, is eventually paired with Joe following Clarence's realisation that the nameless waitress (listed only as 'Girl from Brooklyn' in the credits, initiating this nameless trend), who poured soup over him to attract his attention, is actually his ideal mate. In *On the Town*, Sinatra plays Chip, a city-struck sailor from Peoria, intent on using his twenty-four-hour pass to complete a sightseeing tour of New York. Targeted by sexually aggressive cab driver Hildy (Betty Garrett), he instead assumes the role of passive prey, chased around a yellow cab, and eventually succumbing to the proposition to 'Come up to My Place'. The shore-leave narrative of each film removes the necessity for displays of masculine bravado by these servicemen, an aspect of the films accentuated by their naval rather than army identities – pointedly, the three sailors run from a bulky and aggressive soldier when exiting the subway in *On the Town*. The close-combat experiences of soldiers enabled Hollywood film-makers to represent both heightened masculinity and subsequent emotional damage, and it is notably as ex-soldiers that Sinatra reveals this sense of a shifting post-war masculinity in films such as *Young at Heart* (1954), *Suddenly* (1954) and *Some Came Running* (1958).

Anchors Aweigh (1945): Sinatra uses his inadequate body for male bonding

Anchors Aweigh emphasises Clarence Doolittle's unconventional identity in the opening scenes, as both Clarence and Joe receive the Silver Star for an incident in which Joe dived into the ocean to rescue Clarence, who had been blown overboard during a naval attack. Sinatra's character is again distanced from combat itself, and the account equally draws attention to his physical inadequacy in relation to the role of serviceman. In the context of the musical, this gains heightened significance, as all three musicals Sinatra makes with Kelly require his participation in dance routines, something which is not a feature of his individual star vehicles at MGM. These performances alongside Kelly, Munshin and other leading cast members function as group bonding exercises rather than, more conventionally, as means of seduction, and position Sinatra in ways which point to the genre's objectification of male performers through dance and visual display.

At the same time, however, the sailor suits that emphasise Sinatra's slight frame highlight the shift from his sexually irrelevant body, identified by Parker Tyler, to its inadequacy, visible and underlined in the film musical. Kelly's muscular build and dancing prowess are accentuated by the sailor suits for which he expressed a preference over the soldier's uniform, their close fit and stylishness drawing attention to the dancer's body and providing a sense of extraordinary style.[10] As Steven Cohan argues, the resulting eroticisation of Kelly's body combines with the star's insistent but contrary masculinisation of dance in opposition to the 'sissy' stereotype, and the films' exposure of the characters' performed hyper-masculinity, to create an undoubtedly more ambiguous image of masculinity than Kelly intends, which Cohan defines in camp terms.[11] The narratives, however, certainly stress the sexual appeal of Kelly in his tight-fitting sailor suit, as his characters are on the receiving end of wolf whistles from female admirers in both *Anchors Aweigh* and *On the Town*. In contrast, the uniforms re-emphasise Sinatra's physical inadequacy, just as the dance routines reveal further his limitations for the screen genre. Betty Garrett's inside scoop that Sinatra suffered the indignity of bell-bottom trousers padded at the rear only reinforces the singer's diminished masculinity in this strand. Sinatra's impaired masculinity leaves his characters in an indeterminate gender position in both romantic and buddy relationships, as his image, as well as Kelly's hyper-confusion, resists both traditional male sexual and gender identities and their inverse.

The lesser-known *Take Me Out to the Ball Game* (1949) illustrates the mix of conflicting images around Sinatra in these films that moves his male identity beyond simple ideas of feminisation. Notably co-directed by Busby Berkeley, famous for creating the kaleidoscopic visual spectacle of the female chorus, the narrative characterises Sinatra and Kelly as two baseball players who play the vaudeville circuit as a song-and-dance act during the off-season, both arenas of masculine display. Dennis Ryan (Denny) carries Sinatra's familiar mix of sexual naivety and physical inadequacy to contrast with Eddie O'Brien's (Kelly) confident sexual player, traits which position the star's masculinity in unconventional ways. Moreover, the elements of objectification, neutralisation and the imaginary which surround the character's sexual identity, combined with the shifting gender positions of Denny's relationships with both male and female characters, dictate extraordinary readings of his sexual persona.

The film's negotiation of Sinatra's visual appearance is again key to the screen image being constructed. His light build and slim frame serve as a running gag indicating Denny's fragile masculinity as a variety of opponents knock him out with a single punch. As Eddie comments on the first occasion: 'Every once in a while he gets illusions. He thinks he's got muscles.' The visual objectification of Sinatra goes further to illustrate the neutralisation of his actively self-objectifying sexual image, working with similarly challenging imagery to problematise his male identity. These themes emerge most pointedly in a scene in which Denny is called upon to assume the traditional role of active sexual hunter. Tied to their hotel room as a result of an early curfew instigated by the new owner of 'The Wolves', Katherine (K.C.) Higgins (Esther Williams), Nat Goldberg (Munshin) and Eddie push Denny into romancing her with the aim of arranging a triple date and escaping their enforced confinement. A reluctant Denny is initially advised by Nat to employ a caveman approach in his pursuit, until a quick check of his muscles cancels the advice. Instead, Eddie tells Denny to move onto the balcony – Juliet-style – and act nonchalant as Katherine swims in the pool below. Sinatra's pose, arm placed behind his head and chest forward, initiates the feminine visual placement of the star in the scene, just as his character's clumsy descent down the trunk of a palm tree re-emphasises his physical limitations. Denny's romantic gesture comes in the form of Sinatra's vocal performance of 'The Right Girl for Me'. However, much of the song is performed with Williams out of shot or facing away from the camera, diminishing any sense of active romancing in favour of the visual objectification of Sinatra. He therefore becomes a passive visual spectacle, bathed in light and shadows, and leaning against a trellis, transforming the masculine problematic around his body into a feminised display.

Take Me Out to the Ball Game (1949): Sinatra becomes a feminised visual spectacle

The outcome of the performance, which would ordinarily serve as the genre's narrative route to seduction, highlights the neutralisation of Sinatra's active sexual imaging and the alternative gender relationships this provokes. Denny has earlier indicated that Katherine's appeal for him lies in her traditionally masculine traits, having watched her ably throw a baseball: 'She's the kind of girl I've always dreamed about. Wouldn't it be wonderful to be married to a girl who played baseball?' The imaginary game of baseball that follows Denny's romancing, as the characters throw an invisible ball and pretend to catch each other out, reinforces the mix-up of gender positions and emphasises still further the sexual neutralisation of Sinatra. Just as the star is paired with nameless female characters in both *It Happened in Brooklyn* and *Anchors Aweigh*, Sinatra's sexuality here is bound up in the imaginary, in both male and female relationships, all of which contributes to his constantly shifting gender position.

Denny's relationship with the film's other female character, Shirley (Betty Garrett), follows familiar patterns. Shirley takes the traditional male position of pursuer, sending the 'skinny little runt' candy and flowers

Take Me Out to the Ball Game: Kelly cradles his Romeo in his arms

and chasing him around the bleachers singing 'It's fate, baby, it's fate' until he succumbs later in the film. (The film pointedly makes fun of early suggestions that Sinatra appealed to a feminine desire to nurture, Shirley claiming that her clearly sexual response to Denny is 'just the mother instinct'.) Even Denny's fantasies maintain these transposed positions. He falls asleep asserting women's love of the 'caveman stuff', but once awake describes to Eddie how, in his dream, Shirley hit him over the head with her club, threw him over her shoulder and carried him out of the cave and into the woods, Denny remaining passively unconscious throughout this scene of sexual aggression.

The Sinatra/Kelly imaging in the film similarly revolves around a sense of an unrealised imaginary, and its continued sexualisation through the film's dialogue challenges further gender and sexual conventions. The fantasy element is indicated in the song 'Yes, Indeedy', which duplicates the format of 'She Begged Me' in *Anchors Aweigh* as the characters provide fabricated details of sexual exploits. Following Denny's ineffective 'seduction' scene, Eddie assumes a more traditional approach, climbing *up* to Katherine's balcony – *Romeo*-style – proposing a moonlit walk on the beach and kissing her hand. Observing Eddie's actions from their room, Nat attempts to minimise Denny's disquiet: 'Calm down, will ya. He's just kissing her for you.' Denny's response begins a surprising trend of sexually ambiguous dialogue around the Denny/Eddie relationship: 'Then what? I suppose she'll kiss him and he'll come back and kiss me, huh? Well, I know I won't like it.' This trend continues when Eddie returns to the room and, shielding himself from Denny's preparations for a fight, inadvertently knocks him out. Interrupted by one of the training staff as he cradles Denny in his arms, Eddie attempts to explain away the situation as rehearsals for a Romeo and Juliet scene in their new vaudeville act. Switching positions to take up the role of Juliet, Eddie begins reciting the classic lines to his Romeo. This sexual and gender confusion has its apex in the clambake scene, during which Eddie, in an attempt to seduce Katherine for a bet, describes how Denny had an audible dream about the team's new owner. As Eddie explains it, when he tried to awaken his teammate, Denny embraced and kissed him, as Eddie goes on to demonstrate by kissing Katherine. The gender switching in these imagined relationships positions Sinatra as female in male/female relationships and lends him the male role when set against a feminised Kelly. Denny's test of the viability of a relationship is the 'kick' in his kiss, which fails to ignite Katherine but proves his compatibility with Shirley. This fluid shifting between gender positions and sexual identities leaves the audience wondering whether the greatest 'kick' would perhaps be achieved with Kelly.

Sinatra and the Musical Transformed

Sinatra's screen image in the MGM musical strays so far from conventional notions of masculinity and male sexuality, even within this most accommodating of genres, that his tenure as a contract star was inevitably short. A footnote comes in the intended sequel to *On the Town*, the 1955 musical *It's Always Fair Weather*, which teamed Gene Kelly with Dan Dailey and Michael Kidd in a tale of World War II army veterans reuniting in New York ten years after their return home. The film launched the MGM musical into Hollywood's post-war territory of the problematic resettlement of the veteran, a theme

Sinatra was addressing in screen dramas, including the MGM melodrama *Some Came Running*. Had Sinatra chosen to reprise his role, MGM's developing format and Sinatra's altered star image would have represented a comfortable fit. Moves away from the consistently utopian mythology of earlier musicals and towards more complex representations of male identity occurred alongside shifts in Sinatra's image which highlighted rather than concealed the contradictory elements of post-war masculine identity. Sinatra's development of a potent image of heterosexual, emotionally vulnerable and sexually objectified masculinity in musicals such as *Young at Heart* and *Pal Joey* (1957), and his class-based characterisation in *High Society* (1956) – his return to the MGM musical – contested masculine norms in a genre altering its own narrative thematics. In many ways, however, Sinatra's screen image in the MGM musicals of the 1940s provided an even more challenging spectacle. Roles which combined visual objectification, sexual naivety, gender confusion and physical inadequacy stretched to the limits both accepted notions of masculinity and male sexuality and the narrative and character conventions of the studio-branded musical form. MGM's attempts to neutralise Sinatra's alternative sexual image conversely produced a much more disruptive persona for their star, and equally constructed some fascinating imagery for the MGM musical.

Notes

1. Lewis A. Erenberg, 'Swing Goes to War: Glenn Miller and the Popular Music of World War II', in Lewis A. Erenberg and Susan E. Hirsch (eds), *The War in American Culture: Society and Consciousness during World War II* (Chicago: University of Chicago Press, 1996), pp. 144–69.

2. Kahn's three-part series was later combined with extra material into a book. E. J. Kahn, Jr, *The Voice: The Story of an American Phenomenon, Frank Sinatra* (London: Musician's Press, 1946).

3. 'Frankie Fans Make Poor Wives', *Down Beat*, 26 March 1947. Reprinted in *Down Beat*, August 1988, p. 33. *Down Beat* was poking fun at one psychologist's conclusion that young fans found comfort in the unthreatening 'sexlessness' of the crooners' singing style.

4. Martha Weinman Lear, 'The Bobby Sox Have Wilted, but the Memory Remains Fresh', *New York Times*, 13 October 1974, in Steven Petkov and Leonard Mustazza (eds), *The Frank Sinatra Reader* (New York and Oxford: Oxford University Press, 1995), p. 47. For further discussion, see Karen McNally, *When Frankie Went to Hollywood: Frank Sinatra and American Male Identity* (Urbana and Chicago: University of Illinois Press, 2008), pp. 135–41.

5. Parker Tyler, *Magic and Myth of the Movies*, 1947 (London: Martin Secker & Warburg, 1971), pp. 35–6.

6. Ibid., pp. 36–7.

7. Richard Dyer, 'Entertainment and Utopia', in Steven Cohan (ed.), *Hollywood Musicals: The Film Reader* (London and New York: Routledge, 2002), p. 20.

8. Dyer acknowledges these interventions in passing in 'Entertainment and Utopia' and more substantially in, for example, his study of 'Judy Garland and Gay Men' in *Heavenly Bodies: Film Stars and Society*, 1986 (London: Routledge, 2003).

9. Steven Cohan, *Incongruous Entertainment: Camp, Cultural Value, and the MGM Musical* (Durham, NC, and London: Duke University Press, 2005), p. 60. See also Matthew Tinkcom, *Working Like a Homosexual: Camp, Capital, Cinema* (Durham, NC, and London: Duke University Press, 2002), pp. 35–72.

10. Gene Kelly, interview by Marilyn Hunt, 1975, quoted in Beth Genné, ' "Freedom Incarnate": Jerome Robbins, Gene Kelly, and the Dancing Sailor as an Icon of American Values in World War II', *Dance Chronicle*, vol. 24 no. 1, 2001, p. 89.

11. Cohan, *Incongruous Entertainment*, pp. 164–73.

8 Bloody Mary Is the Girl I Love:
US White Liberalism vs. Pacific Islander Subjectivity in *South Pacific*

Sean Griffin

I wish I could tell you about the South Pacific. The way it actually was.

James Michener[1]

The musical play *South Pacific* opened on Broadway in 1949 to almost universal acclaim. The production ran for over five years, winning eight Tony awards and the Pulitzer Prize for drama. The original cast recording became a gold record, and the 1958 film version made $17.5 million in rentals (when the average successful film made $5 million).[2] Among the reasons for *South Pacific's* high regard was that the play tackled a topic most would have considered too serious and complex for a musical at that time: race relations. Dramatising the detrimental effects of white prejudice against Asians and Pacific Islanders on both sides of the racial divide, songwriters Richard Rodgers and Oscar Hammerstein II, director Joshua Logan and author James Michener (who wrote the Pulitzer Prize-winning *Tales from the South Pacific* on which the play was based) consciously saw themselves and their work as progressive and liberal.[3]

In the hindsight of a half-century, *South Pacific's* reputation as a text has lost some of its lustre. While conservatives in the 1940s and 50s winced at its liberal outlook, the similarities of its post-war white (and male) liberalism to Edward Said's concept of Orientalism have become increasingly apparent. *South Pacific* presents islanders as exotic objects for white audiences to enjoy. Rather than a concrete place with a social and economic system, the island of Bali Ha'i is a dream space where innocent natives wait for white Americans to guide them. Without understanding a word of English, Liat, the daughter of Tonkinese Bloody Mary, happily and mutely falls in love with Lt. Cable. The only other major native characters are literally children – French planter Emile DeBecque's two half-Tonkinese offspring. Further, interracial relationships are still portrayed as tragic – Lt. Cable's prejudices drive him from Liat, and then he dies in combat; DeBecque's Tonkinese first wife has died before the narrative starts. The ideological leap nurse Nellie Forbush must take is marrying DeBecque though he once had sex with a Tonkinese woman. While perhaps bold for 1949, the lingering biases are now somewhat hard to ignore.

Christina Klein's analysis of *South Pacific* describes how Asian and Pacific Islanders are constructed as children in need of kindly parental oversight by white America.[4] This obviously applies to the children Nellie agrees to mother at the play's finale. Klein further argues that Bloody Mary and Liat are presented as childlike – tragedy occurs because Cable is asked to provide *romantic* love rather than *parental* love. While such a dynamic exists, Klein's argument overlooks the fact that Mary *is* Liat's parent. Klein suggests that Cable parallels Nellie (white Americans encountering childlike islanders), but Bloody Mary *also* parallels Nellie: both are independent adult women taking younger people under their care. A happy ending comes when Nellie agrees to parent the half-Tonkinese children; death results from Mary acting as the parental figure, trying to adopt Cable into *her* family. Asians and Pacific

Islanders, the text asserts, need to realise that white America knows what's best for them – not the other way around. Such an analysis pulls Mary out of what might initially seem to be a supporting-character status and into the epicentre of the piece's discussion of race relations, and many of Asian and Pacific descent have zeroed in on her to denounce the text in all its formulations.

This attitude of white liberals bestowing paternal acceptance to Asians and Pacific Islanders extends beyond the text and into its creation. My focus is not on the creation of the original stage production but on its transference to the motion-picture screen, because it was during the filming that a number of people involved were confronted most dramatically with the limitations of their attitudes and assumptions. The history of Twentieth Century-Fox's involvement in putting *South Pacific* on celluloid creates a rival narrative to the one provided by the text itself, showing Pacific Islanders responding to and challenging post-war white liberal misconceptions. In light of this rival narrative, it is then possible to revisit the character of Bloody Mary and see echoes of such resistance.

Bali Ha'i May Call You

South Pacific is not drenched in realism – the characters keep breaking out in song, as non-devotees of the genre regularly complain. Yet, those involved in bringing the musical to the stage consciously strove to invest the piece with as much naturalism as they felt the form could bear.[5] Logan and Hammerstein wrote dialogue that used the slang and profanity common to average enlisted men. Logan blocked the performers to move around in a less stylised fashion during numbers in lieu of explicit choreography. The story itself diverged from the triviality and farce traditionally associated with musical theatre, in favour of a strongly organised dramatic plot. The numbers as well (other than 'Honey Bun', sung as part of a show within the text) serve to drive the story along rather than divert from it. Such realism also served the creators' liberal outlook: to present things as they are, rather than sugar-coating them. For example, Rodgers and Hammerstein stood their ground on keeping the song 'Carefully Taught' in the show, despite complaints by some preview audiences and investors about its discussion of the social construction of racism.

The enormous success of the Broadway production meant that many of the original stylistic decisions were kept when transferring the property to celluloid. With Rodgers and Hammerstein as part of the producing team, and Logan as director, much of the original dialogue was retained, as well as the blocking, such as the final, under the table, hand-holding of Nellie and DeBecque, and the tromping around of the sailors during 'There Is Nothing Like a Dame'. The major difference between the theatrical and film versions of these two moments is that on stage they occurred on sets designed by Jo Melizner, while on film they took place on an actual Pacific island. Location shooting for the film adaptation was a foregone conclusion – partly to help draw audiences to theatres (and away from their TV sets), but also to provide even greater verisimilitude. More than half of the final film was footage shot on or around the Hawaiian islands. Such location shooting allowed the film to expand from the stage play and show some of the military action of the story, aided by the filming of actual naval manoeuvres near Hawai'i during the production.[6]

With all this in mind, a viewer might expect a sober, uncompromising motion picture. Yet, the film is (literally) awash with elements and stylistic choices that continuously undercut the supposed commitment to realism. Most notably, Logan seemed to think that location shooting in Hawai'i would not be sufficiently spectacular, and made the decision to film almost all the musical numbers through coloured filters (rather than tinting or toning the footage in post-production). By and large, whenever anyone starts singing, the environment submerges into bright purple, a sort of lime green or burnt

The obvious matte painting used to represent the island of Bali Ha'i in the film version of Rodgers and Hammerstein's *South Pacific* (1958) indicates the concerted lack of realism used to depict native Pacific environments

umber yellow. Intriguingly, the opening two numbers of the film do not use filters ('Bloody Mary Is the Girl I Love' and 'There Is Nothing Like a Dame'). They first appear when Mary sings for the first time: 'Bali Ha'i'. From this point on, the island of Bali Ha'i and its inhabitants are never seen in anything but the aforementioned burnt umber – whether singing or not. As Bill Osgerby describes, the filters 'heighten the sense of aroused passions in a sultry tropical paradise'.[7] Consequently, such effects are eventually used when white characters experience such emotions and break into song – but the coloured filters primarily filter the coloureds.

Pacific culture is repeatedly and somewhat obviously artificially created. Beyond the filters, the filmmakers 'enhanced' the beauty of the location setting by adding massive amounts of extra greenery and foliage to the surroundings meant to represent Bali Ha'i. Fog machines are also employed in all of the Bali Ha'i footage, mist wafting in everywhere. The mist appears even when Mary is just describing the place while on another island! In long shots, Bali Ha'i is revealed as a pretty blatant matte painting rather than an actual island. While devoting much of the production to location shooting, a number of episodes that take place on Bali Ha'i were eventually filmed back in Hollywood. Such artificiality extended to the people as well. The casting of islanders included a number of ethnic or racial groups – including (to use the terminology of the times) 'mulatto' Juanita Hall as Bloody Mary and Japanese actress France Nuyen as Liat. Mary is actually played by two performers in the film. Although Hall was the original Mary on Broadway, Rodgers decided that he wanted her singing voice to be dubbed by Muriel Smith, who had played the part in the London stage version.[8] When Logan talked with choreographer LeRoy Prinz about chorus girls, he wanted 'good looking Chinese, Tonkinese, and beautiful Japanese girls … that will be adaptable to any native category'.[9]

The image of Pacific Islanders and their culture as happy-go-lucky (but sometime petulant) individuals needing (and gladly accepting) the guidance of more civilised white Americans had dominated western thought over decades of 'discovery', colonisation and commercialisation. This discourse was prominent across the United States during the immediate post-war years (as Klein and others ably and thoroughly recount). Attitudes towards the Hawaiian Islands stand as a strong example. Hawai'i during this period was aptly termed a 'protectorate' of the US. As the federal legislature and popular magazines discussed making Hawai'i a state, supporters often visualised the US bringing the islands into the fold like a child being rewarded for its work during World War II.[10] Department of Labor reports on Hawai'i's workforce stressed that the median age on the islands was much younger than on the US mainland – and Hawai'i worked under a 'paternalistic' plantation structure during the 1800s.[11]

Such descriptions ignored or minimised the will and determination of Hawaiians to assert agency over their lives. As early as 1841, the first labour strike on the islands took place.[12] As soon as World War II ended and federal restrictions about union organising were lifted, Hawaiian workers quickly joined the International Longshoremen and Warehousemen's Union. The ILWU was accused of communist ties throughout the 1950s, and there were constant attempts to deport the group's Hawaiian representatives. The main argument *against* Hawaiian statehood was that it would provide a gateway for Communists to infiltrate the US, seeing the success of the ILWU as naive Hawaiians being duped rather than workers unwilling to be treated like children.[13] The executives at Fox, Joshua Logan, and Rodgers and Hammerstein would confront this clash between mainland discourse and actual Hawaiian labour issues in deciding to film *South Pacific* on the island of Kaua'i – the site of that first labour strike in 1841.

You Have to Be Carefully Taught

The tendency to collapse pan-Pacific cultures probably explains why Fox and South Pacific Enterprises (SPE, founded by Rodgers and Hammerstein to act as the film's official production company) believed Hawai'i was like anywhere in the Pacific. (Many native Hawaiians regard themselves as part of the *North* Pacific.[14]) Yet, an effort *was* made to research what the culture of mythic Bali Ha'i might look like. Asked by Hammerstein what had inspired his idea of the island, Michener revealed that he had thought of the islands of Acthin and Vao off the coast of Malekula, north of New Caledonia.[15] Second unit photographers were duly dispatched to gather research material. They found that 'the people here are almost black and have Negroid features – not brown like the Hawaiians'.[16] Faced with these findings, the film-makers were troubled: 'There are virtually no negroes on [Hawai'i].'[17] Unit production manager Eric Stacey suggested that 'we could use Samoan or local people and put war paint on them'. In the end, the fictional Boar's Tooth Ceremony on Bali Ha'i was shot in Hollywood – where, presumably, it was easier to find extras with 'Negroid features'.[18]

The island of Kaua'i was chosen for a variety of reasons. Location scouts found areas that could accommodate all the various places in the story.[19] Confining the shoot to one island also minimised the expense of shipping equipment and personnel. On the negative side, most unions were based on the island of O'ahu and regarded working on Kaua'i as 'location' work, resulting in a pay increase. In early March 1957, Eric Stacey contacted the local (O'ahu) chapter of the International Alliance of Theatrical Stage Employees (IATSE), which guaranteed sixteen men to work as 'grips, electricians, props [men, and] greensmen' at $3.06 an hour, higher than the standard Studio Scale rate of $2.55 an hour.[20] These negotiations were in accordance with agreements between Fox and IATSE for *all* productions made by the studio. Yet, the shoot would require far more hands than IATSE would be able to supply, and this is where shooting in Kaua'i seemed a smart strategic move. Kaua'i's carpenters and truck drivers had *not* been unionised. Memos reveal that Fox executives felt certain they could pay *less* than standard union scale to Kauaians dazzled by the prospect of working on a big Hollywood film.[21]

This decision was made around the beginning of April 1957, leaving four months for preparation (hiring the vast crew; reconstructing areas on location, including building certain sets;

The Boar's Tooth Ceremony on Bali Ha'i, which was shot in Hollywood rather than Hawai'i because of the difficulty in finding extras who had 'Negroid features' on the island

making or gathering together the vast numbers of costumes for the stars and extras; pre-recording all the numbers; shipping all the equipment – lights, the large and expensive Todd-AO cameras, multi-track magnetic sound recording equipment, 70mm film stock; organising lodging for all the cast and crew coming from outside Hawai'i). Shooting would begin in mid-August (in conjunction with the naval exercises), laying out a two-month stay before the rainy season hit in late October.[22] In other words, once the decision was made, it was practically impossible for the production to change its mind and relocate elsewhere without a substantial loss of both time and money. A detail not nailed down before the pre-production juggernaut was launched was a definitive arrangement for labour on Kaua'i, lending further credence to the theory that white producers stateside assumed native workers would welcome the arrival of a major Hollywood movie as eagerly and uncomplicatedly as Liat fell into Lt. Cable's arms.

Everyone involved generally ignored ongoing efforts by the AFL-CIO to organise carpenters and truck drivers on Kaua'i. According to Robert Weir, from the Kaua'i Chamber of Commerce, 'The AFL's organizational drive has been drastically bogged down, at present, by the refusal of local contractors to permit either an industry wide representation vote or industry wide negotiations.' Attempting to prevent use of the coming 'production as a lever to enforce the establishment of unionization of the building trades', the Kaua'i Chamber of Commerce told the AFL-CIO 'that any organization which hamstrung or stalemated any project that would aid our Island economy could expect to be very thoroughly discredited'.[23] Weir felt that Raymond Aki, the AFL representative on Kaua'i, had given assurances that the union would not attempt to stymie the production – and Weir seemed to regard the AFL as having little power other than to annoy and complain.

This was in May 1957. By the end of June, opinions had been substantially revised: a general strike on the island had been called. Weir wrote to Stacey with his version of events:

> Aki was informed by … Charley Nichols [, one of Aki's superiors in Honolulu, that studio] … rates were going to be paid. Aki organized the building trades by singling out each individual employee and offering him a movie job in return for signing up with the union. When this sign-up was practically 100 percent, Aki began working on the contractors and presented them with the accomplished fact that their employees were already union members. About 12 contractors capitulated and recognized the AFL. The employees of the contractors who refused to recognize the AFL were pulled off their jobs and assigned to the 12 contractors who recognized the union. This put Aki in the position of having a closed shop with 12 contractors plus practically all building trade laborers on the island signed up and taking orders from Aki.[24]

The production team worked to keep this development from destroying plans for the shoot (now less than two months away). In early July, both on-location production manager Eric Stacey and Fred S. Meyer, Fox's Director of Industrial Relations in Hollywood, were involved in the negotiations. While Meyer and Stacey must have kept in contact with each other, the presence of two separate negotiators resulted in different statements and agreements being expressed – which the AFL used to its advantage. Following talks with Arthur A. Rutledge, President of the AFL-CIO's Honolulu chapter, in Hollywood, Meyer thought Rutledge had agreed to a $1.75 per hour wage for construction workers supplied by the union. Unfortunately, Stacey in Hawai'i dealt with Aki, and *he* committed to paying the Studio Scale wage rate of $2.55 per hour given to union workers in Hollywood. Aki possibly knew of this rate due to the shooting of an episode of the TV series *The Life of Riley* on Kaua'i in early 1957. With a much smaller-scale production, the show's producers paid workers the Studio Scale rate for a few days work. Stacey may have been forced to acknowledge that this rate existed, giving Aki a powerful negotiating tool. Once Rutledge learned of this development, he refused to agree to Meyer's earlier negotiation. The revolt extended beyond carpenters and truck drivers. Word got around that extras hired for *The Life of Riley* had been paid about $10 a day, substantially raising what Fox planned to pay the hundreds needed for *South Pacific*.

By mid-July, most of the island was caught up in the brouhaha. An editorial in Kaua'i's local news-paper, the *Garden Island News*, indicates that certain local officials (including probably the Chamber of Commerce) were trying to put the unions in bad light by making it seem they were endangering the potential economic windfall brought by the arrival of Hollywood film-makers. Coming to the work-ers' defence, the editorial declared that the Studio Scale

> rates may well bring to the attention of Kauai [sic] workers the difference between local rates and those paid elsewhere. We wonder if anyone thinks that the rates paid elsewhere are a well kept secret. Anyone who feels that they are should consider the number of people that are leaving Kauai each month to make their homes on Oahu [sic] or the mainland. Also a study of want ads in the Honolulu papers regard-ing employment in the Western Pacific and other areas will quickly dispel such ideas. … It is … our belief that unless more and better jobs are created on this island, there will be an ever increasing number of people leaving Kauai. Kauai can hardly expect to maintain status quo either in population or in wage rates when there are better opportunities available elsewhere.[25]

Trapped in an impossible situation only worsening as negotiations dragged on, Executive Production Manager Sid Rogell informed Stacey on 19 July that 'we have settled the union problems by acceding to all their demands. We didn't salvage a nickel's worth of anything, and I cannot help but feel that somewhere along the line we fumbled the ball a few times.'[26]

However, this did not end their troubles with the unions. Stacey wrote to complain that the union was 'rotating the help' so that 'some more local people could get in on the "gravy" '.[27] Even IATSE workers began causing problems, refusing daily changes of assignments, insisting that once they were assigned a position, they remained in that capacity for the duration. Further, IATSE members refused to be assigned to more general manual labour – meaning that no one was doing toilet detail – and Stacey informed Rogell that 'situation quickly becoming critical [due to] sanitary reasons and ninety degree heat'.[28] Rogell responded that IATSE workers had the right to maintain their position for the day, but could be assigned a different position with each new day. As for toilet detail and other manual labour, Rogell advised assigning AFL workers.[29]

By the end of August, tempers were fraying. Various days of rain had scuttled shooting. While film-ing ocean footage, heavy swells had sunk canoes, a navy whaleboat had developed motor trouble and a Todd-AO camera fell into the water. While shooting the Bali Ha'i sequence, three hundred extras promptly helped themselves to whatever had not been nailed down as souvenirs.[30] Memos from Stacey indicate that Logan was angrily arguing with numerous co-workers. Meanwhile, in Hollywood, Lyle Wheeler, head of Fox's art department, noted that 'To say the least, "Holy Hell" was raised yester-day afternoon when the final budget figures came in and every department had increased their esti-mates.'[31] He brought to Logan's attention 'very forcibly that we're out of money location-wise'. Location shooting finished on 6 October and intriguingly, considering how disillusioned the film-makers and the studio became with the actual island of Kaua'i and its inhabitants, a large portion of the Bali Ha'i scenes were completed in Hollywood, such as the Boar's Tooth Ceremony, the scenes in Liat's hut and the underwater shots during the 'Happy Talk' number. Obviously, back at the studio, it was easier to make the South Pacific look and act as white subjectivity desired.

In recounting this history, one could easily surmise that Kaua'i natives had 'pulled a fast one' on unknowing whites. Yet, that would only replace one oversimplification with another – innocent, happy natives transformed into conniving, inscrutable natives. In fact, the native population of Kaua'i was on various sides of the film's production history. While the bulk of newly unionised workers were of Pacific origin, so too it seems were many of the contractors resisting unionisation. (Evidence suggests, though, that the contractor who resisted unionisation most stubbornly was white – a man named E. F. Nilson.[32]) Further, Kauaians hired as extras included people of both Pacific and European backgrounds. The Bali Ha'i sequence required extras to play natives and to play European nuns and the daughters of European planters. Hence, *both* groups were probably responsible for the large-scale looting of props and greenery from the shoot. Acknowledging these details prevents slippage into another round of racial and ethnic generalisations.

Twin Soliloquies

While islanders used the filming of *South Pacific* to gain greater agency over their lives, such a history went largely unreported outside of Hawai'i, and has been subsequently forgotten. Meanwhile, the problematic representations in *South Pacific* live on – in countless stage revivals (including on Broadway in 2007); the continued popularity of the 1958 film; an American network television version starring Glenn Close and Harry Connick, Jr in 2001; and a 2005 'concert' performance of the piece with Reba McIntyre, Brian Stokes Mitchell and Tom Wopat. Many native Hawaiians have responded to the overwhelming cultural force of *South Pacific* with scorn – particularly in regard to Bloody Mary. For example, poet and scholar Rob Wilson describes her as 'disfigured', 'slobbering' and 'a toxic Asian/Pacific brew of bad English, stinking body, and clownish manners'.[33] Wilson goes on to examine more recent attempts to 'counter the global machinery of … *South Pacific* … [with] the turn within Asian/Pacific literary culture in Hawai'i toward expressing and coalescing into some kind of *oppositional regionalism*'.[34] The 'Bamboo Ridge school' of native poets and authors often 'resists (understandably) national assimilation of self and culture; wants to start over (as it were) by going back to a time when the island economy was not so much caught up in the flows, mongrel mix, and struggles of imperial powers'.[35]

Juxtaposing the film version of *South Pacific* as the binary opposite of the Bamboo Ridge artists highlights how the history of the production has been erased even from the memory of native islanders. Furthermore, while not dismissing his criticism of the character within the text, Wilson's distaste for Bloody Mary does not take into account the real-life inspiration for her. Michener based the character on an actual Tonkinese woman he encountered in the New Hebrides. She got the name Bloody Mary not from chewing betel nuts but from her revolutionary politics, loudly advocating the overthrow of French colonial rule of her homeland off the Gulf of Tonkin – Vietnam.[36] In a letter to *The New York Times* in 1991, Michener described Bloody Mary as 'a 1944 prevision of those stubborn little Vietnamese women of 1965 who played a major role in defeating the entire American Army'.[37]

Thus, contrary to Wilson's assessment, it is possible to read into Bloody Mary the ghost of Asian resistance to white American and European paternalism (such as American Nellie Forbush and French Emile DeBecque overseeing two Tonkinese youngsters). The white American humanism that dominates *South Pacific* works to minimise racial or ethnic difference – it is all 'piffle', as Nellie comes to realise. One can read Mary, though, as resisting that assessment, refusing to be assimilated and asserting cultural distance. Such resistance occurs on multiple levels. Within the diegesis, she continually proclaims

Capt. Brackett (Russ Brown, foreground left) confronts Bloody Mary (Juanita Hall, foreground right) about the 'economic revolution' she is causing on the island

her own identity and agency, and the film version arguably focuses more attention on Mary than the stage version. The original play begins with Nellie and DeBecque sharing brandies and falling in love, then shifts to the beach where Mary and Cable meet for the first time. The film inverts this order, introducing Cable (John Kerr) and Mary first – and not getting to Nellie (Mitzi Gaynor) and DeBecque (Rossano Brazzi) until a half-hour into the picture. In reversing the sequences, the first number of the film is 'Bloody Mary Is the Girl I Love'. While definitely presented as a grotesque amusement (for the sailors and potentially for the audience), Mary is also quickly established as having power – haggling successfully with Billis (Ray Walston) over the price of grass skirts, and inciting Capt. Brackett (Russ Brown) to shout in exasperation, 'You are causing an economic revolution on this island! These French planters can't find a native to pick a coconut or milk a cow because you're paying them ten times as much to make these ridiculous grass skirts!' Mary replies, indignantly, 'French planter stingy stinker! Like you, crummy captain!' Mary remains the empowered one throughout the relationship with Cable, manoeuvring him expertly according to her game plan. She even declares that she will provide economic support for him and Liat upon their marriage.

However, Mary's assertion of independent agency and resistance to assimilation into white culture extends beyond her interaction with characters in the diegesis. The excess of the musical genre creates a space even in this tightly plotted and integrated piece for Bloody Mary to expand beyond her intended function in the narrative, thus often signifying more than her white creators can fully contain.[38] In their introduction to each other, it is Mary's gaze at Cable that is foregrounded rather than the other way around, and the emotions within that gaze are ripe with possibility. Certainly, the shot/reverse-shot structure, the shift to hazy filters and the surge of Rodgers's ethereal music evoke the traditional genre signature for 'love at first sight'. The text attempts to deflect (and thus explain away) the intensity of this moment by eventually introducing daughter Liat; however, the vague sense of something more between Mary and Cable is never completely erased. (It is worth noting that displacing the potential sexual desire towards Cable onto Liat also strengthens parallels between Mary and Nellie – both women are at one remove from actual interracial coupling.) Such an aura of inexplicability surrounds Mary throughout the narrative. Much is left unexplored and kept hidden: why she is drawn to Cable if she does not need his wealth or white privilege; the identity of Liat's father; how she came from the Gulf of Tonkin to Bali Ha'i. Mary only divulges what she wishes to divulge.

Of course, Mary is a fiction created by white authors – but the lack of answers indicates their inability to enter fully into Pacific and/or Asian consciousness. While presented as a slovenly comic grotesque, Mary still remains somewhat elusive to the grasp of her creators. The last scene for Mary and Liat works to reign in (or conquer) Mary's power. Mary finds Nellie, and asks her to help them find Cable, conceding that Liat will not marry anyone but him (not realising he has been killed). The narrative humbles

Mary, showing circumstances (and desires) finally beyond her control. She even stands lower than Nellie, and is framed to the side of the screen while Nellie hugs Liat in the centre. Since she is relegated literally to the sidelines in her final scene, the audience is encouraged not to focus on Mary – and not to recognise how many questions about her are still left unanswered.

Mary is not a revolutionary political figure by any means, and the demeaning stereotypical aspects that critics such as Wilson and Klein have enumerated are not to be dismissed. Yet, Mary does arguably contain an echo of exactly the type of 'regional opposition' that Wilson and the Bamboo Ridge authors champion, and which can be read into the labour strike that greeted the Fox production team in 1957. Hence, a purely hypothetical picture as a final image: director Joshua Logan and his crew desperately trying to get the workers of Kaua'i to 'keep on talkin' happy talk', but finding them on the picket line chanting 'Bloody Mary is the girl I love'.

Notes

1. James A. Michener, *Tales of the South Pacific* (New York: Macmillan, 1947), p. 9.
2. The data on the stage production is from Ethan Mordden, *Rodgers and Hammerstein* (New York: Harry N. Abrams, Inc., 1992), p. 121; the box-office figures for the film are in Aubrey Solomon, *Twentieth Century-Fox: A Corporate and Financial History* (London: Scarecrow Press, 1988), p. 227.
3. See Hugh Fordin, *Getting to Know Him: Oscar Hammerstein II, a Biography* (New York: Ungar, 1977), pp. 269–71; and Christina Klein, *Cold War Orientalism: Asia in the Middlebrow Imagination, 1945–1961* (Berkeley: University of California Press, 2003), pp. 143–90.
4. Klein, *Cold War Orientalism*.
5. Joshua Logan, *Josh: My Up and Down, In and Out Life* (New York: Delacorte Press, 1976).
6. 'Marines to Swarm Ashore Saturday at Barking Sands for "Operation Tradewinds" ', *Garden Island News*, 7 August 1957, pp. 1, 8.
7. Bill Osgerby, 'Beach Bound: Leisure Style and Popular Culture in Post-war America from *South Pacific* to *Beach Blanket Bingo*', in Bill Marshall and Robynn Stilwell (eds), *Musicals: Hollywood and Beyond* (Exeter, Devon: Intellect Books, 2000), p. 133.
8. Hall was not the only one dubbed. John Kerr was voice-doubled by Bill Lee, and Rossano Brazzi had the singing voice of Georgio Tozzi. Of the three, only Tozzi was given screen credit for his work.
9. LeRoy Prinz, Letter to Eric Stacey (18 June 1957) (UCLA Arts-Special Collections, Twentieth Century-Fox production files on *South Pacific* [UCLA]).
10. Klein, *Cold War Orientalism*, pp. 243–52, analyses the discourse over potential statehood after World War II.
11. US Department of Labor, Bureau of Labor Statistics, *Monthly Labor Review*, vol. 78 no. 12, December 1955, was a special issue on Hawai'i. James H. Shoemaker, 'Economic Forces and Growth Prospects', p. 1414, states that 'Hawai'i has an extraordinarily youthful population. The census of 1950 showed that half of the people in Hawai'i were less than 25 years of age; today this figure is even lower. For the Nation as a whole, the average age is slightly over 30.' Edwin C. Pendleton, 'Characteristics of the Labor Force', p. 1416, also makes this point. As for the plantation system in Hawai'i's past, both Thomas H. Ige, 'Working Conditions and Workers' Wages', p. 1424, and Robert Sroat and Ruth W. Loomis, 'Labor Legislation and Enforcement', p. 1432, use the term 'paternalistic' in their descriptions.
12. Sroat and Loomis, 'Labour Legislation and Enforcement', p. 1431.
13. Sroat and Loomis describe the growth of unionisation after the war, but attempt to play down the Communist ties (mention often occurs in footnotes rather than in the text). Klein, *Cold War Orientalism* (p. 248), describes the situation that the Department of Labor seems loath to admit.

14. Rob Wilson, *Reimagining the American Pacific: From 'South Pacific' to Bamboo Ridge and Beyond* (Durham, NC: Duke University Press, 2000), p. x.

15. Oscar Hammerstein II, Memo to Buddy Adler and Joshua Logan (7 March 1957) (UCLA).

16. Lee Crawford, Letter to Bess Lasky (10 June 1957) (UCLA).

17. Eric Stacey, Memo to Ben Kadish (29 July 1957) (UCLA).

18. Daily Production Reports (UCLA) indicate that the ceremony was shot at the Fox lot on 7–8 November 1957.

19. Location Survey Report (no author, completed in March 1957) (UCLA).

20. Sammy K. Arashiro, (IATSE) Local 665, Letter to Eric Stacey (11 March 1957) (UCLA).

21. Location Survey Report, p. 4.

22. Location Survey Report included data on seasonal weather conditions; Schedule (n.d.) (UCLA) lists the start and stop dates for the production.

23. Robert R. Weir, Letter to Eric Stacey (15 May 1957) (UCLA).

24. Robert R. Weir, Memo to Eric Stacey (30 July 1957) (UCLA).

25. 'Competition Has a Part in the Labor Market Also', *Garden Island News*, 17 June 1957, p. 4.

26. Sid Rogell, Letter to Eric Stacey (19 July 1957) (UCLA).

27. Eric Stacey, Letter to Ben Kadish (29 July 1957) (UCLA).

28. Eric Stacey, Telegram to Sid Rogell (12 August 1957) (UCLA).

29. Sid Rogell, Memo to Eric Stacey (13 August 1957) (UCLA).

30. All of this information was gleaned from the Daily Production Reports on the shooting of the film (UCLA).

31. Lyle Wheeler, Memo to John De Cuir (21 August 1957) (UCLA).

32. Among the news reports discussing Nilson's attempts to hire scabs, his refusal to recognise employee votes for a union and the AFL-CIO's countermeasures are 'Union's Election Offer for Nilson Is Rejected', *Garden Island News*, 3 July 1957, p. 5; 'Nilson Rejects Two-Point Union Proposal; Steps Not Yet Taken to End Walkout', *Garden Island News*, 24 July 1957, p. 1; 'AFL-CIO Union Tightens Strike Grip on Nilson with Steps for ILWU Support', *Garden Island News*, 11 September 1957, p. 1.

33. Wilson, *Reimagining the American Pacific*, pp. 173, 180.

34. Ibid., p. 163 (emphasis in original).

35. Ibid., p. viii.

36. James A. Michener, *The World Is My Home: A Memoir* (1992; reprint, New York: Ballantine, 1998), p. 149.

37. James A. Michener, Letter to the editor, *New York Times*, 1 September 1991, Sec. 2, p. 2. Klein, *Cold War Orientalism*, pp. 167–70, also exposes the Vietnam connection to the text and Bloody Mary's real-life inspiration.

38. Elsewhere I have argued that, although the white power structure in charge at Fox tended to resort to stereotypical ideas of race and ethnicity, a number of minority performers were able to negotiate and subtly upend the racial dynamics in these films. See Sean Griffin, 'The Gang's All Here: Generic vs. Racial Integration in the 1940s Musical', *Cinema Journal*, vol. 42 no. 1, Fall 2002, pp. 21–45.

9 The Singing Sixties:
Rethinking the Julie Andrews Roadshow Musical

Brett Farmer

In 1967, Stanley Donen, the choreographer-director responsible for many of the most celebrated MGM musicals of the 1950s and dubbed by at least one critic the 'King of Hollywood musicals', released his twenty-second motion picture, *Bedazzled*.[1] Featuring a light-hearted, episodic storyline about a hapless short-order cook who makes a Faustian deal with the devil in order to win his love's affections, *Bedazzled* would seem on paper to have been the ideal fantasy vehicle for a musical director like Donen and, had it been made a decade earlier, it would very likely have been given the full MGM treatment. Donen, however, made his last musical in 1958 – coincidentally, the Faustian-themed *Damn Yankees* – and by 1967 he had turned his directorial attentions almost exclusively to a string of increasingly frank, contemporary sex comedies that, like *Bedazzled*, he made under the aegis of his own independent production company. *Bedazzled* might thus be taken to substantiate a certain orthodox reading of American film history in which the 1960s is cast as a period of marked decline, if not terminal demise, for the classical Hollywood musical. Patterned on standard evolutionary narratives of genre formation, this reading understands the musical to have reached its artistic and popular peak in the 1940s and early 50s, after which it rapidly lost cultural relevance and marketability, due principally to the dissolution of the studio system and changing taste economies, before finally being left, in the melodramatic words of one recent commentator, 'to wither and wander destitute, demeaned and defrocked throughout the 1960s'.[2] In its stead, Hollywood turned to small, independently produced films like *Bedazzled* whose mix of formal unconventionality, contemporary themes and settings, and youthful iconoclasm seemed better attuned than the glossy escapism of musicals to the changing spirit of the times. Or so the argument goes.

There is, however, another history of the Hollywood musical in the 1960s and it is a history that is also evidenced, albeit pejoratively, in *Bedazzled*. When Stanley Moon (Dudley Moore), the socially inept protagonist of the film, finally agrees to his Faustian contract, he is informed by the Devil, played with deadpan insouciance by Peter Cook, that in exchange for his soul he will be granted seven wishes. To realise these wishes, all he need do is close his eyes and utter the magical incantation, 'Julie Andrews'. A wry in-joke for audiences of the time, this satirical reference to the famous singing star of stage and screen musicals highlights that, in 1967, Julie Andrews was a name, quite literally, to conjure with. Having already appeared in several smash-hit Broadway shows, Andrews shot to global superstardom in the mid-1960s with a number of extraordinarily successful family musicals, most notably *Mary Poppins* (1964) and, what was at the time the highest-grossing film in history, *The Sound of Music* (1965). Firmly middlebrow in form and address with a family-oriented narrative and spectacular but roundly traditional aesthetics, these films not only secured a reputation for Andrews as the reigning box-office queen of wholesome musical fare – a reputation that, as *Bedazzled* attests, was ripe for lampooning from the start – but they also fanned a flurry of industrial emulation that saw the film musical enjoy a brief but intense period of renaissant popularity and unprecedented cultural prestige in the era's distinctive cycle of big-budget, 'roadshow' musicals.[3]

Theatre façades showing the 'special event' theatricality of the Andrews roadshow musical

Dubbed 'super-gigantic block-buster musicals' by the ever-sardonic Pauline Kael, these films were big in every sense, aiming for broad mass-audience appeal via an aura of 'special event' distinction with lavish production values, lengthy running times and state-of-the-art cinematic technologies.[4] In addition, they used the value-adding presentational system of 'roadshowing' to simulate a live theatre-going sense of occasion, with the films screened exclusively at select first-run venues, usually in prime metropolitan locations, on a reserved-seat basis, complete with souvenir programmes, intermissions and specially composed overture, entr'acte and exit music. Defined in these broad terms, the roadshow musical was not strictly new. As a way of marketing select 'prestige' film products, roadshowing had been in use since at least the late silent era and it became particularly widespread in the 1950s when it was redeployed as part of a set of industrial strategies in Hollywood's ongoing battle to lure audiences back from the newly formed suburbs and away from television and other competing leisure pursuits.[5] Generally, however, most earlier roadshown vehicles were drawn from traditional epic genres like historical dramas, adventures, Westerns and war films, with only the occasional musical appearing, albeit with slightly more frequency in the 1950s. The generic balance shifted dramatically in the 1960s, largely due to the commercial under-performance of several roadshow epics, including *The Alamo* (1960), *Cleopatra* (1962) and *The Fall of the Roman Empire* (1964), and the unexpected box-office ascendancy of roadshow musicals such as *West Side Story* (1961), *My Fair Lady* (1964) and, of course, *Mary Poppins* and *The Sound of Music*.[6] Compounding the sense of industrial surprise was the transnational popularity of these films and the fact that they performed exceedingly well, not just at the domestic North American box office, but also in overseas markets that had formerly been notoriously resistant to Hollywood musical product.[7] The 'runaway success' of these films was so phenomenal and apparent that, as Mark Harris writes, suddenly in the mid-1960s it seemed that 'every studio in Hollywood was pushing hard to get a giant roadshow musical, or two, or three, into production'.[8]

Precisely because *Poppins* and *Music* were far and away the most popular – read: profitable – entries in this industrial cycle, Julie Andrews quickly assumed an emblematic status as the star most

Posters for *The Sound of Music* (1965) and *Thoroughly Modern Millie* (1967)

closely associated with the 1960s roadshow musical, a position further cemented by the follow-up success of *Thoroughly Modern Millie* (1967), a lightweight, musical-comedy star vehicle that was hastily reworked in early production as a prestige spectacular to cash in on the roadshow craze and Andrews's meteoric celebrity.[9] It is a synecdochal star–genre coupling that has proved surprisingly enduring. As recently as 2003, a syndicated news article on film musical history could still marshal Andrews as a legible shorthand for the whole era of the roadshow musical, declaring sensationally that 'Julie Andrews killed the movie musical', because roadshow vehicles 'like *Star!* and *Mary Poppins* were so expensive to make that they put the form out of business'.[10] As this excerpt suggests, almost as quickly as it rose, the Julie Andrews roadshow musical and the generic cycle of which it was part waned, and following a number of high-profile failures – *Star!* (1968) and *Darling Lili* (1970) – both Andrews and the roadshow musical were, by decade's close, deemed passé.

It is an assessment that has in many ways become the standard critical take on Andrews and the era of the roadshow musical at large where – in consonance with the generalised reading of the 1960s as the deathbed of the musical referenced above – both are viewed as historical and industrial hiccups, anachronistic throwbacks to earlier forms of stardom and genre. Most generously, the roadshow musical and its principal star are glossed as a nostalgic 'last hurrah' of cultural traditionalism that offered audiences of the time an escapist respite from the social tumult of the 1960s: 'transport[ing] a scarred generation … out of the present's lack of political clarity and social cohesion, back to a past [that] seemed clear and coherent'.[11] Less sympathetically, they are chided as signs of industrial and social reactionism, with Andrews dismissed as 'a cipher for values already lost [and without] the slightest relevance to th[e] period in which [her] films were made',[12] and Hollywood's 'desperate search for the next *Sound of Music*' deemed to 'reveal just how out of step the studios had become, how little studio executives seemed to understand or appreciate the marketplace'.[13] In fact, Barry Langford opines that the Andrews roadshow musical does nothing so much as highlight the 'growing disjunction of the classical musical's formal and thematic direction and both the world and the industry of which it remained a part', concluding that '*The Sound of Music* proved not the harbinger of a new era for the classical musical, but its swansong'.[14]

The net effect of these widespread critical responses is an operative dehistoricisation wherein the Andrews roadshow musical is essentially written out of film and cultural history, defined as a marginalised epiphenomenon, a hangover from an earlier age that was somehow *in* the 1960s but not really *of* the 1960s. It is a historical erasure that is quite literal when one considers the scant attention afforded the Andrews musical in much of the available literature.[15] Yet, the extraordinary popularity of these films – the fact that they clearly spoke to enormously large groups of people in acutely meaningful ways – highlights both their centrality to and embeddedness within their historical milieux. These are films that quite simply 'matter' in historical terms, both in the sense of being significant to their era – *The Sound of Music* was after all the single most successful film of the 1960s and, even today, in inflationary-adjusted figures, remains the third highest-grossing motion picture of all time – and in the sense of emerging out of, and bearing determinant traces of, their specific material locations in time and place. What is thus needed is a critical reassessment that takes stock of this materiality, that apprehends the Julie Andrews musical and, by extension, the whole cycle of roadshow musicals not as an anachronistic refusal of history but as a distinct historical articulation that was directly shaped by and responsive to a complex but determinate set of industrial, cultural and social forces.

The beginnings of such a reassessment can arguably be found in recent revisionist scholarship that challenges the popular view of post-studio Hollywood history in terms of a simple paradigm shift from the 'old' mass-oriented Hollywood of escapist family fare to the youth-oriented 'New Hollywood' of aesthetic innovation and graphic realism – the 'transition from *The Sound of Music* to *Easy Rider*' in the neatly telescoped metonymy of one recent reckoning[16] – on the grounds that it 'produces a partial and misleading picture of the American film industry, its outputs and its audiences in the 1960s and early 1970s'.[17] While agreeing that American cinema, like society at large, experienced profound changes during this time, this newer work holds that the changes were neither as singular nor as absolute as generally imagined, and that a longer historical view reveals a more complicated picture. Of particular significance to the concerns of this paper is the reassessment offered of the changing fortunes of 1960s roadshow musicals.

Against the standard view that the box-office underachievement of roadshow musicals in the late 1960s – such as Andrews's *Star!* and *Darling Lili*, but also other high-profile entries including *Dr Dolittle* (1967), *Finian's Rainbow* (1968), *Hello, Dolly!* (1969) and *Paint Your Wagon* (1969) – evidences the musical's loss of cultural appeal and relevance, recent scholarship points out that, though these films may have posted on-paper losses, many of them actually enjoyed solid box-office returns, frequently featuring in annual lists of the biggest hits. When other, even more profitable examples are factored in – *Oliver!* (1968), *Funny Girl* (1968), *Fiddler on the Roof* (1971) – it is apparent that, as Steve Neale opines, 'big budget road-shown musicals' remained 'popular at the box office throughout the 1960s and early 1970s'.[18] Peter Krämer goes even further, arguing that a popular demand for musicals, and other traditional roadshown fare, endured well into the 1970s and beyond. He cites the successful theatrical re-release of roadshow musicals throughout the ensuing decade – including, importantly, the three hit Andrews musicals (*Poppins*, *Music* and *Millie*), all of which enjoyed highly profitable reissues in 1972/3, with *Poppins* re-released again in 1980 – as well as high-rating TV broadcasts and consistent popularity in audience polls, concluding that 'Roadshow Era superhits remained absolutely central to American film culture' until at least the late 1970s.[19]

Having thus determined that the roadshow musical did not suffer a radical loss of cultural popularity in the 1960s, this revisionist history sets about recontextualising the form's demise not as an effect of sociocultural irrelevance, tectonic generational shift or even diminished marketability, as generally claimed, but rather more prosaically as the simple by-product of convergent economic and industrial factors. As already noted, following the success of *Poppins* and *Music*, Hollywood studios cranked up their production of roadshow musicals. In addition, exponentially increased revenues in the period from the sale of films to broadcast television, especially elite product like roadshow films, enticed a rash of new production companies to enter the field, thus not only 'increas[ing] the supply of films' but, through added competition for properties and talent, 'contributing to the escalation of budgets to a level insupportable by theatrical demand'.[20] Add to the mix the fact that many earlier successful roadshow musicals were still playing throughout this period – *Music*, for example, screened in its original North American release for a record-breaking four and a half years well into late 1969 [21] – and the net effect was a market quickly saturated with 'too many movies … competing for the box-office dollar' and revenue 'spread more thinly'.[22] The oversupply of product was not unique to roadshow musicals – a generalised culture of overproduction plagued the industry as a whole in the late 1960s, with financiers estimating studios were spending double what the market could support – but it impacted roadshown product particularly hard, both because of the scale of fiscal investment in these films, and because of the aura of special distinction on which they traded.[23] When the bubble inevitably burst in the infamous 'crash' of 1969/70, in which the industry posted record losses in excess of $200 million, roadshow musicals were unsurprisingly the first in the line of fire. Amid an intense period of sweeping industrial reorganisation that largely set in place the current Hollywood system of corporate ownership and media conglomerates, existing musical productions were scaled down, slated ones cancelled and the cycle of roadshow musicals that so characterised the mid- to late 1960s dwindled to a mere trickle before disappearing altogether in the early 70s.[24]

While it is not difficult to understand why the studios turned away from roadshow musicals as they did, especially in view of the unstable and panicked industrial climate in which it occurred, it was arguably an 'over-drastic reaction' that created further problems of its own.[25] By relinquishing the road-show musical, Hollywood studios effectively lost one of the few remaining products at the time still geared to a general 'family' audience. Matters weren't helped any by the fact that the studios' newer, leaner production slates were given over almost entirely to the sort of iconoclastic, youth-oriented films dubbed by Paul Monaco the 'cinema of sensation' and Peter Krämer 'taboo breakers' for their accent on graphic violence, sex and other such previously proscribed material.[26] This product was relatively cheap to make, certainly in comparison to roadshow films, and its strong appeal to the burgeoning youth market – which had for some time been emerging as post-war Hollywood's most loyal audience segment and, with the full flush of baby-boomers coming of age in the late 1960s, a statistically ever more significant one – seemed to hold out the promise of more dependable returns. However, it also served to further alienate other key market segments, particularly those that had helped constitute the previous family-audience mainstay such as women, children and older viewers, by fostering a new-found sense of cinema as increasingly agonistic and exclusionary.

Because the roadshow musical was so centrally invested in the mass family market, the alienation of these core audience segments proved irreparably damaging. This is possibly nowhere more true than in relation to the female audience, whose patronage had been pivotal to the success of the 1960s roadshow musical, in general, and the Julie Andrews musical, in particular.[27] While their enormous success suggests that Andrews's films clearly enjoyed wide and diverse audience support, there is strong evidence to indicate that they were especially popular with women. Commentators have frequently drawn attention to the markedly female-dominated profile of Andrews's fanbase.[28] Writing about 'an inspection of audiences at three theaters in Hollywood where [Andrews's] films were playing', a 1967 newspaper profile remarks on the preponderance of 'lovely old ladies' and 'rows of enraptured little girls', with the writer quipping,

I have never seen so many middle-aged housewives in hats gathered together in one place as I saw at a packed afternoon showing of *Thoroughly Modern Millie*. 'Oh, isn't she cute! Isn't she just darling!' they whispered to one another throughout the film.[29]

Moreover, female audiences of the Andrews musical were noted for their astonishing repeat business, with many filmgoers averaging several visits and, in the case of *Music*, some returning to see the film record-breaking numbers of times well into the hundreds.[30] Andrews's strong female popularity was certainly not lost on industrial gatekeepers, with promotional campaigns for her films openly addressing female viewers through both a generalised discourse of feminine thematics, about which more below, and specific exhibition strategies such as coach parties and matinée screenings for women's groups; while extra-textually, publicity stories and interviews with Andrews were widely and strategically channelled to female-oriented publications.

In this context, it could be claimed that the Andrews roadshow musical signals one of the last times Hollywood explicitly geared its big-budget product to a female audience. Where throughout much of the studio era, Hollywood had assumed women as its dominant, or at least most influential, audience and tailored its products accordingly, a shift took place in the 1950s and 60s as the industry increasingly reoriented itself to a new target audience of young men.[31] Richard Maltby contends that this regendering of its assumed audience 'was the real marker of the change from the Classical to post-Classical Hollywood', noting that in 'the two decades after 1970, women were rarely specifically addressed as an audience, and then only by modestly budgeted pictures', and that, as a result, women diminished as an appreciable moviegoing force across this era.[32] One of the indicators frequently cited to evidence this gendered shift is the marked decline in popularity, and by extension industrial power, of female stars. In contrast to earlier times, where women had proved among the most popular, and certainly most iconic, of Hollywood's star commodities, in the 1960s and after, female stardom lost much of its cultural and industrial potency, prompting Paul Monaco to dub the decade 'the twilight of the goddesses'.[33]

Andrews assumes a significant position in this history. Not only was she the last woman to occupy the number one spot in the industry's annual list of top-ten box-office stars, in 1966 and 1967 – a distinction held for over thirty years till Julia Roberts momentarily occupied the position in 1999, the only other woman to do so to date – but publicity discourses of the time drew frequent parallels between Andrews and earlier models of iconic female star dominance.[34] 'She is not just an ordinary movie personality,' gushed *The Hollywood Reporter* in 1965,

> she is a phenomenon. Once there was Mary Pickford, then there was Garbo, now there is Julie. She is very likely going to be the object of one of the most intense and sustained love affairs between moviegoers and a star in the history of motion pictures.[35]

While this widespread association with classical traditions of female stardom possibly fuelled common perceptions of Andrews as old-fashioned and anachronistic, it also encoded her screen persona with a strong dynamic of conferred authority and empowered femininity. Indeed, for all the glib ridicule of the Andrews image as singularly sweet and anodyne – what one critic of the era dubbed 'Miss Sunshine of the Sixties'[36] – a survey of popular press commentaries published during the height of her celebrity reveals a surprising complexity of ascribed characteristics, in which a particular premium is placed on her perceived attributes of strength and capability, with words such as 'determination', 'grit', 'professionalism', 'trouper', 'energy', 'industry' and 'intelligence' abounding. An enthusiastic 1966 profile published in the otherwise soberly middlebrow *Films and Filming* serves as a representative example: summarily titled 'The All-Conquering Governess', it notes Andrews's association with wholesomeness, virtue and what it describes as 'other sickly comforts' but argues these are more than offset by competing qualities of 'common-sense, levelheadedness, independence', all of which 'she conveys ... with a crisp sense of humour' and an air that 'underneath there are always currents running – [that] she might start throwing things like Carole Lombard or vamping like Mae West'. Like these and other 'stars of the 'thirties', it continues, she is 'strong and sensible – and always witty ... What they had and what she has is style, by which I mean discipline.'[37]

A discourse of star-empowered femininity is equally crucial to the intratextual dynamics of the Julie Andrews musical and offers further contextualisation for these films' popularity with women. The Hollywood musical at large has long been noted for an accent on strong performing women and a 'prominence of female stardom' more generally, which, coupled with the genre's 'foregrounding of ... specifically feminine interests and competences', is widely understood to constitute the genre's principal female appeal.[38] It's an appeal that is not without qualification, however, with many critics noting the musical's penchant for ultimately constraining and disempowering female stardom, whether through classic structures of cinematic fetishism, where the female star image is transvalued as a com-modified icon of male desire, or through narrative mechanisms of hymeneal closure, where the female star is yoked to a domesticating structure of marital union. The Julie Andrews musical signals a strik-ing exception, if not challenge, to these tendencies on both counts.

In terms of objectification, while Andrews as star is inevitably the focus of specular attention and dominates the visual field in her films, there is seldom any sense that she is being encoded as a static erotic icon in the way that Laura Mulvey famously critiques the fetishisation of Dietrich or Monroe, say. Indeed, commentaries on Andrews almost uniformly draw attention to what they interpret as the star's patently 'unerotic', even 'sexless' image.[39] A 1966 cover story on Andrews in *Time* magazine starts with the following frank assessment of what it takes to be her lack of conventional erotic allure:

> It is doubtful that the boys in Viet Nam regard her as their favorite pinup … Her curves do not pop the eye. Her legs are a little too lean and a mite long … Her jaw is on the prognathous side. Her feet are a little less than dainty (size 8); when she played Cinderella on TV, her slipper could almost have fit the Prince. And she's got freckles on her nose. … If it is not sex appeal, what is it?[40]

As the metonymic conflation of Cinderella and the Prince here suggests, Andrews's alleged lack of sex appeal – which of course simply means her apparent disregard of normative measures of female desir-ability – frequently registers as a disruption of orthodox scripts of sexual difference, crystallised most explicitly in the category of 'tomboyishness' which informs the Andrews image both at the level of spe-cific role – notably, the rambunctious Maria who 'climbs a tree and scrapes her knee' but also the ener-getic, egalitarian flapper Millie – and general persona: the jolly air of schoolgirl athleticism, no-nonsense pragmatism and, most famously, trademark bobbed hairdo, described by one magazine as her 'depend-able, comfortable tomboy cut'.[41] Moreover, when Andrews did essay more conventionally sexualised roles, the strength of the tomboyish persona was such that it undercut their efficacy. Part of the reason for the relative underperformance of *Star!* and *Darling Lili*, for example, other than the industrial issues mentioned earlier, undoubtedly lies in the difficulty audiences had in accepting Andrews in these films' roles of glamorous showgirl and Mata Hari-esque spy-courtesan respectively.[42]

A similar sense of gender disruption marks the Julie Andrews musical's relations to the genre's other traditional axis of feminine containment: marital union. It is a commonplace to argue that the Hollywood musical is constitutively invested in a teleological system of heterosexual courtship played out through a dual-focus structure between male and female leads that moves inexorably towards creation of the couple and, with it, the reconciliation of thematic and social differences.[43] While this hymeneal imperative is certainly not absent from the Andrews musical, it is problematised on several counts. Looking across the five musicals Andrews made in the 1960s: *Poppins* features no romantic union at all (the film's restoration of the Banks family unit arguably assumes a similar function, but Andrews role therein is ambiguated by the fact that her character flies away); in *Music*, the wedding occurs two-thirds through, with the film ending somewhat indefinitely as the von Trapps cross a mountain peak into an unknown future; while the remaining three – *Millie*, *Star!* and *Darling Lili* – feature what could only be described as weak romantic resolutions. Furthermore, what *is* largely absent from the Andrews musical is the dual-focus structure of gendered parallelism that is typically understood to give the classic musical's hymeneal resolution its textual and ideological weight.

Julie Andrews in the opening sequence of *The Sound of Music*

Almost without exception, the Julie Andrews musical is precisely that, 'the Julie Andrews musical', with male co-stars relegated to a secondary, even marginalised role. It's a dynamic underscored by the fact that Andrews's male co-stars are mostly non-musical performers who either don't sing at all (Richard Crenna in *Star!*, Rock Hudson in *Darling Lili*) or do so peripherally and weakly (Christopher Plummer, dubbed by Bill Lee, in *Music*, and James Fox in *Millie*). Conversely, Andrews, by virtue both of her extraordinary vocal prowess and the film's construction of her as textual fulcrum, dominates the space of musical performance, which, in the film musical, is tantamount to owning the show. Thus, when the men in her films do enter into some sort of romantic or social union with Andrews's characters, it is effectively on her terms.[44]

The Sound of Music is exemplary in this context if only for the fact that, as its title makes plain, it highlights the functional role of musical spectacle in the text's orchestration of character relations and desires. The famous opening sequence, where an accelerative montage of panoramic alpine vistas culminates in a forward aerial shot of Maria/Andrews striding forcefully toward the camera, twirling and then literally singing out her heart in the title song, forges a striking union between the star and the expressive space of the spectacular number. Augmented by the roadshow's epic production values of 70mm widescreen cinematography, Deluxe colour and five-track stereophonic sound, the sequence constructs Maria/Andrews as a powerful figure of authoritative presence who not only dominates the physical landscape around her – in a way that is customary in epic male genres but that, even today, is quite exceptional for female cinematic representation – but arrogates to herself the full weight of what Steve Neale suggestively terms the 'presentational prowess' of cinematic spectacle, 'the overwhelming sensual experience of images and sounds'.[45] That the sequence occurs before the opening credits – something of a common feature of the Andrews musical – and, thus quite literally, outside of the centripetal colonisation of narrativity, further strengthens the sense of Andrews as an authorising force who drives and controls the text rather than the other way round. It is a dynamic that characterises many of the film's subsequent musical numbers, notably Maria's anthem to liberated femininity, 'I Have Confidence', and her parallel emancipatory tutelage of the von Trapp children in the extended 'Do Re Mi' sequence. The vocal and physical exuberance of Andrews's masterful performance in these numbers, combined with the panoramic mobile cinematography and free editing of the film's spectacular roadshow aesthetics, construct a utopian vision of what Richard Dyer describes as 'the world come under the control and determination of the heroine, whose very essence is music'.[46]

Positioned as not only external but inimical to that world, Captain von Trapp seeks to repress Maria and, true to the assonance of his name, contain her within 'his' world of patriarchal order and domesticated propriety. Her subsequent marriage to him, played out not too subtly to the reprised strains of the very song sung earlier by the nuns in the abbey in exasperation over how to 'solve a problem like Maria', might suggest he is successful in that endeavour, and at a certain level he is. An ethos of relative repression marks the final post-hymeneal act of *Music* where the film changes formal gears, effectively moving from the joyous thematics and unfettered mobile aesthetics of the musical into the darker shadings of the war film, a shift with obvious gender implications. The net effect of this change though is to evoke a strong desire for escape from the repressive constraints of Maria's post-marital containment and a return to the exuberant spaces of musical expression that characterise the earlier parts of the film, a desire given narrative rendering through the von Trapp family's flight from the Nazis. That this flight is realised through the narrative agency of Maria and her music, augmented by additional female assistance – the family manage to evade the Nazis by performing in concert, largely singing the very songs Maria has taught them, after which they are hidden and helped across the border by the nuns from her abbey – and concludes with the family back on the mountain top marked so spectacularly as Maria's space in the film's prologue – accompanied musically by a full-throated, female-dominant choral imperative to 'climb ev'ry mountain … till you find your dream' – serve to reassert female primacy and control over the text and to conclude with the utopian fantasy of a feminine-author(is)ed world.

It's not difficult to understand the lure of such a fantasy for many women, especially in historical context. When the Julie Andrews musical first emerged in 1964, it was within the burgeoning context of second-wave feminism and sweeping changes to traditional sexual politics. In the year or two preceding, Betty Friedan had published her groundbreaking critique of 'the problem with no name', lifting the lid on the myth that women were fulfilled in their roles as suburban housewives, and Helen Gurley Brown had penned her equally influential ode to 'the single girl', exhorting women to find self-realisation through a professional, social and sexual life defined in their own terms.[47] The Julie Andrews musical is not of course a direct articulation of these feminist discourses, at least not in an uncomplicated or straightforward manner, but it does emerge out of the same socio-historical milieux and arguably responds to the same sets of cultural-political pressures and anxieties. That it does so ambivalently and contradictorily – which is ultimately the condition of most cultural production, especially in its mainstream variants – does not diminish the fact of its significance as a popular cultural trend that offered an important space for women to cathect feelings and desires that can only be defined as prototypically feminist and assume diverse, even critical, perspectives from which to imagine social and sexual alternatives.[48]

At the end of a generally favourable review of *Darling Lili*, the fifth and final of the Julie Andrews roadshow musicals, Vincent Canby of *The New York Times* appends the following retrospective coda:

> As a historical note, I might also point out that *Darling Lili* is in itself the kind of romantic gesture we're not likely to see again for a very long time. It's the last of the mammoth movie musicals … inspired by the success of *The Sound of Music*. … I doubt that Hollywood, now practically broke and trying desperately to make a connection with the youth market, will ever again indulge itself in this sort of splendidly extravagant, quite frivolous enterprise.[49]

The striking mix here of eulogy and casual dismissal is something that has tended to characterise most responses to the Julie Andrews-led cycle of 1960s roadshow musicals, which is routinely written off as a spectacular but ultimately 'frivolous enterprise' with little correspondence to, let alone significance for, the material social world, especially one as tumultuous and politically charged as the 60s. This paper has attempted to suggest why such a response is inadequate, as well as to begin to lay the grounds for a more productive reassessment. The Julie Andrews films, along with other examples of the 1960s roadshow musical, warrant much fuller analysis than can be given them here. In particular, the question of how these films spoke to women merits deeper and more careful consideration, as does the reception of these films among other audience segments, such as children and gays and lesbians, that have also been crucial constituencies of the Andrews musical and its variable historical circulations.[50] As apologists of the musical frequently stress, far from masking social and historical realities, the extravagant, utopian dimensions of the genre render these realities in aesthetic form, while also providing imaginary scope for the realisation of more capacious alternatives. It is a liberating impulse that the Julie Andrews roadshow musical has extended in ample measure to its enraptured audiences, in the 1960s and beyond.

Notes

1. David Quinlan, *Quinlan's Film Directors: The Ultimate Guide to Directors of the Big Screen* (London: B. T. Batsford, 1999), p. 62.
2. Philip Brophy, 'Where Sound Is: Locating the Absent Aural in Film Theory', in James Donald and Michael Renov (eds), *The SAGE Handbook of Film Studies* (London: SAGE, 2008), p. 429.
3. As John Belton points out, from 'one perspective, the 1960s marked the high point of the musical' in that more musicals won Best Picture Academy Awards during that decade – an astonishing four wins from seven nominations – than in any other before or since. *American Cinema/American Culture*, 3rd edition (New York: McGraw-Hill, 2008), p. 162.
4. Pauline Kael, '*Paint Your Wagon*: Somebody Else's Success', in Joseph Morgenstern and Stefan Kanfer (eds), *Film 69/70: An Anthology by the National Association of Film Critics* (New York: Simon & Schuster, 1970), p. 112.
5. For a history of roadshowing, see: Justin Wyatt, 'From Roadshowing to Saturation Release: Majors, Independents, and Marketing/Distribution Innovations', in Jon Lewis (ed.), *The New American Cinema* (Durham, NC: Duke University Press, 1998), pp. 64–86; and Sheldon Hall, 'Tall Revenue Features: The Genealogy of the Modern Blockbuster', in Steve Neale (ed.), *Genre and Contemporary Hollywood* (London: BFI, 2002), pp. 11–26.
6. Strictly speaking, *Mary Poppins* was not a roadshow film in that, in line with Disney's populist distribution policies, it was exhibited continuously with tickets at 'popular prices' rather than the more restrictive roadshow practice of limited sessions and expensive 'hard ticket' prices. However, with a comparatively lengthy running time of 139 minutes, an accent on cinematic spectacle and special effects, and a major marketing and merchandising campaign, the biggest in Disney's history to that date, *Poppins* was effectively positioned and received as part of the broader roadshow musical trend. Disney-Buena Vista, *Mary Poppins Pressbook and Exhibitor's Manual* (Burbank, CA: Walt Disney Productions, 1964).
7. Thomas Thompson, 'Turning U.S. Musicals to Overseas Box Office', *Life*, 12 March 1965, pp. 55–8.
8. Mark Harris, *Pictures at a Revolution: Five Movies and the Birth of the New Hollywood* (New York: Penguin, 2008), p. 129.
9. For some reason, *Thoroughly Modern Millie* is misrepresented in several sources as a commercial flop. While certainly not in the league of *Poppins* or *Music*, it was a major hit earning domestic rentals of

$16 million and international rentals in excess of $40 million on a production cost of $6 million, sufficient to make it the highest-grossing film to that date in (the releasing studio) Universal's history and the seventh most popular musical of the 1960s. See Lawrence Cohn, 'All-Time Film Rental Champs', *Variety*, 10 May 1993, pp. C76–106, 108; and Stanley Green and Elaine Schmidt, *Hollywood Musicals: Year by Year*, 2nd edition (Milwaukee, WI: Hal Leonard, 1999), p. 240.

10. Gerald Nachman, '60s Flops That (Almost) Killed Musicals on Film', *San Francisco Chronicle*, 24 August 2003. <www.sfgate.com/cgi-bin/article.cgi?f=/c/a/2003/08/24/MO295005.DTL&hw=doting&sn=374&sc=378> (accessed 29 November 2009).

11. Gerald Mast, *Can't Help Singin': The American Musical on Stage and Screen* (New York: Overlook Press, 1987), p. 218.

12. Derek Owen, 'Julie Andrews', *Film Dope*, no. 1, 1972, p. 38.

13. Jon Lewis, *Hollywood v. Hard Core: How the Struggle over Censorship Saved the Modern Film Industry* (New York: New York University Press, 2001), p. 152.

14. Barry Langford, *Film Genre: Hollywood and Beyond* (Edinburgh: Edinburgh University Press, 2005), pp. 95–6.

15. To give but one example, the recent volume on the 1960s in the 'Rutgers Screen Decades' series, whose avowed mission is to 'illuminate … the essential movies that define an era', makes next to no mention of Andrews or her films other than one or two passing comments such as the volume editor's sneering one-line dismissal of *The Sound of Music* as 'a work of calculated sentimental claptrap' that merely serves to demonstrate how Hollywood 'struggled to remain in touch with the decade's burgeoning youth culture'. Barry Keith Grant (ed.), *American Cinema of the 1960s: Themes and Variations* (New Brunswick, NJ: Rutgers University Press, 2008), p. 16.

16. Michael Buening, 'Book Review: Geoffrey Nowell-Smith, *Making Waves: New Cinema of the 1960s*', *Pop Matters*, 4 January 2008. <www.popmatters.com/pm/review/making-waves-by-geoffrey-nowell-smith/> (accessed 29 November 2009).

17. Steve Neale, ' "The Last Good Time We Ever Had?": Revising the Hollywood Renaissance', in Linda Ruth Williams and Michael Hammond (eds), *Contemporary American Cinema* (Maidenhead, Berks.: Open University Press, 2006), p. 91.

18. Neale, ' "Last Good Time We Ever Had?" ', p. 100.

19. Peter Krämer, *The New Hollywood: From* Bonnie and Clyde *to* Star Wars (London: Wallflower, 2005), p. 46.

20. Neale, ' "Last Good Time We Ever Had?" ', p. 103.

21. 'Four-Year Hiatus Due for *Sound of Music*', *Film and Television Daily*, 8 July 1969, p. 1.

22. Richard Maltby, *Hollywood Cinema* (Oxford: Blackwell, 2003), p. 175.

23. Hall, 'Tall Revenue Features', pp. 16–17; Maltby, *Hollywood Cinema*, p. 175; Neale, ' "Last Good Time We Ever Had?" ', p. 104.

24. Hall, 'Tall Revenue Features', pp. 17–18.

25. Krämer, *The New Hollywood*, p. 61.

26. Paul Monaco, *The Sixties, 1960–1969* (Berkeley: University of California Press, 2001), p. 2; Krämer, *New Hollywood*, pp. 47–58.

27. Krämer, *New Hollywood*, pp. 62–3. See also Peter Krämer, 'A Powerful Cinema-going Force? Hollywood and Female Audiences since the 1960s', in Melvyn Stokes and Richard Maltby (eds), *Identifying Hollywood's Audiences: Cultural Identity and the Movies* (London: BFI, 1999), pp. 93–108.

28. See, *inter alia*: Richard Dyer, 'The Sound of Music', in Dyer, *Only Entertainment* (London and New York: Routledge, 1994), pp. 45–59; and Bruce Babington, 'Song, Narrative and the Mother's Voice: A Deepish

Reading of Julie Andrews', in Babington (ed.), *British Stars and Stardom: From Alma Taylor to Sean Connery* (Manchester: Manchester University Press, 2001), pp. 192–204.

29. Jane Wilson, 'Thoroughly Wholesome Julie', *LA Times West*, 15 October 1967, p. 12. Similar observations, often with the same tenor of thinly veiled condescension, are still made today. A newspaper report on the contemporary cult phenomenon of Sing-A-Long-A-*Sound of Music*, for example, notes that the audience, which it facetiously dubs 'the faithful', are 'mostly women in their 40s and 50s' and '[l]ittle old ladies of both genders and all ages'. Martin Knelman, 'The World Is Alive with Sentimental *Sound of Music*', *The Toronto Star*, 18 June 2000, p. E1.

30. Joan Barthel, 'Biggest Money-Making Movie of All Time – How Come?', *New York Times Magazine*, 20 November 1966, pp. 45–84 *passim*; Percy Livingstone, ' "Dim Little Flick" Becomes a World-Beater', *Kine Weekly*, 17 December 1966, p. 9; 'The Sound of Success', *London Times*, 10 January 1967, p. 4.

31. Thomas Doherty, *Teenagers and Teenpics: The Juvenilization of American Movies in the 1950s* (Philadelphia, PA: Temple University Press, 2002). See also Monaco, *The Sixties*, pp. 40–5; Krämer, *New Hollywood*, pp. 58–63.

32. Maltby, *Hollywood Cinema*, pp. 22–4.

33. Monaco, *The Sixties*, p. 120.

34. Eileen S. Quigley, Aaron Dior Pinkham and Dee Quigley (eds), *International Motion Picture Almanac*, 80th edition (Malden, MA: Quigley Publishing, 2009), p. 319.

35. James Powers, 'The Sound of Music', *Hollywood Reporter*, 3 March 1965, p. 1.

36. John Coleman, 'Per Ardua ad Julie', *New Statesman*, 26 July 1968, p. 118.

37. David Shipman, 'The All-Conquering Governess', *Films and Filming*, vol. 12 no. 11, August 1966, p. 20.

38. Ian Conrich and Estella Tincknell, 'Introduction', in *Film's Musical Moments* (Edinburgh: Edinburgh University Press, 2006), p. 2.

39. It is significant to recall that Andrews's screen stardom emerged against the backdrop of her much publicised failure to secure the role of Eliza Doolittle in the film version of *My Fair Lady*, a role she had created on Broadway and in London's West End, ostensibly on the grounds that she was not yet a sufficiently marketable name. That she lost the role to Audrey Hepburn, however, implicitly served to define her screen image from the outset in contradistinction to the sort of auratic feminine glamour and erotic iconicity personified by a more traditionally gendered female star like Hepburn. See Bruce Babington and Peter William Evans, *Affairs to Remember: The Hollywood Comedy of the Sexes* (Manchester: Manchester University Press, 1989), p. 291.

40. 'Stars: The Now and Future Queen', *Time*, 23 December 1966, p. 53.

41. George Haddad-Garcia, 'Thoroughly Modern Julie', *Saturday Evening Post*, January/February 1980, p. 100.

42. The gender non-normative aspects of the Andrews image would find further expression in the cross-dressing musical comedy *Victor/Victoria* (1982), which is one of the few films Andrews made in the long wake of her 1960s heyday that seemed to resonate with audiences and that managed to inflect her star persona in any appreciable way.

43. Rick Altman, *The American Film Musical* (Bloomington: Indiana University Press, 1987); and Jane Feuer, *The Hollywood Musical*, 2nd edition (Bloomington: Indiana University Press, 1993).

44. The subversive nature of this dynamic was not lost on commentators of the time. A 1968 academic article cautioning against 'the depolarization of sex roles in contemporary America' cites as one example: 'Aggressive performers like … Julie Andrews [who] star in musicals which feature male leads who are either innocuous or nonsingers and are puny successors to the male singers, dancers, and comedians who made the American musical our happiest export.' Charles Winick, 'The Beige Epoch: Depolarization of Sex Roles in America', *Annals of the American Academy of Political and Social Science*, vol. 376, March 1968, p. 23.

45. Steve Neale, 'Hollywood Blockbusters: Historical Dimensions', in Julian Stringer (ed.), *Movie Blockbusters* (London: Routledge, 2003), p. 55.

46. Dyer, '*Sound of Music*', p. 45.

47. Betty Friedan, *Feminine Mystique* (New York: Norton, 1963); Helen Gurley Brown, *Sex and the Single Girl* (New York: Bernard Geis, 1962).

48. Here my reading departs dramatically, at least in its conclusions, from Anne McLeer, who apprehends *Music*, as well as *Poppins*, as reactionary texts designed to counter anti-feminist cultural anxieties by returning women to a domesticated femininity and restoring a benevolent patriarchy. While her argument responds to a certain dynamic in these films, it does rather depend on a troublingly limited analytic approach focused almost exclusively on plot with scant attention to the texts' performative, cinematic or even musical aspects, while at the same time allowing for no critical agency on the part of these films' vast female audiences. Anne McLeer, 'Practical Perfection? The Nanny Negotiates Gender, Class, and Family Contradictions in 1960s Popular Culture', *NWSA Journal*, vol. 14 no. 2, 2002, pp. 80–101.

49. Vincent Canby, 'Screen: *Darling Lili* Sets the Stage for Pure Comedy of Roman Gestures', *New York Times*, 24 July 1970, p. 16.

50. For a rudimentary assessment of the historical reception of the Andrews musical among children, see Douglas Brode, F*rom Walt to Woodstock: How Disney Created the Counterculture* (Austin: University of Texas Press, 2004), pp. 24–5; and Raymond Knapp, *The American Musical and the Performance of Personal Identity* (Princeton, NJ: Princeton University Press, 2006), pp. 124, 141–9. On Andrews's reception in queer cultures, see Stacy Wolf, *A Problem Like Maria: Gender and Sexuality in the American Musical* (Ann Arbor: University of Michigan Press, 2002), pp. 131–72; and Brett Farmer, 'Julie Andrews Made Me Gay', *Camera Obscura*, vol. 22 no. 2, 2007, pp. 144–53.

10 The Streisand Musical

Pamela Robertson Wojcik

Over a thirty-six-year film career, Barbra Streisand has appeared in a total of seventeen films. Of those, only six are musicals, ranging from her first film, *Funny Girl* in 1968 to *Yentl* in 1983, two decades before her most recent screen appearance in *Meet the Fockers* (2004) (there are rumours of a forthcoming sequel). Compare Streisand's output to that of Fred Astaire, who made thirty-eight feature films in fifty-four years, interspersed with numerous TV appearances and TV movies. The Astaire oeuvre consists exclusively of musicals for the first twenty-eight films and more than two decades of his career, bookmarked by *Flying Down to Rio* (1933) and *Silk Stockings* (1957). After his ventures into non-musical film, in such fare as *On the Beach* (1959), Astaire still performed in musicals such as *Finian's Rainbow* (1968) and performed musically as a voice actor in TV specials like *Santa Claus Is Coming to Town* (1970), as well as promoting the genre of the musical via appearances as a narrator in *That's Entertainment* (1974) and *That's Entertainment, Part II* (1976). Or put Streisand side by side the star with whom she is most frequently compared, Judy Garland. Garland made over twenty-five musicals in a twenty-seven-year career, with only a few non-musical films, most of those made after she was fired by MGM and following the self-reflexive *A Star Is Born* (1954).[1] Relatively speaking, Streisand seems like a dabbler in the film musical, rather than a major musical star.

It is, perhaps, not surprising that Astaire and Garland have deeper roots in the musical than Streisand, if we bear in mind that their careers traverse the heyday of the classical Hollywood musical. Her career began in the late 1960s during Hollywood's post-classical period, when the musical was more of a speciality boutique item than everyday fare, and when the breakdown of the studio system, in tandem with the rise of the Method, enabled actors to define themselves less by type and more by versatility. Still, consider this: over *his* thirty-four-year career, John Travolta, who has made approximately forty-six films – amid numerous TV appearances – has starred in nearly as many musicals as Streisand – four, against her six – most recently in *Hairspray* (2007). In addition, Travolta had prominent dance numbers in non-musical films, such as *Michael* (1996) and *Pulp Fiction* (1994), and was featured in *That's Dancing* (1985) as part of a new generation of dancers carrying on the tradition of the musical. Even Christopher Walken has punctuated his career with musicals, appearing recently (as Travolta's husband!) in *Hairspray*, as well as in the earlier films *Pennies from Heaven* (1981) and *Puss in Boots* (1988), for which he recorded five songs.

So why do we associate Streisand so strongly with the genre of the musical and align her with such figures as Astaire and Garland, rather than view her career as parallel to Travolta's or Walken's? And, alternately, why don't we consider Travolta and Walken as musical stars? With respect to the latter, it is partly a question of percentages – Travolta and Walken have each made many more movies than Streisand, so their musical output is proportionately less than hers across their careers. However, the first question, as to why we view Streisand as a musical star, is trickier. It relates partly to her career as a singing star in concert, and especially on record. From the soundtrack for her Broadway debut in *I Can Get It for You Wholesale* in 1962, to the 2009 recording *Love Is the Answer*, Streisand has made an astonishing fifty-nine albums. While she dabbles in various genres, such as disco, most of these recordings place Streisand firmly in the world of Tin Pan Alley standards, and/or as maintaining the Broadway vault, as in *The Broadway Album* (1985) and *Back to Broadway* (1993). Thus, she deepens her generic affiliation with the musical by carrying on, as it were, the musical tradition in song, establishing herself as, in some ways, a preserver of traditions and songs from a wide array of film and theatre musicals. However, musical recordings are not the same as the musical genre: Streisand's link to the film musical as genre is not completely explained by her recording career.

Rather than the quantity of musical films in which she appears, or her recording of songs with ties to the musical, the reason we consider Streisand a musical star, and not just a star who dabbles in musicals, may ultimately have to do with the status of her musicals as star vehicles. In other words, we consider Streisand a musical star because Streisand as a star is unthinkable without the musical – her star image is formed in and through the musical – and because her star persona produces a unique variant of the musical genre.

Certainly, Travolta and Walken are stars with distinctive performance styles. However, I would suggest that while they are both very talented musical performers, their roles in musicals are neither irreplaceable – other performers could, theoretically, play the parts equally well, with little adjustment to the overall shape of the role or narrative – nor unique within the genre. There is nothing about the musical films in which Travolta and Walken appear that makes them a Travolta or Walken vehicle, and there is nothing about their presence in those films that is determining. While we might delight in Travolta's performance in *Grease* (1978) or *Hairspray*, it is not unthinkable that another actor could perform the role as well, without significantly altering the film.

By contrast, one could say that both Astaire and Garland produce a variant of the musical genre because their star text is, on the one hand, dependent upon the musical and, on the other, because the films in which they appear function, for the most part, as star vehicles and would be dramatically altered if another star took their roles. We could not exchange an Astaire role in, for instance, *Top Hat* (1935) with a Gene Kelly role in *Singin' in the Rain* (1952), or substitute Garland in *A Star Is Born* (1954) with Julie Andrews in *The Sound of Music* (1965). And, we could not exchange a Streisand role – any Streisand musical role – for a performance by another musical actress.

John O. Thompson's description of the commutation test helps clarify the contrast I am making between the status of Travolta and Walken as musical stars and the status of Astaire, Garland or Streisand.[2] The commutation test consists in imagining one actor in another's role. The more distinctive the star, the more ridiculous and unimaginable the commutation becomes. We can, for instance, substitute one stunt man for another, and one chorus girl for another, and the difference is almost nil, because it is what the actor does and not the actor's persona that matters. But in the case of a star, what the actor does and who she is are deeply interconnected, so that replacing one actor with the other utterly transforms the role. Beyond its obvious parlour-game potential, for Thompson, commutation offers a practical methodology that helps open up a gap between actor and role to highlight the star's distinctive features and the ideology embodied by those features. For me, it also points to the ways in which star image and genre can be mutually determining. In some cases, the actor's star image is tied to certain genres and cannot be commuted into other genres. Imagine John Wayne in a screwball comedy like *His Girl Friday* (1940) and Cary Grant in a Western like *The Searchers* (1956) and the genre expectations that go along with certain star images become clear. It is not only the case that certain stars are better suited to certain genres, but that some stars significantly revise genres and leave their mark on them.

This essay, then, considers Streisand's star image to locate the unique qualities that she brings to the film musical. At the same time, by delineating the unique qualities of Streisand's star persona, I hope to suggest the ways in which she produces a unique variant of the musical, a subgenre that can be categorised as the Streisand musical.

'If a Girl Isn't Pretty'

In order to understand the Streisand variant of the musical, it is first necessary to understand what makes her a unique type. As Stanley Cavell argues, 'What makes someone a type is not his similarity with other members of that type but his striking separateness from other people.'[3] Certainly, Streisand shares qualities with other camp icons and divas – her belting style of singing, an outsized theatricality of gesture and an affiliation with gay cultures. However, Streisand as star differs from other divas and camp icons in ways that mark her as an individual type and that establish the elements of her persona that shape the Streisand musical. Most of the qualities we associate with Streisand exist already or are determined by her performance in *Funny Girl*.

Unlike Judy Garland, whose star image Richard Dyer famously links to 'ordinariness',[4] Streisand's star persona is defined first and foremost through difference and particularly ethnic difference. Instead of Waspy small-town values, Streisand's film roles merge with 'real life' and associate her with Jewishness, urbanity and New York street smarts. Streisand's Jewishness defines her and makes her a star in her initial role as Fanny Brice, who became a star by adopting a Yiddish persona, playing up an accent though she didn't speak Yiddish. Ironically, during the intolerant 1920s, Brice attempted to de-Semitise her image by having a nose job. Dorothy Parker put it simply when she said Brice 'cut off her nose to spite her race'.[5] However, the nose job did not sufficiently de-Semitise her image and *Variety* blamed her 'Hebrew jesting' for the termination of her much-publicised screen career.[6] By contrast, Streisand's portrayal of Brice (with scripts that whitewash these problems) establishes her as the first major female star to command major roles *as* a Jewish actress.

Streisand's Jewishness is often explicitly referred to in her films. In *Funny Girl*, Brice's Yiddish humour and her roots in Hester Street emphasise her Jewish identity. The sequel, *Funny Lady* (1975), includes a sequence in which Brice performs an act based on the very funny notion of a Jewish Little Eva. As Patricia Erens notes, even in films like *A Star Is Born* (1976) where her Jewishness is irrelevant to the plot, she provides herself with a Jewish name, substituting Esther Hoffman for the original Esther Blodgett – and eliminating the name change that's part of the female star's manufacture in earlier versions.[7]

Except for *Yentl*, which deals explicitly with Jewish female identity, Jewish custom and Jewish religion through its portrayal of a girl's desire to study sacred texts and enter a yeshiva, Streisand's Jewishness is taken as an ethnic identity as opposed to a religious or cultural one. Jewish identity in Streisand's star image is conflated with quirks of individual personality associated as much with being a New Yorker and with being Barbra Streisand as with being Jewish – her ethnicity gives her an accent and an attitude, brash, bossy and bold. Very often, Jewishness is sublimated into chutzpah. Ethnicity translates into street savvy and is what makes her fast-talking, funny, ironic and self-deprecating. Ethnicity makes Streisand both an urban character and authentic: 'She is earthy, she is real, she is ethnic,' one fan says in a 1965 *New York Times* article.[8]

Whereas Garland's supposed lack of glamour reads as girl-next-door, Streisand's supposed lack of glamour is equated with the Jewishness of her looks. *Funny Girl* establishes this element of her persona. Her first words on film are the famous 'hello gorgeous' she directs at herself in the mirror preceding her flashback memory of her mother's friends telling her she'll never make it on stage in 'If a Girl Isn't Pretty'. Then, when Mr Keeney fires her because she doesn't look like the other girls, she compares herself to 'a bagel on a plateful of onion rolls'. An article by Judith Crist from 1968, 'The Bagel as Superstar', picks up on this. Stanley Kauffman spoke of 'the social importance of Miss Streisand's face' and said 'she is *Jewish* homely. To disregard both these elements is to disregard the importance of Miss Streisand's emergence.'[9]

Streisand does achieve glamour, but it's a glamour that needs constantly to be rediscovered and reasserted. Crist describes her as 'beautiful ugly. ... a startling piece of pop art.'[10] Shana Alexander defines Streisand's prototype as the 'Ugly Duckling' and calls hers a 'weird, now-you-see-it-now-you-don't beauty' which is achieved only because Streisand insists 'I AM GORGEOUS.'[11] Martha Weinman Lear, similarly, writes: 'Pretty? Heavens, no; but striking, a sow's ear transformed by instinct, hard work and sheer will into a sleek, silk purse of an original.'[12] Streisand's films are permeated by this cycle: in them, she is very often considered to be, or considers herself to be, unattractive; then her beauty is discovered and/or she is transformed.

Streisand's looks are defined constantly and almost exclusively in relation to her nose, a stereotype reappropriated as a mark of her Jewishness and difference. Alexander describes her nose as 'long, Semitic and – most of all – like Everest, There'.[13] In 'If a Girl Isn't Pretty' from *Funny Girl*, Fanny's mother sings, 'Is a nose with deviation such a crime against the nation?' Minutes later, in 'I'm the Greatest Star', Streisand sings, 'Who's an American beauty rose,/With an American beauty nose,/And ten American beauty toes?'. In 'Don't Rain on My Parade', she refers to herself as a 'freckle on the nose of life's complexion'. In films, Streisand is often shot in profile, a shot as typical and indicative in its way as what Dyer identifies as the frequent 'side-long tits and arse' shots of Marilyn Monroe.[14]

In her films, ethnicity is foregrounded as difference and she is the only character who seems to *have* an ethnicity – she differs from a norm that is taken to be non-ethnic through her embodiment of ethnic characteristics. As Dyer argues, 'whiteness secures it dominance by seeming not to be anything in particular'.[15] Even within dominant whiteness, however, there is a hierarchy; and certain national or ethnic identities come into focus against seemingly non-ethnic identities. In certain representations, for example, Italian Americans or Jewish Americans are marked as 'ethnics' while Anglo-Saxon whites are not; and, often, Jewish ethnicity overrides other identities, such as national identities. In Streisand's case, her Jewish identity is figured against the invisible dominance of both Wasp and gentile normativity.

Her ethnicity marks her difference from the men in her films, but their ethnic and/or religious difference from her is masked: rather than an ethnic or religious identity, they are primarily defined by other characteristics, notably class. The pairing of Streisand with Omar Sharif, an Egyptian who converted to Islam, caused great controversy when the Arab–Israeli Six-Day War erupted a few days into the filming of *Funny Girl*.[16] However, in sharp contrast to the constant assertion of Fanny's Brooklyn Jewish identity, the foreignness of Sharif's Nick Arnstein in *Funny Girl* and *Funny Lady* is never mentioned. Instead, Sharif's nationality translates into tropes of 'class' and 'elegance'. He is uptown vs. Streisand's downtown, loafing vs. her work ethic, frilly shirts vs. her store-bought clothes, fancy nightclubs vs. her Hester Street saloon.

This contrast continues across her career. In *The Prince of Tides* (1991), Nick Nolte is marked as a gentile only through his sister's schizophrenic desire to forget her family by taking on a Jewish pseudonym and by Streisand's remarks. Otherwise, he is marked primarily by regional difference (as a Southerner) and class difference (as a football coach). Similarly, Redford's Wasp-ishness in *The Way We Were* (1973) is a given; but rather than register as a religious or ethnic difference, it seems like a difference of personality and character, as a kind of preppy bourgeois mentality which contrasts to her committed politics and ideals. Redford's ethnic or religious difference from Streisand and his Wasp identity translates into a class difference. Sharif and Redford, in particular, also set off Streisand's difference in terms of looks, their perceived prettiness a reminder of her lack.

'The Greatest Star'

Streisand's uniqueness relates not only to her looks but to the type of character she plays and the narrative elements her star image produces, or requires. These aspects of her persona mould what Rick Altman would call the syntax of the Streisand musical as genre, its overall meaning and thematics.[17] They signal some of the ideological differences between the Streisand musical and the musical genre as a whole.

First, we need to define the Streisand character. If part of Garland's ordinariness is that she is a fan, like us, on the outside, Streisand is always already a star. She emerges full-blown as a star in *Funny Girl*, and as a star who asserts her talent in the first number she sings, 'I'm the Greatest Star'. Despite the fact that it's Brice's life, not Streisand's, the star that's born in *Funny Girl* is Streisand and this is the film image that structures her image from then on.

One can see the unique qualities of the Streisand character most clearly by comparing her remake of *A Star Is Born* to the Garland version. Whereas Garland's Esther Blodgett is awed by Norman Maine, the star, and needs him to tell her what we already know, that she too can be a great star, Streisand's Esther Hoffman is, as Pauline Kael says, 'so indifferent to [John Norman Howard's] fame that she doesn't take cognizance of it at any point; she's a little princess from another planet'.[18] When Kris Kristofferson's John Norman stumbles upon Streisand singing, she yells at him for 'blowing' her act. Where James Mason's Norman has to tell Garland how good she is, Kristofferson can only tell Streisand how good her singing makes him feel – she never doubts how good she is. At the end of the 1954 film, Garland's character, who was willing to sacrifice her career to save her husband, subsumes her identity into her dead husband's: the film ends as she announces 'This is Mrs Norman Maine.' Streisand's Esther, by contrast, will sacrifice nothing and never seems to notice that her husband has sacrificed himself for her. Rather than end with the proclamation that she is 'Esther Hoffman Howard', Streisand's Esther goes on to appropriate two of her husband's songs, ending with a cover version that demands recognition for the star: 'Are You Watching Me Now?'.

The Streisand character, defined first and foremost as a star, and as supremely self-sufficient, troubles the usual reliable structure of couple formation in the musical. Unlike the alternation and duality of male and female performance that Altman identifies as a key structural feature of the Hollywood musical,[19] Streisand's dominance on screen diminishes the male leads that are expected to perform with her. A throwback to an older belting performance style, Streisand never finds a singing partner who can approach – let alone, match – her. Often, in her musical roles, she is paired with non-singers like Sharif, Walter Matthau and James Caan (each of whom awkwardly talk-sings a number or two). Yves Montand sings in *On a Clear Day You Can See Forever* (1970) but his Piaf-trained *chansonnier* style can't rival Streisand's more powerful Broadway-inflected belting. Musically speaking, the nearest she comes to an equal is Kristofferson, but this pairing depends on Streisand significantly modifying her style to become a kind of schmaltzy Janis Joplin and, even then, the plot demands that Kristofferson play a fading star with a fading voice, and not a rival to Streisand's talent. In *Yentl*, Mandy Patinkin, who can sing beautifully, doesn't – the film is a musical only in Streisand's mind and the songs function as a kind of voiceover narration to reflect her interiority – an ironic move into solipsism in the film most clearly tied to Jewish identity politics.

Her dominance figures as an issue blocking the successful resolution of the romance plot, and thus works against what Jane Feuer identifies as the myth of integration in the musical, which posits that success in love and success in the musical go hand in hand.[20] Only Walter Matthau in *Hello, Dolly!* (1969) is paired at film's end with Streisand. Others die, go to jail or, in the case of Montand, decide to wait for a reincarnated version of Streisand in some other life. When Streisand does get the guy in *Hello, Dolly!*, it seems unsatisfying, because her youth, difference and strength make him pale by comparison. The torchiest, most romantic Streisand roles in musicals – *Funny Girl*, *Funny Lady*, *Yentl* – are also films in which she ends up alone, or not with the male lead. In these films, her difference and strength attract the men, but ultimately they can't handle it. In the phallic economy of *Funny Girl*, *Funny Lady* and *Yentl*, her added masculinity is perceived as a threat to the man's dominance and individuality. To reaffirm his masculinity, he rejects her.

Streisand's musical films assert again and again that the Streisand character is a person who needs people, or one very special person, a man. Rather than assert her indifference to others, the films expose the conflict in Streisand's persona between needing people and being self-sufficient. The major contradiction in Streisand's persona is that between two modes of desire – the first, romantic longing, and the second a drive for freedom and independence. Romantic longing in the typical Streisand musical produces the conditions for torch, a mode of emotional authenticity linked to hurt and loss. This desire, however, is matched by an equally strong drive toward freedom and independence, which provides a counter to torch's victim discourse and emphasises self-sufficiency.

'Before the Parade Passes By'

Having sorted through aspects of the Streisand persona, we can now distinguish a few specific elements of Streisand's film performance that constitute her performance idiolect and that serve as what Altman would refer to as the semantics, or stylistic vocabulary, of the Streisand musical. I have already mentioned the very typical shot of Streisand's profile as an important feature of her image. Here, I am concerned with four specific motifs that display the conflict in her persona between the desire for romantic love and the drive toward freedom. These consist of specifically cinematic gestures, framing, camera movements and musical numbers that I will call the Streisand gaze, the Streisand solo, the Streisand stride and travel motifs, and the Streisand anthem.

The Streisand gaze

No other female performer has ever done so much for her male co-stars as Streisand. Streisand doesn't just look, she stares. Her stare expresses her deep longing. Her gaze fetishises the man, turns him into an idol. When she gazes, her hand inevitably reaches out toward the man's face, as if to test his reality. Her hand – long slender fingers, long dangerous nails – just brushes his face, seeming simultaneously to express a desire to mark him and to trace the contours of his face. Streisand's gaze is comparative. From the perspective of her difference, equated with non-prettiness, the man seems strange and unnatural in his normality and prettiness. Her gaze reverses the structure of othering: instead of being herself the exotic other, her difference and her desire make the man exotic.

In terms of plot, the gaze appears at two key moments. First, Streisand displays her desire for the man. Picture her looking at Omar Sharif outside the dressing room at Mr Keeney's. Then, the gaze returns again, for a last encounter, the moment of loss. It can happen in the street or alone in a dressing room, but the goodbye is always the same. At the moment of the goodbye, Streisand's gaze marks her recognition and acceptance of the loss. She stares, then stops and makes her resolve to be brave, to admit that it's over. Her gaze, which always involves the gesture of brushing his face at these moments, makes the man seem sorry, and forces him to look back and recognise her.

The Streisand solo

It may be redundant to describe a Streisand solo, since, as I've suggested, her roles on the whole have a solo quality. But certain numbers are specifically demarcated as solos. The solos sometimes take place with Streisand alone on stage in a theatre, and sometimes with an implied audience. Either way, the camera focuses on her alone and eliminates any reverse shot of an audience for the duration of the song, and usually beyond that. In these moments, the Streisand character puts her true self, her true feelings, on display – not for an audience but for herself.

Alan Spiegel links the crucial motif of the Streisand solo to the goodbye scene I mentioned above:

> One awaits the almost ritualistic climax of each film … the moment after the marriage has failed, after she realizes she can go on by herself, triumphant in her grief, the moment when she stands alone before the crowd whose rapport she is so confident of that it becomes her exalted mirror: Streisand asserting her tragic self to her heroic self.[21]

Goodbye solos like 'My Man' in *Funny Girl* or 'Are You Watching Me Now?' in *A Star Is Born* serve to assert Streisand's triumph over grief. In addition to managing grief, the solos also express anger – this can be seen in Fanny's spiteful rendition of 'How Lucky Can You Get?' in *Funny Lady* or the crescendo of resentment in 'I'm the Greatest Star'.

The Streisand stride and travel motif

The stride and the travel motif express a different but related kind of resolve. What I'm calling the stride is a reverse tracking shot in which Streisand walks or, more precisely, marches toward the camera. The stride appears in all the Streisand musicals. Consider the beginning of 'Before the Parade Passes By', where Streisand starts out slowly, then picks up speed, walking directly into the camera, then moving into a march; or, the end of *On a Clear Day*, where she strides gleefully into the camera, before running into a garden of flowers.

Funny Girl (1968): Streisand emerges as a full-blown star in a solo declaring that she is 'the greatest star'

Funny Girl: The movement of the camera up and away from Streisand highlights her mobility and becomes a Streisand trademark shot

The travel motif involves a sound-bridge and shows Streisand running, driving, flying, travelling by boat, car, train and/or plane. The travel sequence ends each and every time with a crane or helicopter shot that moves up and away from Streisand to create a feeling of flight and uplift. The best known of these is probably 'Don't Rain on My Parade' in *Funny Girl*. These two motifs appear in all the musicals except *A Star Is Born* and are, I think, unique to Streisand as a musical performer.

The Streisand anthem

The musicals usually employ these motifs in conjunction with Streisand anthems that express her character's desire – for independence, or, simply, for something more out of life. The anthems often explicitly describe a kind of movement in both literal and metaphoric references to parades and flight. For instance, from 'Don't Rain on My Parade':

> Don't tell me not to live.
> Just sit and putter.
> Life's candy and the sun's a ball of butter.
> Don't bring around a cloud.
> Don't rain on my parade.
> I'm gonna live and live now,
> Get what I want,
> I know how.

In 'Before the Parade Passes By' she sings:

> I want to hold my head up high.
> I need a goal again.
> I need a drive again.
> I want to feel my heart coming alive again.
> Before the parade passes by.

Two Streisand anthems – 'Don't Rain on My Parade' (*Funny Girl*) and 'Before the Parade Passes By' (*Hello, Dolly!*) – initiate the Streisand stride, a forward-moving walk or run with a reverse tracking shot

In *Yentl*, she sings: 'Why have the wings if you're not meant to fly?' and

> What's wrong with wanting more?
> If you can fly and soar?
> With all there is,
> Why settle for
> Just a piece of sky?

These anthems are, in some way, the most important Streisand moments, the moments we wait for and remember, the moments that transform longing into pure undistilled desire. They are anthems for unruliness.

On a Clear Day You Can See Forever significantly modifies the travel motif and anthem but in ways that underscore its necessity in a Streisand film. In that film, Montand rather than Streisand sings what would, in another film, be the travel motif song. His song, 'Come Back to Me', however, still describes her motions, not his, and it functions as a soundover and sound-bridge for a series of shots that show Daisy walking, running and taking cabs through the city. His lyrics could almost be a shot description of scenes from *Yentl* or of Fanny's movements in *Funny Girl* and *Funny Lady*:

> Take a train, steal a car,
> Hop a freight, grab a star …
> Catch a plane, catch a breeze,
> On your hands, on your knees …
> On a mule, in a jet,
> Come back to me.

Despite the reversal of roles, then, Montand's song still functions as a vehicle for Streisand's travel motif. Importantly, despite the iterative form, this number does not contain the Streisand figure's unruliness. Daisy does 'come back' but then she leaves Montand and, shortly after, Streisand sings a reprise of 'On a Clear Day' as she strides into the unknown alone, and, through special effects, soars into the sky.

Conclusion

When Garland's star is born, she is discovered by Norman Maine singing 'The Man that Got Away'. Surely, it is no accident that when the star is born again in Streisand's remake, she sings the song 'Everything': 'Ask what I want/And I will sing/I want everything.' More than anything, it is this demand for more, this privileging of desire, that defines the Streisand type and that underpins the Streisand musical. In the Streisand musical, difference, rather than normativity, dominates. In the Streisand musical, the girl does not always get the guy, and the girl gets angry. She goes it alone, assured of her own talent and strength. The Streisand musical fails to achieve the myth of integration or to produce a couple, but, instead, promotes a fantasy of female independence and unruliness. Streisand only made six musicals, but in those six films, she remade the musical in her image.

Notes

Portions of this essay appeared in 'A Star Is Born Again, or How Streisand Recycles Garland', in Lesley Stern and George Kouvaros (eds), *Falling for You: Essays on Cinema and Performance* (Sydney: Power Institute, 1999).

1. Among her MGM films, *The Clock* (1945) is completely non-musical. The Andy Hardy films are, to my mind, musicals, though their generic status can be debated. Post-MGM, Garland appears in the non-musicals *Judgement at Nuremburg* (1961), *A Child Is Waiting* (1963) and *I Could Go on Singing* (1963) but also provides voice for the animated musical *Gay Puree* (1962).
2. John O. Thompson, 'Screen Acting and the Commutation Test', in Christine Gledhill (ed.), *Stardom: Industry of Desire*, 1st edition (New York: Routledge, 1991), pp. 183–97.
3. Stanley Cavell, 'From *The World Viewed*', in Gerald Mast, Marshall Cohen and Leo Braudy (eds), *Film Theory and Criticism: Introductory Readings*, 4th edition (New York: Oxford University Press, 1992), p. 291.
4. Richard Dyer, *Heavenly Bodies: Film Stars and Society* (London: BFI, 1986), pp. 141–94.
5. Quoted in Barbara Grossman, *Funny Woman: The Life and Times of Fanny Brice* (Bloomington: Indiana University Press, 1991), pp. 148–9.

6. Henry Jenkins, *What Made Pistachio Nuts? Early Sound Comedy and the Vaudeville Aesthetic* (New York: Columbia University Press, 1992), pp. 175–6.

7. Patricia Erens, *The Jew in American Cinema* (Bloomington: Indiana University Press, 1984), p. 269.

8. Martha Weinman Lear, 'She Is Tough, She Is Earthy, She Is Kicky', *New York Times*, Sunday, 4 July 1965, p. 10.

9. Stanley Kauffman, 'Three for Fun', *New Republic*, vol. 159 no. 19, 9 November 1968, p. 22.

10. Judith Crist, 'The Bagel as Superstar', *New York*, 7 October 1968, p. 56.

11. Shana Alexander, 'A Born Loser's Success and Precarious Love', *Life*, 22 May 1964, pp. 52, 54.

12. Lear, 'She Is Tough, She Is Earthy, She Is Kicky', p. 10.

13. Alexander, 'A Born Loser's Success and Precarious Love', p. 52.

14. Dyer, *Heavenly Bodies*, p. 21.

15. Richard Dyer, 'White', *The Matter of Images: Essays on Representation* (New York: Routledge, 1993), p. 141.

16. Nellie Bly, *Barbra Streisand: The Untold Story* (New York: Pinnacle Books, 1994), p. 85, and James Spada, *Streisand: The Intimate Biography* (London: Little Brown and Company, 1995), p. 193.

17. Rick Altman, *Film/Genre* (London: BFI, 1999).

18. Pauline Kael, *When the Lights Go Down* (London: Marion Boyars, 1980), p. 242.

19. Rick Altman, *The American Film Musical* (Bloomington: Indiana University Press, 1987), pp. 28–58.

20. Jane Feuer, 'The Self-Reflexive Musical and the Myth of Entertainment', in Steven Cohan (ed.), *Hollywood Musicals: The Film Reader* (New York: Routledge, 2002), pp. 35–6.

21. Alan Spiegel, 'The Vanishing Act: A Typology of the Jew in Contemporary American Film', in Sarah Blacher Cohen (ed.), *From Hester Street to Hollywood: The Jewish-American Stage and Screen* (Bloomington: Indiana University Press, 1983), p. 272.

PART THREE: Beyond Classic Hollywood

11 The Music and Musicality of Bollywood

Anna Morcom

While the musical is a distinct genre in western films, in India, virtually all commercial films have songs, whether Hindi cinema, including the 'A-list' form known as Bollywood which this chapter describes, or regional cinemas such as Tamil, Telugu, Malayalam, Gujarati, Bhojpuri, Marathi. Some songs are also generally present in 'B' or 'C' grade films in various Indian languages, including horror and/or films that are adult certificate in terms of sexual content. In recent years, songs have been seen creeping into even art or parallel cinema, which previously only had background songs or diegetically performed songs. While the film musical has declined in the West (though songs continue to feature in background scores), in Hindi cinema, the musical format has continued unabated.

In this paper, I explore the music and musicality of Bollywood: big-budget, star-cast Hindi films. As a way of introducing some characteristics of Hindi films and their musical ethos, I examine how the use of songs in Hindi films involves a number of fundamental differences from both western non-musical films and musicals. I then turn to a closer exploration of the Hindi film as a (melo)drama-musical, looking in detail at the classic film *Sholay* ('Flames', directed by Ramesh Sippy, music by R. D. Burman, 1975) and its use of songs.

Songs, Realism, Fantasy and Frivolity

For a large part of its history, the presence of song sequences has been one of the aspects of Hindi films that western audiences have found most difficult, and it has been at the root of the criticism of Hindi cinema as bad cinema by the West and westernised Indian elite, something which has only recently started to change. The use of songs in Hindi films clashes head on with the codes of realism found in Hollywood and art cinema, since they apparently interrupt the narrative: they more often than not involve characters simply breaking into song with no visible diegetic musical context or accompanying ensemble; they are sung by 'playback' singers as opposed to the actors and actresses, who are clearly only lip-synching; and song sequences often move out of the narrative world into at times multiple extra-narrative or fantasy locations. Peter Manuel describes the songs as 'more or less gratuitous insertions into the plot, to be enjoyed for their own sake'.[1] Satyajit Ray wrote of commercial Hindi films in 1948, 'In India, it would seem that the fundamental concept of a coherent dramatic pattern existing in time was generally misunderstood.'[2] While his comment refers to more than just the inclusion of songs, it is the songs that have caused the most controversy.

While the presence of songs in Hindi film has led to accusations that it lacks realism and is therefore bad cinema, at the same time, Hindi films do not fit into the mould of the genre that is particularly focused on fantasy – the musical. As Altman writes, 'too much realism threatens a film's identity as a musical'.[3] He states:

> As a genre, the film musical satisfies the spectator's desire to escape from a humdrum day-to-day existence, each musical subgenre meeting this need for a fuller life in a different way. The show musical involves the

spectator in the creation of a work of art; the fairy tale musical creates a utopian world like that of the spectator's dreams; the folk musical projects the audience into a mythicized version of the cultural past.[4]

Hindi films have been described as escapist fantasies. However, in comparison to American musicals, even if the 'humdrum of day-to-day existence' is absent, some of life's grittier, more violent and nastier sides are very much prominent. Moreover, powerful conflicts surrounding the individual and the social/moral rules of society are also foregrounded. In this sense, the Hindi film involves too much realism, in terms of grit and emotional/moral conflict, to fit the pattern of an American musical. Or looking at this from another point of view, it can be said that while the American musical is fantasy in a light-hearted, playful and frothy sense, a Hindi film, rather, involves fantasy or a lack of realism (in the sense of non-musical Hollywood films) in terms of being melodramatic, where characterisations, emotions and resolutions are larger than life and ideal, and are the focus of the narrative.[5] Hence, while Hindi films focus on romance, as do American musicals,[6] they also generally centre on a struggle between good and evil in the form of heroes and villains, anti-heroes and the law, or family melodramas. In a 'traditional' Hindi film potboiler, therefore, romance exists on a knife-edge, and even in the glossy family melodramas common post the 1990s, it is not frothy, or not for long, as serious problems and obstacles appear that threaten the couple and, moreover, fundaments of the entire moral universe of Hindi cinema such as the family and its core relationships. Therefore, unlike American musicals, song sequences and love and romance are juxtaposed with, interlaced with or even embody heavy melodrama, violence and struggles between good and evil.

In other words, while Hindi films have song or song-and-dance scenes, in terms of plot and aesthetics, they do not resemble western musicals, but, rather, are closer to large-canvas Hollywood social dramas, epics or historicals. While western films imply that musical sequences (and the breaking of narrative realism) are inherently linked to a film being frothy, light, other-worldly, fantastic and centred around love, in Hindi films, there is no conflict between the mixing of heavy melodrama and song and dance, of situations that are blatantly fantastic with those that are very real in terms of the diegesis and the wider social, cultural and moral/emotional world of India. Hindi films and their use of songs, therefore, cross conventions of realism and fantasy and 'serious' versus 'light' entertainment in ways that those brought up on western film traditions find uncomfortable. This results not just in reading Hindi cinema as 'bad cinema', but also in more colonialist/elitist attitudes that focus on audience failure. The presence of songs has been seen as catering for a mass audience 'not ready' for good cinema, that require 'crude' films to meet their unsophisticated entertainment needs.[7]

In recent years, Bollywood films have gained a new level of acceptance, appreciation and presence in the western world along with many other aspects of Hindi cinema and cinematic style, including song, dance, clothes and jewellery. However, in this context, Bollywood tends to be celebrated in the context of postmodern kitsch, loved for its un-realism, its 'over-the-topness', its ebullience. This can be seen as the appropriation of Bollywood into the ethos of an (American-style) musical, reading it in terms of fantasy and light entertainment, a kind of pantomime where even villains are camp caricatures, rather than taking on board the intense emotional and moral turmoil of Hindi films. Thus, the appreciation is more for a parody of Hindi cinema than for Hindi cinema itself. This attitude can therefore also be seen as another form or phase of 'othering' and the exoticisation of Hindi films (adopted by non-Indians as well as many elite and diaspora Indians living in western countries), whereby the culture of the 'other' can only be seen in terms that tend to infantalise it, or at least make it unserious. Again, these attitudes reflect an inadequate understanding of the musicality of Hindi films, or of Hindi films themselves.

An argument also exists in India that songs are merely included for 'commercial reasons'. That songs are crucial to the commercial success of Hindi and other Indian films is true. However, on close examination, this commercial value exists strictly in the context of a symbiotic relationship, where films need songs for commercial success (as the songs market the films), yet songs also require films for commercial success, since the films market the songs. In fact, it is the film that is the stronger partner, with the success of songs depending overwhelmingly on the success of the films.[8] This fact points to a much more integrated relationship between films and their songs, one that sees Hindi films as *musical film (melo)dramas* as opposed to films interrupted or compromised by commercially oriented song sequences – too 'real' and gritty to be musical fantasies, too unrealistic and fantastic to be 'serious' films. Rather than comparing Hindi films to Hollywood non-musicals or musicals, in many ways, the mixture of (melo)drama and music, of intense emotions and impossible conflicts as well as spectacle and entertainment brings Hindi films closer to opera, a genre that has never been criticised for lack of realism.

Songs in Hindi Cinema: Narrative, Drama and Entertainment

Sholay is one of the most successful Hindi films ever made, and the songs have become all-time classics. It is usually described as a 'curry Western', a horseback action story of the fight against a dangerous outlaw, Gabbar Singh (Amjad Khan), who is terrorising a small Indian village from his camp in the dusty and rocky hills nearby. It is at the same time a classic Hindi film melodrama, where the narrative is set in a Manichaean universe of good and evil, as well as a range of other powerful binary oppositions and pairings. Good is represented by Thakur (Sanjeev Kumar), an ex-police officer, and the two anti-heroes, Jai (Amitabh Bachchan) and Veeru (Dharmendra), who are small-time crooks. Evil is embodied in Gabbar, who is one of Hindi cinema's most sadistic, cruel and frightening (as well as popular!) villains. Thakur had previously managed to capture Gabbar, who was put in jail. Gabbar escaped, however, and carried out a horrifyingly cruel revenge against Thakur, killing all members of his family but his younger daughter-in-law, Radha (Jaya Bhaduri), who had gone to the temple when Gabbar arrived and so escaped. The massacre included men (Thakur's two sons), women (his elder daughter-in-law and daughter) and a child (his grandson). The killing of the child is particularly shocking. The boy runs outside to where the corpses are lying on the ground and Gabbar is on horseback with his gun. He stands and stares at Gabbar, who, after an agonisingly long pause, lifts his gun and assassinates the child. When Thakur returns, he rides off in fury and grief to seek out Gabbar, who captures him and ties him between two posts by his hands. After tormenting him with jeering dialogue, he lifts two swords up and, with a roar, brings them down on both arms, cutting them off. This appalling violation of the moral universe is righted during the film, which sees Thakur seek personal revenge, and the rule of law reinstated with Gabbar recaptured by police.

Within this violent action film, with its bloody struggle of good and evil, are five of Hindi cinema's most popular songs. I will describe each of the song sequences, illustrating how they operate with the narrative in terms of emotion, plot and the structuring of the binary oppositions of the film, and how they are integral to the serious drama as well as providing entertaining spectacle.[9]

'Yeh dosti'/'This friendship'

The film opens with Thakur announcing to some police officers that he needs the help of Jai and Veeru, explaining that though they are rascals, they are also decent men. In an extended flashback, Thakur explains why: having arrested Jai and Veeru, Thakur is escorting them back by train when it is attacked by bandits. He frees Jai and Veeru so they can help fight the bandits. When the fight is over,

Jai and Veeru in 'Yeh dosti'

the two prisoners are about to run away when they see that Thakur is wounded; rather than escape, they decide to take him to hospital, thus saving his life but also ensuring that they go to jail. After a brief exchange between Thakur and the officers, the 'Yeh dosti' sequence begins. Although the train sequence introduces – and to a certain extent defines – Jai and Veeru, this song focuses on the emotional aspects of their characters as opposed to their bravery and fighting skills. In this sense, 'Yeh dosti' forms the other side of their introduction. The song shows the heroes to be fun-loving and full of pranks, as they ride through the countryside on a motorbike and side-car, stealing someone's cap who is quietly dozing by the road and then causing chaos in a bazaar as they send carts of fruit flying. Above all, this song is about Jai and Veeru's friendship, and shows the warm affection and loyalty they have for each other, with the lyrics of the refrain sung individually or together: 'I won't leave this friendship,/Even if I lose my strength,/I won't leave your side.' The song returns near the end of the film to underline the emotional core of the friendship as Jai dies after effectively sacrificing himself for Veeru and Veeru's sweetheart Basanti (Hema Malini), marking the pair's journey from carefree pranksters to true heroes; here Veeru sings the refrain (though not in lip-sync) in a slow, heavy, tragic way.

This song also shows the anti-heroes to be good, since they are capable of such love and loyalty. However, more fundamentally, the very fact that this pair sing is a clear marker of their goodness and their status as heroes. As I have argued elsewhere,[10] singing and melody are coded strongly positively in Hindi films, and while heroes and heroines sing (on the whole abundantly), the villain does not (in *Sholay*, for example, Gabbar never sings. As music director Uttam Singh commented when I asked about this characteristic of the Hindi film villain: 'The terror of Gabbar will go off if he sings.'[11] In other words, song itself is involved in the construction of the moral framework of *Sholay*, and Hindi films in general. As I will argue below, singing and not-singing mark out other important aspects of the film's emotional dynamics too.

'Holi ke din dil khil jaate hain'/'Our hearts come to life on the day of Holi'

The next song in the film takes place during the celebrations of the spring festival of Holi. Jai and Veeru have moved to the village and begun the task of fighting Gabbar and his men. Hindi films generally contain at least one big song-and-dance sequence, and a seasonal 'folk' number like this Holi song is one of the forms it commonly takes, especially in films with rural settings. In this sense, this song is generic, an 'item' that entertains with its spectacle, colour and exuberance. However, it is also placed and composed carefully to propel the drama and mark out the characters, their emotions and relationships. This joyful song that involves the whole village in a communal celebration of the spring festival marks it at its happiest. The song, however, is immediately followed by an attack on the village by Gabbar's men, an assault we knew was pending, since the preceding scene had shown Gabbar plotting the attack with his men, and enquiring, with a sadistic smile, 'When is Holi?'. In this way, this song is underpinned with suspense, and leads into the attack with the accelerated repetition of its final chorus.

This song also marks and develops some of the core relationships in this film. Veeru begins singing the song with the playful and vivacious Basanti, making it clear that these two are to form a couple. At one point, Jai is about to sing, as we would expect from a hero. However, he glances up to Thakur's residence and sees Radha, Thakur's widowed daughter-in-law, who as a Hindu widow is excluded from celebration and singing. The Holi song is particularly poignant in marking Radha's tragic state, since as a widow she wears only white, whereas Holi is a vibrant celebration in which coloured powder is playfully thrown around among the celebrants. Jai and Radha fall in love, but unlike Veeru and Basanti who do so amid much singing and dancing, they do not sing or dance, and their developing romance is instead themed by Jai's mournful playing of the harmonica as he sits in the courtyard each night as Radha carries out household duties. The fact that Jai refrains from singing from this point on and thereby attaches himself to Radha, thus empathising with her predicament, is particularly pointed: in the context of Hindi cinema, where love is always expressed and developed in song, their songless love marks the impossible nature of their relationship, since widow remarriage is taboo in the kind of rural context in which the film is set.[12] Thus, the song plays an important part in establishing the contrast between the two leading couples.[13]

'Mehbooba mehbooba'/'My beloved'

Later, Jai and Veeru plan an attack on Gabbar's camp. As with the Holi song and the assault on the village, this action scene takes place around a song sequence, and indeed parallels the Holi sequence. The narrative moves to Gabbar's camp, where a song-and-dance sequence is being performed by some itinerant musicians/dancers. A man sings of his desire for his darling and Hindi film's most famous vamp dancer, Helen, dances in a sequined green Arabian Nights type costume. The song and dance are sexy (and the shooting emphasises this), and Gabbar looks at the dancer lasciviously, clearly enjoying the seductive moves and lyrics. During the instrumental interludes, shots of Jai and Veeru laying explosives and preparing to blow up the camp are intercut with those of the performers and Gabbar. Again, the song builds in speed and intensity, dramatically leading up to the explosion.[14]

Dance at Gabbar's camp, 'Mehbooba mehbooba'

This song also performs a structural function in terms of marking the film's core binary of good and evil. In the context of contemporary India and the Hindi film, this kind of erotic dance is illicit, and shows Gabbar Singh to be of 'bad character' (and the female performer too). Hence, this song opposes the centre to the outside, the wholesome, idyllic village to the camp in the hills. It also opposes the heroes and Thakur to Gabbar and his men, and the heroines to the unchaste dancer.[15] This is the 'bad' song of the camp and Gabbar's lust, and is opposed to the Holi song (the song of the village), as well as the following song, which is sung by Veeru and Basanti. This song, therefore, is very much an 'item', and an excuse to include a sexy Helen number without marking the film as immoral.[16] However, at the same time, it embodies suspense and narrative progression as well as forming part of the binary moral fabric of the film.

'Koi haseena jab ruth jati hai to'/'When a beautiful girl gets angry'

This song sees Veeru finally managing to win over Basanti, who has so far resisted his somewhat crude (and comical) advances. It follows a scene where, using a tube for amplification, Veeru stands behind the god Shiva as Basanti prays, and tells her that she should get together with Veeru. Basanti is at first taken in, but Jai leads her round the back of the statue to where Veeru is standing. Basanti is furious and gets into her *tonga*, followed by the irrepressible Veeru. The number is again a classic of Hindi cinema, the *manao* song where the hero wins over an angry or uppity heroine in a comic sequence. He sings, 'When a beautiful girl gets angry she becomes even more beautiful' in the refrain, and after much tussling in the *tonga*, during which Basanti drives at breakneck speed and cracks her whip – sometimes at her horse and sometimes at Veeru – he subdues her. Hence, this song sees the couple finally get together, covering an important point in the narrative. As discussed above, it is also structured relative to the unsung, tragic love of Jai and Radha, and the illicit lust of Gabbar.

'Jab tak hai jaan'/'As long as there is life in me'

After a breakneck chase in her *tonga*, Gabbar's men capture Basanti and take her to the camp. Gabbar looks her up and down lasciviously, and teases her, asking Basanti to dance for them. Some more of Gabbar's men appear with Veeru, following a failed attempt to save Basanti. Gabbar ties him up. He notes the fondness Basanti and Veeru clearly have for each other, and passes other coarse comments about Basanti, enraging Veeru. He is about to kill Veeru when Basanti screams and runs to him. Again noting the fondness between them in a loaded manner, an opportunity for sadistic play occurs to him: ordering his men to aim their guns at Veeru, he tells Basanti that if she wants the life of her sweetheart, she has to dance for them; as long as she dances, he will live. To have Basanti dance in front of Gabbar and his men is firstly to insult her, to treat her like the dancer in 'Mehbooba mehbooba', a female entertainer of men who would be seen as little more than a prostitute. It also insults Veeru, who is her (we assume) husband-to-be, and he cries out, 'Basanti, don't dance in front of these dogs.' However, in Gabbar's eagerness to stage Veeru's death as an elaborate and sadistic show, he gives Basanti a performative arena, time and space in which to act, and thereby heightened agency, and the song turns into one of the most dramatic sequences of the film. Rather than cowering in shame at having to dance in front of the leering Gabbar and his men, Basanti dances with pride and defiance; instead of playing the role of the dishonoured woman, she assumes the part of the brave and loyal lover who will break normal social rules and sacrifice herself for the safety of the man she loves.[17] She begins to sing the refrain 'As long as I have life I will dance' as the (extra-diegetic) music strikes up and she dances with energy and determination, continuing, 'Love never

Basanti's heroic performance, 'Jab tak hai jaan'

ever dies,/Death is not afraid of it,/We will die and fade away,/Our story will remain.' Amused at first, Gabbar begins to grow angry as she continues to dance and sing in this way, performing love, loyalty and bravery as opposed to the shame and humiliation that he had wanted to see. He signals to one of his men, who throws a bottle onto the ground. There is a pause in the song as Basanti contemplates the broken glass, and the audience wonders whether she will continue to dance or stop, which would trigger Veeru's death. Rising to this even greater challenge, she dances over the broken glass using complex rhythmic footwork, ultimately dancing on one foot when a large piece of glass becomes embedded in the other. Again, she takes this new challenge as an opportunity to perform her love and loyalty for Veeru with added defiance and passion.

Eventually, after one suspense-filled pause where Basanti nearly faints, her strength finally reaches its end. Her voice fades away and she collapses at the feet of Veeru, signalling his death. We hear a shot, and then see the man who was meant to shoot Veeru fall to the ground. Jai has come to the rescue, and this scene leads into the final fight which sees Jai mortally wounded and Gabbar eventually captured. This song hence embodies a scene packed full of passion, defiance and suspense that is, moreover, pivotal to the whole film drama.

'Jab tak hai jaan' utilises dramatically the agency of performance. The performance is set up by Gabbar, who attempts to base it on the model of 'Mehbooba mehbooba', a classic gender/sexuality/power matrix of Indian society which places the female performer as an object of erotic pleasure for the male audience. However, Basanti refuses to accept this format, and being brave enough to directly defy it, uses the agency Gabbar has unwittingly provided to reverse her intended humiliation and, crucially, buy time that allows help to arrive and Gabbar to be finally defeated.

Songs in Hindi films play with and exploit the core link of performance, agency and drama, making them at times among the most dramatic sequences of the film. In other words, they do not just mobilise the emotionality or *affective* potential of music/song/dance for the sake of drama, they tap into the inherent dramatic potential of performance itself.[18] In real-life theatrical or musical performances, roles are generally dictated by cultural norms and traditions, forms of social contract which the performers have an interest in keeping, and the individual's agency can hence be seen as being channelled and shaped within these parameters into artistry, charisma and virtuosity. In the world of the Hindi film, however, since the exigencies of the narrative govern what happens and how it happens, the song-and-dance performances therefore do not follow the authority of conventional social or artistic norms. Indeed, the flouting of normal social rules is what is so dramatically powerful.[19] For example, highly dramatic diegetically performed song sequences where characters take over or 'hijack' the performance to stage their personal drama, in a similar vein to Basanti, are not uncommon. In *Muqaddar ka Sikandar* (Prakash Mehra, 1978), for example, a courtesan is performing a number about love in her salon when the drunk and disturbed hero takes the floor and sings at length about his emotions, leaving the courtesan shocked, overwhelmed and ultimately smitten, and hence transformed into a major player in the narrative. A similar song sequence occurs in the middle of *Raja Hindustani* (Dharmesh Darshan, 1996), in which an itinerant troupe sing of love and separation at the moment when the (rich) heroine is about to leave the (poor) hero and return to the big city with her father (who knows nothing of the 'forbidden' love that has grown between them). The lyrics of the song resonate so strongly with the emotions of the hero that he takes to the floor and sings himself. The heroine is so overwhelmed that she runs into his arms at the end of the sequence, her horrified father looking on, spurring the film into the second half. In the finale song-and-dance sequence in *Pakeezah* (Kamal Amrohi, 1971), the courtesan heroine, tortured by her 'shameful existence', breaks a lantern and dances over the broken glass in a frenzied coda, destroying her dancing feet and her courtesan persona for ever.[20] In *Pardes* (Subhash Ghai, 1997), in a long and complex denouement song sequence, a troupe of *qawwali* singers perform a song about love (with, conveniently, rather more worldly overtones than should exist in traditional *qawwali*) at a Sufi shrine. The *qawwali* resonates with the feelings of love that exist between the hero and heroine, feelings which they cannot express because the heroine is engaged to the hero's friend (who is a bad lot). In the sequence, the diegetic performance and the emotional drama intertwine, the hero tries to deny his love for the heroine, but eventually embraces her as her enraged fiancé turns up with friends in tow to fight.

In such song sequences as these, the personal drama overpowers what in the real world would be expected codes of behaviour for performers and/or audiences, or it subsumes the diegetic performance into itself (as in *Pardes*). The personal drama is thus heightened, foregrounded, shown to be bigger than the rules and conventions of the (fictional representation of) society. In many other songs, the emotional drama of performing protagonists manifestly bubbles beneath the surface, almost bursting out, thereby creating tension and suspense. More generally, in all song sequences, even those not formally staged as in the above examples, a particular aspect of the drama gains the heightened space of a framed performance through its expression in song, the choreographed movement or dance, and usually lavish sets, giving it a privileged position in the narrative.

Conclusions
As this discussion of the Hindi film songs in *Sholay* has shown, song sequences are certainly about entertainment, and constitute special 'items' within the narrative. In a sense, therefore, the Hindi film

can be seen as a 'cinema of attractions',[21] or, as Madhav Prasad has argued, as 'modular' rather than 'serial' in its construction.[22] Yet at the same time, film songs are a part of the narrative, and play distinct roles that extend beyond mere entertainment and spectacle. Songs are a form of emotional expression, and are central to the emotionality of the Hindi film in a way comparable to opera more than the light, fantasy-oriented American musical. Looking in terms of the melodrama of Hindi films, having sung rather than spoken expression amplifies emotions and affect. As director Anil Sharma stated, while the songs in the Hindi film are clearly unrealistic, since people do not sing in this way in real life, they express 'emotions in a better way'.[23] Put simply, many of the key emotional developments of the film are set in song because they are important.

While songs are often interpreted as 'interrupting' the Hindi film narrative (based on the conventions of Hollywood), they in fact provide modes of heightened performativity that enable dramatic agency that may become crucial to the unfolding of the narrative. In this way, songs are significant to the narrative and creation of drama over and above the sheer affect and emotion of music, poetry and dance versus speech and non-choreographed movement. The heightened dramatic agency of song sequences also enables them to play a key role as vehicles for characterisation as well as the common binary structuring of relationships and the film's moral conflicts.

Another key way in which film songs constitute spectacle and entertainment 'items', at the same time as embodying the main narrative and dramatic fabric of the film, is through the use of background style music in the accompaniments, especially the instrumental interludes. Interludes may be, as Anil Sharma put it, 'as per the song', so continuing the idiom of the song, or be 'as per the visuals', acting more like a backing music track.[24] While song sequences are not incompatible with the grittier and more knife-edge aspects of the (melo)drama, singing on its own does not embody evil, chaos or destruction (of good) in Hindi films (as discussed above with reference to the fact that villains do not sing). Rather, it is the orchestral interludes that signify these things, adopting a number of Hollywood codes for the portrayal of on-edgeness, danger and evil.[25] In this way, while singing limits the emotional flavour of a song somewhat, there is no such restriction with interludes.

In this sense, Hindi films are musicals, though not in the same sense as American musicals. Music and musicality are used as a key part of the emotional expression of the film, especially romance. Yet they are also one part of the structuring of the overall Manichaeistic matrix of the film. Also key to the music and musicality of the Hindi film is the mobilisation of the performativity of the song sequence for characterisation and dramatic agency. The Hindi film and the film songs are both imitations of life, and dramatic tension and effect is created through the ways that songs play with, enlarge on, flout and musically dramatise real-life performance. While the song sequences are certainly special parts of the film, they are, more simply, also integral to the overall narrative, although most film songs work extremely well as separate audio or audio-visual sequences. The producer Rajkumar Barjatya of the long-standing production house Rajshri, explained:

a song itself is a scene. In any film, … if a scene can be removed and it does not hamper the last two or three reels which are the main crux of the story, then that scene has no business to remain in the film normally. Sometimes there are extraordinary scenes which are put in as an item, which is there, which is OK. … If the story is not changed by removing a song then that song is not worth keeping, however good a tune it is, however good its lyrics are. So, it should be woven together, and this is only possible when the film is conceived as a musical film.[26]

Notes

1. Peter Manuel, *Cassette Culture* (Chicago: University of Chicago Press, 1993), p. 41.

2. Quoted in Ravi Vasudevan, 'Shifting Codes, Dissolving Identities: The Hindi Social Film of the 1950s as Popular Culture', in Vasudevan (ed.), *Making Meaning in Indian Cinema* (New Delhi: Oxford University Press, 2000), pp. 99–121, p. 100.

3. Rick Altman, *The American Film Musical* (Bloomington: Indiana University Press, 1987), p. 273.

4. Ibid., p. 272.

5. See Rosie Thomas, 'Indian Cinema: Pleasures and Popularity: An Introduction', *Screen*, vol. 26 no. 3–4, 1985, pp. 61–131, and Thomas, 'Melodrama and the Negotiation of Morality in Mainstream Hindi Film', in Carol A. Breckenridge (ed.), *Consuming Modernity: Public Culture in a South Asian World* (Minneapolis and London: University of Minnesota Press, 1995), pp. 157–82, on the Hindi film as melodrama. Ien Ang has argued that melodrama exhibits 'emotional' realism as opposed to 'empiricist' realism, found in some art-house films, or 'classical' realism, characteristic of Hollywood non-musical films, in *Watching Dallas: Soap Opera and the Melodramatic Imagination* (London: Routledge, 1985). This is discussed with reference to Hindi films in Rachel Dwyer, *All You Want Is Money, All You Need Is Love: Sex and Romance in Modern India* (London and New York: Cassell, 2001), p. 107. Peter Brooks's classic work on melodrama emphasises the emotions and moral conflicts as the real players, with psychological realism subsidiary: 'The Melodramatic Imagination', in Marcia Landy (ed.), *Imitations of Life: A Reader on Film and Television Melodrama* (Detroit: Wayne State University Press, 1991), pp. 50–67.

6. Altman, *American Film Musical*, p. 103.

7. This is commented on by Vasudevan, 'Shifting Codes, Dissolving Identities', pp. 101–2.

8. Anna Morcom, *Hindi Film Songs and the Cinema* (Aldershot, Hants.: Ashgate, 2007), pp. 181–206.

9. While it is impossible to find one film that is representative of Hindi cinema as a whole, *Sholay* is a classic *masala* (literally 'spice') film, an iconic Hindi film potboiler. Although there are differences in the way songs are used by different subgenres or different directors, *Sholay* shows well how songs are integrated with the film narrative, and may form a part of its most dramatic moments.

10. Anna Morcom, 'An Understanding between Hollywood and Bollywood? The Meaning of Hollywood-style Music in Hindi Films', in *Music and Meaning*, special issue of *British Journal of Ethnomusicology*, vol. 10 no. 1, 2001, pp. 63–84.

11. Interview, 3 March 2000, quoted in Morcom, *Hindi Film Songs and the Cinema*, p. 177.

12. Near the end, Jai declares his love for Radha, and Thakur agrees to the match (stating that 'times have changed'). However, Jai's death results in the film ultimately upholding conservative values. Presumably, the production team must have decided that to show the easy acceptance of widow remarriage would be too radical for the cinema audience. In contrast, in *Prem Rog* ('The Disease of Love', Raj Kapoor, 1982), which does tackle the subject, remarriage is only allowed after a full film's worth of struggle and sacrifices. In *Sholay*, Radha is left as if twice widowed, which adds to the sadness of Jai's death.

13. This pairing is similar in ways to what Altman describes as the 'dual-focus narrative' structure of the American musical (*American Film Musical*, pp. 16–27). However, with the American musical, which revolves around the binary of the couple, this structuring of dualities is apparently far more extensive than in the Hindi film.

14. This and the Holi song illustrate clearly how it can embody narrative, yet retain its integrity as a song in its aural dimension: on screen, the accelerating tempo clearly builds suspense bio-acoustically, but listened to on recording, it just sounds like an increase in the intensity and excitement of the erotic – or in the case of the Holi song, celebratory – emotion of the song. The balance of 'audio value' with situationality (i.e. narrative function) is one that is given considerable attention in Hindi films (Morcom, *Hindi Film Songs and the*

Cinema, pp. 51–5). In 'Yeh dosti', the balance is achieved in the audio version through the deletion of much of the situational detail of the song, which conveniently happens in the interludes: for example, the skidding around in the bazaar, which is expressed with chromatic 'dizzy' violins and then muted jazzy trumpet.

15. Jerry Pinto discusses the structural, moral role of the vamp in Hindi cinema in *Helen: The Life and Times of an H-bomb* (New Delhi: Penguin, 2006), pp. 85–101.

16. See Asha Kasbekar 'Hidden Pleasures: Negotiating the Myth of the Female Ideal in Popular Hindi Cinema', in Rachel Dwyer and Christopher Pinney (eds), *Pleasure and the Nation: The History, Politics and Consumption of Public Culture in India* (New Delhi: Oxford University Press, 2000), pp. 286–308, for an examination of the Hindi film's disavowal of voyeurism in the erotic display of song-and-dance sequences.

17. Such 'noble sacrifices', where a woman's performance becomes honourable as opposed to marking her as immoral, are discussed by Kasbekar in 'Hidden Pleasures'.

18. Such ideas of performance, action and transformation are explored in much performance theory, notably John L. Austin's theory of the performative in language or 'speech acts', and collaborations between Victor Turner and Richard Schechner. See Richard Schechner, *Performance Studies: An Introduction*, 2nd edition (New York and London: Routledge, 2002), for an introduction and overview of performance theory.

19. Michel Foucault's discussion of executions as spectacle in *Discipline and Punish: The Birth of the Prison* (New York: Vintage Books, 1979) raises the same point of performance as agency. Whereas in a Hindi film, the normal social rules of performance are subordinate to, and in fact used for the sake of, the drama, in the macabre performances of public execution, the main 'protagonist' no longer has any reason to obey any rules set them: 'If the crowd gathered round the scaffold, it was not simply to witness the sufferings of the condemned man or to excite the anger of the executioner: it was also to hear an individual who had *nothing more to lose* curse the judges, the laws, the government and religion. ... In these executions, which ought to show only the terrorizing power of the prince, there was a whole aspect of the carnival, in which rules were inverted, authority mocked and criminals transformed into heroes' (pp. 60–1; my emphasis).

20. Anna Morcom, 'The Pure Voice: Disembodied Performance and Playback Singing in Hindi Films', paper presented at the British Forum for Ethnomusicology one-day conference 'Music and the Body', November 2003.

21. Ravi Vasudevan 'Addressing the Spectator of a "Third World" National Cinema: The Bombay "Social" Film of the 1940s and 1950s', *Screen*, vol. 36 no. 4, pp. 305–24, p. 307.

22. Madhav Prasad, *Ideology of the Hindi Film: A Historical Construction* (Delhi: Oxford University Press, 1998), p. 43.

23. Interview with author, 15 April 1999, quoted in Morcom, *Hindi Film Songs and the Cinema*, p. 15.

24. Ibid., p. 43.

25. This use of Hollywood-style music in ways that code good and evil in Hindi film songs is discussed in detail in Morcom, 'An Understanding between Hollywood and Bollywood?'. I also discuss the 'of the cinema' character of Hindi film songs as lying in the violin-dominated orchestral accompaniments (*Hindi Film Songs and the Cinema*, especially p. 87), and the situational nature of the music which fits around visuals and narrative and adopts many Hollywood-derived scoring techniques (ibid., pp. 130–6).

26. Interview, 30 June 1999, quoted in Morcom, *Hindi Film Songs and the Cinema*, pp. 30–1.

12 Robert Altman and the New Hollywood Musical

Gayle Sherwood Magee

Between 1975 and 1980, director Robert Altman (1925–2006) made eight films, of which three are unquestionably musicals. These three musicals were filmed during one of the most productive and volatile periods in Altman's career, and amid great changes in the film industry. They include one film that is usually described as his masterpiece, one that is largely forgotten and one that initiated his decade-long exile from Hollywood: *Nashville* (1975), *A Perfect Couple* (1979) and *Popeye* (1980). Taken together, these three musicals reflect not only the range of Altman's output, but also his continuing engagement with the film musical, a genre that seemed moribund at the beginning of the 1970s.

In order to understand Altman's relationship to the musical, this study will place these three films within the context of the screen musical of the 1970s. Additionally, each work will be considered in light of its reception in contemporary media, particularly how the film was described and portrayed by Altman and his creative collaborators. Filling out the study will be complementary and contrasting views of these works as represented in material from the Robert Altman Archives at the University of Michigan, primarily press kits and publicity materials aimed at the mass media and at industry insiders. As this multilayered approach reveals, the musical offered Altman unprecedented opportunities for reinvention within the larger context of New Hollywood – a connection between a classic studio-era genre and an emerging industry that, at first glance, might seem paradoxical.

By New Hollywood, I am referring to the concept in both its general and more specific meanings, beginning with but not limited to the post-studio era that emerged in the late 1960s. As Peter Krämer defines New Hollywood, this era includes 'all American films, the film industry and the wider film culture' during the years 1967–76 and represents a break from the previous studio-era model.[1] Thomas Schatz places New Hollywood even later: initiated with *Jaws* in 1975 and continuing through the blockbuster era.[2] At the same time, 'New Hollywood' is commonly used interchangeably with American art or modernist cinema from approximately 1967 until the late 1970s. As an examination of these three films will reveal, Altman's musicals belong to all of these meanings of 'New Hollywood' – the general and the specific – and it is possible to suggest one further meaning as well.

Nashville and the Early 1970s Musical

First, it may prove beneficial to outline the state of the film musical up to 1975 – that is, leading up to the release of *Nashville*. Table 1 presents a representative group of film musicals, organised by origin on stage (usually Broadway or Off Broadway); as screen musicals; or as concert documentaries. As Table 1 illustrates, the old-style stage and screen musical was out of tune with contemporary Hollywood studios, film critics and movie audiences alike in the early 1970s. Part of its failure involved the disconnection between storylines and topics of traditional musicals with the more daring, mature, often more violent films of New Hollywood.

Table 1: Select Film Musicals 1970–5

Year/Origin	1970	1971	1972	1973	1974	1975
Broadway	Song of Norway On a Clear Day You Can See Forever	Fiddler on the Roof	Cabaret Jesus Christ Superstar	Godspell	Mame	Rocky Horror Picture Show
Screen	Darling Lili	Willy Wonka and the Chocolate Factory	Lady Sings the Blues	Lost Horizon		At Long Last Love Funny Lady Tommy Nashville
Concert Documentary	Gimme Shelter Woodstock Let It Be		Elvis on Tour	Jimi Hendrix		

Yet another issue was demographic in origin, in that younger adult viewers flocked to concert documentaries, or what Rick Altman calls the 'the non-filmic rock concert craze of the sixties and seventies'.[3] In addition to straightforward concert documentaries, some films blended elements of concert documentary to create inter-generic hybrids. For example, the nominally narrative film *Tommy* combines barely fictionalised characters with concert-style performances by Elton John and Eric Clapton, among others. On the flip side, an actual concert documentary such as *Woodstock* can be read simultaneously as a narrative musical by focusing on the 'story' of the flower children at the concert, as Rick Altman has shown.[4] Moreover, these films offered studios high returns on low investments – a critical fact at a time of heavy studio losses and even bankruptcies. This fact was particularly true in the case of *Woodstock*, which cost a mere $100,000 and made more than $16 million in rentals, pulling Warner Bros. from the brink of bankruptcy. The film's soundtrack album added to the profits, selling more than 2 million units in the first year alone.[5]

By contrast, films that consciously invoked an older model of the musical generally failed at the box office, while earning mixed or negative media reviews. *The Song of Norway* (1970) reprised an Grieg-scored, operetta-style Broadway show from the 1940s in what reviewer John J. O'Connor described as 'good, clean family entertainment' along the lines of *The Sound of Music* (1965), but with the warning: 'If your stomach was turned by the sweetness and light of *The Sound of Music*, not even Tums will get you through *The Song of Norway*.'[6] *Fiddler on the Roof* (1971) fared somewhat better despite its three-hour running time, although Vincent Canby complained of its 'mechanical and bland' performances that 'let most of the life out of' the original show.[7] *Willy Wonka and the Chocolate Factory* (1971) was deemed 'hollow', 'barely acceptable', 'poorly staged' and 'a terrible letdown' by Gene Siskel.[8]

The seeming incompatibility of innovative, contemporary film-making with the classic musical came to the fore just a few months before the June 1975 release of *Nashville*, with the March release of

Peter Bogdanovich's *At Long Last Love*. The film tried to recreate the 1930s musicals using non-singers Burt Reynolds and Cybill Shepherd along with live-recorded vocal tracks. *At Long Last Love* failed to impress audiences or critics, who inevitably compared it pejoratively to earlier musicals, as in Canby's review:

> *At Long Last Love* is almost entirely devoid of the kind of wit, vigor and staggering self-assurance with which real musical comedy performers – people like Fred Astaire, Ginger Rogers, Ethel Merman, Clifton Webb, Nanette Fabray, Charlotte Greenwood, Jack Buchanan – could turn a leaky rowboat of a show into the Ile de France ... The problem that Mr Bogdanovich set himself in *At Long Last Love* – and which he never solves – is how to top these evocations of the past for our current pleasure.[9]

Siskel opened his review with an even more pointed comparison of the present musical with the past:

> After watching Peter Bodganovich's *At Long Last Love* one wonders what the point is. Is he trying to have fun with the Hollywood musical? It seems that way. But is he trying to kid it, or imitate it? Not the latter, for sure, because the film has been stocked with musical incompetents.[10]

The performers' lack of ability as well as Bogdanovich's use of live, on-the-set recording for the songs brought particular condemnation, with Siskel stating flatly that the 'musical numbers are a mess. Nobody knows how to dance; nobody knows how to sing.'[11]

    With Bogdanovich's very public failure to recreate the classic musical early in 1975, and the reduced currency of the traditional musical overall, it should come as no surprise that Altman's *Nashville* is not identified as such. Indeed, the description of the film as 'a musical' is generally absent from advertising materials aimed at the media, Altman's own promotional interviews that accompanied the film's opening in June 1975 and descriptions by the other members of the creative team. On the contrary, all try to distance *Nashville* from traditional musicals. One interview with Altman paraphrases the director as saying, 'his new film won't be thought of as a musical, but it is loaded with country music songs'.[12] Musical director Richard Baskin told *Newsweek*, 'We did not set out to create a country-Western musical ... We wanted to allow the performers to express themselves in whatever music felt best for them.'[13] (Regardless of the film's promotion, reviewers almost immediately described the film as a musical, beginning with Pauline Kael hailing it as 'a country-western musical' in her pre-release review in *The New Yorker*.[14])

    Baskin's comment relates to often-repeated beliefs concerning the film's songs that challenge traditional ideas of the musical. These claims have persisted since the release of the film in the popular media, in statements by Robert Altman himself and in scholarly sources as well. A particularly pithy description exists in Altman's own description of the songs from 2000, when the LP soundtrack was released on CD as part of the twenty-fifth anniversary of the film's release. 'Each performer wrote their songs from the character's point of view: it lent a reality as well as a theatrical depth to the songs and performances ... for some, it was a first film, and a first singer-songwriter experience.'[15] This portrait of the creative process stands at the centre of *Nashville*'s legacy, and as evidence of Altman's daring challenge to the conventions of the old Hollywood musical of the studio era. The old musical divided the creative labour between professional songwriters, and professional singers and dancers; it often recycled previously written songs; and it maintained a top-down structure in which actors were not encouraged to write their own dialogue, let alone their own songs. In this sense, *Nashville* emerges as a complete challenge to the studio-era musical. *Nashville* thus avoided the label of 'musical' while promoting a new attitude towards the traditional division of labour in the studio-era musical, adhering to the principles of New Hollywood in the incorporation of improvisation and creative process.

Yet the belief that cast members wrote their own songs for the film, 'from the character's point of view', is not true for much of the music that we hear in *Nashville*. Nor were the majority of singers and songwriters inexperienced – far from it, in fact. Just as the film-makers avoided the label of 'musical' despite a classic backstage or show-musical format, the creative process and models for the film are closer to traditional musicals than previously believed. Not once do we see a first-time singer/songwriter perform his or her own song written for the film from the character's point of view.

Not only are most of the film's songs written and performed by professionals, but the soundtrack incorporates at least a half-dozen previously existing songs. These songs were written neither for the film nor from the characters' point of view. Indeed, existing copies of the film's earlier scripts indicate that at least some of the story and characters were built around these pre-existing songs, not unlike the traditional approach to Hollywood musicals such as *Singin' in the Rain* (1952) and *White Christmas* (1954). In effect, there is more of 'old' Hollywood in this New Hollywood masterwork than is generally acknowledged.

A case in point involves two songs written by Keith Carradine that provided the catalyst for *Nashville*. Altman heard Carradine perform the songs, 'It Don't Worry Me' and 'I'm Easy', at a party during the making of another Altman film, *Thieves Like Us*, in Mississippi, and later recalled, 'When I heard them I knew I wanted to base a whole movie around them, a movie that would simply give me an excuse to put them in.'[16] Author Jan Stuart documents that the earliest scripts for *Nashville* include these two songs and, he suggests, 'there is a sense of the screenplay having been constructed around the songs'.[17] The same can be said of a pre-shooting script in the Altman archives that includes cues not only for Carradine's two songs but for Henry Gibson's 'Keep A-Goin", a text written well before the earliest ideas for *Nashville*.

In these scripts, as in the final film, Carradine's previously written songs define character, advance the plot and represent *Nashville*'s central theme. 'It Don't Worry Me' is particularly important as the film's theme song. As Barbara Ching notes, the song voices 'a haunting paean to irresponsibility', and serves 'as a reflection on the lives of the characters' more so than any other song.[18] Carradine's songs, Gibson's 'Keep A-Goin", Ronee Blakley's 'Dues' and other previously composed works dominate the film's LP soundtrack and are among the most highlighted performances – that is, presented in nearly complete form with a minimum amount of competing dialogue. ABC executives financed *Nashville* based on the strength of Carradine's two songs, which Altman played when selling the concept of the film.[19] Altman sold the film's financial backers not on new songs written by amateurs, but on extant songs by Carradine, an experienced singer/songwriter. Carradine's songwriting contribution would be recognised officially, as he won the film's sole Academy Award for 'I'm Easy' in the Best Original Song category.

The importance of pre-existing songs in *Nashville* does not cancel out the film's many innovations. Just in terms of the music, the number of songwriters involved is higher than in the traditional studio-era musical. And, in *Nashville*, several, although not all, of the performers on screen are the song-writers themselves, thus breaking down the old division of labour using the new folk-rock, singer/songwriter model. Yet, for the most important songs and performances, Altman left very little to chance. In building its storyline and characters around pre-existing songs written and performed by professionals, *Nashville* can be seen and heard as an update of the studio musical. Yet this dimension of the film may have been de-emphasised in light of the failure of *At Long Last Love* and similar musicals that reference the classic version of the genre.

What is remarkable about *Nashville* is the presence of two narratives in the film's promotion. The pro-innovation view of *Nashville* – that is, stressing the film's break from the traditional musical – originated in the film's promotional materials circulated to the mainstream press, and through the press to the public. Yet within the industry, the film was marketed as the product of professional musicians. The film's press book and merchandising manual, which appears to have been circulated to industry insiders and exhibitors rather than the media, consistently emphasises the cast's musical qualifications.[20] Within these materials are extensive biographies that summarise and highlight the experience and previous hits of the cast's professional musicians – even those who do not perform significantly within the film. Other promotional materials include a songbook with lead sheets for the main songs, accompanied by detailed profiles of the cast's most experienced singer/songwriters – again, even those who are not featured prominently in *Nashville*.[21] The latter suggests yet another defensive response to the harsh criticisms of Bogdanovich's film and the ineptitude of its performers. As such, these materials underscore the two-pronged publicity efforts for the film: to the public, obscuring *Nashville*'s connections to the traditional backstage musical in favour of the New Hollywood narrative of innovation and process; and for industry insiders, an emphasis on the cast's musical abilities, songwriting skills and singing experience.

At the same time, *Nashville* doesn't look, or sound, like a traditional musical. In fact, *Nashville* updated the musical through visual and aural references to the concert documentary. These references are apparent throughout the film in extended performance sequences. Yet the Parthenon sequence after the shooting stands out as particularly explicit in reproducing a concert-documentary style through the conscious incorporation of out-of-focus shots, obstructed views and anonymous crowd scenes (see select captures in Table 2).

While the camerawork and editing invoke this very contemporary model, the sequence's sound design heightens the effect. As Rick Altman has stated in his study of sound recording, mixing and editing in *Nashville*, the film to this point has used multitrack recording to create a three-dimensional

Table 2: Select Concert Documentary References in *Nashville*

Image				
Timing	2:33:50	2:33:50	2:33:50	2:33:51
Sung Text	'[It don't] worry	me'		

Image				
Timing	2:33:53	2:33:54	2:33:55	2:33:55
Sung Text	'[You may] say, I	ain't		free'

sonic space in which 'overlapping dialogue, competing conversations, interfering media, and other examples of radio-miked twenty-four-track multi-dimensionality' are possible.[22] The end of the film, however, features a single audio channel in contrast to the multitracked soundscape of the remainder of the film, which he describes as the forfeit of 'non-hierarchic openness oriented to spectator choice [that] yields in the end to the narrative logic of the traditional linear model'.[23]

While the sequence may, in fact, capitulate to conventional narrative demands, it is equally possible to see and hear this segment as reproducing standard concert-documentary sound design, in which a monolithic soundtrack suppresses and dominates individual voices. Such canny use of sound amplifies the lyrics sung by those on stage, leaving the crowd voiceless and powerless. The result is a perfect use of sound diegesis to illustrate the theme of *Nashville*: that a lethal combination of religion, politics and popular culture controls the American populace, who unthinkingly sing, 'you may say that I ain't free, but it don't worry me'. Notably, one of Altman's least recognised innovations at this moment and elsewhere in *Nashville* may be combining the old studio musical with the concert documentary to create a genuinely 'new' Hollywood musical – but a musical all the same.

A Perfect Couple and the Disco Musical

Over the next few years, the musical would make a comeback of sorts, as summarised in Table 3. The mega-hit *Saturday Night Fever* (1977) used dance performances as an excuse for nearly constant musical interludes in the realm of the stage musical. Soundtrack sales broke all previous records and marked the mainstream arrival of disco with hits by the Bee Gees. *Grease*, from 1978, revitalised the Broadway-based musical, again with the support of a widely marketed and wildly successful soundtrack – led by the film's title track, a disco hit written and produced by, again, Barry Gibb of the Bee Gees. The success of both films can be seen as the outcome of more than a decade of heavy marketing of music-based films to the 'baby-boomer' demographic that had first emerged with films such as *The Graduate* (1967) and *Easy Rider* (1969).[24] Neither *The Wiz* (1978), *Thank God It's Friday* (1978) nor *Sgt. Pepper* (1978) duplicated this box-office success, despite featuring disco soundtracks. Yet the dominance of

Table 3: Select Film Musicals 1975–80

Year/Origin	1976	1977	1978	1979	1980
Broadway			The Wiz Grease	Hair	
Screen	A Star Is Born	Saturday Night Fever New York, New York	The Buddy Holly Story Sgt. Pepper's Lonely Hearts Club Band Thank God It's Friday	All That Jazz The Rose The Perfect Couple	Fame The Blues Brothers Popeye
Concert Documentary	The Song Remains the Same	ABBA: The Movie	The Last Waltz		

this musical style can be seen by the presence of clear-cut disco, or disco-tinged hits in seven out of ten musicals listed here from 1977 to 1978, including *ABBA: The Movie* (1978), another concert documentary.

Altman's film *A Perfect Couple* from 1979 then emerges against a clear track record of success in, and an industry trend towards, the subgenre of disco musicals. And it is possible to see and hear *A Perfect Couple* as expanding this subgenre by merging a disco-influenced stage musical with the concert documentary – using, again, models from traditional musicals. The film traces an unlikely romance between a singer in a Los Angeles band and her suitor, a conservative middle-aged man whose family clearly prefers classical music. The band's performances provide the film's spine, in what is essentially another backstage musical.

With eleven songs and extended coverage of the band, the film could hardly avoid the 'musical' label. In promoting *A Perfect Couple*, Altman took a step towards acknowledging the film as 'a kind of musical', in his own words.[25] The film's production notes to the media support Altman's label, while straining to emphasise the work's contemporary relevance and its differences from traditional musicals. *A Perfect Couple* is described in these sources as a 'contemporary musical', along with the statement: 'Amid the contemporary America he so likes to reflect, Altman has created his kind of musical.'[26] Musical director Allan Nicholls (who also wrote several of the songs) defended the use of music as relevant to the plot – another clear criticism of the traditional studio musical – as follows: 'The songs underscore every scene … There is always a real reason for the music to be there.'[27]

In keeping with the dominant musical style, some of the film's songs are disco-influenced. However, both songs and ensemble defy easy categorisation, or even explanation (see select screen captures in Table 4). The band contains twelve people, including at least six lead singers. The use of

Table 4: Select Screen Captures from *A Perfect Couple*

Image		
Timing	1:15:15	1:15:48
Image		
Timing	1:30:51	1:45:53

amateur dance at various points in the film may have been intended to express spontaneity and nat-
uralness in contrast to the expert choreography of films such as *Saturday Night Fever*. Yet the comparison works to the detriment of Altman's film, as the performers appear merely inept and untrained.

The songs that dominate the film are part of the problem as well. In fact, they provided the im-
petus for the film, and several of the most prominent songs were previously written – as in the case of
Nashville. Both the songs and the film's band originated in 'Keepin' 'Em Off the Streets', a musical-
theatrical production that debuted in December 1976. The show was organised by Allan Nicholls and
featured an evening of songs performed by professional singer/songwriters and out-of-work actors
with backgrounds in musical theatre.[28] (The title of the band and the show also bears an uncanny, and
possibly unfortunate, resemblance to the 1976 Doobie Brothers hit, 'Takin' It to the Streets'.)
Altman saw the show, and decided to act as producer for more than a dozen performances in 1977.
A review of the theatrical version noted the energy and enthusiasm of the fourteen-piece ensemble,
while criticising the original songs, stating, 'there wasn't a single lyrical or melodic idea that hadn't
been exhausted by 1970 … The music was characterless and banal … and played at a decibel level
designed to destroy brain tissue.'[29]

Altman imported several songs and most of the ensemble intact from the theatrical production for
the scaffolding of *A Perfect Couple*. Despite the differences in musical style and division of labour, the
net result is not unlike the studio-era musical once again. And like *Nashville*, *A Perfect Couple* marries
concert documentary to show musical narrative, but with far less success. In *A Perfect Couple*, the
concert-documentary style – with extended performances and anonymous crowd shots – dominates
the film to such a degree that the narrative has no room to develop. As critic Roger Ebert wrote,

> Altman gets sidetracked by 'Keepin' em Off the Streets' … It's almost as if Altman sees *A Perfect Couple*
> as a promotional film for the group, or a concert film … The music is a distraction, a carryover, maybe,
> from Altman's success with the country music of *Nashville*.[30]

In fact, Altman was considering backing the band in a national tour on the strength of the film, as well
as to promote it. And, the director saw the soundtrack album not only as publicity for the film, but
also as a means to recoup his financial investment. As Altman told one interviewer,

> I had to spend $250,000 out of my own pocket to add the group, but I keep the rights to the music.
> Now I have to try to recoup with the band … I want both the group and the record properly promoted in
> order to help the film … The current dilemma, that of wondering whether to put the music or the film
> out first, is like the old chicken and egg problem. It's not clear yet which is the most efficacious method,
> since this whole business of rock and film is still really a novelty.[31]

Yet by 1979, selling a film through a popular song soundtrack was anything but a novelty. In essence,
Altman was aiming for the kind of synergy that had become standard in the film industry by this time,
as exemplified by the enormous successes of *Saturday Night Fever* and *Grease*. Jeff Smith describes
this approach as the belief that 'a well-coordinated marketing campaign could use a soundtrack album
to generate advance interest in its accompanying film, and vice versa'.[32]

But while the singers are all experienced and relatively professional, the songs are nearly impossible to grasp on first hearing and can last several minutes at a time. The band's ensemble character plus
the songs' stylistic jumble – rock and theatre in addition to disco, sometimes in a single song such as

'Don't Take Forever' – must have challenged the marketing of either the film or the LP soundtrack on mainstream radio. Neither made much of an impact, and both dropped from sight within a few weeks of opening. Despite the film's lacklustre fiscal performance and lukewarm reviews, Altman would later claim, 'I think it's a terrific musical – it's what *I* call a musical.'[33]

Popeye and the Blockbuster Era

Undaunted by this failure, Altman released his third musical just a year later – and this time, he embraced the label of 'musical'. *Popeye* avoids any hint of concert-documentary style, instead playing up its connections to the studio-era incarnation, with a few key changes. As Altman's biggest-budgeted film – costing over $25 million – *Popeye* is now remembered as a monumental failure, a reputation that doesn't match its initial, quite positive critical reception. Based on the classic comic strip, *Popeye* starred Robin Williams, a brand-new mega-star who had just finished his first season on the hit TV show *Mork & Mindy*, along with Altman regulars such as Shelley Duvall.

The film as a whole is in the tradition of the fairy-tale musicals of the studio era, with Popeye as an adventurer to the exotic land of Sweet Haven, and Olive Oyl as the damsel to be conquered and claimed. In effect, Robin Williams and Shelley Duvall are the postmodern reincarnation of Nelson Eddy and Jeanette MacDonald. Unlike their predecessors, however, neither Williams nor Duvall could sing. For the most part, the performance duties in *Popeye* are handed over to amateurs, to create a charming, naive effect. As opposed to *Nashville*, in which the singers were often described as amateurs but were in fact almost entirely professionals, *Popeye* features singers who can't sing, and dancers who can't dance – an unfortunate replication of the same faults as Bogdanovich's *At Long Last Love*. This may have been one of Altman's biggest risks, and one that has contributed to the film's negative reputation. A second risk involved the recording of these singers live on the set, again following in Bogdanovich's footsteps: an understandable, even stylistically consistent approach for the concert-documentary aspects of *Nashville* and *A Perfect Couple*, but a very questionable approach for *Popeye*.

In terms of the songs, it is much easier to define songwriter Harry Nilsson's contributions in the negative. Nilsson writes 'anti-standards' that cannot be fully extracted from the film but are integrated into the drama fully, thus paradoxically replicating elements of the post-*Oklahoma* Broadway musical. Nilsson avoids any categorical musical style such as disco, rock, country, folk or standard musical theatre pop song – a fact acclaimed in a promotional booklet that describes the songs as 'not rock and roll, not old American musical'.[34] What the songs do represent is authentic children's music that is stylistically neutral, easily accessible and memorable to even young children on their first viewing: mostly single-syllable, repeated lyrics; a limited vocal range; and transparent, repetitive melodies.

Thus, *Popeye*'s songs and indeed the film itself embody actual family entertainment by drawing on a very outdated model. By any standards, this synthesis represents a real risk – especially for Altman at this stage of his career, and against the backdrop of the late 1970s. As one contemporary reporter noted, 'the conventional wisdom in Hollywood is that Altman needs a hit film. *Popeye*, starring the phenomenally popular Robin Williams, may be that film.'[35] With too many non-starters such as *A Perfect Couple* behind him, and studio enthusiasm for quasi-independent film-makers like Altman fast disappearing, *Popeye* needed to make a big profit. Judging from the LPs, storybooks and other types of merchandising aimed at the children's market, the film's joint producers, Disney and Paramount, were banking on *Popeye*'s success at the box office and beyond.

Perhaps most telling is Altman's own description of his intent with *Popeye* in the film's enormous press kit: 'What we try to do in the motion picture is … go back to the roots of a genuine American hero. … He's human … imperfect … someone I think we can all identify with. He is not a robot.' Altman further stated that he hoped that *Popeye* would 'bring audiences back from space and down to earth'.[36] In the wake of the record success of *Star Wars* (1977) and *The Empire Strikes Back* (1980), which had dominated theatres during the previous summer, the director seems to be opposing the blockbuster space epics out of which the globalised studio system emerged, and which by some accounts resulted in the (temporary) disappearance from mass circulation of American art film and modernist film-makers such as Altman. From this perspective, *Popeye* arrived either too late, or too early: a family musical fifteen years after *The Sound of Music*, and a Disney-sponsored, child-friendly, fairy-tale musical nine years before *The Little Mermaid* (1989).

Conclusion

Both Altman and the mature, innovative musical went into something of a hiatus during the 1980s. The musical did return, but animated and infantilised, in films such as *The Little Mermaid* and *Beauty and the Beast* (1991). Altman didn't abandon music-based works, but he did give up on film musicals for quite some time. Instead, he worked in opera, directing productions of Stravinsky's *The Rake's Progress* at the University of Michigan and in Lille in northern France, and creating a remarkable cine-operatic segment for the film *Aria* (1987). He collaborated with composer William Bolcom and the Chicago Lyric Opera on *McTeague*, which debuted in 1992, and the operatic adaptation of his own 1978 film, *A Wedding*, which premiered in 2004. Musical performance remained important, even crucial in his later films such as *Short Cuts* (1994) and *Kansas City* (1996), in which diegetic performances lend connective tissue and historical depth, as shown by Krin Gabbard.[37] And dance would make a return engagement, in the ballet film *The Company* (2002), yet another work using the skeleton of pre-existing performance pieces and documentary-style footage merged with a backstage musical. But Altman would really only return to a song-based stage musical in his final film, *A Prairie Home Companion* (2006).

In retrospect, *Nashville*, *A Perfect Couple* and *Popeye* reveal one of the most frequently cited criticisms of the director's oeuvre: his inconsistency. Yet taken with its attendant publicity, each film is fascinating for reflecting its own micro-era. *Nashville*'s identity as a musical remained suppressed under the weight of its public image, even as its appropriations of the concert documentary and some aspects of the traditional musical are now obvious. *A Perfect Couple* represents Altman's sole excursion into disco musicals and a blatant effort to tap into industry and box-office trends. Despite its contemporary musical style, it embodies yet another show musical built around extant songs and filmed as a concert documentary. And *Popeye* offers the least viable musical form of the late 1970s and early 80s – the fairy-tale musical – complete with a big star, amateur performance and children's songs, in what was conceived of as a blockbuster, large studio production.

Beyond this, Altman's three musicals from the 1970s reveal much about this legendary film-maker as well as his relationship to his own time, and to film and musical history. These musicals fall along a continuum between relative box-office success and failure; low-budget, independent film-making and the new studio monopoly of the blockbuster era, with its higher costs and break-even points; the large ensemble cast vs. the star vehicle; and between critical acclaim and commercial failure. Inherent in this continuum is the move of Hollywood film-making from a system in which American art cinema aimed at mature audiences could co-exist with more overtly commercial fare, to the era of blockbusters and sequels. And, each represents a unique synthesis of elements drawn from studio-era musicals with contemporary trends, musical styles and industry conditions to create a novel genre: Altman's very own 'new' Hollywood musical.

Notes

For access to materials housed in the Robert Altman Archives, I am grateful to Peggy Daub, Director of the Special Collections Library at the University of Michigan, Ann Arbor, and to the Estate of Robert Altman.

1. Peter Krämer, *The New Hollywood: From Bonnie and Clyde to Star Wars*, Short Cuts: Introductions to Film Studies (London: Wallflower, 2005), p. 2; see also the discussion of the various meanings of 'New Hollywood' on pp. 1–4.
2. Thomas Schatz, 'The New Hollywood', in Jim Collins, Hilary Radner and Ava Preacher Collins (eds), *Film Theory Goes to the Movies*, American Film Institute Film Readers (New York: Routledge, 1993), pp. 8–9.
3. Rick Altman, *The American Film Musical* (Bloomington: Indiana University Press, 1987), p. 114.
4. Ibid., pp. 102–3.
5. R. Serge Denisoff and William D. Romanowski, *Risky Business: Rock in Film* (New Brunswick, NJ: Transaction Publishers, 1991), p. 715.
6. John J. O'Connor, 'Damsels to Dickens to Grieg', *Wall Street Journal*, 6 November 1970, p. 8.
7. Vincent Canby, '*Fiddler* on a Grand Scale', *New York Times*, 4 November 1971, p. 52.
8. Gene Siskel, 'There's Gold in Willy Wonka Chocolate Bars', *Chicago Tribune*, 18 July 1971, p. E1.
9. Vincent Canby, '*At Long Last Love* Evokes Past Films', *New York Times*, 7 March 1975, p. 22.
10. Gene Siskel, '*At Long Last Love* is a Labor Lost', *Chicago Tribune*, 21 March 1975, p. B12.
11. Ibid.
12. Don Safran, 'Altman and Beatty', unidentified newspaper clipping, in Box labelled G129, Yellow Nashville Scrapbook, Robert Altman Archives, Special Collections Library, University of Michigan, Ann Arbor.
13. Charles Michener and Martin Kasindorf, 'Altman's Opryland Epic', *Newsweek*, vol. 85, 30 June 1975, p. 49.
14. Pauline Kael, 'The Current Cinema. Coming: *Nashville*', *New Yorker*, 3 March 1975, p. 79.
15. Robert Altman, Liner notes to *Nashville: The Original Motion Picture Soundtrack*. Various artists. LP released 1975 (ABC Records ABCD-893): CD re-release 2000 (MCA 088 170 1332). Altman's commentary is dated 18 February 2000.
16. Reported in Jan Stuart, *The Nashville Chronicles: The Making of Robert Altman's Masterpiece* (New York: Simon & Schuster, 2000), p. 35.
17. Ibid., p. 37.
18. Barbara Ching, 'Sounding the American Heart: Cultural Politics, Country Music, and Contemporary American Film', in Pamela Robertson Wojcik and Arthur Knight (eds), *Soundtrack Available: Essays on Film and Popular Music* (Durham, NC: Duke University Press, 2001), p. 207.
19. See Robert Altman and David Thompson, *Altman on Altman* (London: Faber & Faber, 2006), pp. 88–9; also reported in Stuart, *Nashville Chronicles*, p. 43.
20. *Paramount Press Book and Merchandising Manual*, Box labelled 21 Nashville, Folder labelled Nashville/Advertising, Altman Archives.
21. *Nashville Songbook*, unpublished bound sheet music, Box labelled 21 Nashville, Folder labelled Nashville/Songbook, Altman Archives.
22. Rick Altman, '24-Track Narrative? Robert Altman's *Nashville*', *Cinémas: Journal of Film Studies*, vol. 1 no. 3, Spring 1991. <www.revue-cinemas.umontreal.ca/vol001no03/08-altman.htm>.
23. Ibid.
24. Quentin James Schultz, Roy M. Anker, *et al.*, *Dancing in the Dark: Youth, Popular Culture, and the Electronic Media* (Grand Rapids, MI: Wm. B. Eerdmans, 1991), pp. 93–4 state: 'The vitality and profitability of youth culture continued to thrive through the 1970s … The mild economic surge generated in the seventies by

emphasis on youth finally exploded in 1977–8 with *Saturday Night Fever* and *Grease*. Each film earned Paramount over $100 million. The two soundtracks together sold over 42 million units worldwide; *Saturday Night Fever* became the largest-selling LP in history.'

25. Rory O'Connor, 'Sound Track: Strike up the Band', unidentified newspaper clipping in Box 10, labelled A Perfect Couple, Altman Archives.

26. Press kit for *A Perfect Couple*, Box 34 labelled California Split, Perfect Couple: Production Notes, p. 1.

27. Ibid., p. 2.

28. The playbill for the March productions are preserved in Box 10, labelled A Perfect Couple, Altman Archives. Additional background material on the theatrical version is included in press clippings in the same location.

29. Lawrence Christon, 'At The Roxy: "Off the Streets", A Vanity Showcase', *Los Angeles Times*, 19 March 1977, p. 8.

30. Roger Ebert, '*A Perfect Couple*', *Chicago Sun-Times*, 9 April 1979. <rogerebert.suntimes.com/apps/pbcs.dll/article?AID=/19790409/REVIEWS/60419001/1023#at>.

31. O'Connor, 'Sound Track'.

32. Jeff Smith, *The Sounds of Commerce* (New York: Columbia University Press, 1998), pp. 186–7.

33. Altman and Thompson, *Altman on Altman*, p. 118.

34. Advance promotional booklet for *Popeye*, Box 13 labelled Popeye, Altman Archives: Biography of Harry Nilsson, p. 15.

35. Colin Covert, 'Movies: Robert Altman: He Is What He Is, And That's All That He Is', *Passages*, January 1981, p. 8; copy preserved in Box 13 labelled Popeye, Altman Archives.

36. Press kit for *Popeye*, 27 October 1980, in Box 13 labelled Popeye, Altman Archives: Production notes, p. 8.

37. Krin Gabbard, '*Kansas City* Dreamin': Robert Altman's Jazz History Lesson', in James Buhler, Caryl Flinn and David Neumeyer (eds), *Music and Cinema* (Hanover, NH: University Press of New England, 2000), pp. 142–57; idem, *Jammin' at the Margins: Jazz and the American Cinema* (Chicago: University of Chicago Press, 1996).

13 The Musical as Mode:
Community Formation and Alternative Rock in *Empire Records*

Kevin John Bozelka

Now that a spate of films beginning with the success of *Moulin Rouge!* (2001) has given rise to procla-
mations of the rebirth of the Hollywood musical,[1] the genre's decreased popularity in the last third of
the twentieth century needs to be re-examined. Too often, scholars conceive this era as the latest stage
in an endless series of falls from grace into hopeless amounts of commodification and fragmentation,
with film and popular music audiences united only in their antipathy to the musical and its communal
spirit. But even if we are to take the genre's death in the late 1960s as gospel, it seems unreasonable
to suggest that its supposedly unique structures, as well as the utopian energies that powered it, simply
evaporated from the cinematic arsenal at one historical juncture. Instead, I argue that these structures
and energies comprise a mode that has thrived even in fallow years for the genre, namely the 1980s
and 90s.[2] As Christine Gledhill defines it, 'mode' refers to an 'aesthetic articulation adaptable across a
range of genres, across decades, and across national cultures'.[3] So the aesthetic articulation of the
musical constitutes a mode that takes up residency in disparate genres and texts long after the 'death'
of the musical as a genre. The first section of this essay, then, traces the presence of musical modality
in *Empire Records* (Allan Moyle, 1995), most crucially in its attempt to integrate a community through
alternative rock.

I choose *Empire Records* because, while it flopped in its theatrical run, it has since enjoyed a cultish
second life on cable and video/DVD, inspiring tribute websites, discussion groups and fan fiction as well
as prompting the release of the *Empire Records Remix! Special Fan Edition* DVD in 2003. Its status as
both a failure and a success can help restore some of the complexity of responses to the musical in an
era when it supposedly disappeared. So the second section of the essay argues that the appearance of
musical modality within *Empire Records* accounts for the film's failure with its target demographic –
fans of alternative rock, an audience resistant to direct address solicitations to invest in a musical community. But those eager, even manic solicitations have endeared the film to audiences with no subcultural allegiance to alternative rock, a younger generation more open to the film's strong images of
incorporation. The final section will then situate *Empire Records* at a provocative midpoint among shifts
in film and popular music in the 1990s to account for the film's belated success.

Musical Modality in Empire Records

If a film is in the musical mode, then it will appear both like and unlike a musical. As Alistair Fowler
notes, 'modal terms never imply a complete external form. Modes have always an incomplete repertoire, a selection only of the corresponding (genre's) features, and one from which overall external structure is absent.'[4] *Empire Records* is unlike a musical in that it has shed a crucial feature of the musical
genre – the spontaneous outburst of song. Characters in the film play albums and sing and dance
along to them instead of spontaneously bursting into song and dance. When an unseen source of
instrumentation appears on the soundtrack, it takes the form of non-diegetic songs which 'sing' for,
and sometimes to, the characters.

The spontaneous outburst of song disappeared almost entirely in Hollywood films starting in the late 1980s, by which point the musical had long since been declared dead.[5] This shift suggests that, for many audiences, the spontaneous outburst of song became the most important element in defining the musical.[6] It should come as no surprise, then, that *Empire Records* is rarely, if ever, referred to as a musical. The film's advertising bills it as a comedy and most reviews followed suit, sometimes specifying a 'teen comedy' while frequently noting the centrality of music. For instance, a blog post identifies the film as one of five 'Teen Cult Movies I Wish Would Be Turned into a Musical'.[7] And in a review of the *Remix!* DVD, Patrick Naugle refers to the film as a 'musical … err, I mean comedy'.[8] So, in other words, with *Empire Records*, the musical mode has taken up residency within the teen-comedy genre.

But the extent to which modulation infiltrates a text varies. If *Empire Records* is unlike a musical in the absence of a spontaneous outburst of song, then it is like a musical in that musical modulation infiltrates the film to a large degree. This should not be viewed as incommensurate with the film's popular status as a comedy. After all, as Fowler explains, 'a mode announces itself by distinct signals, even if these are abbreviated, unobtrusive, or below the threshold of modern attention'.[9] So in the remainder of this section, I will detail how distinct signals of the musical (its utopian ideals, community integration through song and dance, paradigmatic structure, direct address) appear in *Empire Records* and work together towards the creation of a utopian community through music.

Richard Dyer's classic essay 'Entertainment and Utopia' is most useful in this regard, because he moves beyond the representational characteristics of the musical number by sketching out its more modal aspects – how it presents a better world, often in contrast to the world 'as it is now' of a realist narrative. Instead of providing a model for how this better world could be organised, however, the musical displays how such a utopia might feel. Dyer outlines the utopian solutions, this feel, which the musical offers and the needs being met in the process as follows: Abundance for Scarcity; Energy for Exhaustion; Intensity for Dreariness; Transparency for Manipulation; and, most crucially for *Empire Records*, Community for Fragmentation. But musical entertainment orients itself around only certain categories, because 'with the exception perhaps of community (the most directly working class in source), the ideals of entertainment imply wants that capitalism itself promises to meet. Thus abundance becomes consumerism, energy and intensity personal freedom and individualism and transparency freedom of speech.'[10]

Quite fascinatingly, *Empire Records* fits this description better than most classical Hollywood musicals, because it attempts to meet the needs outlined above through the blatantly capitalist act of selling albums at the title record store. The film puts forth the hope that alternative music (as a genre and an ideology) will transform the workplace into a utopia, and here a brief detour explaining alternative is in order. Extremely popular (and almost synonymous) with Generation X in the early 1990s, alternative finds its roots in the American independent, or indie, bands of the 1980s. Popish but uncompromisingly punky and/or noisy groups like X, Hüsker Dü, The Minutemen, The Replacements, Mudhoney, The Pixies and others enjoyed critical praise and rabid devotion from fans but never sustained commercial success, despite many eventually moving from independent to major labels. With the breakthrough of grunge gods Nirvana (previously Sub Pop labelmates with Mudhoney) in 1991, however, indie was at last commercially validated and the term 'alternative' helped connote the music's vexed relationship with Top 40 success, especially in the experience of its largely Generation X fans. 'Sell out' returned as a crucial buzzword in determining whether or not a band had retained its uncompromising credentials while seizing the mainstream.[11]

New Regency, the independent company that produced *Empire Records*, and A&M, the record company that released the soundtrack a month before the film's opening, explicitly acknowledged using the popularity of alternative to build interest in the film.[12] And the film's poster blatantly advertises the ideology of alternative with the tagline, 'They're selling music but not selling out.' The advertising suggests that the ideology of alternative, that to sell out is the most grievous sin, will bring together the community within the film, which, as with the musical, ideally includes the audience in the theatre or at home. The narrative makes this point obvious with its paradigmatic structure, a key characteristic of the musical genre. Lucas (Rory Cochrane), night manager of Empire Records, puts the forward, syntagmatic pull of the narrative in motion when he discovers papers in his manager Joe's (Anthony LaPaglia) desk hinting that the store will soon become a Music Town chain (clearly invoking the ubiquitous, at the time, Musicland chain across the United States). He takes the evening's deposit to an Atlantic City casino in order to win the cash to save Empire Records from a corporate takeover. But he loses it all at the roulette wheel. So the narrative asks the question, how can Lucas raise the money to keep on selling music without selling out to Music Town?

But most of the subsequent scenes stall the progression towards this resolution. In the meantime, the film's project is to bring the disparate employees together so they can ultimately band behind Lucas. Thus, *Empire Records* showcases a multiple-focus structure in contrast to the dual-focus structure of most classical Hollywood musicals, which centre around the heterosexual couple.[13] Some of the Empire Records employees have been in conflict since before the story starts; others will be as the film progresses. But all will be united in their desire to save Empire Records from selling out, which can happen only once the conflicts are resolved. As in most musicals, the paradigmatic structure overshadows any syntagmatic thrust, taking over to demonstrate to the audience the resiliency of the Empire Records community and thus how to sell music without selling out. In short, it explains not only how to be alternative but also that alternative can replace fragmentation with community.

Even before these community-building scenes, however, Lucas has already engaged us with direct address, another characteristic of the musical.[14] Spouting mock-mystical aphorisms 'like the Chinese guy from *The Karate Kid*' (as one co-worker puts it), Lucas serves as the 'sage' character that Rick Altman identifies as crucial to the functioning of multiple-focus narratives.[15] His two instances of direct address bookend the film, practically bringing the narrative in and out of existence. And throughout the film, he will 'help [viewers] understand the thematic value of the other characters' lives', i.e. reasserting the necessity to band together to save Empire Records.[16]

Another employee, Mark (Ethan Randall), engages in direct address as well in order to help shape the Empire Records community for the viewer. His two instances of direct address serve to familiarise the audience with various Empire Records rituals – playing music in the store and catching shoplifters. In the former instance, the employees pick M&Ms to determine who will choose the music to start off the day. Mark wins and selects Queen Sarah Saturday's 'Seems', an obscure alternative song, the first line of which he sings directly into the camera. Everyone has different morning tasks to perform in different areas of the store. But they all sing along with the song,

Empire Records (1995): Mark (Ethan Randall) sings along to Queen Sarah Saturday's 'Seems' directly into the camera

The Empire Records community

cementing the Empire Records community through music. And in a veritable model of democracy, everyone can exercise one veto a day, thus inflecting community-building with their own particular tastes in music.[17]

But not everyone can join the Empire Records community, which needs a negative example in order to solidify its image. One character not only poses a formidable challenge to the community but also serves to strengthen the definition of alternative. Rex Manning (Maxwell Caulfield) is a pop star past his prime who still enjoys a rabid following and has come to Empire Records for an in-store promotion. A real-world approximation might be Tom Jones – a fortysomething cheeseball with stiff, blow-dried hair and a black velvet suit who sings ridiculously lascivious lyrics in his hit song 'Say No More (Mon Amour)'.

Everyone at Empire Records hates Rex and his music except Gina (Renée Zellweger) and, especially, Corey (Liv Tyler). Corey's infatuation with Rex is a problem for the Empire Records community, since Rex represents the antithesis of alternative. He has sold out from the start, shamelessly tailoring his music to the (99 per cent female) masses. Thus Corey must be made to see Rex the way the rest of the Empire Records staff sees him – as a sleazy has-been whose music is most decidedly not alternative. This is effectuated through Corey's plan to give up her virginity to Rex, which backfires when Rex ignores her romantic intentions and knowingly puts her off. Corey is now properly repulsed by Rex. But the incident causes even more problems, creating rifts between Corey and both A.J. (Johnny Whitworth), who had planned on telling Corey today that he loved her, and Gina, who does have sex with Rex. Rex's presence must then be eradicated before all these disparate disputes can be settled. Thus, Joe eventually throws Rex out of the store.

With most of the conflicts resolved, the climactic fund-raising concert that saves Empire Records represents a synthesis number. Here, 'all the beautiful little tattooed, gum-chewing freaks', to borrow Lucas's words, of Empire Records are able to retain their individual characteristics, since they have effectively prevented servitude as worker drones for Music Town. Gina and another employee, Berko (Coyote Shivers), perform 'Sugar High' (a punky pop number that could pass for alternative) for a wildly disparate crowd of clearly demarcated subcultures (bikers, hippies, skaters, punks, etc.) and age groups (ranging from a young boy buying his first picture disc to a duo of old women in hair curlers enjoying a beer). And everyone is brought together under the aegis of alternative.

Alternative

The presence of musical modality within *Empire Records* accounts for the film's failure to address an alternative rock audience. If selling out stands as the most grievous sin in alternative ideology, then 'selling to' will never sit well with the audience for alternative. The fact that the film issues direct solicitations to join the Empire Records community and offers alternative as a utopian energy source doomed the project from the start, because, as Eric Weisbard notes:

> Alternative rock … is anti-generationally dystopian, subculturally *presuming* fragmentation: it's built on an often neurotic discomfort over massified and commodified culture, takes as its archetype bohemia far more than youth, and never expects that its popular appeal, such as it is, will have much of a social impact.[18]

In this respect, alternative rock functions as the quintessential manifestation of the theory that *all* popular music (if not all popular culture, period) has become grossly commodified to the point where it can no longer build coalitions or elicit political commitment. Lawrence Grossberg sums up this environment well, making it clear that what he calls a 'postmodern structure of feeling' has become dominant by the early 1990s, especially for Generation X (also labelled 'post-baby boomers'):

> Now everything has come under the antiaura of the inauthentic, everything is already co-opted, already an act. The result is that one's responsibility is only located within a realm of affective sovereignty and individual choices where it does not matter what you invest in, as long as you invest in something. Consequently there is a tendency to keep everything at a distance, to treat everything ironically, with no investment in one's investment.[19]

Empire Records' direct address is bound to fail in this kind of affective climate. It elicits investment for community from a viewer rooted firmly within this non-invested structure of feeling which places one's needs at a distance. Moreover, it elicits that investment actively, even earnestly. Something is too hyper about this strategy, not distanced enough in its explanations of and entreaties to join its putatively cool filmic community.

    In this, the Empire Records employees seem hardly more capable of investment. Indeed, they are all dancing and singing along to 'Seems' in the film's first 'number'. But A.J. cuts short the number by exercising his veto power and turning off the song after its first chorus. 'Mark, listening to this crap is guaranteed to make you sterile,' he explains even though he was singing and dancing along to it mere seconds before. Later, A.J. plays Rex's 'Say No More (Mon Amour)' and gets everyone in the store dancing to it, including Debra (Robin Tunney) whose initial veto protests he ignores. Mark, Debra and most of the other employees have delivered their negative appraisal of Rex's authenticity in no uncertain terms. But again, the investment in that judgment carries only a decentred affective investment. Here, another quote from Grossberg seems particularly instructive:

> Rather than being the affective center and agency of people's mattering maps, music's power is articulated by its place on other mattering maps, by its relation to other activities, other functions. Rather than dancing to the music you like, you like the music you can dance to.[20]

Some critics have extended this postmodern structure of feeling to film audiences as well. Seen from this perspective, the failure of *Empire Records* mirrors a more notorious Hollywood failure – *Heaven's Gate* (1980). Timothy Corrigan has written on the centrality of this film for understanding what he might call post-Vietnam cinema spectatorship. He describes this mode of viewing in much the same way as Grossberg does the postmodern structure of feeling in this era: 'The dynamics within (contemporary) views and viewings indicate a decidedly contradictory blend of nostalgia for the older rituals of seeing epic movies and a refusal to believe in those images and unifying rituals.'[21] As with the nostalgia for the Western in *Heaven's Gate*, *Empire Records* offers a nostalgia for the musical and its rituals of bringing the audience into the filmic community.

    But the film's attempt to posit alternative as a unifying energy triggers that refusal to believe in those images and unifying rituals. For the bizarre truth of the matter is that the film cannot sustain a workable definition of alternative. The songs that provide the soundtrack for most of the key numbers are not alternative. Even stranger, the diverse groups represented in the film are not even unified by these particular songs. For instance, at a point of particularly high stress, Joe retreats to his office drum kit and pounds along to AC/DC's 'If You Want Blood (You've Got It)', a hard-rock anthem from 1979. He plays the song on his office jukebox, but Lucas places the backroom phone on intercom so that everyone in the store can hear it. Once the song kicks into gear, however, the scene cuts back and forth between the backroom jollies and a pan across the store's listening booths. The pan reveals several different social types/activities: a bleach-blond white grunge boy thrashing about to Picasso Trigger's raw, riot grrrl-esque *Fire in the Hole*; a hip black cat grooving to his own selection (with a copy of Ten City's soulful house music album *State of Mind* in the background); a white heterosexual couple making out; a hippyish white boy and girl lost in romantic bliss (rather improbably to the raucous Cheap Trickery of The Chainsaw Kittens's *Pop Heiress*); and a white girl raining tears on a Carpenters' record (*Made in America*, the final one to be released during Karen Carpenter's lifetime). But they are separated not just from one another in their respective booths but also from the AC/DC rocker blaring throughout the store – they are all wearing headphones. Everyone here is either listening to a completely different song or decentring the song, as per Grossberg's analysis, by other activities (e.g. making out).[22]

An equally confused scene of attempted unification occurs a few minutes later to Dire Straits's 'Romeo and Juliet', an AOR song with even fewer claims to being alternative. Its creaky, Dylan-esque vocals initially provide the soundtrack for A.J.'s failed attempt at courting Corey. But the scene cuts to a white girl practising ballet moves with headphones on at a listening kiosk, and then to an Asian woman performing more arty gestures at her own kiosk. Only the black UPS worker seems to be hearing 'Romeo and Juliet' as she bops out of the store. And, of course, as already discussed, everyone dances along to Rex's explicitly non-alternative 'Say No More (Mon Amour)'.

But even within in these already ambiguous efforts to include everyone in the Empire Records musical community, the film stereotypes the diverse groups represented within – there simply is not enough time to develop them. Even more disconcerting, the same fate awaits the Empire Records employees. The multiple-focus structure renders them more signposts for alternative than fully realised characters. With little time to form character arcs, their stories become trivialised due to an almost surreal telegraphing. In this respect, then, *Empire Records*, and presumably most Hollywood product of the post-Vietnam era,

> must aim to 'undifferentiate' the desires of different audiences, usually by emphasising the importance of that investment *in and of itself* (the presence or use of computer animation or of an expensive star) rather than what they may be able to represent (new spaces or depths, for instance).[23]

Corrigan's quote here echoes Grossberg's 'it does not matter what you invest in, as long as you invest in something', that 'something' being alternative in *Empire Records*. The different audiences represented in the film are so telegraphed and ambiguously integrated via alternative, however, that they point to a failure to conceive of this inconceivable audience that is everyone (or as many markets as possible). Like *Heaven's Gate*, *Empire Records* apparently failed because 'it seemingly appealed to no one because of its attempts to appeal to everyone (which is of course no one)'.[24]

With *Empire Records*, though, its failure rises to the surface more egregiously like a scar on the text. The scores of Rex Manning fans lined up for autographs are all women save for a fluttering queen beside himself in fanaticism. Most of Rex's fans have failed to gain any distance from their object of idolatry, most hilariously the woman who belts out 'Say No More (Mon Amour)' as an opera aria at the altar of Rex. Indeed, Corey's one apparent flaw is that she is not properly insincere with her Rex Manning worship. These fans, then, are a glaring excess within the textual system. The energy of alternative that mobilises so many disparate groups in the film, albeit again quite ambiguously, cannot mobilise the Rex Manning fans, since they are all guilty of supporting the one thing alternative can never mobilise – selling out. Ultimately, it fails to include everyone in the Empire Records community, keeping them separated by listening booths or eradicating them from the system altogether along with Rex Manning.[25]

So given *Empire Records*' eager direct address, character-flattening multiple-focus structure and confused attempts to forge community via music, it is entirely understandable how this film would fail with the audience for alternative rock if not the fragmented post-Vietnam (or postmodern, depending on the critic) audience overall. Borrowing from Corrigan again, one might conclude that *Empire Records* 'accurately reflects the contemporary trouble with representing *any collective history* for an audience that, at least since Vietnam, has only the most temporary sense of itself as a singular historical image along an unprecedented plethora of cultural and historical images'.[26]

The problem with these post-everything jeremiads, however, is that while they do indeed accurately characterise some film and popular music audiences in the 1990s, they are written from an adult perspective. And that matters when it comes to a youth film like *Empire Records*. They fail to take into account a youth audience that does not presume fragmentation, that does not keep everything at a distance, and that believes fervently in unifying rituals. Moreover, for such an audience, it *does* matter what they invest in. Only with *Empire Records*, that investment is less alternative than a utopian vision of entering the workforce – e.g. at the minimum-wage level of a record-store employee. And by placing the film in a wider film and popular music history of the 1990s, a clearer picture of this audience and the pleasures they take in the film emerges.

Beyond Alternative

Timothy Shary has noted that the late 1980s saw a significant decrease in the number of successful American youth films: 'Teens in American films had been entirely reconfigured, if not often extinguished, as increasing emphasis fell on portraits of the post-teen "20-something" generation in movies after *Slacker* in 1991 (examples include *Singles* in 1992 and *Reality Bites* in 1994).'[27] Interestingly, Shary traces this decline in part to a previous Allan Moyle film, the decidedly single-focus *Pump up the Volume* (1990), which espoused revolutionary rhetoric that seemed to raise the ante too high for teen films to sustain.[28] By 1995, however, Hollywood took a renewed interest in teen films, 'partially due to the recycling pattern of most film genres, but also in an effort to lure youth back to theaters and away from the proliferation of cable-TV channels and new teen-oriented Internet sites'.[29] But the turn from '20-something' slackers to a younger generation could just as easily be chalked up to the waning of alternative by the time of *Empire Records*' release.

With art/commerce tensions eating at its insides, alternative was doomed to enjoy an abbreviated zeitgeist. In Weisbard's words, 'alternative culture was about the least profitable mainstream variant ever, a product that practically begged to be taken off the shelf'.[30] And that is precisely what happened. More and more unchallenging bands were lumped into alternative radio/video formats, rendering the term meaningless. The soundtrack to *Empire Records* is a perfect example. One did not need to suffer any art/commerce anxieties while enjoying its flagship single, The Gin Blossoms's 'Til I Hear It from You', or, indeed, almost any of the music in the film. The song's easy, mid-tempo jangle is so blatantly pop that it becomes impossible to ascertain, as with so many songs in this era, just what it poses an alternative to. If it offends, it does so only in its inoffensiveness.

And by the time of the film's release, the bohemian, anti-pop ethos alternative briefly installed on the pop charts began to recede. The big successes of 1995 were the jolly, proudly mainstream Hootie and the Blowfish and the riot grrrl-lite of Alanis Morissette. Released on Madonna's Maverick label, Morissette's *Jagged Little Pill* translated female rage and disillusionment for the masses and became the second-best-selling album of the 1990s. For many, her ascendancy (not to mention her misunderstanding of irony in her hit 'Ironic') was the final nail in alternative's coffin. Soon Local H's devastating 'All the Kids Are Right' and albums like Everclear's *So Much for the Afterglow* were looking back on alternative from a mournful, even self-flagellant distance. And the final years of the decade ushered in one of the greatest eras of shameless pop with an explosion of boy bands (Backstreet Boys, 'N Sync) and bubblegum princesses (Christina Aguilera and Britney Spears).

In retrospect, then, *Empire Records* seems to fit more comfortably with this latter era of pop than the alternative belch that preceded it. Its gushing, sugar-high optimism finds kinship with shiny, happy pop masterpieces such as Hanson's 'MMMBop' and Aqua's 'Barbie Girl' (both 1997) more than any grunge anti-anthem. And given the film's introductory-course view of alternative, it feels like the cultural property of a younger generation, perhaps the siblings of the Empire Records employees. Sceptical viewers in particular have noted this aspect of the film. A comment on the alternative newsweekly *The Nashville Scene*'s website about a multi-band concert tribute to the film's soundtrack states that '*Empire Records* was more for the post-*Dookie*, post-*In Utero* school of youngsters all jazzed about this new "alternative" music',[31] referencing key Green Day and Nirvana albums released respectively in 1994 and 1993. And as Matthew Webber notes of the film's celebration of avoiding corporate takeover, 'it's one small step for readers of *Spin*, one giant leap for future readers of *Pitchfork*!'[32]

The impulse here would be to lay out the tensions between *Empire Records*' fans and haters, between alternative rock in the early 1990s and a pop paradise at decade's end, as a clash between Generation X and Generation Y. The late-1990s boom in both teen films and teen pop reflected a baby boom in the 1980s and 90s that created the swelled ranks of Generation Y (also known by the rather threatening name of 'Echo Boomers'). Buoyed by a healthier economy, their larger demographic made for a much more confident zeitgeist, with performers such as Justin Timberlake and Britney Spears determined to stay on top to this day.[33]

Although strict demographic figures remain unavailable, the comments on Amazon, IMDb and numerous discussion groups and Internet forums suggest that *Empire Records* targeted Generation Y much more successfully. Furthermore, many of the fans' comments pinpoint various aspects of the film's musical modality, particularly its rituals of community formation, as its most attractive elements. The most common response is some variation on 'it made me want to work in a record store/at Empire Records' with an Amazon comment like 'you somehow can't help placing yourself within Empire Records itself; you are powerless against this urge to "join in"' typical.[34] In the remainder of this section, then, I want to look at how it creates this urge through images of incorporation which heighten the film's direct address.

In a scene lodged awkwardly towards the end of the film, Mark is eating hash brownies received from another employee, Eddie (James 'Kimo' Wills), and watching a video by the theatrical thrash metal band GWAR. The lead singer, Oderous Urungus, looks directly at the camera and yells, 'Hey Mark! You love GWAR! Why don't you join the band?' A cut reveals that Mark has suddenly appeared in the video playing guitar with the band. Mark watches himself on screen, understandably baffled. But the scene ends with him giggling and saying 'I love you, Eddie,' grateful for this hallucination. As with many numbers in a musical, this scene 'wastes time' and could easily be cut from the film.

But thematically, it exemplifies the strong degree of incorporation in the film, one of several scenarios in which fans transcend various boundaries to become part of a musical community.

For instance, the audience is treated to a plethora of images of Rex Manning before he appears in the store – album covers (which Gina licks in lust at one point), cardboard standees, posters, music videos, etc. His signing at Empire Records gives his fanbase the occasion to witness itself, to share a commonality in the same space previously separated by mass media. Manning's appearance also occasions Corey's seduction scene. Where once she could only enjoy Manning from the distance of album covers and television shows, now she has him in the store's 'count out' room where she plans to give him her virginity. That the seduction does not go well is appropriate given Manning's ideological status in the film. But even here, Corey's transcendence of the limits of mass media has a positive effect. In a subsequent scene, she yanks off in disgust the red bra she wore for the seduction. Coming face to face with Manning has made Corey realise the masculine economy of vision surrounding him and has opted out of the impoverished roles available to women within it (e.g. as one of the sex objects populating his videos).

Finally, any fan wanting a job at Empire Records has one undeniable surrogate in Warren (Brendan Sexton), a juvenile delinquent who robs the store. After being taken away by the police, Warren returns with a gun at the film's climax. He shoots up the store in a rage but eventually reveals that all he ever wanted was a job at Empire Records. When Joe realises he means no serious harm, he offers Warren a job, sealing the deal with a name tag. Ann Powers has registered the centrality of Warren to the film: 'I was like Warren (minus the gun) when I was fifteen, buying my Elvis Costello albums at Tower Records in Seattle and gawking at the coolness of the guys who took my cash.'[35] Crucially, Warren is younger than the Empire Records employees, probably sixteen. And his taste in music is suspect – he steals rap and metal CDs (and Whitney Houston, presumably for his girlfriend). That he is still welcomed on as an employee suggests a relative elasticity to the Empire Records community and its alternative ideology, despite excommunicating Rex Manning. Warren's incorporation undergirds the film's musical modality, making it easy for viewers to feel a part of its community.

But while this feeling may come easier to a younger generation who have not yet had their first job, *Empire Records* need not be viewed solely as their province. Even viewers turned off by the film's 'alternasploitation' acknowledge its compulsive watchability.[36] This is because *Empire Records* offers investment in a vision of work as a font of abundance, energy, intensity, transparency and community. Going one better than the classical Hollywood musical, Joe even begins to suggest how this utopia could be organised when he speaks determinedly near the end about acquiring the start-up capital to buy out Empire. That start-up capital comes unexpectedly from Mitch (Ben Bode), the dreaded owner of Empire, who, exasperated by the masses dancing all over his store, sells it to Joe for the night deposit raised at the concert finale. The move is a cheap deus ex machina, but the Empire Records community has found something that eluded the alternative nation – a utopia in the heart of commerce, selling records. And it achieves this utopia through music – the buying and selling of human time frequently succumbs to the lyrical time of music with its repetitions and narrative-halting pauses. Within the oscillation between these two

Joe (Anthony LaPaglia) offers Warren (Brendan Sexton) a job, while A.J. (Johnny Whitworth) looks on

orders of time lie new forms of public discourse and existence – what musicals, in modal and generic form, offer at their best.

A Graceful Continuum

As bricks-and-mortar record stores give way to mp3s sold and shared on the Internet, it becomes easy to slip into nostalgia for *Empire Records*' conditions of existence. Indeed, in his recent study of Guns N' Roses' 1991 *Use Your Illusion*, Eric Weisbard, the most astute commentator on alternative and its woes, comes perilously close to a nostalgia for the Musicland chain that threatened the Empire Records of the land with extinction.[37] He explains that Musicland was eventually undone by monster retailer Best Buy, 'notorious for undercutting record chains with album promotions that used the lower prices as loss leaders to entice customers to come in and contemplate far pricier fare'.[38] Where once youth was decentring music, now record stores were following suit. So Weisbard reminiscences about fans lining up at midnight to purchase a pretentious two-volume CD like *Use Your Illusion* in the environmentally unsound long cardboard box as a way to measure a consensus that no longer exists in the niche markets of today.

But as the complex address of *Empire Records* makes clear, any era will waver between fragmentation and consensus or collectivity. If this essay calls for more attention to that wavering in all eras of film and popular music, it is not to paint a rosier picture of the present; rather, it is to gain a clearer idea of historical shifts and community formations. In this regard, the current spate of musicals would appear less as an overdue rebirth than different modulations along a vibrant, graceful continuum.

Notes

I would like to thank David Gurney and Janet Staiger for their helpful comments on this essay.

1. See, for instance, Susan Wloszczyna, 'Mamma Mia!: Musicals Big News at Box Office Again', *USA Today*, 19 March 2008. <www.usatoday.com/life/movies/news/2008-03-19-musicals-main_N.htm> (accessed 21 March 2008).

2. I want to make it clear from the start that I do not view the musical mode as beginning at one particular point in time, e.g. after the classical Hollywood era. Rather, I see it as merely dominant in certain eras. Mode is a concept meant to preserve the dynamism of history. So I see a film like *Christmas Holiday* (released in 1944 during peak years for the musical genre) as very much a film in the musical mode. For more recent examples, see *Mean Streets* (1973), *The Big Chill* (1983), *The Breakfast Club* (1985), *Romy and Michele's High School Reunion* (1997), *Ghost Dog: The Way of the Samurai* (1999), *Outside Providence* (1999), *The Royal Tennenbaums* (2001), *Love Don't Cost a Thing* (2003) and *She's the Man* (2006).

3. Christine Gledhill, 'Rethinking Genre', in Christine Gledhill and Linda Williams (eds), *Reinventing Film Studies* (London: Arnold, 2000), p. 229.

4. Alistair Fowler, *Kinds of Literature: An Introduction to the Theory of Genres and Modes* (Cambridge, MA: Harvard University Press, 1982), p. 107.

5. Near as I have been able to determine, 1984, 1987 and 1988 saw no Hollywood films featuring characters spontaneously bursting into song. The 1990s fared even worse. The *only* years with Hollywood films featuring a spontaneous outburst of song were 1990 (*Cry-Baby*), 1992 (*Sarafina!*), 1995 (*Monster Mash: The Movie*) and 1996 (*Cannibal: The Musical*, *Evita* and *Everyone Says I Love You*).

6. See Box Office Mojo's definition of 'Musical Movies', 3 February 2008. <www.boxofficemojo.com/genres/chart/?id=musical.htm>.

7. 'Teen Cult Movies I Wish Would Be Turned into a Musical', *Youth Ministry Blog*, 11 June 2009. <blog.digitalorthodoxy.com/?p=1155>.

8. Patrick Naugle, '*Empire Records: Remix! Special Fan Edition*', *DVD Verdict*, 23 June 2003. <www.dvdverdict.com/reviews/empirerecordsremix.php>.

9. Fowler, *Kinds of Literature*, p. 107.

10. Richard Dyer, 'Entertainment and Utopia', in Rick Altman (ed.), *Genre: The Musical* (London and Boston: Routledge and Kegan Paul, 1981), pp. 184–5.

11. For a history of Amerindie, see Michael Azerrad, *Our Band Could Be Your Life* (Boston and New York: Little, Brown and Company, 2001).

12. Carrie Borzillo, 'A&M Soundtrack Plants Hopes with the Gin Blossoms', *Billboard*, 5 August 1995, p. 103.

13. For the paradigmatic, dual-focus structure of the musical, see Rick Altman, 'The American Film Musical: Paradigmatic Structure and Mediatory Function', in Altman (ed.), *Genre: The Musical*, pp. 197–207.

14. Jim Collins, 'Toward Defining a Matrix of the Musical Comedy: The Place of the Spectator within the Textual Mechanisms', in Altman (ed.), *Genre: The Musical*, pp. 134–46.

15. Rick Altman, *A Theory of Narrative* (New York: Columbia University Press, 2008), p. 253.

16. Ibid.

17. These instances of direct address are more convincing than the examples from the Fred Astaire/Ginger Rogers numbers that Jim Collins uses to explain this aspect of the musical – 'Let Yourself Go' (*Follow the Fleet*, 1936), 'Shall We Dance' (*Shall We Dance*, 1937) and the waltz from *Swing Time* (1936). Collins states that 'the characters address the diegetic audience but, in the process of reframing that audience becomes invisible and the characters talk directly to the viewer'. But never do Astaire and Rogers's characters talk (or sing) directly to the viewer. In fact, they seem to consciously avoid looking directly into the camera, continuing to address the diegetic audience to the sides and even below. By contrast, Lucas and Mark do look directly into the camera. And they address no diegetic audience in the first place, thus augmenting the *histoire-as-discours* quality associated with the musical. Collins, 'Toward Defining a Matrix of the Musical Comedy', p. 139.

18. Eric Weisbard, 'What Is Alternative Rock?', in Eric Weisbard and Craig Marks (eds), *Spin Alternative Record Guide* (New York: Vintage, 1995), pp. vii–xii, pp. vii–viii.

19. Lawrence Grossberg, 'Is Anybody Listening? Does Anybody Care? On "The State of Rock" ', in Andrew Ross and Tricia Rose (eds), *Microphone Fiends: Youth Music & Youth Culture* (New York: Routledge, 1994), p. 53.

20. Ibid., p. 56.

21. Timothy Corrigan, *A Cinema without Walls – Movies and Culture after Vietnam* (New Brunswick, NJ: Rutgers University Press, 1991), p. 14.

22. Of course, stating absolutely that an AC/DC song is not alternative goes against the better instincts of this essay. Indeed, AC/DC have an entry in the *Spin Alternative Record Guide*. If one is going to talk about alternative modality, then one should take into account its ability to reignite genres like hard rock and heavy metal with new meaning. Nevertheless, the way the number is shot underlines the film's hapless attempts to mobilise alternative. See Natasha Stovall, 'AC/DC', in Weisbard and Marks (eds), *Spin Alternative Record Guide* , pp. 5–6.

23. Corrigan, *Cinema without Walls*, p. 21 (emphasis in the original).

24. Ibid., p. 13.

25. In a deleted scene included in the extras on the *Special Fan Remix!* DVD, however, Rex Manning himself appears at the integrated fund-raiser. Significantly, he is dressed down in a jean jacket and good-naturedly joins Berko's band in a punky desecration of 'Say No More (Mon Amour)'.

26. Corrigan, *Cinema without Walls*, p. 15 (emphasis in the original).

27. Timothy Shary, *Generation Multiplex: The Image of Youth in Contemporary American Cinema* (Austin: University of Texas Press, 2002), p. 21.

28. Ibid., p. 59.

29. Ibid., p. 10.

30. Eric Weisbard, 'Generation Ex', *Village Voice*, 13 July 1999. <www.villagevoice.com/2005-10-18/specials/generation-ex> (accessed 30 August 2009).

31. 'Tribute to *Empire Records*', 28 April 2009. <blogs.nashvillescene.com/nashvillecream/2009/04/may_13_mercy_lounge_tribute_to.php#comment-3880996>.

32. Matthew Webber, 'Goodwill Hunting: *Empire Records* – The Unified Theory of *Empire Records*', *Erasing Clouds*, 2008. <www.erasingclouds.com/wk0608empire.html>. *Spin* was the magazine most associated with alternative during its popularity; *Pitchfork* is currently the premier Internet music publication specialising in indie rock.

33. For a fantastic piece laying out these tensions, see Weisbard, 'Generation Ex'.

34. 'Mr A. M. Field's review of Empire Records', 7 May 2006. <www.amazon.com/review/ROKAM1VP92LCC>.

35. Ann Powers, *Weird Like Us: My Bohemian America* (New York: Simon & Schuster), pp. 158–9.

36. See the first comment on '*Empire Records* (the movie) – C or D?', 16 May 2003. <www.ilxor.com/ILX/ThreadSelectedControllerServlet?boardid=41&threadid=17286>.

37. Eric Weisbard, *Use Your Illusion I and II* (New York: Continuum, 2007).

38. Ibid., p. 22.

14 'A Musical Dressed up in a Different Way': Urban Ireland and the Possible Spaces of John Carney's *Once*

Matthew J. Fee

> How do I make a little film that appeals to a younger audience – a musical dressed up in a different way?[1]
>
> Writer-director John Carney

When journalists and critics would sing the praises of John Carney's *Once* (2007), they would simultaneously dance around the film's status as a musical. For example, while *The Village Voice* notes that the film lacks 'the sheen (or arrogance) of most cinematic musicals', *Variety* describes it as a 'full-blown musical without anyone bursting into song'.[2] The *Los Angeles Times*'s 'covert musical' is similarly qualified by *Time* as not being 'the kind of musical you'll sing in the car on the way home', but rather, 'the kind you'll debate … before you pop in the soundtrack'.[3] Further underscoring the extent to which the film sheds the generic dressings of the musical, *USA Today* likewise finds the two main actors' performances 'honest and convincing, forgoing the stilted feel of classical musicals'.[4] *Film Ireland* cautions against even describing the film as a musical in the first place, as 'it would be misleading and potentially injurious to the film to classify it as a "musical" ' – yet a review of the film in that same issue fails to share such concern, declaring *Once* 'a modern-day musical set in contemporary Dublin'.[5] But it is perhaps *The New York Times* that supplies one of the most explicitly genre-based qualifications in reviewing the film:

> Periodically – about twice a year, by my calculation – someone tries to breathe new life into the movie musical by putting together a lavish song-and-dance spectacle like the ones they used to make, full of big numbers and bigger emotions. … [*Once*] makes a persuasive case that the real future of the genre may lie not in splashy grandeur but in modesty and understatement. … [*Once*] does not look, sound or feel like a typical musical. It is realistic rather than fanciful, and the characters work patiently on the songs rather than bursting spontaneously into them.[6]

Although John Carney's *Once* emerges in the midst of the recent swell in the musical genre dominated by film adaptations of Broadway musicals such as *Dreamgirls* (Bill Condon, 2006), *Hairspray* (Adam Shankman, 2007) and *Sweeney Todd: The Demon Barber of Fleet Street* (Tim Burton, 2007) – a resurgence noted in the preceding *New York Times* review – as well as by the popularity of the *High School Musical* franchise, *Once* charts largely unexplored terrain in the specific landscape of Irish cinema. For while industrial, critical and even academic attention has shifted towards film genres as an optic through which to envision and engage with Irish film, the musical has been virtually absent across all of these arenas, with gangster films, urban thrillers and romantic comedies dominating such discourses.[7] Indeed, in surveying Irish cinema's representational field, arguably the two sole examples of what one could consider 'Irish musicals' would be Francis Ford Coppola's 1968 adaptation of the Broadway musical *Finian's Rainbow* starring Fred Astaire, and Alan Parker's cinematic translation of Roddy Doyle's *The Commitments* (1991). This is a paradoxical silence when one considers not only how breaking into song and dance has come to signify Irish conviviality, but also how Irish artists such as U2, Enya, Sinead O'Connor and The Corrs – not to mention the global popularity of Riverdance – have dominated the international music stage.

Having premiered at the Galway Film Fleadh in 2006 and released internationally in 2007, *Once* dwells at the intersection of two distinct roads – one global, and one more local – in the production of genre cinema. On the one hand, Carney's film circulates alongside a contemporary upsurge in the musical genre and its attendant lavishness, while on the other, *Once* results from the concerted efforts of the Irish film industry to focus its funding strategies upon low-budget, digital films as part of a 'micro-budget initiative'.[8] But regardless of where one chooses to locate the incredible success of Carney's film – having earned back fifty times its production budget one year after its release – its engagement with the musical genre proves key to more than simply proving the viability of a genre and/or a funding strategy. The musical provides a unique generic framework within which *Once* maps Ireland – particularly Dublin – and the attendant complexities of contemporary Irish identity.

Once portrays a week in the lives of a Dublin busker (street musician) and a Czech immigrant (referred to as 'Guy' and 'Girl' in the film's closing credits).[9] The Guy (Glen Hansard) resides at home with his father and works in their Hoover repair shop, while the Girl (Markéta Irglová) lives off Mountjoy Square on Dublin's northside with her mother and young daughter, earning a living through cleaning houses and by selling flowers as well as copies of *Issues* magazine on Grafton Street. A classically trained pianist – trained by her orchestra violinist father back in the Czech Republic, before he committed suicide due to arthritis – the Girl now practises on a borrowed piano in a local shop off Grafton Street, since she cannot afford her own instrument. But these two characters share more than a passion and talent for music, with both of their romantic lives complicated by long-distance attachments: his girlfriend Catherine has left him and moved to London, while her husband (and daughter's father) remains in the Czech Republic.

One night on Grafton Street, the Girl approaches the Guy after having observed him performing one of his original songs. Soon they begin collaborating musically, he teaching her one of his songs (on which they ultimately duet) and she, in turn, writing lyrics for one of his pieces. As a result of her persistence and indefatigable support, the Guy decides to travel to London to reunite with his girlfriend, but not before he produces a professional demo tape to take with him. The Girl helps the Guy secure funding and negotiate a session at a recording studio, and they produce a recording of the Guy's various songs with the assistance of some additional buskers. The Guy leaves for London, while the Girl – whose husband has responded to her invitation to rejoin her in Dublin – continues to play the piano, albeit now in her apartment and on her own piano, purchased for her by the Guy before he departed.

Digitally filmed over the course of seventeen days in January 2006 and from a sixty-page script, *Once*'s ultimate budget was approximately $200,000, with funding secured primarily through the Irish Film Board/Bord Scannán na hÉireann, and supplemental monies contributed by RTÉ (Ireland's national broadcasting service) and Samson Films. Prior to pursuing a career in film, writer-director John Carney was in the band The Frames with Glen Hansard during the early 1990s, and Carney asked his former bandmate to write and adapt a few songs for the 'modern musical' he was working on. Realising that he would prefer to have 'singers who could act' as opposed to actors who could sing, Carney ultimately cast Hansard in the role of 'The Guy', with Hansard's friend and musical collaborator, the Czech musician Markéta Irglová, cast as 'The Girl'.[10]

Although *Once* was declined by numerous festivals such as Edinburgh, Locarno, London, Rotterdam, Telluride and Toronto, it premiered to positive acclaim at Sundance in January 2007, winning the World Audience Award. Having acquired the film's distribution rights (for everywhere but Ireland) for $1 million, Fox Searchlight Pictures distributed *Once* to relatively strong critical acclaim, winning an Academy Award for best original song for 'Falling Slowly' and even stirring Steven Spielberg to declare: 'A little movie called *Once* gave me enough inspiration to last the rest of the year.'[11]

Critical accolades – such as those I mentioned at the beginning of this essay – may have consistently attempted to distance *Once* from the musical genre, but closer examination of Carney's film reveals a rather traditional incarnation of some of the genre's most standard tropes. First, the film locates a musically inclined, heterosexual couple at the centre of its narrative who articulate their feelings and share narrative information via song. In addition, while not exactly a 'backstage musical', *Once*'s narrative trajectory similarly culminates with the characters combining their talents and creating a completed musical production. Finally and most obviously, characters throughout *Once* break into song, and the film alternates between narrative and musical numbers. In this essay, I will examine each of these areas where *Once* embraces the musical and uniquely reshapes its generic elements. However, Carney's film does not merely create a contemporary, somewhat deconstructed iteration of the genre, but rather, a film musical whose generic manipulations, particularly its handling of space, articulate dimensions of contemporary Irishness and its urban character.

First, *Once* shares in the generic inheritance of the musical's focus upon the heterosexual couple and the genre's tendency both to articulate characters' feelings and to impart narrative information through musical interludes, with Carney seeking to create a film in which 'the music was actually the chief way the characters were communicating'.[12] The most explicit example of this communicative function for the music is found in the Guy's singing of 'Broken Hearted Hoover Fixer Sucker Guy'. Specifically, as the Guy and the Girl ride a city bus to his father's house, he responds to her enquiries concerning his ex-girlfriend ('What did she do to you?', 'Where is she?' and 'You're not going to go get her?') through the lyrics of this song as well as two brief accompanying pieces, each of a different musical style.

The Guy's use of this song to croon about his ex-girlfriend in London instead of the Girl sitting next to him cues us to a further fine-tuning of the genre's elements by Carney. Throughout *Once*, the Guy and the Girl sing of heterosexual romance, but their melodic pinings concern their feelings for and relationships with their separated lovers, as opposed to one another. Recall how their first conversation in the film overtly references this fact when the Girl asks, 'Tell me of the girl that you wrote this song for', after hearing him sing 'Say It to Me Now'. The Guy has written numerous songs for his estranged girlfriend Catherine (Marcella Plunkett), with his performances voicing emotion for this distant lover, instead of the Girl standing right in front of – indeed singing alongside – him. The lyrics of the songs 'All the Way Down' and 'Lies' aurally articulate this focus on his ex-girlfriend, and are visually supported by the interspersion of images of Catherine while the Guy sings. Similarly, the Girl's performances of 'If You Want Me' and 'The Hill' invoke her feelings towards her distant, older husband. Hence, and as is standard in the musical, the male and female leads in *Once* sing with one another about romantic endeavours, but not those which would potentially join them together.

To be sure, certain musical numbers, most notably the Guy and Girl's duet 'Falling Slowly', hint at the romantic undercurrents of their relationship (for example, 'I don't know you/but I want to/all the more for that'). But recall that the Guy's decision to travel to London to reconnect with his ex-girlfriend follows his performance of 'Lies', and that the Girl's call to her husband to 'work things out'

follows shortly after her rendition of 'The Hill', a song that she tells the Guy was written for her husband. 'Falling Slowly' thus sounds a regretful note about the impossibility of their relationship, a fact
compounded by its reprise as the non-diegetic closing to the film, as we cut between the Guy in
London on his way to meet up with Catherine, and the Girl newly reunited with her husband in
Dublin.

Second, *Once* is reminiscent of Hollywood's 'backstage musicals' and their focus on the characters
and behind-the-scenes machinations that come together to produce a show, although in Carney's film
we get backstage for the production of a demo tape (e.g. securing a loan, creating a band, practising
songs, renting a space, staying up all hours, etc.).[13] But this is not the only adjustment to the film's
nods toward the backstage plot, as this subgenre of the musical would concomitantly situate the completion of the show with the union of the heterosexual couple. As Jane Feuer notes: 'In a typical backstage musical, the success of the couple will be placed in a metaphorical relationship to the success of
the show.'[14] In much the same way that *Once* takes the genre's focus on the heterosexual couple and
its singing of romance and modifies it – the Guy and Girl sing of love, but not for one another – so too
does the film adjust this generic element: the Guy and Girl do 'put on a show' and produce a demo
tape at the end of the film, yet the successful completion of this project does not ensure the success
of their relationship, for they part ways immediately afterward. If anything, given that both of their
attempts to reconnect with their distant lovers are narratively positioned as subsequent to their singing
about these persons as opposed to one another, music in *Once* precipitates the failure, and not the
success, of the lead couple's potential romance.

The Guy and Girl's final exchange on Grafton Street succinctly sums up the film's rehearsal of both
of these generic elements – on the one hand, recalling the backstage musical's ethos of musical collaboration, yet on the other, failing to ensure that the successful completion of this musical project will
necessarily result in the Guy getting the Girl. The Guy invites the Girl over to his place that night (for
what both of them admit will likely involve 'hanky panky'), but the Girl initially protests, indicating that
their coming together romantically would be 'worthless'. While her judgment could be understood in
relation to the impending return to/of their significant others, her declaration shortly before that there
is no need for her to come over to his place, since the demo has been completed ('But we [*sic*] done
our work'), also implies that their coming together romantically is unnecessary, now that the narrative
demands surrounding the demo's production have been completed. Put another way, the songs in
Once establish the Guy and the Girl as a couple solely in the realm of musical collaboration, instead of
through heterosexual romance.

Third, it is through its musical numbers and their cinematic rendering that *Once* most interestingly
engages with the genre. Considerations of film musicals often engender questions surrounding the
supposed realism of a narrative in which people spontaneously burst into song (and most often dance
as well), and the attendant challenges that these moments pose for the cinema audience. In fact, in
the DVD commentary for the film, writer-director Carney explicitly acknowledges this challenge when
describing the creative impulse behind *Once*:

> I guess the idea was to make a kind of a musical film that would appeal to a younger audience of people,
> a more modern audience of people who wouldn't necessarily accept the Gene Kelly/Frank Sinatra break-
> ing into song that I happen to actually really enjoy. ... a more modern audience won't get past the fact
> that people are breaking into song walking down the street unless the film is very ... self-consciously
> made.[15]

Once helps its 'more modern audience' get past these breaks into song from its very opening. An in-progress rendition of Van Morrison's 'And the Healing Has Begun' aurally interrupts the silence of the black screen upon which the opening production credits gradually become visible. The image track of the film itself then abruptly appears, halting the credits and revealing a busker belting out the tune on a crowded Grafton Street in the heart of Dublin. The film thus commences with a rather literal incarnation of arguably the musical's most significant, defining element – and source of Carney's concern – as a busker's profession entails earning a living through (literally) breaking into song on the street. *Once* thus foregrounds, yet simultaneously qualifies its engagement with, an essential component of the musical genre, in the process establishing a pattern for the film's subsequent musical sequences: characters will break into song throughout the film, but these musical numbers will be indisputably justified by the film's narrative.

Musical performances reverberate throughout *Once*, with the film containing a broad array of musical pieces that are frequently performed in their entirety by the Guy and the Girl. But there are additional, more abbreviated bursts of music throughout the film as well. For example, when the Guy and Girl meet with a small-loan manager in order to secure funding for the studio rental, the manager breaks into a song declaring, 'I want to be free/I want to be me'. An abrupt cut punctuates this unexpected and brief musical performance of a white-collar worker sharing his own plaintive musical aspirations, but there are other points throughout the narrative where song – most often in-progress – diegetically breaks out within the film: during the opening pre-credit sequence with the Guy and the heroin addict; when the Guy plays a recording for the Girl in his room; when the band drives to the beach with the studio's sound engineer for the 'car test'; and when the Guy shares his music with his father, just prior to announcing his departure for London.

Yet with the exception of the non-diegetic closing reprise of 'Falling Slowly', all of these musical sequences – abridged or complete, directly performed by characters or technologically mediated by tape recorders and car speakers – arise from the demands of the narrative itself, with *Once* thus recalling the dynamics of Hollywood's 'integrated musicals' in which 'song, dance, and story ... artfully blended to produce a combined effect'.[16] In fact, Carney has remarked that one of his strategies for producing an 'unselfconscious musical' was through having the musical sequences 'stitched into the drama of the piece ... justified by the events that were taking place and by the characters' state of mind in the film'.[17]

Characters break into song at numerous points throughout *Once*, yet the narrative motivations for these musical occasions are clearly justified within the context of the film. For example, musical performances result from the Guy's job as a street musician ('And the Healing Has Begun' and 'Say It to Me Now'); from the Guy and Girl collaborating, writing lyrics and sharing songs ('Falling Slowly', 'If You Want Me', 'Lies' and 'The Hill'); from a group of friends singing at a party ('Gold'); and from the band rehearsing and ultimately recording a demo tape in a studio ('Trying to Pull Myself Away', 'When Your Mind's Made Up' and 'You Must Have Fallen from the Sky').

Moreover, although *Once*'s narrative does not as explicitly precipitate additional songs such as the Guy's 'All the Way Down' and 'Broken Hearted Hoover Fixer Sucker Guy', the fact that he is a musician handily explains the presence of these numbers. In other words, given that he has already performed a number of songs in the film, the Guy's reflecting upon and summarising his relationship with his ex-girlfriend via, respectively, a private performance of 'All the Way Down' and the spontaneously composed 'Broken Hearted Hoover Fixer Sucker Guy' on a city bus are, in essence, 'keeping in character' and do not significantly challenge the realm of narrative possibility.

A number of additional cinematic strategies complement these practical justifications for characters' singing in *Once*, and serve to enhance their realistic dimension. For example, shooting – often shakily – with digital video cameras as well as via long/medium long shots and long takes not only recalls the 'authenticity' of documentary film and home video, but also allows the musical numbers to transpire in actual locations, in real time. Hence, the film's musical numbers are clearly distinguishable from the deliberate and measured opulence of Hollywood's more elaborate musical sequences, as well as from the frenetic editing that has come to be associated with the musical's contemporary relative, the music video.[18]

In addition, *Once* frequently and reflexively highlights the constructed nature of its musical performances through focusing on moments when characters write lyrics and practise songs in the lead-up to the performances themselves. For example, performances of 'If You Want Me' and 'Lies' are introduced by the Girl and the Guy writing and editing the songs' respective lyrics. 'Falling Slowly' starts with the Guy teaching the Girl the lyrics and chords, while the Girl is initially reluctant to perform 'The Hill' for the Guy because of its unfinished lyrics. Similarly, *Once* lays bare the technical as well as technological practicalities necessary to produce such music in the first place, as the musical sequences require the replacement of batteries when they are dead, the use of an in-store piano when one cannot afford one's own instrument and the miking of instruments in the studio. Music does not simply burst forth in *Once*; it is practised and produced with effort.

However, I would argue that it is through *Once*'s handling of space and its movement between narrative and performance that Carney's film provides the strongest cinematic complement to the realism of its narratively integrated musical numbers, especially when one considers how the Hollywood musical's methods of manipulating space became a significant component of the genre's unrealistic associations. Moreover, *Once*'s rendering of cinematic space proves noteworthy not simply for the realistic ways that it 'dresses the musical up differently', but also for the ways that its integration of musical and non-musical spaces – a hallmark of the musical genre – becomes a means for articulating the complexities of Irishness that reverberate after the economic boom of 1990s 'Celtic Tiger' Ireland.

While the Hollywood musical's camerawork, particularly musical sequences directed by Busby Berkeley, would often expand the cinematic space into fantastical locations that extended beyond the narrative realm, affording visual perspectives not physically possible – 'impossible [numbers] from the standpoint of the realistic discourse of the narrative'[19] – *Once* limits our visual access to its performances, and consistently reminds us of our limited possibilities of perspective. The musical sequences in Carney's film do not extend the space of the narrative, as compared to, for example, Hollywood musicals, in which a number opens onto an indefinite space that stretches behind the stage's proscenium, and hence beyond the initial view of the audience. On the contrary, *Once* frequently makes us aware that we are, in fact, viewing musical performances situated in, and tethered to, authentic locations in and around Dublin.

Framing, camera position and cinematic technique continuously emphasise the fact that we are grounded in actual locations in and around Dublin's city centre. For example, vans and passers-by obstruct our opening vista of the Guy singing 'And the Healing Has Begun', while Carney's reliance on long shots clearly locates this performance within the teeming crowds that comprise the reality that is the hustle and bustle of Grafton Street, Dublin's busiest shopping area. In fact, the only way that this initial musical performance 'opens out' occurs when the heroin addict steals the Guy's money, interrupting the performance and leading the Guy on a chase along Grafton Street, through the entrance of an HMV music store and into St Stephen's Green.

As noted earlier, this number establishes the film's dominant tendency to justify its musical performances narratively, as the Guy's work as a busker requires that he break out into song on the street. In a similar manner, this opening sequence cues us to subsequent patterns in the film and its handling of space. This pre-credit sequence establishes a number of constants for the cinematic strategies through which musical numbers will be envisioned for the remainder of Carney's film: numbers grounded in spatial reality, often with observers serving as narrative surrogates for the cinema audience. *Once*'s subsequent musical numbers are all very 'possible', logically stitched into the narrative fabric and clearly located in Dublin's contemporary reality, whether that reality be found on Grafton Street, in the claustrophobic bedroom/living room of one's childhood home, in a piano shop, on a city bus or the night-time streets of Dublin's northside.

While the musical sequences in the classical Hollywood musical – specifically the iconographic offerings of Busby Berkeley – would begin in the narrative reality, and then expand out into 'unreal' and 'impossible' realms and perspectives, *Once* inverts this movement between the narrative and the musical numbers, as it *moves into* and focuses in on the musical action via camera movement and framing. Moreover, this reversal of the movement between narrative and performance continues at the end of these musical interludes. Camera movement and framing, as well as the use of editing and sound-bridges, move us out of the performance, and back to the narrative reality – instead of returning us to the performer him/herself. In other words, as with Hollywood musicals, cinematic technique renders *Once*'s musical numbers as distinct from the narrative proper, but instead of accomplishing this separation through a moving out/moving in, *Once* inverts this establishment of space, moving into the performances and then ultimately moving out of them in order to return us to a story very clearly located in contemporary Dublin.

The number 'Say It to Me Now' provides us with a clear example of this reversed movement. This scene returns us to the Grafton Street of the pre-credit sequence as we open on a long shot of the Guy passionately singing the song, the performance aspect accentuated by the way the camera frames him in the proscenium-like arch of the alleyway, illuminated by the green and blue glow of the storefronts' neon lights. The night-time street is completely empty, allowing us an unobstructed view of the performance, as opposed to the pre-credit sequence during which, as we have seen, vehicles and passers-by persistently hindered our view. Slowly, the camera begins to track into the Guy, closing off our view of the street as it privileges our access to his fervent performance in a medium close-up. As the song concludes, the camera slowly tracks back, revealing that the Girl has been watching his performance. When the sequence next cuts to a shot/reverse-shot exchange between the two of them, pedestrians are now visible behind them on Grafton Street, as the noises of passing crowds become apparent. Performance over, we are returned to the bustling commerce of Grafton Street.

Once (2007): at the conclusion of musical numbers, we are often returned to the narrative via the introduction of spectators – in this case 'the Girl' – who have observed these performances

Subsequent musical sequences likewise follow this general pattern for segueing between the narrative and the performances themselves: we cut to an establishing shot of the space of the performance, framing and camera movement focus our attention on the performance itself (although we are often reminded of its physical location through additional elements within the frame), and then we are returned to the narrative itself, often through the reintroduction of non-performing Dubliners who have observed this performance. In some instances, the conclusion of the musical number will return us to the narrative via reframing back to the overall space, to a re-establishing shot of the location in which the performance took place, while in others, a sound-bridge will remove us from that space entirely, most often returning us to Dublin and its city centre. Still other sequences remove us from the performance via majestic camera movements, such as the crane shot at the conclusion of 'If You Want Me', along with the final crane shot that concludes the film itself. Consequently the musical numbers in *Once* are narratively rationalised, yet the editing and framing make us aware of their status as performances, with their re-establishing shots and sound-bridge transitions functioning not only as a strategy for resituating us back into the narrative, but also a means of reintroducing contemporary Dublin.

For example, the Guy's performance of 'All the Way Down' begins with a cut to an establishing shot of him playing the song in his room, followed by a succession of shots that alternate between him on the bed, a medium close-up of him calling his ex-girlfriend, a close-up of her photo, a shot of him on the bed and then back to a long shot of him sitting on his bed, playing the song. But this sequence moves out even further than the confines of his bedroom, as the song becomes the underscore for the life of a busker, playing underneath scenes of the Guy in the Hoover shop and performing on Grafton Street for drunken spectators and hare krishnas. In a similar manner, 'Falling Slowly' gradually focuses on the performance from two specific camera angles (one behind the Guy's shoulder and one on the Girl's side of the piano) and moves into close-ups of the Guy and Girl performing the song. Towards the end, however, we are returned to the narrative 'reality' through a cut to a reaction shot of the store owner and a later sound-bridge that transforms the song into underscore for the Guy and the Girl's stroll down the St George's arcade.

Once: camera movements such as the film's concluding crane shot remove the spectator from the musical number and relocate her/him in contemporary Dublin

Later musical sequences also use framing and camera movement to situate these musical performances firmly within their Dublin environs, whether those surroundings are a city bus with views of the suburbs passing by (as in 'Broken Hearted Hoover Fixer Sucker Guy') or the streets of Dublin's northside surrounding Mountjoy Square, visualised via long takes and following shots (as in 'If You Want Me'). Even when ostensibly restricted to the private spaces of a living-room table or a friend's apartment, as with the respective numbers 'Lies' and 'Gold', a montage of home-video mpegs and a motorcycle trip to Killiney Hill move these performances beyond their initial 'stages'.

To be sure, the musical numbers in *Once* do not exhibit uniform strategies for integrating narrative and performance. For example, those musical sequences at the studio are primarily restricted to the confines of one particular space. However, the 'car test' on the way to the beach does allow us to venture beyond the limits of the studio, and the cutaway to the sound engineer's reaction to the band's performance of 'When Your Mind's Made Up' recalls earlier instances in the film when we were similarly reintegrated into the narrative by way of cutaways to characters' reactions.

But consideration of the earlier numbers, as well as of the concluding reprise of 'Falling Slowly', enables us to appreciate how *Once's* movement between narrative and performance underscores the film's role as a chronicle of contemporary, urban Dublin, and hence engages with larger conversations concerning Irish representation in film. *Once's* return to its narrative at the conclusion of the musical performances simultaneously serves as a strategy for introducing and traversing the varied urban environs of present-day Dublin. As a result of this movement, Carney's film consequently contributes to a representational tradition that has prevailed across Irish cinema for approximately the past two decades, a visual field preoccupied with contemporary Ireland's – particularly Dublin's – urban character.

Alongside the rapid economic growth that characterised the Celtic Tiger Ireland of the 1990s, contemporary Irish cinema likewise witnessed a transformation and became captivated by urban stories, itself a noteworthy shift in the canon of Irish filmic representation. Even though the earliest filmed images of Ireland prioritised the urban milieu of Dublin at the turn of the twentieth century – and are marked 'by a structured absence of rural life' – a romantic tradition of depicting Ireland through recourse to its lush bucolic landscapes, especially visualising the rural settings found in the western areas of the Republic, nonetheless dominated subsequent renderings of Ireland and the Irish in cinema.[20] However, one of the major features of Irish cinema of the past two decades has been an increasing focus on 'cityscapes' instead of landscapes, with Dublin-based films, in particular, providing the *mise en scène* for what Martin McLoone describes as a 'hip hedonism' manifested in consumerist acquisition and sexual freedom.[21] I would further develop McLoone's appraisal of these films by noting how the genres of the urban thriller and the romantic comedy (or 'rom-coms') have specifically provided the foremost generic structures through which to examine, respectively, either the dark underside or the carnal amusements of this hedonism.

Contrary to these earlier films and their polished cityscapes and metropolitan dwellers, the urban tale of *Once's* struggling musician and triply employed Czech immigrant proves more reminiscent of recent films that have focused on those Dublin inhabitants excluded from the glossy narratives of Ireland's boom years. For example, films such as *Adam & Paul* (Lenny Abrahamson, 2004) and *Pavee Lackeen: The Traveller Girl* (Perry Ogden, 2005) portray the everyday experiences of, respectively, heroin addicts and travellers during this era. With its Czech protagonist whose Polish neighbours learn English through watching the soap opera *Fair City*, and with its Irish lead emigrating to London to find success after the end of Ireland's economic boom, *Once* is very much another 'snapshot of modern Dublin'.[22] *Film Ireland* editor Lir Mac Cárthaigh eloquently enhances this snapshot:

Once represents a cultural byproduct of Ireland's boom years in the 1990s. … In a property-obsessed society, both protagonists live in unglamorous circumstances with one of their parents. No one in the film (apart from Eamon the record producer) uses a mobile phone or drives a car; no one drinks a cappuccino, eats parma ham or rocket, uses an ipod or goes online. … the trappings of the new disposable income that we are all supposed to be enjoying are noticeable by their absence.[23]

But it is not simply what *Once* represents (or fails to represent) that enables Carney's film to envision early twenty-first-century Dublin. Taking into account the metropolitan shine of urban thrillers and romantic comedies, as well as the supposedly corrective realism of films depicting those marginalised by Ireland's economic transformation, *Once*'s musical addition to the existing corpus of generic representation supplies a more complex articulation of Ireland's urban character. If, as Jane Feuer notes, 'the world is a stage'[24] when musical performances move outside of the theatre, Carney's film reveals post-Celtic Tiger Dublin as an assortment of stages, for *Once*'s shifts between narrative and performance are concomitantly movements between the heaving commerce of Grafton Street and a host of other not-so-thriving locales in addition to the living spaces described above: public transportation; a piano shop with unaffordable instruments; a Hoover repair shop overrun with broken machines, yet void of customers; a sizeable home where the Girl dusts and polishes silverware; and the multicultural streets of Dublin's northside. *Once* thus chronicles an urban topography more apt for navigating the lives of those persons struggling to reside in post-Celtic Tiger Ireland, a generic mapping that contrasts with the 'conspicuous winners' who dwell in the cityscapes of thrillers and romantic comedies.[25]

Once: musical numbers underscore the many possible spaces and attendant social realities of contemporary Dublin in the aftermath of the Celtic Tiger's economic boom

Musicals become cinematic sites where we can explore the dynamic interplay of 'multiple realities', of the relationship between the narrative and the musical numbers/dream sequences/show performances, for 'The musical's multiple levels of reality contrast the stage with the world, illusion with reality.'[26] These 'realities' of contemporary Ireland have been fraught with contradiction. A country historically defined by centuries of emigration became home to thousands of immigrants from Africa and Eastern Europe. Moreover, the economic boom of the 1990s – in which 'People running around with mobile phones did very well, [while] others just found life got more expensive'[27] – translated into a turn-of-the-century building and borrowing fervour that ultimately developed unaffordable properties. Now in the midst of a global economic downturn, the spectre of Irish emigration again haunts the Emerald Isle (for both those born in Ireland as well as for the more recently arrived), while the burst in the property bubble and decrease in consumer spending signify a final silencing of the Celtic Tiger's roar. *Once's* embrace of the musical consequently becomes a fitting genre for examining these shifting dimensions of contemporary Ireland, as it provides the film with a generic framework within which to dynamically situate these disparate realities in conversation with one another.

Once's musical performances may be 'dressed up differently', and not as illusory or dreamlike as in many Hollywood musicals, but the correlation between its differing levels of 'reality', as demarcated by cuts and camera movements into and out of performances, along with sound-bridges that remove us from them and into other spaces, prove nonetheless significant in linking the numerous social realities that define Dublin post-boom and at the start of a new century. Although various cinematic strategies have envisioned urban Ireland over the past two decades, ranging from thrillers and rom-coms to the supposed realism of films focusing on those excluded from the boom, I would argue that it is actually a film musical that has best voiced the realities of early twenty-first-century Dublin by staging its numerous *possible* spaces.

Notes

1. Quoted in Carole Horst, 'Musicals Orchestrate a Global Movement', *Variety*, 3–9 December 2007, p. B1.
2. Robert Wilonsky, 'Busker Love', *Village Voice*, 16 May 2007, p. 68; Dennis Harvey, '*Once*', *Variety*, 5–11 February 2007, p. 102.
3. Kenneth Turan, '*Once*', *Los Angeles Times*, 16 May 2007. Online. <xml.latimes.com/entertainment/news/business/cl-et-once16may16,1,2148073.story> (accessed 29 November 2009); Rebecca Winters Keegan, 'What Makes a Modern Movie Musical Sing?', *Time*, 17 May 2007. Online. <www.time.com/time/arts/article/0,8599,1622288,00.html> (accessed 29 November 2009).
4. Claudia Puig, 'For *Once*, Songs Fuel the Musical', *USA Today*, 17 May 2007, p. E4.
5. Lir Mac Cárthaigh, '*Once*: From the Heart', *Film Ireland*, March/April 2007, p. 13; Jennifer Saeger Killelea, '*Once*', *Film Ireland*, March/April 2007, p. 40.
6. A. O. Scott, 'Some Love Stories Have a Better Ending Than the Altar', *New York Times*, 16 May 2007, Section E, p. 9.
7. For recent attempts to analyse Irish cinema through genre theory, see Brian McIlroy (ed.), *Genre and Cinema: Ireland and Transnationalism* (New York and London: Routledge, 2007). See also Dervila Layden, 'Generic Migrations: The Productive Relationship between Ireland and Hollywood', *Film Ireland*, March/April 2008, pp. 24–6.
8. For a discussion of Ireland's 'micro-budget initiative', see Ruth Barton, *Irish National Cinema* (London: Routledge, 2004), p. 110.
9. In fact, most of the characters are identified in the closing credits with generic names, e.g. 'Heroin addict'.
10. John Carney, Audio commentary, *Once*. Dir. Carney. Perf. Glen Hansard and Markéta Irglová. 2006. DVD. Twentieth Century Fox Home Entertainment, 2007.
11. Quoted in Adam Dawtrey, '*Once* Director Remains Close to His Roots', *Variety*, 20–6 August 2007, p. 8.
12. Carney, Audio commentary, *Once*.

13. Martin Rubin, 'Busby Berkeley and the Backstage Musical', in Steven Cohan (ed.), *Hollywood Musicals: The Film Reader* (London and New York: Routledge, 2002), pp. 53–61.

14. Jane Feuer, *The Hollywood Musical*, 2nd edition (Bloomington: Indiana University Press, 1993), p. 80.

15. Carney, Audio commentary, *Once*.

16. John Mueller, 'Fred Astaire and the Integrated Musical', *Cinema Journal*, vol. 24, no. 1, 1984, p. 28.

17. Carney, Audio commentary, *Once*.

18. Steven Cohan, 'Introduction', in Cohan (ed.), *Hollywood Musicals*, p. 1.

19. Rubin, 'Busby Berkeley', p. 57.

20. Kevin Rockett, '(Mis-)Representing the Irish Urban Landscape', in Mark Shiel and Tony Fitzmaurice (eds), *Cinema and the City: Film and Urban Societies in a Global Context* (Oxford: Blackwell Publishing, 2001), p. 219.

21. Martin McLoone, *Film, Media and Popular Culture in Ireland: Cityscapes, Landscapes, Soundscapes* (Dublin and Portland, OR: Irish Academic Press, 2008), pp. 37–50.

22. Ray Pride, 'Hear My Song', *Filmmaker*, Spring 2007, p. 56.

23. Mac Cárthaigh, '*Once*: From the Heart', p. 13.

24. Feuer, *Hollywood Musical*, p. 24.

25. McLoone, *Film, Media and Popular Culture in Ireland*, p. 50.

26. Feuer, *Hollywood Musical*, p. 68.

27. David Williamson, 'Irish Luck Runs Out', *Wales on Sunday*, 15 March 2009, p. 28. For more on the collapse of Ireland's economy post-Celtic Tiger, see Fintan O'Toole, *Ship of Fools: How Stupidity and Corruption Sank the Celtic Tiger* (London: Faber & Faber, 2009).

15 Christophe Honoré's *Les Chansons d'amour* and the Musical's Queer-abilities

David A. Gerstner

Homage-Frottage

To write about the film musical as an *objet de queer* is, in short, redundant.[1] The genre, Steven Cohan notes, has 'achieved considerable subcultural status as an object of camp, especially for gay audiences'.[2] Such recognised standing in popular culture and the scholarship that has rigorously announced the campy pleasures the musical evokes ostensibly leaves little room to pry open fresh queer conceptualisations about the genre. To be sure, gay and lesbian studies since the 1970s illuminated homopleasure possibilities with the classical Hollywood genre. Since the 1990s, moreover, academic intervention with the rise of queer studies arguably prepared the stage for new representational modes in musical production.[3] With the likes of John Greyson's *Zero Patience* (1993) and Todd Haynes's *Velvet Goldmine* (1998), queer subjects took the wheel behind the musical's narrative force and rewrote the terms for a narratively hetero-inflected genre. Hence, the traditional musical genre that once made way for campy-queer reception now took shape in the hands of (*openly*) queer film-makers.[4] Queers now put on the show for *and* by queers. This is a decidedly marked movement from 'camping' a hetero-assertive mode of production to a mode of film production in which queers insert non-heterosexual images, romances, intrigues and affirmations into the traditional genre.

This essay looks to a queer-subject musical directed by the prolific French director and novelist, Christophe Honoré. His film, *Les Chansons d'amour* (*Love Songs*, 2007), is the second in the director's unofficial 'Paris Trilogy' (*Dans Paris*, 2006; *Les Chansons*, 2007; and *La Belle Personne*, 2008). Before returning in detail to the film and the queer-abilities it offers the film musical, I wish briefly to situate Honoré within the tradition of French film-making to which he aspires and that which he queers.

Often referred to as a descendant from the Nouvelle Vague and, hence, a consecrated member of the 'Nouvelle-Nouvelle Vague', Honoré has directed a number of films, including *Ma mère* (2004, his adaptation of Georges Bataille's posthumously published novel) and *Tout contre Léo* (2004; alternately translated as *Close to Leo* and *All against Leo*).[5] Tracing his cinematic heritage to the 'Nouvelle Vague', specifically with regard to making *Les Chansons*, Honoré aligns himself with Jean Luc Godard and Jacques Demy. Godard's *Une Femme est une femme* (1961), and its playful turn on the American musical, as well as Demy's provincial musical trilogy – *Lola* (1961), *Les Parapluies de Cherbourg* (1964) and *Les Demoiselles de Rochefort* (1967) – most fully resonate across Honoré's Parisian trilogy.[6] Godard's film saturates *Les Chansons*' cinematic world, since the film

Fixed-character tracking shot: Jacques Demy's *Les Parapluies de Cherbourg* (1964)

Fixed-character tracking shot: Christophe Honoré's *Les Chansons d'amour* (2007)

echoes the same Parisian district (the 10th *arrondissement*) where Honoré shot his film.[7] The most obvious cinematic references to Demy include *Les Chansons*' tripartite-chapter structure and fixed-character tracking shots. And, like both Godard and Demy, Honoré incorporates a knowing cinematic wink to the American-musical enterprise.

Though Honoré pays homage to his cinematic forefathers, he most provocatively embraces Demy in *Les Chansons*. Like Demy, the corporeal-emotional transformations that take place in Honoré's film occur through *and because of* the director's genre techniques. In many ways, Honoré follows Demy's much-considered use of camera movement and music to express a character's existential position. Consider, for example, Lola (Anouk Aimée), Geneviève (Catherine Deneuve) and Delphine (Deneuve again), and Demy's strategic direction of tossing one's hair, tilting one's head, or rehearsing a song and how these choreographed events intimately intersect with, most often, a range of mobile camera shots. His imbrication of genre technique and prescient homage, along with precise corporeal-emotional direction, illuminate what we shall see are Honoré's cinematic queer-abilities.

Demy's links to contemporary queer culture are also important for Honoré. Demy not only reinvigorated the musical's sentient qualities that queers readily camped, he passed away from AIDS in 1990, a disease with which queers have been stigmatised but, nonetheless, successfully politicised, in part, by aestheticising. Although not explicit in *Les Chansons* (the film, as Nick Rees-Roberts points out, is, however, dedicated to a friend who died from the disease), AIDS is at the narrative core of Honoré's television movie, *Tout contre Léo*.[8] Honoré's rubbing-up against French film history and his relationship to contemporary queer French culture is thus where this frottage awakens queer spectatorship with an already familiar genre.

Honoré, for example, plays with similar Nouvelle Vague themes while expressing them through new mediated terms. If Godard earlier illuminated the 'truth' limitations that image, word and sound achieve through cinematic representation, Honoré – and this is crucial to his queer sensibilities – redirects Godard's challenges to these forms of communication by querying the 'truth' behind bodily performance-expression. Though each gesture is carefully choreographed in *Les Chansons* (particularly in a musical that contains little or no dancing), Honoré's cinematic bodies – like Godard's word-montage – confound any easy reading about meaning that draws conclusions associated with 'real' desire or 'true love'.[9] The scripted gestures in concert with visceral song lyrics, in fact, reaffirm through their staging the ambiguity that all forms of expression emit. Erotic desire is, therefore, inexplicable. Although Alex Beaupain's lyrics for *Les Chansons* attempt to communicate desire in tandem with bodily expression, their purpose merely serves to articulate the struggle to, in fact, articulate desire. Bodily touch and performance may indeed evoke immediate sensation and gratification. They do not fully explain it.

This does not mean, for Honoré, desire is inexpressible. To express the inexplicable, and not dissimilar to Demy's direction, Honoré commingles and *moves* bodies, gestures and lyrics through *mediated* devices, including the cinematic apparatus. In Demy's world, for example, big white American

Love mediated from a distance: *Les Chansons d'amour*

cars (*Lola*), roulette wheels (*La Baie des anges/ Bay of Angels*, 1963) and abstract paintings (*Rochefort*) merge cinematic space, time and bodies to allow desire an aestheticised outlet. This cinematic mediation does not prove entirely satisfying for our protagonists but, nevertheless, facilitates a means with which they might *act on* desire. Similarly, for Honoré, sites and devices that cinematically mediate bodily relations – such as mobile phones, parks and cemeteries (*Les Chansons*), depart-ment store windows and motor scooters (*Dans Paris*), a handwritten note and a record player (*La Belle Personne*) – bring bodies together only to demonstrate the all-too brief but ever-present affectiveness modern technology has on intimate relations.

Through dissolves, camera movement and strategic long shots, Honoré's affective mediation, cho-reographed as Demy might, takes place through chance and circumstance. In *Dans Paris*, for example, Jonathan's three sexual encounters over the course of a day in Paris begin because he bumps into a woman on a motorbike in a city tunnel, while a former girlfriend crosses his path in a park and, finally, another woman appears to him in front of a department store window's Christmas spectacle. In *Les Chansons*, two boys who are about to develop a sexual relationship sing to each other on their mobiles while standing not 20 feet from one another on the same street. Honoré uses mobile telephones else-where when Paul (Romain Duris) and Anna (Joana Priess) hope to express their fraught love in *Dans Paris*'s only musical number. It should be noted that *La Belle Personne*'s only musical number takes place just prior to a protagonist's suicide – the ultimate form of mediation where the body moves between life and death.

Following Demy, Honoré's mediated interventions channel abstract, yet undeniably materialist, expressions of and for human desire. Significantly, it is the varied cinematic tools, when in Honoré's hands, that display the erotic commingling of bodily materiality with elusive desire. *Les Chansons*, in other words, unfolds the film genre as itself a mediation device through which inexplicable desires (bodily, erotically, emotionally, sexually) are expressed. Like Demy's employment of the dissolve in a film, such as *La Baie des anges* that ironically cements Jackie (Jeanne Moreau) and Jean's aleatoric romance

Visual and aural euphoria: Claude Mann and Jeanne Moreau in *La Baie des anges* (1963)

(Claude Mann) with the roulette wheel, Honoré evokes the dead lover's body in *Les Chansons* through dissolves that allow the apparition to cinematically hover over and through her still-living boyfriend in the Montparnasse cemetery. In addition, the cine-matic dissolve is euphorically punctuated with music: Demy with Michel Legrand, Honoré with Alex Beaupain. It is precisely this bundling of cinematic properties that, when converged with the film's material world – whether roulette wheels or bodies – reaches for an expression of the inexplicable.

Why have you come so late?

Visual and aural hauntings: Ludivine Sagnier in *Les Chansons d'amour*

What makes *Les Chansons* notably queer, and decidedly shifts Honoré from Demy's cinematic impulses (no matter how ambiguous Demy leaves his story endings), is that Honoré's films resist narratives that end with fixed coupling.[10] Characters and spectators are hence not duped into believing that a comprehensive or transcendent truth exists for (hetero/homo) love or (hetero/homo) sexual desire. We are, we shall see, left on the precipice of desire.

Moving through, or Genre's Translatabilities

In addition to film-making, Honoré is a well-known author in France.[11] In film and novel, death and taboo-erotics cut across his narratives. Moreover, his multimedia practices, informed by his immersion in French film history, are key to Honoré's queer practices; this is to say, he remains acutely sensitive to the affective and deconstructive erotic interplay available to him precisely because he works across media. Mobilising media in the ways described above to express malleable desire, intimacy, sentiment and identity links, formally, with Honoré's films and novels.[12] To describe his own movement through media, Honoré often relies on double or multiple entendres in interviews to relay the way he envisages his own corporeal entanglements as he transports himself between writing and film-making. In a recent interview he was asked:

> *Le Monde*: How do you move from literature to film? Is it necessary to separate these domains in your head? Are there connecting passages?
> Honoré: I move, the verb is accurate and just. I move through novels to films like crossing a frontier where, nevertheless, I must take a position from where I come. The territory changes – a new language, a new culture – but, ultimately, I do not change. I move through but the '*I*' remains; this is movement, not a new identity.[13]

Elsewhere, Honoré describes a similar *moving through* media – specifically the cinema – where his queer identity takes its place. When discussing the music for *Les Chansons* and working with his 'long-term' friend, once-lover, and film's composer and lyricist, Beaupain, Honoré exposes a vital aspect involved with his queer cinematic 'touch', a touch he finds penetratively indissoluble with the genre:

> [Beaupain's] songs touch me particularly because I recognise a lot of elements from my own life in them. Starting from his songs does several things – it creates a certain Romanesque *distance for me* in the work, and also allows me to talk about myself while *going through him*.[14]

Honoré's kinetic mediation through the musical genre allows him to 'talk about' himself precisely because Beaupain's music yields both distance and visceral intimacy. The musical, therefore, queerly transforms the 'frontier' through which Honoré mobilises the 'I' that 'remains'. His description of the 'I' recalls the fixed-character tracking shot where characters are attached to the tracking apparatus yet are made mobile through city streets. If the 'I' remains because one 'must take a position' with one's authorial identity (sexuality, for instance), the mediated landscape, then, generates multiple 'crossing[s]' and transformations for the 'I' to '[go] through'.

Hence, the musical genre's landscape offers something quite different with regard to cinema's mediating possibilities. To be sure, the genre's history with queer camp reception is readily recognised for the multiple ways it deconstructs meaning. Honoré, I argue, enters the genre through fresh choreography and geography: that is, strategic *queer-abilities*. When he tells us *Les Chansons* is 'less a musical comedy than a film with song', he indicates his queer position in relationship to the genre where the director's intervention passes through a regenerated but nevertheless recognisable 'frontier' that he creates from a 'distance' while, simultaneously and intimately, he goes through it.[15]

Moving through the musical genre's cinematic space and time involves a seductive gesture, one that '[awakens]' the 'queer musical' to 'an afterlife', as Samuel Weber puts it in a different context.[16] Weber goes on to tell us that the 'presentation of an idea' – the musical is/as 'queer' in this instance – need not remain firmly fixed once and for all. To affix the moniker 'queer' to the musical is to, in effect, make the genre something less than queer. How is it possible to, and in what way does, Honoré breathe queer 'afterlife' into a genre that appears to have suffered the fate of commodification (queer and otherwise)? 'What defines the world in its heterogeneity – divine, human, non-human', Weber proffers, 'is precisely the diversity of translatability, which in turn entails the ability to impart: to partition, take leave of oneself in order to transpose a part of that self elsewhere, thereby altering it.'[17] For Honoré, queer desire necessarily remains inexplicable but translatable, expressible, queer-able. His intercourse with the cinematic musical 'imparts' ('translatability') affective and sensuous queer-abilities through an authorial moving-through, a fixed-character ('I') tracking shot, an imparting where one '[takes] leave of oneself in order to transpose a part of that self elsewhere, thereby altering it'. The musical, we might say, not only gives life to queer sensibilities for the homo 'I' that 'remains'; the musical's affective imparting offers a glimpse into a queer and mutable real (Honoré will lead us back to this remarkable and sudden possibility).

If queer-abilities resuscitate the musical's queer life, then are such queer doings only reserved at the author's behest? Is he alone the one who revives the genre's frisson*ic* possibilities? I wish to suggest that *Les Chansons*, in Honoré's hands, significantly contributes to a camp queer reception to the extent that the queer director interferes with the expectations such reception depends upon. The queer auteur's cinematic frottage, in other words, engages queer spectatorship to the extent that the spectator's pleasure involves a sensual experience of re-producibility where what is reproduced is, quite simply, desire.

Cinematic Frottage

How do we get at or experience queer cinematic frottage? To address Honoré's cinematic queer-abilities around matters of genre, I turn to Walter Benjamin's generative theory, the 'author as producer'. Benjamin incisively challenges key concerns with which theorists (past and present) have grappled. Because he is less anxious than most when discussing 'intention', Benjamin is more pliable and, therefore, more sensitive to the affective possibilities (ideologically, materially, politically) that cultural authorship yields.[18] For Benjamin, a theory that provides materialist 'afterlife' necessarily situates the author *within* the spatial and temporal forces found in the work of art, not at its margins. Thus, instead of asking, 'What is the attitude of a work *to* the relations of production of its time?' Benjamin poses a more prodding question: 'What is its position *in* them?'[19] In other words, by reformulating a question

Love on the edge: Louis Garrel and Grégoire Leprince-Ringuet in *Les Chansons d'amour*

that sets critics adrift and meandering through political quicksand, Benjamin identifies aesthetic possibilities through formal 'techniques' that the author-as-producer puts to use. Techniques 'affect' not only the 'conventional distinction between genres, between writer and poet, between scholar and populariser, but also revise[s] the distinction between author and reader'.[20] What does this nuanced revision pose? 'What matters', Benjamin asserts, 'is the exemplary character of production, which is able, first, to induce other producers to produce, and second, to put an *improved apparatus* at their disposal. And this apparatus is better, the more consumers it is able to turn into producers – *that is readers or spectators into collaborators.*'[21]

By drawing Benjamin's theory into a queer study, we might propose that if the ideologically fixed spectator longs to be satisfied with, *to know once and for all*, a narrative resolution that meets the demands for reproduced hetero-sanctioned concerns, Honoré's queer cinematics lead us away from such conclusions so as to bring us toward a cinematic (l)edge. His cinematic frottage, therefore, pulls away, pulls out, and leaves us – quite literally – on the edge of a building. Hence, when in *Les Chansons*' final scene, two boy lovers declare intimate feelings for one another, they are filmed – first in medium close-up – on the edge of a building where – in a quick cut to a long shot – we hear one boy say to another: 'Love me less, but love me a long time,' we are left a very long way from the tradition of hetero-monogamous and eternally reproduced love.

We are, instead, moved by and through cinematic means – an 'improved apparatus' – that dissolve, yet linger, once we leave the theatre and pour into the streets. Reproducibility is a force that awakens, not strict repetition. Honoré thus strokes the generative possibilities that the 'film with song' sets off among queer author, spectator, aesthetics and genre. To produce this collaborative frisson requires the author-as-producer to prod, turn, evoke, penetrate, edge and unfold (*déroulement*) 'conventional distinctions'. To be sure, the queer author-as-producer's stroking 'the conventional' brings us toward something less urgent and less declarative than a closing or, indeed, the longed-for money shot. Instead, the author-as-producer's sensuous hand leaves an afterlife precisely from the work's frisson – *not resolution* – where tingling queer-thinking-spectator-as-collaborators return to the world in which they are 'immersed' and move through.

Love, Death and a Song

For the remainder of this essay I attend closely to the text, *Les Chansons d'amour*, to concentrate on the following: 1) the resonant queer-abilities that the author-as-producer leaves behind; 2) the erotic tensions stimulated by and through the songs sung where Eros and Thanatos convene; and 3) the queer 'I' Honoré identifies in relationship to a *un queer réel*.

Les Chansons takes place in the 10th *arrondissement*, a young, trendy and multiracial neighbourhood in which, not unimportantly, the director resides. The film tells the story of transient, though sincere, intimacies that take place among lovers and family members. Like much of Honoré's oeuvre, the sentiment that brings together these mobile yet penetrating relationships hinges on kinetic impulses that occur when sexual desire and death – Eros and Thanatos – enter the scene. The story opens with a triangular romance that includes Ismaël (Louis Garrel), Julie (Ludivine Sagnier) and Alice (Clotilde Hesme). Ismaël and Julie were intimately involved before Alice joined the relationship. Alice is Ismaël's colleague at an independent political newspaper, though, like the relationships in *Les Chansons*, the film's politics remain ambiguous.[22] Ensconced in commodity culture's hold on emotional intimacy (movies, bars, books), romantic idealism does not simply evaporate for our young lovers. The cheesy and commodified sentiment that marks *Les Chansons* is part and parcel of the critical query about desire that Honoré brings to the cinematic spectacle.

Not long after meeting our threesome, and just at the moment when Ismaël and Julie indicate they may return to a traditionally hetero-monogamous relationship, the three lovers head to a club, L'Étoile, where *Les Chansons*' composer, Beaupain, performs. The young and attractive crowd listens attentively to the music and lyrics that long for a romanticised elsewhere (New York) while, at the same time, they cruise for love and sex in the here and now. While the three intimates reformulate their love affair, Beaupain performs the song 'Brooklyn Bridge'. The song's lyrics conjure a love eternal in a fantastical place: 'Comme une éternité qui plane/Central Park a nous deux' ('Like an eternity that hangs/Central Park holds us both'). Evoking Manhattan's garden to elicit a romantic 'eternity' that purportedly holds lovers together illustrates the intimate-distance that *Les Chansons* both embraces and troubles.

Unexpectedly, while Beaupain sings, Julie takes ill just as it appears the couple is about to anchor themselves qua couple. Quickly, Julie leaves the club to get some fresh air. With Ismaël following close behind, she reaches the outdoors, collapses, then dies. Surrounded by paramedics and police, who cast a suspicious eye on Ismaël (alcohol? drugs? physical abuse?), it is subsequently determined that Julie died from cardiac arrest. It is not an insignificant death, particularly when we consider the pleasure Honoré takes in uncoiling multiple meanings within cinematic time and place. Julie and Ismaël have just decided to fix (arrest) their romance (their hearts) for one another. Under the stars (les étoiles) at the club, they cling to each other while Alice, who has been set adrift from the threesome, makes her way toward another lover, Gwendal (Yannick Renier). Gwendal, we soon discover, is Erwann's brother (Grégoire Leprince-Ringuet), who, in turn, becomes Ismaël's lover and who, as a couple, are responsible for the precarious position at the film's end in which the spectator is left. If the ephemeral song's lyrics seek to ground lovers in eternal, yet artificial, time and space (Manhattan's Central Park), Julie's death brings such overdetermined and over-romanticised – indeed, over-commodified – versions of love to an abrupt end. And yet, her death releases her lovers to explore new sentiment that not merely leads to fixed re-couplings; instead, Julie's death ushers Ismaël, Alice and Erwann (among others) toward a range of erotic possibilities. Death, a passing through, inaugurates desire.

Julie's death is *Les Chansons* narrative centrepiece to the extent that Eros and Thanatos ignite generatively erotic possibilities. The film's storyline thus kills hetero-idealised coupling through an attack precisely on the body's organ (the heart) that is historically and metaphorically saddled with trenchant hetero-idyllic commodification. In this way, Julie's cardiac arrest awakens our young romantics from the cinematic sleep induced precisely by the generic romanticisation *Les Chansons* passes through. At the moment when 'conventional distinction' appears to assert itself, Honoré poisons affirmative coupling so that the terms for love expand outward. Poison is, in fact, necessary for love's expansion.

Some time after Julie's death, while Ismaël still mourns, he and Alice erotically engage each other's bodies at the newspaper office. As they entwine, the lovers' lyrics dig deep into corporeal delights to express, to sensually engage, to grasp the inexplicable – Eros and Thanatos – that feeds their sexual arousal. Together they sing, 'Il Faut Se Taire' ('Silence is Necessary'). As Godard taught, if words fail to articulate meaning as such, Honoré demonstrates this in relation to emotion. During the number, Alice and Ismaël fondle and caress, guided by lyrics that emphasise an expressive voice-sound for their feelings over functional communication. 'Il Faut Se Taire' redeploys the tongue's use through an Honorific punning on the homonymic 'tongue' (langue) and 'language' (langue). Hence, since '[Their] tongues are tired' ('[Ses] langues se fatiguent'), the lovers' lyrics punctuate 'Promises without a voice' ('Des promesses aphones'). 'Let's spare the tongue against language' ('Pour se faire langue contre langue') they sing, while they grope, so as to 'preserve' their 'saliva' that they can 'finally take down [their] throats, like sweet poison' ('Gardes ta salive/Que je puisse enfin la faire couler dans ma gorge/Comme un doux venin').[23]

The 'film with song' is thus an intimate cinema, one where inward poisonous penetration *and* outward sucking reach toward that which is ultimately unreachable through words but nevertheless visceral and meaningful. Throughout the film, Beaupain's lyrics emphasise body parts and bodily functions (feet, asses, blood, breasts, saliva, tongues, odours). Forgoing words to express the inexplicable or, rather, hoping to express the inexplicable through a song, lovers rely on the genre's queer-abilities to get through to one another. When Ismaël and Erwann finally come together, it is, in part, to help Ismaël purge Julie's very prescient spectre. Erwann willingly accepts the terms for the sexual encounter ('you want a body, that's ok,' he sings to Ismaël). As the boys undress and roll through the sheets, they sing, again, about using tongues (the langue/langue homonym reappears) to 'wash' (lave) clean their bodies and memories ('lick me clean'/'Du bout de ta langue nettoie-moi partout').

By introducing into the musical the Eros–Thanatos riddle, and the vexing limitations the spoken word has when expressing the Freudian-inflected dynamic, Honoré unreels 'conventional distinctions' in order to display queer desires through a staggering, often debilitating, range of emotional and physical contacts. To *lyricise* corporeality, or to make corporeality musical, evokes the spirit of inexplicable desire and gives life to queer-abilities.

Why is this important when we rethink the film musical's relationship to queer culture? David Bordwell introduces a helpful analysis about music's relationship to cinema or, more accurately, the historical analogy between music and cinema. Bordwell's theory considers the music-cinema analogy as one that requires us to revisit cinema's claims to representation pure and simple:

> What permits this examination [the analogy between music and cinema] is, precisely, cinema as a *mixed* representational mode, its unyielding impurity. The analogy turns inside out: instead of music operating as an overarching formal model holding representation in check, representation – reconsidered as a social process – places music and, indeed, formal autonomy within a wider context. If we want to know how cinema may work upon the social and the suprasocial, the musical analogy must persist, for it crystallises the drive of film form toward multiple systems. But these systems must be situated with the process of cinema's heterogeneity.[24]

The music-cinema analogy for Bordwell is thus a dynamic one. His argument re-pitches cinema's formal autonomy as a fixed medium structured along specific properties that yield ideal representation, because, as he positions it, cinema is more accurately conceived as a '*mixed* representational mode'. Cinema's 'unyielding impurity', Bordwell tells us, intermingles with the 'social and the suprasocial' (impure themselves) thereby giving way to the suggestion that the cinematic experience is, *mutatis mutandis*, multiple, heterogenous and mutable. It is fixed, yet translatable.

Seen this way, the music-cinema analogy proves crucial – if not literal – for the way Honoré's cine-matic queer-abilities marshal what I take to be Bordwell's use of the terms 'social and suprasocial'. Honoré raises, for example, the spectre of AIDS, the incest taboo, or adolescent anger and desire through assorted media and most presciently through song. His turn to a musical-cinematic concep-tualisation hence explores the inexplicable, or as one reviewer pejoratively called *Les Chansons*' story: 'implausible'. For this reviewer, such implausibility (inexplicability?) could only be found in a 'setup that couldn't be more French'.[25] Nationalist stereotypes aside, the playful, or perhaps giggly, unease with which we see Honoré's young lovers partake of one another's bodies in bedroom scenes and on street corners brings to life the implausible or, to be sure, the queer. This is why word-language does not suf-fice and dishearteningly fails (cardiac arrest) the sentiments that feed expansive emotions, desires and loves.[26] And in Honoré's frontier, the queer-abilities stretch from the corporeal to the musical. Implausible? Certainly. Queer? Indeed.

Cinematic Queer-abilities in a Generic Landscape

> The distinction between such a book as M. Zola's *L'Assommoir* and such a book as Balzac's *Illusions Perdues* is the distinction between unimaginative realism and imaginative reality …
>
> Oscar Wilde[27]

For Honoré, not unlike Balzac, the commingling of cultures, bodies, aesthetics, families, erotics and sexualities destabilise, while generating, what I have been calling queer-abilities. These productive, yet unbalanced, intertwinings lead Honoré toward what he suggests is a queer real, or what Wilde refers to as 'imaginative reality'. To add realism into the discussion this late in the game, I realise, is a bit daunting. Nonetheless, Honoré' invokes it when he speaks about making his 'film with song'. In an interview promoting the release of *Les Chansons*, Honoré makes clear his directorial concerns about the film's 'geography' (the director's neighbourhood in Paris):

> In musical comedies, one often has the feeling of being in a kitsch bubble, with sharp references, songs that produce a separation from reality. When the outside world is there, it [the real] is invoked. In *Les Chansons d'amour*, I invoke the world less than I [simply] make do with it. I think that filming the city where I live profoundly changes things. In *Dans Paris*, Paris performed as a 'museum'. For *Les Chansons d'amour*, on the contrary, I chose to limit myself to the 10th *arrondissement* in Paris. The 10th is a unique *arrondisse-ment* where one works outside with the people who unload delivery trucks … *the streets are not blocked for turns [and because of this], I wanted this life to infiltrate as much as possible the script, and also respect the geography of the place. I gave myself constraints not only to produce an effect of realism that prevents film as [merely] fantasy.* (My translation, emphasis added)[28]

Not only, then, is *Les Chansons* a queer's intrusion into a genre already marked as something less than real. Honoré, moreover, asserts the everyday realm as both circumstantial and cinematic. Though the everyday world is a consequence with which the director must contend (delivery trucks and everyday street life; images we see in the verité-style title-sequence montage), it preserves an 'effect of realism' that keeps sheer musical-genre fantasy at bay. Like the characters in *Les Chansons*, the film's *mise en scène* straddles uneasy parameters set by 'realism' and the 'musical'. The realism effect gives certain life to the 10th's kinetic pace while a film-musical production (the purportedly *not real*) 'infiltrate[s]' the place where, not insignificantly, the director *lives*. Once again, Honoré/'I' moves through, recording from a distance, so as to penetrate and cinematically intrude the familiar material world of genre and the everyday. In other words, Honoré's 10th *arrondissement* evokes *un réel queer*, an uncanny experience where truck drivers unload, Ismaël and Erwann break into song, and French film history imbrues its streets. In this cinematic frottage – consider Demy's similar designs on Rochefort where Delphine strolls down the street while choreographed townspeople spontaneously break into dance; or recall Godard directing Anna Karina's walk down the very streets Honoré gives over to Ismaël, Julie, Alice and Erwann – Honoré's 'I' is thus locatable within the malleable geographical sphere he calls home as well as the homage-frottage he expends on Godard and Demy. The cinema-musical-world (heterogenous representation) thus makes available a queer 'imaginative reality', as Wilde coins it.[29] Honoré's 'film with music' that positions the author-as-producer *in* a generative mode of production yields sensuality where a queer real awakens.

Notes

1. The title for my essay and its theoretical impulses derive from Samuel Weber's book, *Benjamin's-abilities* (Cambridge, MA: Harvard University Press, 2008). Additionally, I thank Julien Nahmias for his good counsel on queer French culture and his translation suggestions. Samuel Weber assisted with translations as well. Nonetheless, I take full responsibility for any linguistic faux pas that may appear in these pages.

2. Steven Cohan, *Hollywood Musicals: The Film Reader* (London: Routledge, 2001), p. 103.

3. Susan Sontag, in 'Notes on Camp' (pp. 53–65), identified early on the Busby Berkeley spectacles as 'camp'. Richard Dyer reaffirmed her claims in his 1976 essay, 'It's Being So Camp as Keeps Us Going (pp. 110–16), where he added Nelson Eddy and Jeannette MacDonald to the list (Sontag and Dyer reprinted in Fabio Cleto, *Camp: Aesthetics and the Performing Subject* (Detroit: University of Michigan, 1999). Later, with the political stakes heightened because of AIDS and homophobia, a new film-musical scholar entered the scene who moved the argument about camp from a reception-mode to camp as mode-of-production. For queer writers tutored under queer theory, the avant-garde was ahead of the curve in this regard (See Matthew Tinkcom's 'Warhol Camp' in Cleto, *Camp*, pp. 344–55).

4. This is key to Tinkcom's book, *Working Like a Homosexual: Camp, Capital, Cinema* (Durham, NC: Duke University Press, 2002).

5. On his relation to the Nouvelle Vague, see 'Outtakes with Christopher [*sic*] Honoré and Louis Garrel', *Time Out*. <www.timeout.com/film/newyork/features/show-feature/4454/take-five-with-christopher-honor-and-louis-garrel.html> (accessed 6 July 2009).

6. Demy's themes and formal devices are clearly showcased in *Les Chansons*' tripartite chapter breakdown; see Gérard Lefort's review, '*Les Chansons d'amour* de Christophe Honoré avec Louis Garrel, Ludivine Sagnier, Clotilde Hesme', *Libération*, 19 May 2007. <www.liberation.fr/cinema/0101102606-honore-enchantant> (accessed 6 July 2009). Honoré, however, confirms that Godard's *A Woman Is a Woman* was so influential for *Les Chansons* that he nearly titled the film *A Man Is a Man*. (Interview with Michelle Orange, 'Talking with Christopher [*sic*] Honoré and Louis Garrel', *Village Voice*, 18 March 2008. <www.villagevoice.com/2008-03-18/film/talking-with-christopher-honore-and-louis-garrel> (accessed 6 July 2009).

7. When asked about the connections between his and Godard's films, Honoré gleefully responded: 'Yes, you know *A Woman Is a Woman* was shot in the same neighbourhood in Paris as we shot' ('Talking with Christopher [*sic*]').

8. For an overview, see Nick Rees-Robert's *French Queer Cinema* (Edinburgh: Edinburgh University Press, 2008); on Honoré specifically, see pp. 109–12.

9. 'They [the musical numbers] were extremely rehearsed. In the scene with the two boys in bed, for instance, every single gesture was mapped out' ('Talking with Christopher [*sic*]').

10. It is true that many of Demy's characters, particularly women, depart the film expressing ambiguous feelings about the men with whom they exit. It is worth noting that Honoré's fixed-character tracking shots are composed with a couple.

11. His novels include *Tout contre Léo* (the 1996 novel on which the 2004 television film was made), *L'Infamille* (1997), *La Douceur* (1999) and *Scarborough* (2002).

12. I use the term 'sentiment' to evoke the French, *sentement*. It more presciently conjures Honoré's much-insisted phenomenological qualities he associates with words.

13. 'Comment passez-vous de la littérature au cinéma? Faut-il cloisonner les domaines dans sa tête? Y a-t-il des passerelles? Je passe, le verbe est précis et juste. Je passe des romans aux films, comme franchissant une frontière, où évidemment je dois déclarer d'où je viens. C'est un changement de territoire, une nouvelle langue, une nouvelle culture, mais moi, finalement, je ne change pas. Je passe, mais le "*je*" reste identique, c'est un mouvement, ce n'est pas une nouvelle identité' (translation mine). Interview with Florence Noivelle, 'La Littérature est partout dans le cinéma', *Le Monde*, 15 May 2009, p. 25.

14. 'Talking with Christopher [*sic*]' (my emphasis).

15. Ibid.

16. Weber, *Benjamin's-abilities*, p. 10.

17. Ibid., p. 47.

18. Ibid., p. 229.

19. Walter Benjamin, 'The Author as Producer', *Selected Writings, Volume 2: 1927–1934*, translated by Rodney Livingstone *et al.* (Cambridge, MA: Belknap Press of Harvard University, 1999, pp. 768–82, p. 770.

20. Ibid., p. 772.

21. Ibid., p. 777 (my emphasis).

22. Some have criticised Honoré's less than 'political' position in this and his other films. See David Calhoun in *Time Out* who calls *Les Chansons*' characters 'depraved and representative of all that is wrong with France' ('Cannes Latest: Reviews of "Control", "The Banishment", and "Les Chansons d'amour" ', 18 May 2007. <www.timeout.com/film/news/1889> (accessed 27 July 2009).

23. 'Il Faut Se Taire', lyrics by Alex Beaupain (my translation).

24. David Bordwell, 'The Musical Analogy', *Yale French Studies*, vol. 60, 1980, p. 156.

25. Anonymous, 'Cannes Latest: Reviews of *Control*, *The Banishment*, and *Les chansons d'amour*', *Time Out*, 18 May 2007. <www.timeout.com/film/news/1889/> (accessed 8 July 2009).

26. Across his work, family members share beds, seductively caress one another during emotionally fragile moments and, then, depart. The title of *Tout contre Léo* reveals these tensions, since it may be translated in one of two ways (as most English translations do): 'Close to Leo' or 'All Against Leo'. Colloquially, however, while 'Tout contre' translates as 'all against', it also suggests 'to cuddle' or 'to hold close'. Honoré most breathtakingly renders this ambiguity when Pierre (Garrel) masturbates at his mother's (Isabelle Huppert) coffin in *Ma mère*. The director frames Pierre, waist up, from behind the casket. We presume Pierre is weeping. He is indeed performing something more.

27. Oscar Wilde, 'Balzac in English', *Pall Mall Gazette*, 13 September 1886, p. xliv. Reprinted in Richard Ellman (ed.), *The Artist as Critic: Critical Essays of Oscar Wilde* (Chicago: University of Chicago Press, 1982), pp. 29–33, pp. 28–9.

28. 'Dans les comédies musicales, on a souvent la sensation d'être dans une bulle un peu kitsch, avec des références acidulées, des chansons qui produisent un décollement du réel. Quand le monde extérieur est là,

il est convoqué. Dans *Les Chansons d'amour*, je convoque moins le monde que je ne fais avec. Je pense que le fait de filmer la ville où je vis change profondément les choses. Dans *Dans Paris*, il s'agissait d'un Paris "musée". Pour *Les Chansons d'amour* au contraire, j'ai choisi de me limiter au Xème arrondissement de Paris. Le Xème est l'un des rares arrondissements où l'on travaille dehors, avec des gens qui déchargent des camions de livraisons … il ne s'agissait pas de bloquer des rues pour tourner, je voulais que la vie s'infiltre le plus possible dans les plans, et aussi respecter la géographie des lieux. Je m'étais donné cette contrainte non pas tant pour produire un effet de réel que pour m'empêcher de fantasmer un film.' Interview with Christophe Honoré. <www.christophe-honore.net/films/Chansonsitw2.html> (accessed 29 June 2009). He later describes the Paris of *La Belle Personne* (the 16th) as 'an empty area where you never see anybody' ('Outtakes with Christopher [*sic*] Honoré').

29. For recent reconsiderations on the topic of realism, see Tom Gunning, 'Moving Away from the Index: Cinema and the Impression of Reality', *differences*, vol. 18 no. 1, 2007, pp. 29–52.

16 'Dozing Off During History':
Hairspray's Iterations and the Gift of Black Music

Matthew Tinkcom

Penny: 'Being invited places by colored people!'
Tracy: 'It feels so hip!'

Introduction

Writing in the late 1980s, James Snead speculated on the future challenges of racial representations for a dominant white imagination: 'it will be interesting to see in the coming years whether the oppositional aesthetics and thematic of their earlier "independent" films [i.e. African-American-produced films manufactured outside Hollywood] can be adapted for mass-market consumption'. Important for the account that follows, Snead added that 'some would doubt whether white Americans can ever learn to see blacks and themselves from a black, and not a white, vantage point'.[1] We might revisit Snead's prescient comments now in light of the fact that, in the past few decades, Hollywood cinema seems to lose no opportunity to congratulate itself on its ostensibly progressive racial politics, but we should pause to take seriously his admonition about whether representations of race continue to be shaped from a position of white privilege. Further, we might wonder how even seemingly progressive accounts of race in dominant depictions do not in fact seem to service the sense that non-white perspectives can move entirely into a Hollywood product; they appear too often to frame their historical depictions through the sense that changes – and especially positive changes – in race in US culture are consistently brought about by the motives and intensions of well-meaning white people. This article takes up Snead's challenge by examining two popular representations of the civil rights era in US history – the two film versions of the musical *Hairspray*, made in 1988 and 2007, films which offer ostensibly progressive versions of the period in question but which do so with highly vexed relations to their fantasies of black popular music of the period.

The role of African-American musical performance in dominant US cinema has, since almost the first moments of US corporate film, been fraught by the anxiety of the larger white culture's ambivalence about the meanings of black music – for black and white listeners. Arthur Knight theorises musical performance by African-Americans within cinema in terms of W. E. B. Du Bois's notion of 'the gift'. By this, Knight understands Du Bois to mean that black music is not solely the sense of gift-as-talent, but the sense that music is a gift because its production disrupts the economy of trade by having no equal. As Knight comments, 'gift suggests an alternative moral and ethical economy of mutuality, reciprocity, and acknowledgement; one gift calls forth another, and gifts become ties of communication and community'.[2] The fact of music's long-standing strong presence in African-American cultures since the inception of slavery was, for Du Bois, the opportunity to understand that African-Americans had something to offer a larger (and, by implication, white) American culture (in addition to the labour of blacks that had contributed to the wealth of the United States). As Knight suggests, though, the technological and economic developments of mass culture made these contributions more complicated and ambiguous because of the ways that black musical genres might, on the one hand, devolve into simplistic, stereotypical and racist notions (for example, that all blacks are musically gifted, and, by implication, the presence of an African-American in a Hollywood film thus nearly guarantees a musical performance by him/her) and, on the other hand, that black musical performance might be unlinked from actual black performers, relegating them to the function of being, at best, acoustic backdrop to narratives of white culture. As Knight writes,

> under mass mediation, music does not simply float as sound carried through air away from its giving, producing, social bodies; rather; it is captured and carried away, to be re-presented under circumstances whose relation to the sound's 'original' affiliated sight and story may be very different. As a consequence, music can seem to become wholly invisible, disembodied, and sui generis.[3]

Put another way for the analyses I am making of the two cinematic versions of *Hairspray*, we can say that there is a representational crisis within both the films over the problem of depicting black dance styles and black vocal performances as they are achieved by black performers *simultaneously*: each film, in its own way, insists on the divorce of black music and dance from black performers that Knight's analysis of the technologies of mass culture articulates, and each film manages the 'problem' of having black culture linked to actual black people for the white imagination – the problem that James Snead describes at the beginning of this chapter – in different ways. For the 1988 version of *Hairspray*, the reconnection of black dance to black musical styles in the name of 'integration' occurs in order to sanction the white fantasy of its liberatory effects for blacks, while, for the 2007 adaptation, 'integration' means musical integration around the tropes and styles of the Broadway mega-musical, a style that expunges actual black popular music of the

Divine and Jerry Stiller in *Hairspray* (1988)

John Travolta and Nikki Blonsky in *Hairspray* (2007)

1950s and 60s in order to preserve that same fantasy of white political agency in the liberation of black subjects.

I

Hairspray's iterations imagine the civil rights era through the period's popular recorded music and its related adolescent subcultures as they emerged in the context of area-local broadcast television in early 1960s America. As Renee Curry writes about the 1988 version, '[Waters] sets out to renegotiate the racist events of one moment in time through the art of film. His film emphasizes a desire for the way it could have been.'[4] In brief, their narratives depict the ascendance of the heroine, Tracy Turnblad, from ordinary fat girl to local television celebrity. In the 1988 version, Tracy (Ricki Lake) is seen watching *The Corny Collins Show*, a teenaged dance programme, with her best friend, Penny Pingleton (Leslie Ann Powers). After Penny comments that Tracy is as talented as anyone on the programme, Tracy auditions for the show, is accepted and quickly becomes one of its most popular figures; her primary rival is blonde and spoiled Amber von Tussle (Colleen Fitzpatrick), whose racist parents enjoin with the show's producers to prevent African-American teens from being included its cast. At her high school, because of her outlandish hair, Tracy is forced into a class of mostly black pupils who are discriminated against by being described as 'special ed' students; she befriends Seaweed, a young black man whose mother, Motormouth Maybelle, is a local celebrity and record-shop owner. (The role of Maybelle is performed by R&B star Ruth Brown, who herself was in fact one of the most prominent of African-American musical artists of the 1950s.) Joining forces with Maybelle, Tracy protests the segregation of *The Corny Collins Show*, whereupon she is arrested and imprisoned. After Maybelle secures her release, in the film's final act Tracy crashes the Baltimore Motor Show, where the teen-pageant queen is to be crowned, and seizes the throne from Amber, the abiding historical lesson emerging that Amber – the ostensible ideal of the white 1950s American teenager as blonde and privileged – is being supplanted by a new teenager of the 1960s, who is fat, cool and unwilling to tolerate segregation, at least in the sphere of popular music and television.

Written and directed by 'trash auteur' John Waters (who already had achieved a measure of notoriety for having directed such midnight art-house films as *Female Trouble*, *Desperate Living*, *Polyester* and *Pink Flamingos*), the 1988 version of *Hairspray* is a fairy-tale account of US race politics at mid-twentieth century, with the television programme *The Buddy Dean Show* (which aired in Baltimore from 1957 to 1964) serving as *Hairspray's* real-life historical model for *The Corny Collins Show*. On both the fictional TV show and its real-life counterpart, the premise is simple: while a disc jockey plays dance music on vinyl 45s, teenagers dance for the TV camera. The larger implication of this practice, and one on which *Hairspray* bases its heroic narrative of racial justice, is that being shown on television conveys (however local) recognition, celebrity and power, and the white teenagers who appear on the programme become an elite, the so-called 'Council', who rule the social pecking-order of teenagers throughout the city. Tracy's aspiration to appear on the programme – given her status as a fat adolescent woman – is as remote for her as it is for the black teenagers of Baltimore, who are similarly prohibited from televisual stardom because of racial segregation typical of the period.[5] *Hairspray* conjoins Tracy's status as a fat girl who wills herself into the public arena of television with that of the civil rights struggles of the period; in sum, Tracy is said to understand racial injustice because of her size, and ultimately her alliance with her black cohorts brings about the integration of black teenagers onto the show.

Vexing *Hairspray's* rendering of racial discrimination and exclusion is the fact that the television programmes – both in 1960s Baltimore's *Buddy Dean Show* and in Waters's fantastic recreation of it in *The Corny Collins Show* – showcased on the soundtrack the musical productions of African-American artists who were just then assuming a more visible position as producers of American popular music. This emergence was made possible both by the longer-standing civil rights movements, dating at least from the early 1950s, and by the new technologies of mass-distributed sound recording and playback on 33 and 45 vinyl, and by radio and television broadcast. Thus, while the visual component of the television show disseminated images of white teenagers dancing, the soundtrack recognised the ways that musical tastes – both among white and black American consumers – were changing under the pressure of the social and technological forces coming to bear in the historical period, changes that included the music of black recording artists. Part of the complicated story of race that *Hairspray* attempts to tell is how television was responsible for broadcasting a depiction of adolescent subculture that orchestrated the work of African-American producers (the music track) with that of white teenagers at their leisure (the image track).

It is within this story that *Hairspray* extends Waters's widely noted fascination with what he has called 'the good taste of bad taste': namely, the domain of the culturally debased that excites the privileged consumer by its energies, its seeming recklessness and its failure to abide by the normative codes of what constitutes 'good taste'.[6] Yet, not just any bad taste will do: the 'good taste of bad taste' is, unlike the naive version of bad taste (what more commonly has been called 'kitsch'), meant to offend the sensibilities of the good-taste aesthetic. In the 1988 version of *Hairspray*, two aspects of such deliberate bad taste come to the foreground, one tacit and the other more explicit. The first takes the form of how association with black culture, and black music in particular, is prohibited to white teenagers on the grounds of taste (rather than, say, one of justice or politics): that is, the fascination by white teenagers with black culture and the people who produce it is inappropriate not because of explicit racist ideologies that are seldom articulated, but because it is 'simply' distasteful to white normative notions of good taste – therefore all the more appealing to white teenagers in rebellion against their parents. This problem is made into a joke in the 1988 version in Mrs Pingleton's hysterical response to her daughter's romantic liaison with Seaweed, the film's male African-American lead. In one sequence in the film, Mrs Pingleton follows her daughter to an African-American neighbourhood in Baltimore where Maybelle, Seaweed's mother, owns a record shop. The comic tone of the sequence derives from the fact that Mrs Pingleton is one of the sole white racists who will in fact articulate her fear and disgust with black culture and black people; the wild-eyed, paranoid performance by actress Joann Havrilla as she 'rescues' Penny from black culture (and subsequently imprisons her in her bedroom) makes evident that most of the whites rely upon a discourse of good taste in order to mask the racist ideologies that organise their everyday life. Given this prohibition, the white teenaged consumers within the film reach out to embrace black cultural productions not primarily because they have any particular political affiliations with the civil rights movements of the period, but because they know it will alarm their parents.

The more explicit practice of bad taste by whites within the film that draws ours and the director's attention is hair, and especially big hair. Baltimore has, according to Waters, long maintained a unique status as a place where hair and its coiffing has gone to extremes, in colour, texture and size, and what makes Tracy especially appealing as a potential performer on *The Corny Collins Show* is her bulk, both in body and in hair. Waters transposes the unarticulated distaste of the racialised body – more customarily seen in racist ideologies of black identity as 'animal' and 'excessive' – onto the figure of the fat white teenager, who becomes, in her devotion to the black popular music showcased on the *The Corny Collins Show*, the story's heroine and the girl who wins the boy. In her willingness to embrace black music, Tracy overcomes the distastefulness of racial discrimination – but, she ultimately affirms registers of taste and status discrimination by asking us to see how bad taste (vis-à-vis hair) is the best taste of all.

Waters's fascination with the question of taste preferences as they relate to identity politics is part of a longer historical tendency for queer intellectuals, and the sustained interest in bad taste extends from his version of the *Hairspray* narrative to its subsequent interpretation for Broadway and later film adaptation. This should come as no surprise, but I admit to my surprise that this in fact came about; in my book on the subject of gay male camp and post-World War II cinema, *Working Like a Homosexual: Camp, Capital, Cinema*,[7] I argue that Waters was historically a pivotal figure for bringing camp's fascination with bad taste to a larger audience than that of gay urban subcultures, but at the moment of writing that book, I saw his work as a terminus for camp's appeal. While I examined Waters's earlier 'underground' films – those that established his reputation as the 'pope of trash' – I concluded the book's historical arc (from Hollywood in the 1940s to the 90s) with the suggestion that camp has perhaps become an outdated relic of a category for making sense of current cultural practices, inasmuch as the historical forces that had given rise to it, not least the covert nature of same-sex subcultures, seemed no longer pertinent. Camp, while important to the survival of gay men during a markedly homophobic period in US history, was not necessarily a meaningful sensibility in the era of 'out' identity politics.

The fact that, subsequent to that book's publication, a broadway musical based on Waters's 1988 film was staged in 2002, and ran for seven years with a travelling US tour and a West End London production, seems to have made my prognosis for camp a bit premature. Further, given that the Broadway version of *Hairspray* won eight Tony awards (the most highly esteemed honours within American live performance) and eleven Olivier awards (its British counterpart), its rendering of race history and show-casing of the good taste of bad taste has clearly formed a strong appeal for its audiences. That said, it is worth noting that the differences between Waters's 1988 film and the subsequent modifications in the Broadway adaptation and the 2007 film based on it can reveal something important about the function of African-American popular music for the different historical narratives of racial desegregation that *Hairspray*'s iterations seek to tell.

If the 1988 version of the film organised its fantasy of desegregation around the inclusion of black recorded voices – via the vinyl 45 – into the spaces of white teenaged leisure, the subsequent stage and film adaptations of *Hairspray* markedly eliminated the use of these recorded songs from the historical period in favour of a score that follows the conventions of what Jessica Sternfeld has called the Broadway 'megamusical'. This musical form emerged most discernibly, according to Sternfeld, in the 1980s, with the importing of a series of productions from the UK: starting in the 1970s with *Jesus Christ Superstar* and developing over the next several decades with such immensely profitable and popular vehicles as *Cats*, *Les Misérables*, *Starlight Express*, *The Phantom of the Opera* and *Miss Saigon*. According to Sternfeld, the mega-musical is defined by its scale, more specifically its 'bigness': big casts, epic historical narratives, expensive publicity campaigns, and long runs on Broadway and on tour in the US and globally. Recognising that many of the elements of the mega-musical she describes might seem to pertain to prior instances of the musical theatre, Sternfeld argues that the peculiarly defining aspect of the form is that it

> is not just big inside the theatre; it is big outside as well. New megamusicals, especially in the 1980s, were cultural events marketed with unprecedented force. British producer Cameron Mackintosh … sold the megamusicals like any other product, complete with logos, theme songs, and advertisements saturating newspapers, radio, and television. By the time a new megamusical opened, massive advance ticket sales testified to the effectiveness of these intense marketing campaigns.[8]

Barring the fact that it did not originate on the London stage but rather as a Broadway product, *Hairspray*'s reinvention as a Broadway live mega-musical might encourage us to interpret the stage musical and the 2007 film version as having replaced the popular songs with a custom-written book and lyrics as simply part of the historical tendencies at work in the mega-musical that Sternfeld describes. However, I would argue that we might pause in the face of this explanation and wonder whether the disappearance of the African-American popular songs here is because the adaptations are trying to tell a different race narrative from the one in Waters's original film. More bluntly, the story that Waters tells in the 1988 version is one of how white teenagers become liberal, tolerant subjects after their encounter with black music and black Americans; the adaptation seeks to ameliorate the questionable race politics of this historical fantasy (i.e. the problem that it is the white subject in the Hollywood narrative who seems to suffer most at the hands of racial discrimination) by erasing any trace of the music that is purportedly what drives *Hairspray*'s storyline. Paradoxically, the later version attempts to give the African-American characters a greater prominence in the struggle to racially integrate television by making one of the central numbers, 'I Know Where I've Been', resonate more explicitly with civil rights discourse of the period, an alteration that I discuss at greater length below.

I should emphasise that my interest here is not solely to argue that one version of the film or live musical should be judged as superior or inferior based on whether it achieves something more like the actual historical developments of (partial) integration of American institutions in the era in which the story is set – that is, the problem of historical fidelity is not only what organises my critique of the films, but instead my goal here is to understand the uses to which history is put as a nostalgic (and, to my mind, anodyne) reworking of the civil rights struggles of the 1960s as the films enact the gift of African-American musical performance which Du Bois and Knight theorise. The differing versions of the historical events discovered in the two versions of *Hairspray* are fantasies, and it seems to me that a more generative question is to ask: what are these different fantasies saying black musical perform- ance in the US post-World War II period was about? When the adaptations differ from the 1988 film by replacing the musical styles of black popular culture of the late 1950s and early 60s with the pop- orchestral style more typical of the Broadway mega-musical, this fact becomes crucial to making sense of the later version's racial politics, because the 2007 adaptation erases the idea that there ever *was* a black popular culture.

II

As argued earlier, the two cinematic versions of *Hairspray* handle the ostensible problem of black sig- nification – that is, the crisis brought about in the liberation narrative when the voice of the African- American performer is recognised as located within the performer's labouring body – in different but related ways; the 1988 film privileges recorded music by African-American performers at the expense of their being seen as the producers of this very same music, while the 2007 adaptation substitutes a Broadway-style integrated score at the expense of the actual music around which the narrative of *Hairspray* is organised. Here, I want to examine in comparative terms *Hairspray*'s two iterations by way of corresponding moments in their narrative; this will, I think, help to illuminate the distinction I am drawing above as it emerges within the formal dimensions of the films.

'The Madison' and 'Ladies' Choice'/'Nicest Kids in Town'

In order to foster a sense of the exclusion of black teenagers from white leisure space in mid-century Baltimore, Waters stages a scene in which the white adolescents from *The Corny Collins Show* perform a highly choreographed dance to the Ray Bryant Combo's immensely successful single 'The Madison'. Essentially a script for line-dancing, the song directs the dancer's body in specific terms of movement, and the performance of the Madison organises the white dancers' bodies and the related *mise en scène*: a series of shots shows the grid-like organisation of the troupe from wide high angles that emphasise the cohesion of the group and low close-up shots on their legs and feet that make plain the highly synchronised choreography that the song evinces among the dancers. Because of this, it is

'The Madison' from *Hairspray* (1988)

the ideal setting in which to witness Tracy's first attempts at integrating herself into the clique and their dance; prompted by her pal Penny, she swayingly inserts her way into the front row and between the idealised couple of Link and Amber.

It would not be a mistake to understand Tracy – as a fat girl – serving as a substitute for the black adolescents who, in an earlier shot in the sequence, we see being turned away at the door by a segregationist police officer

'Ladies' Choice' from *Hairspray* (2007)

and, indeed, the moment opens up the larger story in which Tracy will push for greater and greater inclusion, of herself and of African-Americans, into the white dance culture of Baltimore. The historical circumstances under which 'The Madison' was often danced to would seem to trouble this account, though; Ruth Brown, according to Waters, told him that the dance was often performed in a more complicated version: black and white dancers were, according to Brown, sometimes allowed to dance to the song in the same venue as long as they stayed on separate sides of a rope placed in the middle of the dance floor; in many instances, according to Brown, by the end of the song the rope would have come down.[9]

By invoking this detail of a historical circumstance which *Hairspray* uses to tell its story, I do not want to suggest that it is not necessarily any less dispiriting to contemplate the practice of segregation that Brown recounted to Waters, but it is important to notice how the 1988 version expunges a detail that one of the film's African-American performers knew about and described to the director. What is more, in the 2007 adaptation, this detail resurfaces in more explicit fashion in the sequence where, again, Tracy attempts to integrate into the white clique of *The Corny Collins Show*; in this version, though, African-American teenagers dance, as Brown's account recalled, in a space partitioned by a rope. Telling about the sequence is that, with the inclusion of black performers – dancing to a 'live' performance by a white band (led by Zac Efron) in the 'Ladies' Choice' number – we might expect to see the problem of integration seemingly marginalised; instead, the 2007 version emphasises that it is Tracy alone who might introduce a black-invented dance style to the ensemble by performing a dance we have seen her learning earlier from Seaweed, the 'Peyton Place'. As Tracy enters the dance hall, she gestures to Seaweed across the rope that he, the inventor of this dance, should perform it with her, but he defers to her by saying this is impossible and 'that's just the way it is'. He then suggests that she might 'borrow it for a second', and thereby sanctions her use of the dance to integrate herself into the white clique and, subsequently, as a cast member of the television programme. Du Bois's notion of black music as gift was never more confirmed and simultaneously qualified.

'Nothing Takes the Place of You' and 'The Blacker the Berry'

My analysis of the 1988 version of *Hairspray* has until now emphasised the role of recorded music within the film's diegesis; the sound recording technologies of the late 1950s and early 60s make possible the migration of African-American artists' productions into segregated spaces that prohibit black consumers from participating in the leisure practices of white teenagers. However, there is one important exception to this within the film, and it bears critical scrutiny because, in its anomaly, it demonstrates the centrality of black performances for the white imagination at work in the film. That exception is the live performance (within the diegesis) by African-American artist Toussaint McCall of his 1967 single, 'Nothing Takes the Place of You', which enjoyed a moment on the R&B chart in the year of its release.[10]

Unlike the bulk of the numbers on *Hairspray*'s soundtrack, we see McCall perform his own song within the film; the narrative motivation for this occasion is an African-American dance event which Tracy, Penny and Link sneak into. Unlike the prohibitions which black teenagers encounter in the opening of the 'Madison' number, the white characters are warmly embraced by the black teens, and are seen at the front of the stage looking admiringly when Motormouth Maybelle, who is dj-ing the dance, introduces McCall. The melancholic strains of McCall's ballad, a hymn to an absent lover, ushers two couples, Tracy and Link and the interracial Penny and Seaweed, into an alley adjoining the dance hall, where they kiss and embrace under a full moon. The film then provides a remarkable sound-bridge of the song, shifting its performance from McCall's version of it to that of a passing African-American man, who croons it as he walks by the spooning teenagers in the alley. So saturated is the moment with ostensible black authenticity of feeling that we hear Link whispering to Tracy, 'I wish we were black,' and her response, 'our skin may be white but our souls are black.'

On the DVD director's commentary accompanying the film, Waters explains that his intention was to lampoon the white fantasy of black authenticity that seemed a large part of the historical moment's zeitgeist, and there is little doubt that the sequence is played for laughs at the expense of the white characters. However, it is worth pausing to reflect that we might also read the scene as one in which the intensity of white affect – the need to be legitimised by African-Americans – is so marked that, for once, the black voice is reunited with its performance by a black person. In Du Bois's terms, the gift of black music for white listeners (and, we might add, white heterosexual romance) becomes so powerful that it contravenes the more usual logic of erasure of the black performer that the film relies upon.

As a way of measuring the intensity of this gift, we might recall the other depiction of live musical performance within the film, when the white band The Lafayettes perform 'Life's Too Short' on *The Corny Collins Show*. Their performance, in contrast to McCall's, puts no blessing upon the fantasy of black-souls-within-white-bodies, but rather plays out the social antagonisms among the white teenagers; thus, it comes as no surprise that the villainous Amber displays her attraction to the white lead singer of the band. Further, the performance that Waters stages in the 1988 version – unlike the McCall number later in the film – is not the band's members, but actors who impersonate them.

If McCall's performance in the 1988 version of the film extends his voice to multiple spaces in order to confirm the 'hip' status of white teenage consumers and their fantasies of inclusion in black musical culture, the 2007 version stages the sole vocal performance by a black male performer, Seaweed, in order to perform a similar function within the narrative but by resorting to a confirmation of an essentialist notion of black identity. After inviting Tracy, Penny and Link to his mother's record shop, and Tracy's excited response that 'it feels so hip' to go, Seaweed (Elijah Kelley) sings that

I can't see
Why people look at me
And only see the color of my face
And then there's those
That try to help, god knows
But have to always put me in my place
Now I won't ask you to be color blind
'Cause if you pick the fruit
Then girl, you're sure to find …
The blacker the berry
The sweeter the juice
I could say it ain't so
But darlin', what's the use?

The darker the chocolate
The richer the taste
And that's where it's at …
… now run and tell that!

The song's lyrics are directed to Penny (whose whiteness is diverted into the category of 'people') and flirtingly suggest that she may be associating him with all of the more customary stereotypes of black identity, but, more pertinent for my analysis, the song and its performance affirms white (and, I would argue, racist) fantasies of black identity. Further, the number includes a virtuoso dance performance by the black cast ensemble for the three white teens whose spectatorial gaze in turn anoints the legitimacy of the song.

'I Know Where I've Been'

As a counterpart to Toussaint McCall's performance in the 1988 version of the film, in the 2007 remake, Motormouth Maybelle (Queen Latifah) and an ensemble of mostly African-American performers sing the gospel-styled number, 'I Know Where I've Been'. This sequence, which takes the appearance of a protest song, has no counterpart in the 1988 version. Here we see a crowd of black protesters joining with Maybelle on a march through Baltimore to the television station which airs *The Corny Collins Show*; their aim is to protest about the programme's segregation. The number breaks with the larger Broadway mega-musical style of the film in order to showcase Latifah's voice, and the montage editing of the number evokes documentary film footage of the civil rights protests of the 1950s and 60s. In this regard, the number breaks with the stylistic integration of the 2007 film and its live-stage progenitor, and yet it fulfils the terms of the present argument by being the sole number in the film that does not contain dance. If, once again, we discover Du Bois's gift of black music, once again we discover the conditions under which it can be imagined through the dominant aesthetics of contemporary Hollywood: in order for black voices to emerge in a recognisable idiom of the era – gospel harmonies – the bodies of the performers are denied the very terms of recognition (the dance) that the narrative insists must be granted to all subjects.

Queen Latifah in *Hairspray* (2007)

The fact that the 2007 version showcases black vocal performance is, according to the film's composer, no accident; Marc Shaiman offers that 'I Know Where I've Been' was written because 'we simply didn't want our show to be yet another show-biz version of a civil rights story where the black characters are just background'. Of particular interest for this account, he adds,

> and what could be more Tracy Turnblad-like than to give the 'eleven o'clock number' to the black family at the heart of the struggle? It never dawned on us that a torrent of protest would follow us from almost everyone involved with the show. 'It's too sad … It's too preachy … It doesn't belong … Tracy should sing the eleven o'clock number.' Luckily … the audiences embraced this moment, which enriches the happy ending to follow, and it is our proudest achievement of the entire experience of writing *Hairspray*.[11]

Despite Shaiman's sense that the number was motivated by the hope to have black characters become more than 'just background' to the civil rights struggle, the narrative arc of the 2007 version of *Hairspray* suggests that white privilege is still at the heart of the matter. This is borne out in two moments. The first occurs in the scene in which the protest around which 'I Know Where I've Been' is conceived, where we see Tracy in Maybelle's record shop. When Maybelle reports that the *The Corny Collins Show* is discontinuing the monthly 'negro day' broadcast, Tracy asserts that black teenagers can dance with whites on the show (i.e. that the programme needs to be racially integrated), to which Maybelle responds, 'have you been dozing off during history [class]?' After answering in the affirmative, Tracy suggests that 'if we can't dance, maybe we should just march', and thus it emerges that the protest is a political action birthed by a white character – the protests by African-Americans during the 1960s apparently part of the history lesson through which not only Tracy but the film's producers have slept. The second instance in which this aspect of the narrative becomes even more pronounced appears at the start of the 'I Know Where I've Been' sequence. Tracy has sneaked out of her house to join the protest, and the song (and the march) begins with Maybelle gazing affectionately into her face and singing, 'there's a light in the darkness', as if to confirm that it is Tracy's rebellion that has made possible the march for inclusion on television. If the earlier idea of Tracy's central role in the civil rights protest has been lost on the audience, the music track now drives home the point.

III

By way of conclusion, a remarkable fact from the actual *Buddy Dean Show* might serve to remind us just how far the musical fantasies of *Hairspray*'s racial depictions are from the events of the period. There were, in fact, protests at WJZ-TV in Baltimore in the mid-1960s that sought to bring non-white amateur dancers into the show's broadcast image but, unlike the outcome witnessed in *Hairspray*'s iterations, the programme was taken off the air in 1964 in order to avoid such integration. As Waters himself notes, the outcome of the real programme's attempt to include African-American teenagers in its production was a dismal one – the show's producers preferred to cancel it rather than allow blacks to become a part of its televisual *mise en scène*. Further complicating the matter, as Waters admits, the programme would never have included someone of Tracy's size in its idealised version of white, middle-class adolescent culture.

The more pressing issue for scholars of the musical and the contributions of African-Americans to this cultural form is the paradoxical cost of the gift of black music to the film-musical genre, at least in the instances I discuss here. By this I mean to say that we should continue to press the ways that black musical idioms are put to use – sometimes with seemingly the best of intentions – through the erasure of the historical circumstances that gave rise to them in the first place. Anything else and we, too, are dozing off during history.

Notes

1. James Snead, *White Screens, Black Images: Hollywood from the Dark Side* (New York: Routledge, 1994), p. 119.

2. Arthur Knight, *Disintegrating the Musical: Black Performance and American Musical Film* (Durham, NC: Duke University Press, 2002), p. 5.

3. Ibid., p. 6.

4. Renee Curry, '*Hairspray*: The Revolutionary Way to Restructure and Hold Your History', *Literature/Film Quarterly*, vol. 24 no. 2, 1996, p. 165.

5. Waters comments on the DVD director's commentary for the 1988 version of *Hairspray* that Baltimore was essentially a Southern city in the period the film depicts, and thus by implication the city inherited the Jim Crow style de facto segregation more typical of the Deep US South.

6. See John Waters, *Shock Value* (New York: Delta Books, 1981).

7. Matthew Tinkcom, *Working Like a Homosexual: Camp, Capital, Cinema* (Durham, NC: Duke University Press, 2002).

8. Jessica Sternfeld, *The Megamusical* (Bloomington: Indiana University Press, 2006), p. 3.

9. John Waters on the DVD director's commentary, *Hairspray*. New Line Pictures Home Video, 2001.

10. I am setting aside the problem that it is a historical anachronism within the film, given that McCall's song was released five years after the film's ostensible setting.

11. Mark O'Donnell, Thomas Meehan, Marc Shaiman and Scott Wittman, *Hairspray: The Roots* (London: Faber & Faber, 2003), p. 142. The 'eleven o'clock number' to which Shaiman refers is, in the parlance of the film and stage musical, the solo number customarily reserved for the main character prior to the finale, the latter sung often by the ensemble cast of the production; the 'eleven o'clock number' is often thought to function didactically, offering an ethical reading of the narrative and how it has affected the character who sings it.

Index

List of Illustrations

Whilst considerable effort has been made to correctly identify the copyright holders, this has not been possible in all cases. We apologise for any apparent negligence, and any omissions or corrections brought to our attention will be remedied in any future editions.